THE CLAY SANSKRIT LIBRARY

FOUNDED BY JOHN & JENNIFER CLAY

www.claysanskritlibrary.com

www.nyupress.org

Artwork by Robert Beer.
Typeset in Adobe Garamond Pro at 10.25 : 12.3+pt.
XML-development by Stuart Brown.
Editorial input from Chris Gibbons,
Ridi Faruque & Tomoyuki Kono.
Printed and bound in Great Britain by
T.J. International, Cornwall, on acid-free paper.

THE QUARTET OF CAUSERIES

by ŚYĀMILAKA, VARARUCI, ŚŪDRAKA & ĪŚVARADATTA

EDITED AND TRANSLATED BY

Csaba Dezső &
Somadeva Vasudeva

NEW YORK UNIVERSITY PRESS
JJC FOUNDATION
2009

First Edition 2009

The Clay Sanskrit Library is co-published by
New York University Press
and the JJC Foundation.

Further information about this volume
and the rest of the Clay Sanskrit Library
is available at the end of this book
and on the following websites:
www.claysanskritlibrary.com
www.nyupress.org

ISBN-13: 978-0-8147-1978-7 (cloth : alk. paper)
ISBN-10: 0-8147-1978-3 (cloth : alk. paper)

Library of Congress Cataloging-in-Publication Data
Caturbhāṇī. English & Sanskrit.
The quartet of causeries / by Śyāmilaka, Vararuci, Śūdraka & Īśvaradatta ;
translated by Csaba Dezső & Somadeva Vasudeva. -- 1st ed.
p. cm. -- (The Clay Sanskrit library)
Sanskrit texts with parallel English translations on facing pages.
Includes bibliographical references.
ISBN-13: 978-0-8147-1978-7 (cl : alk. paper)
ISBN-10: 0-8147-1978-3 (cl : alk. paper)
1. Sanskrit farces. 2. Erotic drama, Sanskrit. 3. Sanskrit farces--
Translations into English. 4. Erotic drama, Sanskrit--Translations
into English. 5. Pimps--India--Drama. 6. Sex customs--India--Drama.
I. Dezső, Csaba. II. Vasudeva, Somadeva.
III. Śyāmilaka. Pādatāḍitaka. English & Sanskrit.
IV. Vararuci (Dramatist). Ubhayābhisārikā. English & Sanskrit.
V. Śūdraka. Padmaprābhṛtaka. English & Sanskrit.
VI. Īśvaradatta. Dhūrtaviṭasaṃvāda. English & Sanskrit. VII. Title.
PK3794.C375E5 2009
891'.2'2--dc22
2009004559

CONTENTS

CSL CONVENTIONS

Sanskrit Alphabetical Order

Vowels:	*a ā i ī u ū ṛ ṝ ḷ ḹ e ai o au ṃ ḥ*
Gutturals:	*k kh g gh ṅ*
Palatals:	*c ch j jh ñ*
Retroflex:	*ṭ ṭh ḍ ḍh ṇ*
Dentals:	*t th d dh n*
Labials:	*p ph b bh m*
Semivowels:	*y r l v*
Spirants:	*ś ṣ s h*

Guide to Sanskrit Pronunciation

a	b*u*t
ā, â	f*a*ther
i	s*i*t
ī, î	f*ee*
u	p*u*t
ū, û	b*oo*
ṛ	vocalic *r*, American p*ur*dy or English p*re*tty
ṝ	lengthened *ṛ*
ḷ	vocalic *l*, ab*le*
e, ê, ē	m*a*de, esp. in Welsh pronunciation
ai	b*i*te
o, ô, ō	r*o*pe, esp. Welsh pronunciation; Italian s*o*lo
au	s*ou*nd
ṃ	*anusvāra* nasalizes the preceding vowel
ḥ	*visarga*, a voiceless aspiration (resembling the English *h*), or like Scottish lo*ch*, or an aspiration with a faint echoing of the last element of the preceding vowel so that *taiḥ* is pronounced *taih*^{i}
k	lu*ck*
kh	blo*ckh*ead
g	*g*o
gh	bi*gh*ead
ṅ	a*n*ger
c	*ch*ill
ch	mat*chh*ead
j	*j*og
jh	aspirated *j*, he*dgeh*og
ñ	ca*ny*on
ṭ	retroflex *t*, *t*ry (with the tip of tongue turned up to touch the hard palate)
ṭh	same as the preceding but aspirated
ḍ	retroflex *d* (with the tip

	of tongue turned up to touch the hard palate)
ḍh	same as the preceding but aspirated
ṇ	retroflex *n* (with the tip of tongue turned up to touch the hard palate)
t	French *t*out
th	ten*t h*ook
d	*d*inner
dh	guil*dh*all
n	*n*ow
p	*p*ill
ph	u*ph*eaval
b	*b*efore
bh	a*bh*orrent
m	*m*ind
y	*y*es
r	trilled, resembling the Italian pronunciation of *r*
l	*l*inger
v	*w*ord
ś	*sh*ore
ṣ	retroflex *sh* (with the tip of the tongue turned up to touch the hard palate)
s	hi*ss*
h	*h*ood

CSL Punctuation of English

The acute accent on Sanskrit words when they occur outside of the Sanskrit text itself, marks stress, e.g., Ramáyana. It is not part of traditional Sanskrit orthography, transliteration, or transcription, but we supply it here to guide readers in the pronunciation of these unfamiliar words. Since no Sanskrit word is accented on the last syllable it is not necessary to accent disyllables, e.g., Rama.

The second CSL innovation designed to assist the reader in the pronunciation of lengthy unfamiliar words is to insert an unobtrusive middle dot between semantic word breaks in compound names (provided the word break does not fall on a vowel resulting from the fusion of two vowels), e.g., Maha·bhárata, but Ramáyana (not Rama·áyana). Our dot echoes the punctuating middle dot (·) found in the oldest surviving samples of written Indic, the Ashokan inscriptions of the third century BCE.

The deep layering of Sanskrit narrative has also dictated that we use quotation marks only to announce the beginning and end of every direct speech, and not at the beginning of every paragraph.

CSL Punctuation of Sanskrit

The Sanskrit text is also punctuated, in accordance with the punctuation of the English translation. In mid-verse, the punctuation will not alter the sandhi or the scansion. Proper names are capitalized. Most Sanskrit meters have four "feet" (*pāda*); where possible we print the common *śloka* meter on two lines. In the Sanskrit text, we use French *Guillemets* (e.g., *«kva saṃcicīrṣuḥ?»*) instead of English quotation marks (e.g., "Where are you off to?") to avoid confusion with the apostrophes used for vowel elision in sandhi.

SANDHI

Sanskrit presents the learner with a challenge: *sandhi* (euphonic combination). Sandhi means that when two words are joined in connected speech or writing (which in Sanskrit reflects speech), the last letter (or even letters) of the first word often changes; compare the way we pronounce "the" in "the beginning" and "the end."

In Sanskrit the first letter of the second word may also change; and if both the last letter of the first word and the first letter of the second are vowels, they may fuse. This has a parallel in English: a nasal consonant is inserted between two vowels that would otherwise coalesce: "a pear" and "an apple." Sanskrit vowel fusion may produce ambiguity.

The charts on the following pages give the full sandhi system.

Fortunately it is not necessary to know these changes in order to start reading Sanskrit. All that is important to know is the form of the second word without sandhi (pre-sandhi), so that it can be recognized or looked up in a dictionary. Therefore we are printing Sanskrit with a system of punctuation that will indicate, unambiguously, the original form of the second word, i.e., the form without sandhi. Such sandhi mostly concerns the fusion of two vowels.

In Sanskrit, vowels may be short or long and are written differently accordingly. We follow the general convention that a vowel with no mark above it is short. Other books mark a long vowel either with a bar called a macron (*ā*) or with a circumflex (*â*). Our system uses the

VOWEL SANDHI

Initial vowels:	*Final vowels:* a	ā	i	ī	u	ū	ṛ	e	ai	o	au
a	' â	" â	y a	y a	v a	v a	r a	e '	ā a	o '	āv a
ā	' ā	" ā	y ā	y ā	v ā	v ā	r ā	a ā	ā ā	a ā	āv ā
i	' ê	" ê	' î	" î	v i	v i	r i	a i	ā i	a i	āv i
ī	' ē	" ē	' ī	" ī	v ī	v ī	r ī	a ī	ā ī	a ī	āv ī
u	' ô	" ô	y u	y u	' û	" û	r u	a u	ā u	a u	āv u
ū	' ō	" ō	y ū	y ū	' ū	" ū	r ū	a ū	ā ū	a ū	āv ū
ṛ	a' r	a" r	y ṛ	y ṛ	v ṛ	v ṛ	' ṝ	a ṛ	ā ṛ	a ṛ	āv ṛ
e	' âi	" âi	y e	y e	v e	v e	r e	a e	ā e	a e	āv e
ai	' āi	" āi	y ai	y ai	v ai	v ai	r ai	a ai	ā ai	a ai	āv ai
o	' âu	" âu	y o	y o	v o	v o	r o	a o	ā o	a o	āv o
au	' āu	" āu	y au	y au	v au	v au	r au	a au	ā au	a au	āv au

CONSONANT SANDHI

Permitted finals:							(Except āḥ/aḥ)			
k	ṭ	t	p	ṅ	n	m	ḥ/r	āḥ	aḥ	*Initial letters:*
k	ṭ	t	p	ṅ	n	ṃ	ḥ	āḥ	aḥ	k/kh
g	ḍ	d	b	ṅ	n	ṃ	r	ā	o	g/gh
k	ṭ	c	p	ṅ	ṃś	ṃ	ś	āś	aś	c/ch
g	ḍ	j	b	ṅ	ñ	ṃ	r	ā	o	j/jh
k	ṭ	ṭ	p	ṅ	ṃṣ	ṃ	ṣ	āṣ	aṣ	ṭ/ṭh
g	ḍ	ḍ	b	ṅ	ṇ	ṃ	r	ā	o	ḍ/ḍh
k	ṭ	t	p	ṅ	ṃs	ṃ	s	ās	as	t/th
g	ḍ	d	b	ṅ	n	ṃ	r	ā	o	d/dh
k	ṭ	t	p	ṅ	n	ṃ	ḥ	āḥ	aḥ	p/ph
g	ḍ	d	b	ṅ	n	ṃ	r	ā	o	b/bh
ṅ	ṇ	n	m	ṅ	n	ṃ	r	ā	o	*nasals* (n/m)
g	ḍ	d	b	ṅ	n	ṃ	r	ā	o	y/v
g	ḍ	d	b	ṅ	n	ṃ	*zero*[1]	ā	o	r
g	ḍ	l	b	ṅ	l̃[2]	ṃ	r	ā	o	l
k	ṭ	c ch	p	ṅ	ñ ś/ch	ṃ	ḥ	āḥ	aḥ	ś
k	ṭ	t	p	ṅ	n	ṃ	ḥ	āḥ	aḥ	ṣ/s
gg h	ḍḍ h	dd h	bb h	ṅ	n	ṃ	r	ā	o	h
g	ḍ	d	b	ṅ/ṅṅ[3]	n/nn[3]	m	r	ā	a[4]	*vowels*
k	ṭ	t	p	ṅ	n	m	ḥ	āḥ	aḥ	*zero*

[1]ḥ or r disappears, and if a/i/u precedes, this lengthens to ā/ī/ū. [2]e.g. tān+lokān=tā̃l lokān.
[3]The doubling occurs if the preceding vowel is short. [4]Except: aḥ+a=o '.

macron, except that for initial vowels in sandhi we use a circumflex to indicate that originally the vowel was short, or the shorter of two possibilities (*e* rather than *ai*, *o* rather than *au*).

When we print initial		before sandhi that vowel was
	â,	*a*
	î or *ê*,	*i*
	û or *ô*,	*u*
	âi,	*e*
	âu,	*o*
	ā,	*ā*
	ī,	*ī*
	ū,	*ū*
	ē,	*ī*
	ō,	*ū*
	ai,	*ai*
	āu,	*au*
	', before sandhi there was a vowel *a*	

When a final short vowel (*a*, *i*, or *u*) has merged into a following vowel, we print ' at the end of the word, and when a final long vowel (*ā*, *ī*, or *ū*) has merged into a following vowel we print " at the end of the word. The vast majority of these cases will concern a final *a* or *ā*. See, for instance, the following examples:

What before sandhi was		is represented as
	atra asti	*atr' âsti*
	atra āste	*atr' āste*
	kanyā asti	*kany" âsti*
	kanyā āste	*kany" āste*
	atra iti	*atr' êti*
	kanyā iti	*kany" êti*
	kanyā īpsitā	*kany" ēpsitā*

Finally, three other points concerning the initial letter of the second word:

(1) A word that before sandhi begins with *ṛ* (vowel), after sandhi begins with *r* followed by a consonant: *yatha" rtu* represents pre-sandhi *yathā ṛtu*.

(2) When before sandhi the previous word ends in *t* and the following word begins with *ś*, after sandhi the last letter of the previous word is *c*

and the following word begins with *ch*: *syāc chāstravit* represents pre-sandhi *syāt śāstravit*.

(3) Where a word begins with *h* and the previous word ends with a double consonant, this is our simplified spelling to show the pre-sandhi form: *tad hasati* is commonly written as *tad dhasati*, but we write *tadd hasati* so that the original initial letter is obvious.

COMPOUNDS

We also punctuate the division of compounds (*samāsa*), simply by inserting a thin vertical line between words. There are words where the decision whether to regard them as compounds is arbitrary. Our principle has been to try to guide readers to the correct dictionary entries.

Exemplar of CSL Style

Where the Devanagari script reads:

कुम्भस्थली रक्षतु वो विकीर्णसिन्धूररेणुर्द्विरदाननस्य ।
प्रशान्तये विघ्नतमश्छटानां निष्ठ्यूतबालातपपल्लवेव ॥

Others would print:

kumbhasthalī rakṣatu vo vikīrṇasindūrareṇur dviradānanasya /
praśāntaye vighnatamaśchaṭānāṃ niṣṭhyūtabālātapapallaveva //

We print:

kumbha|sthalī rakṣatu vo vikīrṇa|sindūra|reṇur dvirad'|ānanasya
praśāntaye vighna|tamaś|chaṭānāṃ niṣṭhyūta|bāl'|ātapa|pallav" êva.

And in English:

May Ganésha's domed forehead protect you! Streaked with vermilion dust, it seems to be emitting the spreading rays of the rising sun to pacify the teeming darkness of obstructions.

("Nava·sáhasanka and the Serpent Princess" I.3)

Wordplay

Classical Sanskrit literature can abound in puns (*śleṣa*). Such paronomasia, or wordplay, is raised to a high art; rarely is it a *cliché*. Multiple meanings merge (*śliṣyanti*) into a single word or phrase. Most common are pairs of meanings, but as many as ten separate meanings are attested. To mark the parallel senses in the English, as well as the punning original in the Sanskrit, we use a *slanted* font (different from *italic*) and a triple colon (⁝) to separate the alternatives. E.g.

> yuktaṃ Kādambarīṃ śrutvā kavayo maunam āśritāḥ
> *Bāṇa|dhvanāv* an|adhyāyo bhavat' îti smṛtir yataḥ.
>
> It is right that poets should fall silent upon hearing the Kádambari, for the sacred law rules that recitation must be suspended when *the sound of an arrow ⁝ the poetry of Bana* is heard.
>
> (Soméshvara·deva's "Moonlight of Glory" I.15)

INTRODUCTION

The Quartet of Causeries

THE FOUR PLAYS translated here are traditionally transmitted together in a group as the prime examples of a comical dramatical sub-genre, the "causerie" *(bhāṇa)*, where a single actor speaks all of the parts. The four plays are called "The Kick" *(Pādatāḍitaka)* by Shyámilaka, "The Mutual Elopement" *(Ubhayābhisārikā)* by Vara·ruchi, "The Lotus Gift" *(Padmaprābhṛtaka)* by Shúdraka, and "Rogue and Pimp Confer" *(Dhūrtaviṭasaṃvāda)* by Íshvara·datta.

Scholastic Definitions of the Causerie

The definitions of this sub-genre offered by Sanskrit rhetoricians agree substantially on the character of the protagonist and the general mode of presentation. The oldest among these is that of the "Treatise on Acting" (*Nāṭyaśāstra*, second–fourth century CE):[1]

> *Next I will define the Causerie. The Causerie has many parts but it is performed by a single actor who narrates his own experiences and also recounts what has happened to others. The speech of others is performed by the actor himself with replies, dialogues, speaking to others as if they were present (lit. "speaking to people in the sky"), gestures and mime. Experts should by all means introduce rogues and pimps in it, make it contain various situations and a single act, and make it eventful.*

This passage is cited nearly verbatim in the eleventh chapter of Bhoja's "Light on the Erotic Sentiment" (*Śṛṅgāraprakāśa*), showing that the scholiasts found little to add over time. Similarly intertextual are the two definitions found in the "Ten Dramatic Genres" (*Daśarūpaka*) of Dhanan·jaya and the "Illumination of Feelings" (*Bhāvaprakāśana*) of Shárada·tánaya; the latter defines the Causerie as follows:[2]

> *A causerie is a play in which a single, witty and learned pimp recounts the deeds of rogues, experienced by himself or by others. He addresses people and speaks their replies employing "speaking to the sky" (i.e. conversing with people imagined to be present). He depicts the aesthetic sentiments of heroism and love by referring to valor and conjugal passion. The "verbal style"* (bhāratī vṛtti) *of presentation predominates, the plot is fictive and performed in a single act.*

The Pimp

The "Manual of Erotics" (*Kāmasūtra* 1.4.32) defines the pimp *(viṭa)* as follows:[3] "The pimp has used up his funds, he has good qualities and a wife, is respected in the brothel and in society, and he lives off these." The *viṭa* as a persona is defined in *Nāṭyaśāstra* 35.76–77:[4]

> *The pimp should be skilled in attending courtesans, charming, affable, a poet, an expert in the true meaning of the sciences and conversant with harlotry, capable of arguing pro and con, eloquent and shrewd.*

His knowledge is less universal according to other texts, e.g. the *Bhāvaprakāśana* states:[5] "The pimp has mastered one science: he is versed in erotics."[6]

We have experimented with various names covering one or another aspect of a *viṭa*'s personality, e.g. "rake, gourmet, bon vivant." We could also have chosen a term introduced in that famous book most of us have probably read, and could have named the *viṭa* a "Connector,"[7] since he has an impressive collection of acquaintances and he loves cultivating his casual social connections, his "weak ties." Finally we chose "pimp," which seemed to be a suitable name for someone whose favorite haunt is the red-light district and who arranges rendezvous between prostitutes and their clients. We should keep in mind, however, that these pimps are refined, witty, extremely sociable and generally amiable characters.

Historical Relevance and Dates

"The Kick" is set in Ujjain, the ancient capital city of the Gupta empire. As SCHOKKER has already noted,[8] THOMAS dated it to the time of Harsha or the later Guptas. This is based on a number of mutually supportive pieces of internal evidence. Firstly, there is no mention of either Muslims or Gurjaras, hence it must have been composed before ca. 550 CE. The Latas however are prominent and contempt is poured on the Guptas. Finally there are many affinities with the poetic works of Bana who was patronized by Harsha.

Various attempts have been made to arrive at a more precise dating by identifying characters named in "The Kick" with known historical personages.

BURROW[9] dated the play to the early fifth century CE. He notes that both Shakas (Scythians) and Huns are mentioned, and identifies the character Bhadráyudha who puts in a brief appearance in "The Kick" as none other than the *mahā/pratīhāra Bhadrāyudha,* lord of the Báhlikas, Karúshas and Maladas who conquers Málava, Aparánta and the Shakas for the royal family of Mágadha (i.e. Chandra·gupta II). It is further possible that the character Indra·varman/Indra·svamin is Indra·datta, the first king of Aparánta (Konkan).[10] Tellingly, verses 60–61 of "The Kick" resemble Skanda·gupta's Bhitari inscription.[11] Skanda·gupta's campaign and Bhadráyudha's conquests took place in 455–456 CE. The historical events alluded to in "The Kick" are thus as follows: Bhadráyudha conquers Aparánta, probably dispossesses Indra·datta, and Dahra·sena is installed towards the end of 456 CE. After this Indra·datta is apparently still active as a *viṭa.*[12]

D. SHARMA[13] has claimed that Indra·datta is the successor of Vyaghra·sena of the Traikútaka dynasty (489 CE), though SCHOKKER thinks this improbable. He further identifies the character Bhatti Makha·varman, the son of general Sénaka, as the son of general Dhara·sena I of the Máitraka dynasty of Válabhi (fl. 475–502 CE).

MOTI CHANDRA & AGRAWALA accepted BURROW's date of ca. 410 CE, and further suggested the identification of Harish·chandra with Hari·chandra, the commentator of a standard medical work by Cháraka. According to the lexicon "Light on Everything" (*Viśvaprakāśa*), this Hari·chandra was the physician of king Sahásanka, who is none other than the Gupta emperor Chandra·gupta II (376–414 CE).

On lexicographical grounds Shyámilaka is supposed to be at least a younger contemporary of Kali·dasa (ca. 415–

445 CE). D. SHARMA proposed ca. 510 as the *terminus ante quem* for "The Kick," since by that time the Huns had destroyed the city of Ujjain.

To summarize, the story of "The Kick" is set in the second half of the fifth century, and it was written either then or at a time when the memory of the historical characters and milieu was still current.

Much less material that can be tied in with known historical events is available in the other three causeries. "The Lotus Gift" is also set in Ujjain in the springtime. The main characters of the play belong more to the realm of legend than recent history. The pimp is the friend of none other than the legendary rogue and authority on *ars amatoria*, Mula·deva, also known as Mula·bhadra, Kalánkura, Karni·putra, and Karni·suta.[14] The *viṭa*'s name is Shasha,[15] he is called Shashin in the "Ocean of the Rivers of Story" (*Kathāsaritsāgara*) and the "Flowering of the Long Story" (*Bṛhatkathāmañjarī*). Mula·deva's beloved, the hetaera Deva·datta also figures in various versions of the "Long Story" (*Bṛhatkathā*), and Dandin also seems to refer to her in the introductory verses of his "Avánti·súndari" (*Avantisundarī*) as a principle character in Mula·deva's story, together with Naráyana·datta.[16] Bana mentions in "The Deeds of King Harsha" (*Harṣacarita*) that Mula·deva killed Sumítra, the elder brother of Agni·mitra (son of Pushya·mitra),[17] and from Dandin's novel we know that the Shunga Pushya·mitra, the general who murdered his lord, Brihad·ratha, the last Maurya emperor, also killed Mula·deva in battle.[18] Thus the story of "The Lotus Gift" seems to be placed around 200–190 BCE, which is confirmed by a reference to a Mauryan prince called Chandródaya. The play itself, however, might have been written much later, since Mula·deva's adventures (together with its historical details) were well-known even to Dandin around 700 CE.

"Rogue and Pimp Confer" is set in Pátali·putra in the rainy season. WARDER (§1115) thinks it unlikely that its author Íshvara·datta is the usurper of that name who temporarily ejected Rudra·simha I from Ujjain. "Rogue and Pimp Confer" appears to WARDER older than "The Lotus Gift," and he surmises that it was written during the Murúnda regime in Mágadha (third century CE).

"The Mutual Elopement" is also set in Pátali·putra but in spring. WARDER (§1101), dating it somewhere between the first century BCE and the second century CE, believed it might be the earliest Indian play extant. He places it into the period of the Shaka conquest resulting in a line of rulers known as the Murúndas who became vassals of the Kushánas probably in the time of Kaníshka.

MOTI CHANDRA & AGRAWALA date all four *bhāṇa*s to the Gupta period. They think[19] that "The Lotus Gift" and "The Mutual Elopement" were written during the reign of Kumára·gupta I (r.c. 415–455), since both contain references to him: *mahendra* (Kumára·gupta's title) in "The Lotus Gift," *apratihata/śāsana* ("whose commands are not opposed") in "The Mutual Elopement," which, like *apratigha* ("unvanquished"), might have been a title of Kumára·gupta, although it is unknown as such.

Not much can at present be said about the evident intertextuality among the four causeries, though such studies hold much promise. SCHOKKER thinks that "Rogue and

Pimp Confer" verse 28 may refer to "The Kick" verse 7, but the connection is very general. He further surmises[20] that the "The Lotus Gift" borrows from "The Kick." One such supposed borrowing is the passage with the cacophonous aorists and desideratives (*mā sprākṣīḥ* etc.). One should take into consideration, however, that in "The Lotus Gift" these forms are very appropriate and naturally follow from the fact that Datta·kálashi is a grammarian, unlike Vishnu·naga in "The Kick."

The Authors

An anonymous and undateable *āryā* verse at the end of a South Indian manuscript[21] names the four authors in a group: "Vara·ruchi, Íshvara·datta, Shyámilaka and Shúdraka, these four composed causeries, what talent did Kali·dasa have?" SCHOKKER notes that the "Pimp's Dream" (*Viṭa-nidrā*, fourteenth century?) refers to the authors of the four causeries as a group but without naming them.[22]

LIENHARD notes the legend that Vara·ruchi was known as one of the nine jewels at the court of Vikramáditya of Ujjain (= Chandra·gupta II? 376–415 CE).[23] There were, however, other poets with the same name. The earliest of these authored two lost poems entitled "Chárumati" (*Cārumatī*) and "The Necklace" (*Kaṇṭhābharaṇa*).[24] Some also identify this earliest Vara·ruchi with Katyáyana, the third-century BCE author of the "Annotations to Pánini's Grammar" (*Vārttikasūtras*; he is notably mentioned as a poet by the grammarian Patánjali).[25] The colophon of a Trivandrum manuscript of the "Avi·máraka" (*Avimāraka*), one of the so-called "Bhasa Plays," names the author of the play (in the instrumental case) as *kā<tyā>yanena* (*tyā* is not clearly legible), on the basis of which Unni accepts Kátyayana-Vara·ruchi as the author of the *Avimāraka* and the "Mutual Elopement."[26] Another Vara·ruchi working in eastern India authored the "Light on the Prakrit Language" *(Prākṛta-prakāśa).*

Shúdraka is credited with the authorship of three surviving plays: the "Little Clay Cart" *(Mṛcchakaṭika),*[27] "Vásava·datta's Lute Lesson" *(Vīṇāvāsavadatta),* and "The Lotus Gift." According to the Prologue of the "Little Clay Cart," Shúdraka was a king as well as a scholar versed in many sciences from mathematics to harlotry, who lived one hundred years and ten days. In Bana's novel "Princess Kadámbari" (*Kādambarī*),[28] Shúdraka's capital city is said to be Vídisha,[29] while in the verse summary of Dandin's novel, the "Epitome of Avánti·súndari's Story" (*Avantisundarīkathāsāra* 5.144), he is referred to as "king of Malwa" (*Mālava/rāja*). According to Dandin's novel, Shúdraka's original name was Índrani·gupta. He was born as a Brahman, but he strove for royal power which, after many adventures, he won. In battle he captured alive Svati, the Andhra *(Sātavāhana)* prince, then reinstated him in his father's kingdom, and himself ruled the whole world for one hundred years.[30]

Schokker pointed out that there are certain parallels between "The Lotus Gift" and the "Charu·datta" (*Cārudatta*), one of the so-called "Bhasa Plays," which are not found in the "Little Clay Cart."[31] In an article Schokker suggested that the "Little Clay Cart" is an expansion of Shúdraka's original "Charu·datta," and the "Charu·datta" ascribed to

Bhasa is merely an adaptation of the original to the Kerala stage.[32]

Concerning Íshvara·datta, KRISHNAMACHARIAR speculates that he may be the same as the Ábhira king Íshvara·sena (third century CE).[33] A recently found coin of this king is dated Shaka 154 = 232/33 CE.[34]

From the colophons of the manuscripts of "The Kick" we know that *ārya Śyāmilaka* was a northerner and son of Vishvéshvara·datta. He is quoted by Kashmirian rhetoricians (Ábhinava·gupta, Ksheméndra, etc.) making it possible that he also was a Kashmirian.

The *Ḍiṇḍin*s

Judging from "The Kick" Ujjain was a melting pot of people belonging to various denominations, regions and social groups. The *ḍiṇḍin*s stand out of this medley as a particularly colorful group whose exact identity is, however, far from certain.

The *ḍiṇḍin*s are said to be not very different from goblins or monkeys. They vandalize banners, paintings and whitewashed walls with their graffiti, breach the rules of propriety, and don't care about "becoming an object of fear and loathing for civilized people." Shyámilaka, the author of the play, is himself announced by the director as a "*ḍiṇḍin* poet," a master of "skilled jibes."

It is noteworthy that the *ḍiṇḍin*s are associated with the Lata country in southern Gujarat, where Karóhana was located, the place of origin of the Pashu·pata sect where Shiva's *avatāra*s took place. In the original *Skandapurāṇa*, Dindi·munda is the name of Shiva's incarnation in the Treta age at Karóhana (modern Karvan in Gujarat, not far from the Narmada, north-northeast from Bharuch).[35]

Dindi·mundi (or *Diṇḍi*) is also one of the forty Shaiva sites *(pañcāṣṭaka)* taught in various Shaiva sources: people who die at one of these sites are reborn in the paradise of the same name.[36] Its location is unknown but seems to be connected with modern Eksāl in Gujarat.[37]

In the third act of "Minister Yaugándharáyana's Pledge" (*Pratijñāyaugandharāyaṇa*), a play attributed to Bhasa, Vasántaka enters disguised as a *ḍiṇḍika*, and his behavior is just as mischievous as that of the *ḍiṇḍin*s appearing in "The Kick:" he accuses Shiva of stealing his begging bowl full of sweets and tries to wipe out the bowl at the Lord's feet painted on the temple wall. On the other hand, the introductory verses found in the manuscripts of the Keralan performance version of this act tell us that Vasántaka as a *ḍiṇḍin* carries a staff, his body is white with ashes and he has the Shaiva sectarian mark on his forehead: in other words he looks remarkably similar to a Pashu·pata mendicant ascetic.[38]

The *ḍiṇḍin*s' close link with the Pashu·pata milieu is also evident from the "Emperor of the Sorcerers" (*Bṛhatkathāślokasaṃgraha* 18.202ff.),[39] where they appear as mercenary shaved (*muṇḍa*) Pashu·patas and are portrayed as bellicose braggers. The behavior of the *ḍiṇḍin*s in "The Kick" is comparable to the second stage of the Pashu·pata mendicant's life as described in the third chapter of the "Pashu·pata Aphorisms" (*Pāśupatasūtra*s): abandoning his sectarian marks he was to invite the censure of others by ridiculous, improper or seemingly mad actions. In this way he gave his bad karma to those who abused him and took their good karma from them, thus purifying himself.

This does not mean necessarily that all *ḍiṇḍin*s were disguised Pashu·pata ascetics in their second stage of life. The word "*ḍiṇḍin*" might have become a label for those who had a loose tongue and a liking for eccentric behavior, just as 'stoic' can mean someone who endures pain without complaining.

We translate *ḍiṇḍin* as "cynic," which might be considered as a modern *interpretatio Graeca*. Actually, as INGALLS pointed out, the Indian Pashu·pata and the ancient Greek Cynic traditions do show remarkable similarities, especially in their practices. As INGALLS observes, "it seems possible [...] that the two cults over the course of the centuries from time to time discovered each other."[40] One such discovery might have happened when Onesicratus, a disciple of the Cynic philosopher Diogenes, accompanied Alexander the Great to India, where he talked to Indian wise men whose views sound "as much like Pāśupata doctrine as Cynic."[41] One of these Indian teachers is called Dandamis or Mandanis in the Greek sources,[42] and it is certainly very tempting to connect him with the *ḍiṇḍin*s or Diṇḍimuṇḍa, Shiva's above-mentioned *avatāra* at Karóhana. As for deriving one tradition from the other, one should be more cautious. As INGALLS writes, "I doubt that the evidence permits one to speak of a genetic relation. If Cynicism was borrowed *as a cult* from India or if the Pāśupata was borrowed *as a cult* from Greece one would expect more evidence of its foreign background within each cult. It seems to me best to regard the two cults as parallel."[43]

The four causeries offer a colorful panorama of two ancient Indian capital cities, Pátali·putra and Ujjain, and a cross section of Indian urban society around 300–500 CE. In "The Mutual Elopement" we are introduced, among others, to a flirtatious philosopher girl, a seasoned bawd, and a transvestite called Ms Delicate. In "The Lotus Gift" the pimp meets more than a dozen characters (e.g. a poet, a grammarian, a parasite), with the representatives of typical female characters among them (e.g. *proṣita|patikā*: "whose lover is away;" *kalah'|ântaritā*: "separated by a quarrel," etc.). Shyámilaka parades more than fifty characters coming from all parts of the Gupta empire. His style is perhaps the sauciest among the four authors, sometimes bordering on the disgusting, but his description of the pimps' assembly is pricelessly funny. Finally, in the "Rogue and Pimp Confer" we find an Indian parallel of the Platonic dialogue on love, the Symposium, with such topics discussed as the superiority of kindliness to beauty and of immediate earthly love to uncertain heavenly pleasures.

Notes

1 *Nāṭyaśāstra* 18.107cd–110: *bhāṇasy' âpi tu lakṣaṇam ataḥ paraṃ saṃpravakṣyāmi. ātm'/ânubhūta/śaṃsī para/saṃśraya/varṇanā/ viśeṣas tu, vividh'/āśrayo hi bhāṇo vijñeyas tv eka/hāryaś ca. para/ vacanam ātma/saṃsthaṃ prativacanair uttar'/ôttara/grathitaiḥ, ā-kāśa/puruṣa/kathitair aṅga/vikārair abhinayaiś c' âiva. dhūrta/viṭa/ saṃprayojyo nān"/âvasth"/ântar'/ātmakaś c' âiva, ek'/âṅko bahu/ ceṣṭaḥ satataṃ kāryo budhair bhāṇaḥ.*

2 *Bhāvaprakāśana* 8.258cd–265 (p. 244f.): *bhāṇas tu dhūrta/caritaṃ sv'/ânubhūtaṃ pareṇa vā, yatr' ôpavarṇayed eko nipuṇaḥ paṇḍito viṭaḥ. sambodhan'/ôkti/pratyuktī kuryād ākāśa/bhāṣitaiḥ, sūcayed vīra/śṛṅgārau śaurya/saubhāgya/saṃstavaiḥ. bhūyasā bhāratī vṛttir ek'/âṅkaṃ vastu kalpitam.* Cf. *Daśarūpaka* 3.49ff.

3 Quoted in SCHOKKER p. 46: *bhukta/vibhavas tu guṇavān sa/kala-tro veśe goṣṭhyāṃ ca bahu/matas tad/upajīvī ca viṭaḥ.*

4 Quoted in SCHOKKER p. 44, note 135: *veśy"/ôpacāra/kuśalo ma-dhuro dakṣiṇaḥ kaviḥ, śāstr'/ârtha/tattva/vedī ca nipuṇo vaiśikeṣu ca, ūh'/âpoha/kṣamo vāgmī caturaś ca viṭo bhavet.* In the edition of the *Nāṭyaśāstra* this passage is preceded by the half-verse *sū-tradhāra/guṇair yuktaḥ sarva eva prayoge yaḥ*, which also seems to describe the pimp. However, in the old Nepalese palm-leaf manuscript of the *Nāṭyaśāstra* (NGMCP Reel no. A 18/22–19/1) this line reads as follows (fol. 249 verso): *sūtradhāra/guṇair yuk-tāḥ sarva eva prayoginaḥ*, which makes more sense than the other reading and which does not refer to the *viṭa*. The half-verse beginning with *śāstr'/ârtha/tattva/vedī...* is omitted in this Nepalese manuscript.

5 *Bhāvaprakāśana* 4.185cd (p. 94): *eka/vidyo viṭas tasya kāma/tan-treṣu kauśalam.*

6 He is called *eka/vidya* in other texts, too, e.g. *Daśarūpaka* 2.13, Rudraṭa's *Kāvyālaṅkāra* 12.15, Rudrabhaṭṭa's *Śṛṅgāratilaka* 1.41, *Nāṭyadarpaṇa* 4.14, etc. Bhoja in the *Śṛṅgāramañjarī*, however,

defines the viṭa as *sakala/vidyā/pāraṃ/gata*, "one who has mastered all sciences" (cf. SCHOKKER p. 45, note 135).

7 See MALCOLM GLADWELL (2000: 30ff).

8 SCHOKKER (1966: 19).

9 Quoted in SCHOKKER (1966: 20–23).

10 Cf. the attribution: *pārvatīyaḥ prathamo 'parānt'|âdhipatir Indra-varmā* = the Traikūṭaka king Indra·datta; a coin of his son Dahra·sena is dated to 456 CE.

11 Bhadrāyudha is the *pratīhāra* of King Vikramāditya of Ujjain, son of Mahendrāditya in *Kathāsaritsāgara* CXX, 53ff. This is the Gupta emperor Skandagupta, son of Kumāragupta I.

12 These dates are not undisputed. In his *History of the Traikutakas: Based on Coins and Inscriptions* (New Delhi, 1998), DILIP RAJGOR has revisited the chronology based on the study of Traikūṭaka coins and inscription. He endeavors to establish that the dynasty belongs to the *śaka* era of 78 CE and not the Kalachuri-Chedi era of 248–49 CE. This would lead to a back-dating of the dynasty by 170 years.

13 D. SHARMA (1956–57), quoted in SCHOKKER (1966: 23ff.).

14 Cf. BLOOMFIELD's article (1913) on Mūladeva.

15 Cf. *Kādambarī* p. 19, describing the forest on the Vindhya: *Karṇīsuta/kath" êva sannihita/vipul'/âcalā śaś'/ôpagatā ca*, "Like the story of Karni·suta and his companions Vípula and Áchala, along with Shasha, it is bordered by extensive mountains and full of hares."

16 *Avantisundarī* p. 2, verse 8: *sa/Nārāyaṇadattā yā Devadatt"/āśrayā kṛtiḥ Mūladevodi*⊔ (the ⊔ sign represents a gap in the manuscript.)

17 *Harṣacarita* p. 269: *atidayita/lāsyasya ca śailūṣa/madhyam adhyāsya mūrdhānam asi/latayā mṛṇālam iv' âlunād Agnimitr'/âgrajasya Sumitrasya Mūladevaḥ. Agnimitr'/âgrajasya* is the reading of

MSS A and B (both Devanāgarī, the second one copied in 1643 CE from an ancient palm-leaf manuscript) and *Mūladevaḥ* is the reading of A, B and T (palm-leaf, Grantha characters). FÜHRER accepted the readings of the other manuscripts: *Agnimitr'|ātmajasya* and *Mitradevaḥ*, but Agnimitra's son is called Vasumitra (and not Sumitra) in Kālidāsa's *Mālavikāgnimitra* (translated by DÁNIEL BALOGH & ESZTER SOMOGYI, Clay Sanskrit Library, forthcoming), and Mūladeva is known to have been an enemy of Puṣyamitra (Agnimitra's father) from Daṇḍin's novel as well.

18 *Avantisundarī* p. 184: *punaḥ samuddhṛtya Puṣyamitro nāma Śuṅgas tasy' âiva senā|patir brāhmaṇāyano bhartṛ|lakṣmī|rāga|dur|mada|dur|mantrī vīta|bhaya|bhañjano jvalita|Maurya|vaṃśañca (°vaṃśaś ca?) Mūladevaṃ yudhi nihatya ṣaṭ|triṃśatiṃ samāḥ sthāsyati kṣitim.*

19 MOTI CHANDRA & AGRAWALA (1959: 8).

20 SCHOKKER (1966: 31ff.).

21 M1, GOML, R2725, quoted by SCHOKKER (1966: 13): *Vararucir Īśvaradattaś Śyāmilakaś Śūdrakaś catvāraḥ. ete bhāṇā babhaṇuḥ. kā śaktiḥ Kālidāsasya?*

22 SCHOKKER(1966: 13).

23 LIENHARD (1984: 17 n. 47).

24 LIENHARD 1984: 80).

25 See SHOKKER (1966: 296). In the *Avantisundarī* (pp. 179ff.) we read about a Vararuci, a child genius, who was a contemporary of Mahāpadma Nanda, the infamously greedy king of Magadha (fourth century BCE).

26 UNNI (2001: 97).

27 Translated by DIWAKAR ACHARYA, Clay Sanskrit Library, 2009.

28 Translated by DAVID SMITH, Clay Sanskrit Library, forthcoming.

29 *Kādambarī*, p. 6.

30 See *Avantisundarīkathā* pp. 200f., *Avantisundarīkathāsāra* 4.175ff.

31 SCHOKKER (1966: 27).

32 SCHOKKER (1968).

33 KRISHNAMACHARIAR (1937: 571 n. 2).

34 SALOMON (1998: 185).

35 See BISSCHOP (2006: 33). Shiva incarnated himself at Karóhana as Bhara·bhuti in the Krita age, as Ashádhi in the Dvapara age, and as Lágudi *(=Lākuli, Lakulīśa)* in the present Kali age.

36 BISSCHOP (2006: 27ff.).

37 Cf. note ad 1.8 below.

38 SCHOKKER (1966: 143f.).

39 Translated by SIR JAMES MALLINSON, Clay Sanskrit Library, 2005.

40 INGALLS (1962: 296).

41 INGALLS (1962: 296 n. 30).

42 E.g. Plutarch, "Life of Alexander," 65; Strabo 15.1.64, 68.

43 INGALLS (1962: 296).

Abbreviations

v. = verse

corr. = correction

em. = emendation

conj. = conjecture

vl. = variant reading (*varia lectio*)

ac = before correction (*ante correctionem*)

pc = after correction (*post correctionem*)

MSS = all manuscripts

edd. = all editions

CDIAL = TURNER (1962)

Bibliography and References

PRIMARY WORKS

Avantisundarī of Ācārya Daṇḍin, ed. K.S. MAHĀDEVA ŚĀSTRĪ, Trivandrum Sanskrit Series no. 172, Trivandrum 1954.

Avantisundarīkathāsāra, ed. C. HARIHARA SASTRI, Madras: Kuppuswami Sastri Research Institute 1957.

Buddhacarita of Aśvaghoṣa, ed. and transl. H. JOHNSON, Calcutta 1936.

Buddhacarita of Aśvaghoṣa = Life of the Buddha by Ashva·ghosha, tr. by PATRICK OLIVELLE, Clay Sanskrit Library, NYU Press & JJC Foundation 2008.

Bhāvaprakāśana of Śāradātanaya, ed. YADUGIRI YATIRAJA SWAMI and K.S. RAMASWAMI SASTRI, Gaekwad's Oriental Series no. 45, Baroda 1968.

Śrīharṣacaritamahākāvyam. Bāṇabhaṭṭa's Biography of King Harshavardhana of Sthāṇvīśvara, with Śaṅkara's Commentary, Saṅketa, ed. A.A. FÜHRER, Bombay Sanskrit and Prakrit Series no. LXVI, Bombay 1909.

Kâdambarî by Bâna & His Son, ed. PETER PETERSON, vol. I. Containing the Sanskrit Text, Bombay Sanskrit Series no. XXIV, Bombay 1889.

Kāvyālaṅkāra of Bhāmaha, ed. and tr. P.V. NAGANATHA SASTRY, Delhi 1970.

Kuttani-Matam or Shambali-Matam (A Didactic Poem Composed about AD 755–786) by Damodara Gupta, ed. T.M. TRIPATHI, Bombay 1924.

Nāṭakalakṣaṇaratnakośa of Sāgaranandin, ed. MYLES DILLON, London 1937; tr. M. DILLON, M. FOWLER, V. RAGHAVAN, Philadelphia 1960.

Nāṭyaśāstra of Bharatamuni, with the Commentary "Abhinavabhāratī" by Abhinavaguptācārya, vol. I: Chapters 1–7 illustrated, rev. and crit. ed. K. KRISHNAMOORTHY, Gaekwad's Oriental Series 36, Vadodara 1992.

Nāṭyaśāstra of Bharatamuni, with the Commentary "Abhinavabhāratī" by Abhinavaguptācārya, vol. II: Chapters 8–18, ed. M. RAMAKR-

ISHNA KAVI, rev. ed. V.M. KULKARNI and TAPASVI NANDI. Gaekwad's Oriental Series 68, Vadodara 2001.

Kalhaṇa's Rājataraṅgiṇī. A Chronicle of the Kings of Kaśmīr, ed. and tr. M.A. STEIN, vol. I. Sanskrit Text With Critical Notes, Bombay 1892; tr. Vols. I–II, Westminster 1900.

Saundarananda = Handsome Nanda by Ashva·ghosha, tr. by LINDA COVILL, Clay Sanskrit Library, NYU Press & JJC Foundation 2007.

The Sundarakāṇḍa: The Fifth Book of the Vālmīki Rāmāyaṇa: The National Epic of India, ed. G.C. JHALA, Oriental Institute, Baroda 1966.

SECONDARY WORKS

BISSCHOP, PETER C. 2006. *Early Śaivism and the Skandapurāṇa: Sects and Centres*. Groningen.

BLOOMFIELD, M. 1913. "The Character and Adventures of Mūladeva." *Proceedings of the American Philosophical Society*, vol. 52, no. 212, 616–50.

BURROW, T. 1946. "The Date of Śyāmilaka's Pādatāḍitaka." *Journal of the Royal Asiatic Society*, 46–53.

DE VREESE, K. 1971. Review of SCHOKKER (1966) [= Sed]. *Indo-Iranian Journal,* XIII, no. 1, 44–47.

GLADWELL, MALCOLM. 2000. *The Tipping Point.* Abacus.

INGALLS, DANIEL H.H. 1962. "Cynics and Pāśupatas: The Seeking of Dishonor." *Harvard Theological Review*, vol. 55, no. 4, 281–98.

JANAKI, S.S. 1974. "Caturbhāṇī—Literary Study." *Indologica taurinensia,* 2, 81–106.

KRISHNAMACHARIAR, M. 1937. *History of Classical Sanskrit Literature*. Delhi.

LIENHARD, S. 1984. *A History of Classical Poetry, Sanskrit - Pali - Prakrit*. Wiesbaden.

SALOMON, R. 1998. *Indian Epigraphy.* Oxford University Press.

SCHOKKER, G.H. 1968. "Śūdraka, the Author of the Original Cārudatta." *Pratidānam: Indian, Iranian and Indo-European Studies presented to Franciscus Bernardus Jacobus Kuiper on his Sixtieth Birthday.* Eds. J.C. HEESTERMAN et al. The Hague, 585–600.

SHARMA, D. 1956–57. "The Date of the Pādatāḍitaka: about 500 AD." *J.G. Jha Res. Inst.*, XIV, 17ff.

THOMAS, F.W. 1924. "The Pādatāḍitaka of Śyāmilaka." *Journal of the Royal Asiatic Society*, 262–65.

TURNER, R. 1962. *A Comparative Dictionary of the Indo-Aryan Languages*. London. [= CDIAL]

UNNI, N.P. 2001. *Bhāsa Afresh. New Problems in Bhāsa Plays*. Delhi.

WARDER, A.K. 1977. *Indian Kāvya Literature. Vol. 3: the Early Medieval Period (Śūdraka to Viśākhadatta)*. First edition. Delhi.

———. 1990. *Indian Kāvya Literature. Vol. 2: The Origins and Formation of Classical Kāvya*. Second revised edition, Delhi.

Note on the Edition

MANUSCRIPTS

The following manuscripts are known to transmit the "Quartet of Causeries":

M1 = Government Oriental Manuscripts Library, Madras, R. 2725, Devanāgarī transcript on paper made in 1918–19. It contains part of the "The Kick," "The Lotus Gift," and part of "The Mutual Elopement."

M2 = Government Oriental Manuscripts Library, Madras, R. 2726, Devanāgarī transcript on paper made in 1918–19. It contains "The Mutual Elopement," "The Kick," and "The Lotus Gift."

T1 = Travancore Manuscripts Library of Trivandrum, no. 5968, palm-leaf, Malayālam script. It contains "The Kick," "Rogue and Pimp Confer," "The Mutual Elopement," and the first half of "The Lotus Gift." This manuscripts does not appear in the *Alphabetical Index of Sanskrit Manuscripts in the Oriental Research Institute and Manuscripts Library, Trivandrum*, University of Kerala, vol. V (A to Ta) 1988, vol. VI (Da to Ra) 1995, vol. VII (Ra to Ha) 2000.

T2 = Travancore Manuscripts Library of Trivandrum, no. 17604, palm-leaf, Malayālam script. It contains "The Mutual Elopement," "Rogue and Pimp Confer," "The Kick," and part of "The Lotus Gift."

T3 = Travancore Manuscripts Library of Trivandrum, no. 20497, palm-leaf, Malayālam script. It contains "The Kick," "The Mutual Elopement," "The Lotus Gift," and part of "Rogue and Pimp Confer."

B = Oriental Institute Library of Baroda, no. 13746, palm-leaf, Malayālam script. It contains "The Mutual Elopement," "Rogue and Pimp Confer," "The Kick," and part of "The Lotus Gift."

H = Library of the Vishveshvarananda Vedic Research Institute, Hoshiarpur, no. 4377, palm-leaf, Malayālam script. It contains "The Kick" and "The Lotus Gift."

EDITIONS

Ted = *Caturbhāṇī*, ed. M. Ramakrishna Kavi and S.K. Ramanatha Sastri, Trichur 1922. The editors probably used T2 and the manuscripts on which M1 and M2 were based.

Led = *The Padmaprābhṛtakam. An Ancient Bhāṇa Assigned to Śūdraka*, ed. and transl. J.R.A. Loman, Amsterdam 1956. This critical edition is based on M1, M2, and transcripts of T1 and T3.

MAed = *Caturbhāṇī*, ed. Moti Chandra and V.S. Agrawala, Benares 1959. The editors used Ted and data supplied by Raghavan from M1 and M2.

VWed = *The Ubhayābhisārikā or "Both Go To Meet." A Satirical Monologue or Bhāṇa by Vararuci*, ed. and transl. T. Venkatacharya and A.K. Warder, Madras 1967. The editors used Ted and MAed.

Sed = *The Pādatāḍitaka of Śyāmilaka. A Text-Critical Edition, Part I*, ed. G.H. Schokker, The Hague/Paris 1966. Schokker prepared his critical edition on the basis of M1, M2, T1, T2, B, H.

Ghed = Manomohan Ghosh, *Glimpses of Sexual Life in Nanda-Maurya India*, Calcutta 1975. This edition is based on MAed.

Kuiper collated for the *Padmaprābhṛtaka* B, H and a transcript of T3, plus M1, M2 and T1 on the basis of Loman's ed. up to *hanta idānīṃ dattaḥ pradeyakaḥ. svairam ayantritaś ca cara* in F.B.J. Kuiper, "The *Padmaprābhṛtaka*," in: *Indo-Iranian Journal* vol. 32, no. 2 (1989), pp. 115–40.

We collated T2 for the *Padmaprābhṛtaka*, *Ubhayābhisārikā* and *Dhūrtaviṭasaṃvāda*, and T3 for the *Pādatāḍitaka*, *Ubhayābhisārikā* and *Dhūrtaviṭasaṃvāda*. Our edition cannot claim to be a full-fledged critical edition, and the textual notes at the end of the volume contain only a selection of those variants we considered significant.

◊

A
tetractinal *vade*
mecum of genteel
comedies, *sive* a quaternion of
veritable GOSPELS among *tractati*
on *ars amatoria* transumed from the pe-
culiar Sunskreet language of the natives of
HINDOSTAN & recast with due pertinence and circumspection
for the discerning au-
dience of mod-
ern taste.

◊

◊

SER-
MONUM
QUADRIGÆ, SIVE
QUATTUOR LIBELLI IN-
DICI PLENI DELECTATIONIS
ET FIDE DIGNI DE ARTE AMA-
TORIA CONSCRIPTI E SANSCRITO
IN SERMONUM ANGLO-
RUM CONVERSI ET
ANNOTATION-
IBUS IN-
STRUCTI

◊

THE QUARTET OF CAUSERIES

PĀDATĀḌITAKA

THE KICK

1.1 *nāndy|ante tataḥ praviśati* SŪTRA|DHĀRAḤ.

SŪTRA|DHĀRAḤ:

deha|tyāgena Śambhor
nayana|hutavahe mānito yena kopaḥ
s'|Êndrā yasy' ânuśiṣṭiṃ
srajam iva vibudhā dhārayanty uttam'|âṅgaiḥ
pāyāt Kāmaḥ sa yuṣmān
pravitata|vanitā|locan'|âpāṅga|śārṅgo
bāṇā yasy' êndriy'|ârthā
muni|jana|tapasāṃ sādhakā^bhedakāś ca.

api ca,

sa|bhrū|kṣepaṃ sa|hāsaṃ stana|nihita|karām
īkṣamāṇena Devīṃ
saṃtrās'|ākṣipta|vāgbhiḥ saha gaṇa|patibhir
Nandinā vanditena
pāyād vaḥ Puṣpaketur vṛṣa|pati|kakud'|
âpāśraya|nyasta|doṣṇā
yasya kruddhena bāhyaṃ karaṇam apahṛtam
Śambhunā na prabhāvaḥ.

Then, at the end of the benediction, enter the DIRECTOR. 1.1

DIRECTOR:

Immolating his body in the sacrificial fire
of Shambhu's eye, he paid reverence
to his wrath;*
his ordinances the gods headed by Indra bear
upon their heads like wreaths:
May Kama protect you—
his bow is formed by the drawn out arches of
women's eyes,
his arrows—the objects of sense—
are both lure* and ruin
to the mortification of ascetic hordes.

Furthermore,

May flower-marked Kama safekeep you,
stripped of his faculties of action, but not
of his might, by wrathful Shiva,
his arm reposing on the hump-perch
of his lord of bulls,
lauded by Nandin and the lords of the hosts,*
their voices choked by terror,
gazing laughingly at the Goddess,
his eyebrows astir,
as she draws her hand to her chest.

1.5 evam ārya|miśrān śirasā praṇipatya vijñāpayāmi yad vayam ārya|Śyāmilakasya kṛtiṃ Pāda|tāḍitakaṃ nāma bhāṇaṃ prayoktuṃ vyavasitāḥ. tat tasya kaver mati|pariśramam avadhāna|dānen' ânugrahītum icchāmaḥ. kutaḥ?

«idam iha padaṃ mā bhūd, evaṃ
  bhavatv, idam anyathā,
kṛtam idam, ayaṃ granthen' ârtho
  mahān upapāditaḥ»
iti manasi yaḥ kāvy'|ārambhe
  kaver bhavati śramaḥ
sa|nayana|jalo rom'|ôdbhedaḥ
  satāṃ tam apohati.

tataḥ,[×]

nirgamyatāṃ baka|biḍāla|sama|pracārair
  āryaiś ca rāja|sacivaiḥ śama|vṛttibhiś ca.
tiṣṭhantu ḍiṇḍi|kavi|narma|kalā|vidagdhā,
  nirmakṣikaṃ madhu pipāsati dhūrta|goṣṭhī.

kutaḥ?

1.10 na prāpnuvanti yatayo ruditena mokṣaṃ,
  svarg'|āyatiṃ na parihāsa|kathā ruṇaddhi.
tasmāt pratīta|manasā hasitavyam eva
  vṛttiṃ budhena khalu kaurukucīṃ vihāya.

So, taking a reverential bow, I announce to this gentle audience that we have decided to stage the causerie called "The Kick," a work of the genteel Shyámilaka.* We make bold to ask that the poet's creative labors be complimented with the gift of rapt attention. Why? 1.5

"This word must not be used here,
let it be like this, this must be different,
  this is perfect,
here the text yields an excellent sense":
the inner exhaustion of the poet
  as he sets about writing poetry
is lifted by the tearful goosebumps
  of a worthy audience.*

Therefore,

Begone! Noble courtiers and serene puritans—
you deport yourselves like herons and cats!*
Let those tarry
  who can appreciate a cynic mendicant poet's
  skilled jibes,*
the party of ribalds will drink wine
  without flies.*

For,

Anchorites do not attain deliverance by wailing, 1.10
  an amusing story dashes no hopes of heaven.
Therefore the wise should set aside hypocrisy
  and just laugh with mirth.

ko nu khalu mayi vijñāpanā|vyagre śabda iva śrūyate? *(karṇaṃ dattvā)* hanta vijñātam! eṣa hi sa viṭa|maṇḍapaṃ praviśya dhūrta|cākrikaḥ khalati|Śyāmilako ghaṇṭām āhatya ghoṣayati. ya eṣaḥ—

vyatikara|sukha|bhedaḥ
kāminī|kāmukānāṃ
divasa|samaya|dūto
dundubhīnāṃ purodhāḥ
kalam uṣasi *kharatvād*
yasya kaṇṭhī|ravāṇāṃ
balavad abhinadanto
gardabhā n' ânuyānti.

kiṃ ca tāvad anena ghuṣyate? *(karṇaṃ dattvā)*

NAIPATHYE:*

jayati Madanasya ketuḥ
kāntaṃ praty udyato *vilāsinyāḥ*
śirasā prārthayitavyaḥ
s'|ālaktaka|nūpuraḥ pādaḥ.

1.15 *niṣkrāntaḥ.*

sthāpanā.

What is this ruckus I hear while I compère? *(listens)* Oh! I see! Here comes that bald Shyámilaka, the rogues' bard. He enters the hall of pimps,* whacks his gong,* and clamors loudly.

He is the bane of lovers' union,
the herald of daybreak,
the high priest of kettledrums.
It is because of his *raucousness : donkey-nature*
that the loudly braying donkeys
do not sing in harmony with the soft cooing
of doves* at daybreak.

Well, what does he proclaim? *(listens)*

OFFSTAGE:

Triumphant is the standard of Kama:
the foot of *Párvati : the coquette**
adorned with anklets
and reddened with lac,
poised to threaten her lover
demanding supplication by his head.

Exits. 1.15

End of Prologue.

tataḥ praviśati VIṬAḤ.

VIṬAḤ: mā tāvad bhoḥ! kim atra ghoṣayitavyam? yad evam

praṇaya|kalah'|ôdyatena
  srast'|âṃśuka|darśit'|ōru|mūlena
jitam eva mada|kalāyā
  nūpura|mukhareṇa pādena.

1.20 aye! ken' âitadd hasitam? *(vilokya)* Dadruṇamādhavo 'py atr' âiva! aṃgho Dadruṇamādhava, kim atra hāsya|sthānam?

kiṃ bravīṣi? «pratyakṣaṃ hi me tad yad atīte 'hani tatra| bhavatyā Surāṣṭrāṇāṃ vāra|mukhyayā sa|madanayā Madanasenikayā tatra | bhavāṃs Tauṇḍikokir Viṣṇunāgaś caraṇa|kamalena śirasy anugṛhītaḥ» iti.

suṣṭhu khalv idam ucyate: eti jīvantam ānando naraṃ varṣa| śatād ap' îti. Viṣṇunāgo 'pi nām' âivaṃ sarva|kāmi|jana| sādhāraṇaṃ caraṇa|tāḍana|saṃjñakam śirasy abhiṣekaṃ prāptavān.

kiṃ bravīṣi? «kuto 'sya tāni bhāga|dheyāni yaḥ sa īdṛśānāṃ praṇaya|kalah'|ôtsavānāṃ pātraṃ bhaviṣyati? sa hi tasyā veśa|devatāyās taṃ saṃmāna|viśeṣam avamānaṃ manyamānaḥ krodha|parivyakta|nayana|rāgaḥ prasphurita| bhru|kuṭī|vakraṃ lalāṭaṃ kṛtvā śiro vinirdhūya daśanair oṣṭham abhidaśya pāṇinā pāṇim abhihatya dīrghaṃ niḥśvasy' ôktavān: ‹hā dhik puṃścali, an|ātmajñe! yayā tvayā mam' âsmin

Then enter the PIMP.

PIMP: Now wait a minute! What is newsworthy about this? In fact,

The foot of a tipsily humming woman,
tinkling with anklets,
raised up in a lovers' tiff,
revealing the base of her thigh
as her garment slips back,
has already triumphed.

Hey! Who's laughing? *(looking)* Why, Dádruna·mádhava* is here too! Hi Dádruna·mádhava, what's so funny about this? 1.20

What are you saying? "It is still before my eyes how yesterday, mistress Mádana·sénika,* the passionate odalisque from Surat, ennobled with her lotus-foot the head of the honorable Taundi·koki Vishnu·naga."*

The saying is clearly true: a man will find joy in this life, even if he has to wait for a hundred years. So even Vishnu·naga has received on his head that consecration common to all lovers, known as "the kick."

What are you saying? "Why should fate be so benevolent to bless him with such a bonanza of love-quarrels? In actual fact he took this special grace of the Goddess of the Courtesans' Quarter to be a slight: his eyes were distinctly red with anger, he frowned with quivering eyebrows, shook his head, bit his lip, slapped his hands and snorted: 'Accursed harlot, you don't know your place! For,

prayata|karayā mātrā yatnāt
prabaddha|śikhaṇḍake
caraṇa|vinate pitr" āghrāte
śiśur guṇavān iti
sa|kusuma|lavaiḥ śānty|ambhobhir
dvijātibhir ukṣite
śirasi caraṇo nyasto garvān
na gauravam īkṣitam.›

1.25 evaṃ c' ânen' ôktā virajyamāna|saṃdhyā|rāg" êva rajanī varṇ'|āntaram upagatā, atiprabhāta|candra|niṣprabhaṃ vadanam udvahantī,

vyapagata|mada|rāgā
bhraśyamān'|ôpacārā
‹kim idam?› iti viṣādāt
svinna|sarv'|âṅga|yaṣṭiḥ
bhaya|vigalita|śobhā
vānta|puṣpeṇa mūrdhnā
‹na punar› iti vadantī
pādayos tasya lagnā.

praṇipāt'|âvanatā c' ânena nirdhūy' ôktā: ‹carṣaṇi, mā sprākṣīḥ! kardanena na māṃ ḍhaukitum arhasi!› iti.»

Its top-knot has been meticulously tied
by my mother with sanctified hands,*
my father has kissed it when I bowed
at his feet, saying "Good boy!,"
brahmins have sprinkled it
with holy water mingled with flowers—
but you, haughtily,
regardless of my prestige,*
put your foot on my head.'*

When he reviled her in this way, she changed color as does the night when the red of twilight fades. She lifted up her face, as lackluster as the moon at the close of dawn, 1.25

Her passionate flush drained away,
her compliance was undone.
'What's this?' she asked,
her slender body awash in perspiration with
despair.
Fear melted away her beauty,
and she pressed her forehead,
shedding its flowers,
against his feet saying: 'Never again.'

Spurning her as she bowed down and humbled herself by falling at his feet, he said: 'Don't touch me, you perfidious woman! Keep your distance with your flatulent rumbling!'"

kaṣṭaṃ bhoḥ! kokilā khalu kauśikam anuvartate. Madanasenik" âpi taṃ puruṣa|vetālaṃ kadaryam apavīryam anuvartata iti bhavati me vismayaḥ. bhavati ca punar mahāmātra|putro rājñaḥ śāsan'|âdhikṛta iti na dāna|kāmāv avekṣate. śabda|kāmāḥ khalv etā bhavanti. kāme hi prayojanam anekavidham ity upadiśyate.

kiṃ bravīṣi? «labdhaṃ khalu śabda|kāmayā *śabda/pradhān'*|ârjanāc chabdasya vyasanam iti. sā hi tapasvinī,

1.30 tiryak|trap"|âvanata|pakṣma|puṭa|pravāntair
dhaut'|âdhara|stana|mukhī nayan'|âmbu|pātaiḥ
sv'|âṅgeṣv alīyata navaiḥ sahasā stanadbhir
udvejitā jala|dharair iva rājahaṃsī.» iti.

na ca bhoś citram idam, śrotavyam śrutaṃ. na ca khalv asmābhir vidit'|ârthair apy atītaṃ pṛṣṭam. tatas tataḥ?

kiṃ bravīṣi? «tataḥ sa mayā nirbhartsy' ôktaḥ: ‹aye vaiyākaraṇa|kha|sūcin, su|manaso musalena mā kṣautsīr vallakīm ulmukena mā vādīr vāk|kṣureṇa kisalaya|klībāṃ mā cchetsīr matta|kāśinīm!› iti. evam ukto mām anādṛtya viṭa|mahattara|Bhaṭṭi|Jīmūta|gṛhaṃ gataḥ. tataḥ sā tapasvinī kara|kisalaya|paryasta|kapolam ānanaṃ kṛtvā praruditā. tata utthāpya may" ôktā: ‹sundari, na vānaro veṣṭanam arhati, gardabho vā vara|pravahaṇaṃ

Alas! The cuckoo was chasing the owl. I am frankly appalled that even Mádana·sénika might chase after that tight fisted, impotent, human zombie. On the other hand, he is the son of a minister* and is authorized to issue royal writs,* so evidently she cares not for either love or money. Such women love nothing but titles. As has been taught: the motivation of love is various.

What are you saying? "That woman, fond of titles, winning *a man whose only value is a title : an eminent title*,* has been subjected to the iniquity of harsh speech.* The poor wretch,

Her lower lip, breasts and face bathed in tears 1.30
streaming from eyelids narrowed to slits
with eyelashes lowered in shame,
she cowered like a female flamingo
startled by the new clouds' sudden thunder."

This is hardly a revelation, I've heard this news. And anyway, it is not the case that I, being conversant with a matter, would ask you about what happened. Go on!

What are you saying? "Then I rebuked him like this: 'Hey, you bungling grammarian,* don't triturate flowers with a pestle,* don't plectricate the lute with a firebrand, don't divellicate a ravishing woman, as timorous as a sprout, with your razor-like words!' When I addressed him in this way, he ignored me and went to the house of Bhatti Jimúta, the Prime Pimp. Then the poor woman burst into tears, burying her cheeks in her sprout-like hands. I helped her up and said: 'Sweetheart, a monkey

voḍhum. alam alaṃ ruditena. hāsyaḥ khalv eṣa tapasvī, n' âivaṃ mahāntam śiraḥ|satkāram arhati.

kiṃ kāmī na kaca|grahair yam abalāḥ
klíśnanti mattā balād
yaṃ badhnanti na mekhalābhir athavā
na ghnanti karṇ'|ôtpalaiḥ?
pakṣe tasya tu Manmathaḥ sukṛtinas
tasy' ôtsavo yauvanaṃ
dāsen' êva rahasy apeta|vinayāḥ
krīḍanti yen' âṅganāḥ.›

evaṃ c' ôktā smita|puraḥ|saram apāṅgena me vacaḥ pratigṛhya sa|śiraḥ|pādam avakuṇṭhya vāsasā śayana|talam alaṃkṛtavatī. aham api kāmi|pratyavarasya duś|caritam anucintayan prabhātam iti rājñaḥ prabhāta|nāndī|svanair utthāpitaḥ kṛta|kartavyas tad eva duḥ|svapna|darśanam iv' âpanetuṃ brāhmaṇa|pīṭhikāṃ gataḥ. tasyāṃ ca brāhmaṇa|pīṭhikāyāṃ pūrva|gataṃ kīrṇa|keśaṃ Viṣṇunāgam ev' ārta|rūpam ātma|karm'|ācakṣamāṇam ‹asāv ahaṃ bhoḥ, evaṃ|karmā. taṃ māṃ vṛṣalyāḥ pād'|âvadhūta|śiraskaṃ trātum arhanti traividya|vṛddhāḥ› ity uktavantam apaśyam.

does not deserve a turban, nor does a donkey deserve to pull a deluxe coach. Please stop crying! This wretch is simply ridiculous, he does not merit such an exalted distinction* for his head.

Is he really a lover,
whom impassioned women do not abuse
by violently pulling his hair,
whom they don't bind with their girdles
or slap with their lotus ear-ornaments?
On the contrary,
Kama stands by that fortunate man,
his youth is a festival
whom shameless women
treat like a slave in their private games.'

When I had consoled her in this way, she smiled, assented to my words from the corner of her eye, and lay down attractively on the bed that was adorned from its head to its legs with her cloak. As for me, I was pondering the malfeasance of that worthless lover when I was roused by the sound of the king's morning hymns heralding dawn. My duties done, I went to the brahmins' council to drive away the afterimage of that nightmare, so to say. And in that brahmin council I saw that very Vishnu·naga: he had arrived earlier, his hair was disheveled and he looked careworn as he was relating his story: 'Here I am, this is what happened to me! Will you, principals of the Vedic scholars' council, please defend me whose head has been polluted by the foot of a whore!'*

1.35 evaṃ c' ôktā brāhmaṇāś cala|kapola|sūcita|hāsam anyonyam avalokya muhūrtam iva dhyātv" ôktavantaḥ: ‹bhoḥ sādho, avalokitāny asmābhir Manu|Yama|Vasiṣṭha|Gautama|Bharadvāja|Śaṅkha|Likhit'|Āpastamba|Hārīta|Praceto|Devala|Vṛddhagārgya|prabhṛtīnāṃ maha|rṣīṇāṃ dharma|śāstrāṇi, n' âsy' âivaṃ|vidhasya mahataḥ pātakasya prāyaścittam avagacchāmaḥ› iti. evaṃ c' ôkto viṣaṇṇatara|vaktra ucchritya hastāv upākrośat: ‹bho bhoḥ, caturtho varṇa iti na mām arhatha bhūmi|devāḥ parityaktum! kutaḥ?

āryo 'smi śuddha|carito 'smi kul'|ôdgato 'smi
śabde ca hetu|samaye ca kṛta|śramo 'smi
rājño 'smi śāsana|karo na pṛthag|jano 'smi.
trāyadhvam ārtam agatim, śaraṇ'|āgato 'smi.›

evaṃ c' ôktāyāṃ tasyāṃ pariṣadi,

Thus addressed the brahmins looked at each other, their quivering cheeks betraying their mirth, and, after ruminating for a minute or so, they said: 'Look here, good man, we have consulted the law books of Manu, Yama, Vasíshtha, Gáutama, Bharad·vaja, Shankha, Líkhita, Apastámba, Haríta, Prachétas, Dévala, Vriddha·gargya and other great sages: we are not aware of a propitiatory ritual for such a great sin.' When he heard these words his face became morose, he lifted up his hands and shrieked: 'For pity's sake! You are Gods on earth, please consider that I am a Brahmin and don't forsake me! For, 1.35

I am a noble man of pure conduct,
born in a respectable family,
I have exerted myself in the sciences
of grammar and logic,
I frame the king's edicts,
I'm not just some commoner.
Rescue me, I am distressed and helpless:
I appeal to you for refuge.'

After he addressed the council with these words,

kaiś cid ‹gaur ayam› ity aratni|calanair
anyonyam āghaṭṭitaṃ.
‹syād unmatta› iti sthitaṃ smita|mukhaiḥ
kaiś cic ciraṃ vīkṣitam.
kaiś cit ‹kāma|piśāca› ity api tṛṇaṃ
dattv" ântare dhik|kṛtaḥ
kaiś cid ‹duṣkṛta|kāriṇ"› îti ca punaḥ
s" âiv' âṅganā śocitā.

evam|avasthāyāṃ ca saṃsadi tasyāṃ pratipatti|mūḍheṣu brāhmaṇeṣu prāyaścitta|vipralambha|vihvale krośati Viṣṇunāge teṣām ekatama ācārya|putraḥ svayaṃ c' ācāryo daṇḍa|nīty|ānvīkṣikyor anyāsu ca vidyāsv abhivinītaḥ kalāsv api ca sarvāsu paraṃ kauśalam anuprāpto vāgmī c' ântevāsi|gaṇa|parivṛtaḥ parihāsa|prakṛtiḥ Śāṇḍilyo Bhavasvāmī nāma brāhmaṇaḥ savy'|êtaraṃ hastam udyamya smit'|ôdagrayā vācā pariṣadam āmantry' ôktavān: ‹aye bho Viṣṇunāga, na bhetavyam, alam alaṃ viṣādena! ast' îdaṃ dharma|vacanaṃ yathā deśa|jāti|kula|tīrtha|samaya|dharmāś c' āmnāyair aviruddhāḥ pramāṇam iti. ato viṭa|jātiṃ saṃnipātya viṭa|mukhyebhyaḥ prāyaścittaṃ mṛgyatām. te hi tvām asmāt kilbiṣān mocayiṣyanti.› ity ukte sādhu|vād'|ânuyātram ūrdhv'|âṅguli|pranṛttam avartata tasyāṃ pariṣadi. tad śrutvā Viṣṇunāgo 'py anugṛhīta iti prasthitaḥ. tvaṃ c' âpi viṭa|saṃnipāta|karmaṇi niyuktaḥ» iti. bāḍham.

Some elbowed each other, saying
  'This man is an ox.'
Others, smiling, gaped at him for a long time,
  thinking, 'Perhaps he's mad!'
Some reviled him:
  'He must be an erotomaniac demon!'
  and gave him blades of grass.*
But others pitied that woman, saying,
  'She must have committed a sin.'*

While the council was thus thrown into chaos, and the brahmins were at a loss about which course to follow, and Vishnu·naga, shocked by the impossibility of a propitiatory ritual, kept on wailing, one of them, the son of a teacher and himself a teacher, the brahmin called Shandilya Bhava·svamin, learned in politics, reasoning, and other sciences and, what's more, supremely proficient in all arts, eloquent, surrounded by a throng of his students, and of facetious nature, lifted up his right hand and, with a mirthful, lively voice, saluted the assembly and said: 'Listen here, Vishnu·naga, fear not, you need not be depressed! There is this ruling: the covenants of a country, caste, family, or sect are deemed authoritative, so long as they do not contradict the scriptures. Therefore organize a meeting of the caste of pimps and apply to the chief pimps for a reparatory ritual. They will surely free you from this sin.' When he had spoken raised fingers began to dance in the assembly, attended by a chorus of acclamations. When he heard this, Vishnu·naga said thank you and set off. As for you, you are commissioned to convene the pimps." Agreed.

1.40 kiṃ bravīṣi? «ke punar iha bhavato viṭāḥ saṃmatāḥ?» iti. nanu bhavān eva tāvad agre viṭaḥ.

kiṃ bravīṣi? «katham! aham api nāma viṭa|śabden' ânugṛhītaḥ?» iti. kaḥ saṃśayaḥ? śrūyatām:

divasam akhilaṃ kṛtvā vādaṃ
saha vyavahāribhir
divasa|vigame bhuktvā bhojyaṃ
suhṛd|bhavane kva cit
niśi ca ramase veśa|strībhiḥ
kṣipasy api c' āyudhaṃ
jalam api ca te n' âsty āvāse
tath' âpi ca katthase.

tat kathaṃ tvam a|viṭaḥ?

kiṃ bravīṣi? «yady evam anugṛhītaḥ. saṃnipātayiṣyasi viṭān. viṭa|lakṣaṇaṃ tāvac chrotum icchāmaḥ.» iti. prathamaḥ kalpaḥ. śrūyatām:

1.45 svaiḥ prāṇair api vidviṣaḥ praṇayiṇām
āpatsu yo rakṣitā
yasy' ārtau bhavati sva eva śaraṇaṃ
khaḍga|dvitīyo bhujaḥ
saṃgharṣān madan'|āturo mṛgayate
yaṃ vāra|mukhyā|janaḥ
sa jñeyo viṭa ity apāvṛta|dhano
yo nityam ev' ârthiṣu.

What are you saying? "Whom do you esteem here as pimps, sir?" To begin with, your honor is clearly a first class pimp. 1.40

What are you saying? "What? Do you privilege even my humble self with the title of pimp?" You have doubts? Listen:

After arguing all day with businessmen,
you have dinner in the house of a friend
  somewhere at the end of the day.
At night you have fun with courtesans and,
  what's more, fight duels.
You don't even have water at home
  and yet you boast.

So how could you not be a pimp?

What are you saying? "If so, I am obliged. If you are about to convene the pimps I would first like to hear how you define a pimp." Good idea. Listen:

Who shields his dear ones from the enemy 1.45
  even at the expense of his life,
whose refuge in trouble is his own, sword-wielding
  arm,
whom high-class courtesans,
  lovesick because of jealousy, beseech:
he is to be known as a pimp,
  whose wealth is always available to supplicants.

api ca,

caraṇa|kamala|yugmair arcitaṃ sundarīṇāṃ
sa|makuṭam iva tuṣṭyā yo bibharty uttam'|âṅgam
sa viṭa iti viṭa|jñaiḥ kīrtyate yasya c' ârthān
salilam iva *tṛṣ"/ārtāḥ* pāṇi|yugmair haranti.

kiṃ bravīṣi? «uktaṃ viṭa|lakṣaṇam. viṭān idānīm upadeṣṭum arhasi.» iti. śrūyatām: tatra|bhavān Kāmacāro Bhāṇuḥ, Lomaśo Guptaḥ, amātyo Viṣṇudāsaḥ, Śaibya Āryarakṣitaḥ, Dāśerako Rudravarmā, Āvantikaḥ Skandasvāmī, Hariścandro bhiṣag, Ābhīrakaḥ Kumāro Mayūradattaḥ, Mārdaṅgikaḥ Sthāṇuḥ, Gāndharvasenakaḥ, Upāya|Nirantakathaḥ, pārvatīyaḥ prathamo 'parānt'|âdhipatir Indravarmā, Ānandapurakaḥ kumāro Makhavarmā, Saurāṣṭriko Jayanandakaḥ, Maudgalyo Dayitaviṣṇur ity evam|ādayo yathā|saṃbhavaṃ saṃnipātyāḥ.

kiṃ bravīṣi? «sarvaṃ tāvat tiṣṭhatu. Dayitaviṣṇur api bhavato viṭaḥ saṃmataḥ?» iti. kaḥ saṃdehaḥ?

1.50 kiṃ bravīṣi? «eṣa yo 'yaṃ rājño baleṣv adhikṛtaḥ pāraśavaḥ kaviḥ?» iti. bāḍham, evam ev' âitat.

Furthermore,

Pimpologists accredit him as a pimp
who is pleased to carry his head,
which has been honored
by the pairs of beautiful women's lotus-feet,
as if it bore a diadem;
and whose wealth the *needy* take with pairs of hands,
as *those tormented by thirst* take water.

What are you saying? "You have given the definition of a pimp. Please enumerate the pimps now." Listen: the honorable Kama·chara Bhanu, Lómasha Gupta, the minister Vishnu·dasa, the Shaibya* Arya·rákshita, the Dashéraka* Rudra·varman, Skanda·svamin from Avánti,* the physician Harish·chandra, the Abhíraka* prince Mayúra·datta, the drummer Sthanu, Gandhárva·sénaka, Upáya Niránta·katha, the first king of Aparánta: Indra·varman from the mountains,* prince Makha·varman from Anánda·pura,* Jaya·nándaka from Suráshtra,* and Dáyita·vishnu descendant of the sage Múdgala: these and others should, if possible, be gathered together.

What are you saying? "Wait a minute! You also consider Dáyita·vishnu a pimp?" You have doubts?

What are you saying? "You mean the king's colonel, the bas- 1.50
tard poet?" The same, that's right.

kiṃ bravīṣi? «mā tāvad bhoḥ!

yaḥ saṃkucaty upahita|praṇayo 'pi rājño,
  yo maṅgalaiḥ svapiti ca pratibudhyate ca,
dev'|ârcanād api ca gulgulu|gandha|vāsā
  yo 'sau kiṇa|traya|kaṭhora|lalāṭa|jānuḥ,

api ca,

deva|kulād rāja|kulaṃ
  rāja|kulād yāti deva|kulam eva
iti yasya yānti divasāḥ
  kula|dvaye saṃprasaktasya,

1.55 katham asāv api viṭaḥ?» iti. ā evam etat. ast' îdam asya viṭa|bhāva|pratyanīka|bhūtaṃ purāṇa|ghṛta|gandha iva. kiṃ tu

pūrv'|Âvantiṣu yasya veśa|kalahe
    hast'|âgra|śākhā hṛtā
  sakthnoḥ saṃyati yasya Padma|nagare
    dviḍbhir nikhātāv iṣū
bāhū yasya vibhidya bhūr adhigatā
    yantr'|êṣuṇā Vaidiśe
  yo vājī|karaṇ'|ârtham ujjhati vasūny
    ady' âpi vaidy'|ādiṣu,

What are you saying? "No way!

He who recoils even from the king
if he shows him affection,
who falls asleep and wakes up to prayers,
and, what's more, whose clothes reek of guggul
and whose forehead and knees are hard
with triple calluses due to his worship of gods,

And furthermore,

Who goes from temple to palace
and from palace to temple, nowhere else:
his days slip by in this way,
so attached is he to both houses,

How could he also be a pimp?" Yes, that is true. Such factors 1.55
call into question his status as a pimp, as if they were the smell of rancid ghee. However,

His finger was lopped off in a skirmish
in the courtesans' quarter in East Avánti,
the enemy buried arrows into his thighs
in a battle in Padma·nágara,*
his arms were penetrated by a crossbow bolt*
as it shot to the ground in Váidisha,*
and to this day he fritters away money on
physicians
and others so that they will make him a stallion.

yasmād dadāti sa vasūni vilāsinībhyaḥ
kṣīṇ'|êndriyo 'pi ramate rati|saṃkathābhiḥ
tasmāl likhāmi dhuri taṃ viṭa|puṃgavānāṃ
rāgo hi rañjayati vittavatāṃ na śaktiḥ.

katham asāv a|viṭaḥ?

kiṃ bravīṣi? «evaṃ ced agra|ṇīr viṭānām!» iti. tasmād ev' âyaṃ dhuri likhitaḥ. gacchatu bhavān, svasti bhavate. sādhayāmas tāvat.

1.60 *(parikramya)* eṣo 'smi nagara|rathyām avatīrṇaḥ. aho nu khalu Jambū|dvīpa|tilaka|bhūtasya sarva|ratn'|āviṣkṛta|vibhūteḥ sārva|bhauma|narendr'|âdhiṣṭhitasya Sārvabhauma|nagarasya parā śrīḥ! iha hi,

saṃgītair vanitā|vibhūṣaṇa|ravaiḥ
krīḍā|śakunta|svanaiḥ
svādhyāya|dhvanibhir dhanuḥ|svana|yutaiḥ
sūn"|âsi|śabdair api
pātrīṇāṃ gṛha|sārasa|pratirutaiḥ
kakṣy"|ântareṣu svanaiḥ
saṃjalpān iva kurvate vyatikarāt
prāsāda|mālāḥ sitāḥ.

Since he presents riches to coquettes, and,
though his senses are weak,
finds pleasure in talking about sex,
therefore I reckon him the leader of pimp-bulls,
for it is passion, not potency,
that satisfies the rich.

How could he not be a pimp?

What are you saying? "If it is so then he is the foremost pimp!" That's why I reckon him as the leader. You may go, sir, all the best. I'm on my way now.

(walks about) Here I descend on the high street. Ah! Truly 1.60
the city of Sarva·bhauma,* where the emperor reigns, is supremely magnificent! It is the head-ornament of the continent of Jambu, and its opulence is betrayed by all kinds of treasures. For here,

White rows of mansions seem to gossip with each
other
by means of concerts, the tinkle of women's
jewels,
the cries of pet birds, the sound of Veda-
recitations,
the ringing of knives in the butchery
mingled with the twanging of bows,
and the clatter of dishes in the inner rooms
answered by the cries of tame cranes.

api ca,

giribhyo 'raṇyebhyaḥ
salila|nidhi|kacchād api maror
narendrair āyātair
diśi disi niviṣṭaiś ca śatasaḥ
vicitrām eka|sthām
an|avagata|pūrvām avikalām
iha Sraṣṭuḥ sṛṣṭer
bahu|viṣayatāṃ paśyati janaḥ.

Śaka|Yavana|Tukhāra|Pārasīkair
Magadha|Kirāta|Kaliṅga|Vaṅga|Kāśaiḥ
nagaram atimudā|yutaṃ samantān
Mahiṣaka|Colaka|Pāṇḍya|Keralaiś ca.

1.65 *(vilokya)* aye ko nu khalv eṣo 'vamukta|kañcukayā dhavala|śibikay" êbhya|vidhavā|līlāṃ viḍambayann ita ev' âbhivartate? *(vimṛśya)* bhavatu, vijñātam. eṣa hi sa vetra|daṇḍa|kuṇḍikā|bhāṇḍa|sūcito vṛṣala|caukṣo 'mātyo Viṣṇudāsaḥ. anena hy evaṃ mahaty api prāḍvivāka|karmaṇi niyuktena dhyān'|âbhyāsa|paravattay" ôpekṣā|vihāriṇ" êva bhikṣuṇā n' âtyarthaṃ rāja|kāryāṇi kriyante. tathā hi,

Furthermore,

Kings have arrived from mountains, jungles,
the seashore, and even from the desert,
and settled all over the place by the hundreds:
thanks to them people can observe here the
amazing, concentrated,
never before experienced,
sheer diversity of the Creator's creation.

The city overflows with joy thanks to the
Shakas,* Greeks, Tukháras,* Persians,
Mágadhas, Kirátas,* Kalíngas,* Vangas,*
Kashas,* Mahíshakas,* Chólakas, Pandyas, and
Kéralas.*

(looks around) Hey, who can this be, coming my way in 1.65
a white palanquin with open curtains, parodying the comportment of a rich man's widow? *(reflecting)* Aha, I see. This must be the minister Vishnu·dasa, a low-born *chauksha.** I recognized him by his cane staff and water-pot. Though he has been appointed to the important post of a judge, he certainly does not overtax himself to meet his liabilities towards the king as he is always absorbed in meditation, like a Buddhist monk who delights in indifference. For,

kara|vicalita|jānuḥ kaiś cid ardh'|āsana|sthaiḥ
samavanata|śirobhiḥ kaiś cid ākṛṣṭa|pādaḥ
adhikaraṇa|gato 'pi krośatāṃ kāryakāṇāṃ
vipaṇi|vṛṣa iv' âiṣa dhyāti nidrāṃ ca yāti.

tat kāmaṃ viṭa|jana|pratyanīka|bhūtam asya darśanam tath" âpi dharmam upadiśann abhigamya eva. kā gatiḥ? upasarpāmy enam. eṣa khalu dūrād eva mām avalokya śibikām avatāry' âvatarati. aye bhoḥ, marṣayatu bhavān, n' ârhasy asmān upacāra|yantraṇayā vijanī|kartum.

kiṃ bravīṣi? «kaś ca bhavantam upacarati? ācāro 'yam asmābhir anuvartyate.» iti. mā tāvad bhoḥ! evam upacaratā yuktaṃ nāma bhavatā tatra|bhavatīm Anaṅgasenām Anaṅga|senām iva praṇay'|âbhimukhīṃ tathā vimukhayitum?

kiṃ bravīṣi? «kiṃ mayā na tasyāḥ praṇay'|ânurūpaḥ saṃparigrahaḥ kṛtaḥ? paśyatu bhavān. sā hi mayā

1.70 svast' îty uktvā vandanāyāṃ kṛtāyām
āsīnāyāṃ vācitaṃ yoga|śāstram
netre c' âsyā vāyun" êv' ēryamāṇe
saṃprekṣy' ôktā putri sarpiḥ pib' êti.

Some shove his knees with their hands
while forcing their way half on to his seat,
others lower their heads and pull his feet:
though he came to judge the cases of shouting litigants,
he ruminates and falls asleep
like a bull in the market.

Needless to say his appearance is at variance with that of a pimp. Nevertheless he must be approached as someone who gives legal advice. What to do? I shall go up to him. Apparently he has spotted me from afar, orders the palanquin to be put down, and alights. I beg your pardon, sir, you needn't be sociable just because courtesy constrains you to do so.

What are you saying? "Who is being courteous with you? I am just being perfunctorily civil." This will not do! If you are so civil, was it appropriate that you repulsed the honorable Anánga·sena the way you did, as if she really were Kama's army, even though she was ready for love?

What are you saying? "Didn't I receive her in a way that befitted her affection? Look, sir,

When I was introduced to her I said: 1.70
'How do you do?'*
When she had sat down I recited the Yoga sutras.
And when I noticed her eyes rolling,
presumably through an imbalance of her wind-humor, I said: 'Drink ghee, my girl.'

tat katham na sampratigṛhītā mayā?» iti. aho kāminyā *lalita|saṃparigrahaḥ* kṛtaḥ! eṣa māṃ prahasya caukṣ'|ôpāyanena bīja|pūrakeṇa prasādayati. aye bho, yuṣmad|antevāsina eva vayam īdṛśeṣu prayojaneṣu n' ôtkoṭanābhir vañcayituṃ sakyāḥ. sarvathā, īdṛsa ev' âstu bhavān. sādhayāmas tāvat.

(parikramya) eṣa bho aneka|deśa|sthalaja|jalaja|sāra|phalgu|paṇya|kraya|vikray'|ôpasthita|strī|puruṣa|saṃbādh'|ântar'|āpaṇāṃ Sārvabhaumasya vipaṇim anuprāptaḥ. aho bat' âsyāḥ

śakunīnām iv' āvāse
pracāreṣu gavām iva
janānāṃ vyavahāreṣu
saṃnipāto mahā|dhvaniḥ.

tathā hi,

1.75 svaraḥ s'|ânusvāraḥ
paripatati karmāra|vipaṇau,
bhram'|ārūḍhaṃ kāṃsyaṃ
kurara|virutān' îva kurute,
dhṛtam śaṅkhe śastraṃ
rasati turaga|śvāsa|piśunaṃ,
samantāc c' āpnoti
krayam api jano vikrayam api.

So how did I not receive her hospitably?" Oh, you indeed provided *a kindly reception : easy money* for that woman! He smiles at me and proffers a citron, an offering worthy of a *chauksha*. Oh! I am merely your pupil, I cannot be bribed* in such affairs. By all means, may you keep well. I must go on now.

(walks about) Oh! I've arrived at the market of Sarva·bhauma where the shops are crowded with women and men who came to buy and sell both cheap and costly produce of both the land and the water of various regions. Oho, here

The throng of people doing business
is raucous like a flock of nesting birds
or a herd of cows on the pasture.

For,

The din in the smith's shop reverberates 1.75
with echoes,
brass held to the grindstone shrieks
like an osprey,
the hissing of a knife held against a conch-shell*
reminds one of a horse's snorting.
People are buying and selling things everywhere.

api c' êdānīm

> sumanasa imā vikrīyante
> hasantya iva śriyā,
> carati caṣakaḥ pān'|âgāreṣv
> ataḥ paripīyate.
> kara|dhṛta|tṛṇair māṃsa|krāyair
> apāṅga|nirīkṣitā
> nagara|vihagāḥ sūnām ete
> patanty asi|mālinīm.

api ca,

> aṃsen' âṃsam abhighnatāṃ vivadatāṃ
> tat tac ca saṃkrīṇatāṃ
> sasyānām iva paṅktayaḥ pracalitā
> nṝṇām amī rāśayaḥ.
> dyūtād āhṛta|māṣakāś ca kitavā
> veśāya gacchanty amī
> saṃprāptāḥ paricārakaiḥ sa|kusumaiḥ
> s'|āpūpa|māṃs'|āsavaiḥ.

1.80 tad yāvad aham ap' îdānīṃ mahā|jana|saṃmarda|durgamaṃ vipaṇi|mārgam utsṛjy' êmāṃ puṣpa|vīthikām antareṇa pān'|âgārāṇy apasavyam upāvartamānaḥ Pūrṇabhadra|śṛṅgāṭakam avatīrya Makara|rathyayā veśa|mārgam avagāhiṣye. tat kāmam asaṃgṛhīta|māṣakasya veśa|praveśo nirāyudhasya saṃgrām'|âvataraṇam ity ubhayam apārthakaṃ kevalam ayaśase c' ânarthāya ca. kiṃ tu

Furthermore now

Flowers are sold here,
so beautiful they seem to laugh;
the wine-cup does its rounds in the taverns
and is drained.
Holding grass in their hands,*
people buying meat cast a sidelong glance
at the city-birds alighting on the knife-garlanded
butchery.

Furthermore,

Here,
jostling each other with their shoulders,
bargaining and buying this and that,
crowds of people undulate like rows of corn.
These gamblers here have won some coins at dice
and now they are making their way
to the courtesans' quarter,
accompanied by servants carrying flowers,
cakes, meat and liquor.

So now I too shall leave the market-street, impassable with 1.80
pressing crowds, and, sauntering past the taverns to the right of this flower-market and crossing the Purna·bhadra* plaza, follow the Mákara high street and emerge into the street of the courtesans' quarter. Now it is indisputable that both entering the courtesans' quarter without money and joining a battle unarmed are both pointless, embarrassing, and unprofitable. Nevertheless I must by all means accomplish the instructions of my

suhṛn|nideśo 'yam asmābhir avaśyaṃ nirvartayitavyaḥ. viśeṣeṇa hi bhūyād veśe viṭa|saṃnipātaḥ. *(parikramya)*

aye ko nu khalv eṣa Rohitakīyair mārdaṅgikaiḥ kaṃsa|pātra|veṇu|miśrair Yodheyaka|varṇair upagīyamāna eka|śravaṇ'|âvalambita|kuraṇṭaka|śekharo viralam apasavyam ākula|daśam uttarīyam apavartikayā saṃkṣipan muhur muhuḥ prakaṭ'|âika|sphik savyena pāṇinā madya|bhājanam utkṣipya nṛtyann āpāna|maṇḍapaṃ hāsayati? *(nirvarṇya)* ā jñātam! eṣa hi sa Bālhika|putraḥ sarva|dhūrta|parihās'|âika|bhājana|bhūto veśa|kukkuṭo Bāṣpo dhāntraḥ. bhoḥ! yat satyaṃ na kadā cid apy enam amattam apītaṃ vā paśyāmi. samaṃ c' âyam amṛkṣita|hasto māṣak'|ârdhen' âpi. tat kuto 'sy' âitad upapadyate? *(vitarkya)* hanta vijñātam! eṣa hi puro|bhāgī lajjā|viyuktaḥ sarvaṃ|kaṣaḥ sārvajanīnatvāt.

ābaddha|maṇḍalānāṃ
 pibatām upadaṃśa|muṣṭim ādāya
pravišati Bāṣpo madhyaṃ
 naṭa|naṭi|ceṭ'|âśva|bandhānām.

aho nu khalv asya pān'|ôpārjane vijñānam! tad alam anen' âbhibhāṣitena. ito vayam. *(parikramya)* idam aparaṃ jaṅgamaṃ jīrṇ'|ôdyānaṃ viṭa|janasya. eṣā hi purāṇa|puṃścalī Dharaṇiguptā nāma Kāma|dev'|āyatanād devatāyā upayācitaṃ nirvartya sphuṭita|kāśa|vallarī|śvetam

friend: "Have the pimps convene in the courtesans' quarter!" *(walks about)*

Hey! Who is being celebrated here with Yodhéyaka songs* by drummers from Róhitaka* accompanied by cymbals and bamboo flutes? A wreath of yellow amaranth flowers dangles from one of his ears as he clasps with a fibula* his threadbare, frazzle-hemmed toga that covers his right side.* One side of his buttocks is bared again and again as he dances, lifting up a wine-cup with his left hand, and makes the tavern-hall laugh. *(looking)* Aha! I know! This fellow* is the son of the Bactrian, the prime target of the ridicule of all rogues, the rooster of the courtesans' quarter: Mr Steam! Upon my word, I've never seen him sober or without a drink, but, at the same time, not even a halfpence ever rubs his hand. How can he manage this? *(reflects)* Bingo! I've got it! It is because he is obtrusive, shameless, and universally overbearing.

With a handful of snacks
Mr Steam plows into the circle of drinking dancers,
danseuses, servants and stablemen.

What an expert he is at scrounging liquor! Well, I'd rather not speak to him. Off we go. *(walks about)* Here is another walking garden of the pimps gone to seed. For this is the ancient courtesan called Dhárani·gupta. She has petitioned the deity in Kama's temple,* and now she circumambulates the Mákara post,* putting back on her shoulder her flopping hair, white as a blossoming sugarcane, wearing freshly washed clothes, replacing on her shoulder the cloak that has slipped down, and casting a

āgalitam aṃsa|deśād upari keśa|hastaṃ vinyasyantī sadyo|dhauta|nivasanā vigalitam uttarīyam ek'|âṃse pratisamādadhānā bali|vikṣep'|ôpanipatitair bali|bhṛtaiḥ parivṛtaṃ mayūraṃ nṛtyantam apāṅgen' âvalokayantī makara|yaṣṭiṃ pradakṣiṇī|karoti. bhoḥ! yat satyam ady' âpy asyāś cir'|âtikrāntaṃ yauvana|vibhramaṃ vilāsa|śeṣaṃ kathayati. tathā hi

śvetābhir nakha|rājibhiḥ parivṛtau
vyāvṛtta|mūlau stanau;
sṛkvaṇyoḥ śithilaś ca madhya|gaḍulo
niṣpīta|pūrvo 'dharaḥ;
sa|bhrūkṣepam udāhṛtaṃ paricayād
ady' âpi yukt'|ôttaraṃ:
rūpaṃ hi prahṛtaṃ prasahya jarayā,
n' âsyā vilāsā hṛtāḥ.

1.85 tan na śakyam enām anabhibhāṣy' âtikramitum. eṣā hy asmākaṃ priya|vayasyaṃ mārdaṅgikaṃ Sthāṇumitraṃ mitraṃ vyapadiśantī krauñca|rasāyan'|ôpayogam ātmanaḥ prakāśayati. tat katham enām upasarpāmi? *(vicintya)* ā jñātam! asyā h' îtas tṛtīye 'hani tapasvī Sthāṇumitraś cumban'|âtiprasaṅgāt tayā bībhatsam anubhūtavān. aho dhig akaruṇo rāgaḥ!

cumbana|raktaḥ so 'syā
daśanaṃ cyuta|mūlam ātmano vadane
jihvā|mūla|spṛṣṭaṃ
khāḍ iti kṛtvā nirasthīvat.

tat kāmaṃ veśam avatitīrṣus tīrtham idam atikrāman vañcitaḥ syām, tath" âpi tv āviṣkṛtam asyāḥ Sthāṇumitra|va-

sidelong glance at the dancing peacock surrounded by crows that alighted when the *bali* offering was laid out. Well, upon my word, even now the remainders of her romances speak of the impetuosity of her youth. For,

Her sagging breasts are encircled
by white lines of nail-marks;
her lower lip, sucked dry in former times,
is flaccid at the corners and puffy in the middle;
out of habit she responds appropriately even now
with knitted eyebrows:
old age has indeed robbed her of all her beauty,
but left her flirtatiousness.

I cannot pass by without speaking to her. She calls my buddy, the drummer Sthanu·mitra, her friend and thus betrays that she takes the "Curlew-elixir."* So how shall I approach her? *(reflecting)* All right, I know! Two days ago poor Sthanu·mitra had a disgusting experience with her thanks to their inordinately zealous kissing. Alas! Passion knows no mercy. 1.85

He was passionately kissing her
when with the root of his tongue
he felt her dislocated tooth in his mouth,
choked, and spat it out.*

Well, although I am depriving myself if I fail to honor this holy woman on my way to the courtesans' quarter, nevertheless, the story about her tooth falling into Sthanu·

dane danta|nipatanam, tan n' âbhigamanena vrīḍāṃ punar|uktī|karomi. sarvathā namo 'syai. sādhayāmy aham.

(parikramya) eso 'smi veśam avatīrṇaḥ. aho nu khalu veśasya parā śrīḥ! iha hy etāni pṛthak|pṛthaṅ|niviṣṭāni rucira|vapra|nemi|sāla|harmya|śikhara|kapota|pālī|siṃha|karṇa|gopānasī|valabhī|puṭ'|âṭṭālak'|âvalokana|pratolī|viṭaṅka|prāsāda|saṃbādhāny asaṃbādha|kakṣyā|vibhāgāni bhāge nimitāni sunirmita|rucira|khāta|pūrita|sikta|suṣira|phūtkṛt'|ôtkoṭita|lipta|likhita|sūkṣma|sthūla|vivikta|rūpa|śatāni baddhāni baddha|saṃdhi|dvāra|gavākṣa|vitardi|saṃjavana|vīthī|nirvyūhakāny eka|dvi|tri|pādap'|âlaṃkṛta|madhyak'|ôddeśāny uddeśya|vṛkṣaka|haritaka|phala|mālya|ṣaṇḍa|maṇḍitāni puṇḍarīka|śabalita|vimala|vāpī|toyāni toy'|ântara|vihita|dāru|parvata|bhūmi|latā|gṛha|citra|śāl"|âlaṃkṛtāni par'|ârdhya|muktā|pravāla|kiṅkiṇī|jāl'|āviṣkṛta|pariṣkarāṇy ucchrita|saubhāgya|vaijayantī|patākāny utpatant' îva gagana|talam avani|talād bhavana|var'|âvataṃsakāni vāra|mukhyānām. yatr' âite

mitra's mouth is an open secret, and I had best not embarrass her again by approaching her. Anyway, she has all my respect. Let's move on.

(walks about) I have reached the courtesans' quarter. Ah, the supreme splendor of the brothel quarter! Here the garlands of the hetaeras' exquisite mansions, set apart, reach from the surface of the earth up to the firmament; they are endowed with splendid foundations, verandas, walls, palatial turrets, eaves with dove-figures, window-decorations in the shape of lion's ears, curved rafters, horseshoe-like dormers, towers, balconies, gates, fillets, and terraces; the rooms in their apartments are spacious; their proportions are balanced; they are equipped with hundreds of clearly delineated, massive and filigreed figures which are well-designed, daintily carved out and filled in, sprinkled, their apertures blown through, roughened, plastered, and painted; their doors, windows, verandas, courtyards, galleries, and balconies are well-jointed; the spaces between their quadrangles and groves are beautified with one, two, or three trees; they are adorned with orchards planted for particular purposes, lawns, plenty of fruits and flowers; the clear water in their reservoirs is speckled with lotuses; they are decorated with wooden islands placed in water, underground chambers, bowers, and picture galleries, and they are conspicuously ornamented with exquisite pearls, corals, and nets of tiny bells. Here

āsīnair avalīḍha|cakra|valayair
mīladbhir Āvantikair
dhāryā rūḍha|Kirāta|saṃgata|dhurās
tiṣṭhanti karṇī|rathāḥ
ete ca dvi|guṇī|kṛt'|ôttara|kuthā
nidr"|âlas'|ādhoraṇāḥ
Kāmbojāś ca kareṇavaś ca kathayanty
antar|gatān svāminaḥ.

1.90 api c' âsmin veśe

nayana|salilair yair ev' âiko
vrajann abhivāhyate
pratata|visṛtais tair ev' ânyo
gṛhān atinīyate.
a|kṛśa|vibhaveṣv āsām āsthā
tath" âpi kṛta|vyayāḥ
samanupatitā nirbhartsyante
balāt kila mātṛbhiḥ.

(parikramya)

iyam anunayati priyaṃ kruddham, eṣā priyeṇ' ânunītā prasīdaty. asau sapta|tantrīr nakhair ghaṭṭayantī kalaṃ kākalī|pañcama|prāyam utkaṇṭhitā valgu|gīt'|âpadeśena vikrośati.
iyam upahita|darpaṇā kāminā maṇḍyate kāminī, kāmino maulim eṣā nibadhnāty, asau śārikāṃ spaṣṭam ālāpayaty, eṣa matto mayūro 'nayā cūta|puṣpeṇa saṃtarjito nṛtyati.

Rickshaws, ready to be drawn,
their poles held by tall Kirátas,
stand still with sleepy, seated Avántikas
resting on the rims of the wheels,
and here horses from Kambója* and elephants,
with folded housings and drivers fast asleep
betray that their masters have gone inside.

Furthermore here in the brothel quarter 1.90

The same copious flow of tears brings back a man
who was already leaving, and sends another
home.
These women live off the rich,
but when they nevertheless run into expenses,
their mothers, it is said, track them down
and harshly rebuke them.

(walks about)

Here a woman conciliates her irritated lover,
while this woman here, conciliated by her lover,
calms down.
There a lady plucks her lute's seven strings
with her nails and passionately yowls a tune
full of *kákali·pánchama* notes*
pretending it to be a lovely song.
Here a lover adorns his beloved who holds a mirror,
there a girl styles her lover's hair,
that woman teaches her mynah bird to speak clearly,
there an impassioned peacock dances
while a lady trains it with a mango flower.
What! This woman here overtaxes herself

katham! iyam atikanduka|krīḍayā madhyam āyāsayaty alpam. eṣā priyeṇ' ôpaviṣṭā sah' âkṣaiḥ parikrīḍati, yoṣitā c' ânay" âitat svayaṃ likhyate citram ākhyāyik" âsau punar vācyate.

alam alam atisaṃbhrameṇ' āsyatāṃ vāsu. bhadre, cirād dṛśyase. kiṃ bravīṣy? «adya taṃ praṣṭum arhasy ahaṃ yena mugdhā tathā vañcit" êti.» prasādy" âsi naḥ. svasti te sarvathā, sādhayāmo vayam.

(parikramya) idam aparaṃ suhṛt|pattanam upasthitam. eṣa hi sa Bālhikaḥ Kāṅkāyano bhiṣag Aiśānacandrir Hariścandraś candra iva kumuda|vāpīṃ veśa|vīthīm avabhāsayann ita ev' âbhivartate. tat kim asy' êha prayojanam?

1.95 *(vicintya)* ā jñātam! eṣa hi tasyāḥ pūrva|praṇayinyā Yaśomatyā bhaginīṃ Priyaṅguyaṣṭikāṃ kāmayate. asmān api rahasyen' âtisaṃdhatte. tan na śakyam enam apratipadya gantum. yāvad upasarpāmi.

(upagamya) aṃgho veśa|bisa|van'|âika|cakravāka, kuto bhavān?

in the ball game and strains her slender waist.
Here sits a lady playing dice with her lover,
and there a woman paints a picture herself,
and has a story recited.
Please don't trouble yourself! Remain seated,
darling.
It has been a while since I last saw you, my dear.
What are you saying?
"You must right away go and have words
with that man who deceived an innocent girl
like me in such a way."
I will have to owe you one.
Anyway, my best wishes to you. I'm moving on.

(walks about) Here is another paragon of a friend.* For here comes Harish·chandra,* son of Íshana·chandra,* the physician from Balkh, follower of Kankáyana,* illuminating the courtesans' quarter in the way the moon shines upon a lily-pond. Well, what is he up to here?

(reflecting) Aha! I know! He is in love with Priyángu·yásh- 1.95
tika, the sister of my former beloved, Yasho·mati. He hides his secret even from me. I cannot walk on by without accosting him. I'll go nearer.

(approaches) Ho, you lonesome *chakra·vaka* bird in the lotus-forest of the courtesans' quarter! Where are you coming from?

kiṃ bravīṣi? «eṣa hi tasyāḥ priya|sakhyās te kanīyasīṃ Priyaṅguyaṣṭikām auṣadhena saṃbhāvy' āgacchāmi» iti. na khalu tasyāḥ surata|subhikṣāyā āmay'|âvasanno madan'|âgniḥ? tasya dīpanīyakam uddiṣṭavān asi?

kiṃ bravīṣi? «muktaḥ parihāsaḥ. kaṣṭā khalu tasyāḥ śiro|vedanā» iti. vayasya, yat|satyam?

kiṃ bravīṣi? «kaḥ saṃdehaḥ? kṛcchra | sādhyā» iti. evam etat. śiro|vedanā nāma gaṇikā|janasya lakṣya|vyādhi|yautakam. paśyatu bhavān:

1.100 lalāṭe vinyasya
kṣataja|sadṛśaṃ candana|rasaṃ
mṛṇālaiḥ krīḍantī
kuvalaya|palāśaiḥ sakamalaiḥ
salīlaṃ bhrū|kṣepair
anugata|sukha|prāśnika|kathā
viraktā raktā vā
śirasi rujam ākhyāti gaṇikā.

kiṃ bravīṣi? «sad" âpi nāma tvaṃ karkaśa | parihāsaḥ. eṣa khalu tām auṣadhaṃ prāpāyy' āgacchāmi» iti. yuktam etat. asaṃśayaṃ hi—

What are you saying? "I am coming from Priyángu·yáshtika, the younger sister of your girlfriend. I've provided her with medicine." She has an abundant supply of sex: I hope illness has not tempered the fire of her passion? Did you prescribe her a digestive stimulant?

What are you saying? "Stop joking. She genuinely has a severe headache." My dear friend, are you sure?

What are you saying? "Undoubtedly! It's hard to cure." That is a fact. Such headaches indeed belong to the courtesan's dowry of sham illnesses. Observe, sir:

After smearing blood-like sandal-paste on her forehead, 1.100
the courtesan fools around with lotus-fibers,
and water-lily petals mixed with lotuses,
she punctuates the words of those who enquire after her health with a playful knitting of her eyebrows,
and complains of headache
no matter if she *is infatuated : menstruates* or *not.*

What are you saying? "You have a crude joke for every occasion. I really did administer medicine to her and now here I am." Perfectly reasonable. For undoubtedly

dhūnvantyāḥ kara|pallavaṃ valayinaṃ
ghnantyāḥ padā kuṭṭimaṃ
bibhrantyāś cyutam aṃśukaṃ sa|raśanaṃ
nābher adhaḥ pāṇinā
tasyā dīrghatarī|kṛt'|âkṣam apibaḥ
keśa|grahair ānanaṃ
sā vā tvad|daśana|cchad'|âuṣadham
alaṃ bālā tvayā pāyitā.

kiṃ bravīṣi? «vayasya eva tathā vidhāsyati» iti. cora, yadi na punar asmān rahasyen' âvakṣepsyasi. kiṃ tv adya sarva|viṭaiḥ sarva|viṭa|mahattarasya Bhaṭṭi|Jīmūtasya gṛhe kena cit prayojanena saṃnipatitavyam. tad vayasyo 'py a|hīna|kālam āgacchet.

kiṃ bravīṣi? «viditam ev' âitad viṭa|janasya yathā Viṣṇunāga|prāyaścitta|dānāy' âparāhṇe samāgantavyam iti. tad gacchatu bhavān. aham apy āgacchāmi» iti. tathā nāma. svasti bhavate. sādhayāmas tāvat.

1.105 *(parikramya)* katham? idaṃ sarva|viṭair viditam! tena hy alpa|pariśramo 'smi saṃjātaḥ. kevalaṃ veśyā|suhṛt|samāgamaiḥ kālo 'nupālayitavyaḥ. aye kasya khalv ayam a|Hūṇo Hūṇa|maṇḍana|maṇḍita ārya|ghoṭakaḥ Pāṭaliputrikāyāḥ Puṣpadāsyā bhavana|dvāram āviṣkaroti?

She shook her braceleted sprout-like hands,
  stamped her foot on the floor, and
  held with her hand the girdled garment
  as it slipped below her navel.
While you drank in her face,
  you stretched long her eyes
  by pulling back her hair.
Did you not make that girl drink copiously
  the medicine of your lips?

What are you saying? "Only you, my friend, are capable of such a thing." Thief! I'll make sure you will not get rid of me again by keeping me in the dark! But today all pimps must gather with a certain objective in the house of Bhatti Jimúta, the principal of all pimps. So you, too, my friend, must come in good time.

What are you saying? "The pimps already know that they should gather in the afternoon to impose a propitiatory ritual for Vishnu·naga. Then you may go, sir, all the best. I shall come as well." OK. All the best. I'm moving on now.

(walks about) How can it be? All the pimps are in the know! 1.105
Then my workload is lessened, I just have to while away time meeting courtesans and friends. Hey! Whose is this Aryan horse which marks the door of Pushpa·dasi of Pátali·putra? It is not a Hun horse, yet it is decked out with Hunnish accoutrements.

(nirvarṇya) ā jñātam! ebhir ih' ābaddha|śveta|kāṣṭha|karnikā|prahasita|kapola|deśair baddha|karair a|sajjam apy a|sakṛt sajjam iti s'|âñjali|prativādibhir Lāṭa|ḍiṇḍibhiḥ sūcitaḥ senā|pateḥ Senakasy' âpatya|ratnaṃ Bhaṭṭi|Makhavarmā bhaviṣyati. tan na śakyam enam an|abhibhāṣy' âtikramitum. atikrāman hi sneha|mādhyasthaṃ darśayeyam. yāvad enam upasarpāmi.

(upetya) bhoḥ kaḥ suhṛd|gṛhe? *(karṇaṃ dattvā)* eṣa khalu Bhaṭṭi|Makhavarmā mām āhvayati.

kiṃ bravīṣi? «vayasya, kim ady' âpy apūrva|pratihār'|ôpasthānena cir'|ôtsanno rāja|bhāvo 'smāsv ādhīyate? sthīyatāṃ muhūrtam, āgacchāmi» iti. sakhe, sthito 'smi. *(vilokya)* ita ito bhavān. eṣa khalu pulin'|âvatīrṇa|vṛṣabha|pad'|ôddharaṇa|khelaiś caraṇa|vinyāsair bhavana|kakṣyām alaṃkurvann ita ev' âbhivartate Bhaṭṭiḥ. aho nu khalv asya vilāseṣv abhyāsaḥ! athavā veśo vilāsa ity upapannam etat. api ca,

vilola|bhuja|gāminā
        rucira|pīvar'|âṃs'|ôrasā
vilāsa|catura|bhruvā
        muhur apāṅga|viprekṣiṇā
anena hi nar'|êndra|sad-
        ma viśatā padair mantharair
a|vīṇam a|mṛdaṅgam e-
        ka|naṭa|nāṭakaṃ nāṭyate.

(looking) Ah! I know! It must be Bhatti Makha·varman,* the noble son of general Sénaka: he is given away by these cynic ascetics from Lata* whose cheeks laugh with white wooden earrings,* who join their hands in supplication and incessantly protest that something is ready though it is not. It is impossible to pass by without speaking to him. By ignoring him I would show indifference to friendship. Let's go closer then.

(approaches) Hello, is someone in my friend's house? *(listens)* I hear Bhatti Makha·varman greeting me.

What are you saying? "Comrade, why after all this time do you restore me to my long obsolete royal rank* by assuming the role of such an extraordinary doorkeeper? Hold on, I'm coming." I'm waiting, my friend. *(looking)* This way, sir, this way. Here comes Bhatti, gracing the inner apartments with his footfalls that imitate the cavorting of a bull that has descended the sandy riverbank. Lo, his mastery of frivolity! Or rather, this is appropriate since the courtesans' quarter is synonymous with frivolity. What's more,

Striding with swinging arms,
his shoulders and chest splendid and robust,
his eyebrows adept at flirting,
repeatedly shooting side-glances,
he performs a one-man play without lutes
and drums, as he enters a royal palace with stately bearing.*

1.110 yāvad enam ālapāmi. Bhaṭṭi|Makhavarman, kim ayam ati|divā|vihāreṇa suhṛj|jana utkaṇṭhyate? sādhu, muhūrtam api tāvad yuṣmad|darśanen' ânugṛhyeta.

eṣa khalu vihasann ākul'|âpasavya|paridhānaṃ śvāsa|viṣamit'|âkṣaraṃ svāgatam ity añjalin" âbhyupaiti. bho yadā tāvad anen' âdy' âiva Puṣpadāsī puṣpavat" îti mahyam ākhyātā, tath" âpi katham upabhukt" âiva? *(vicintya)* Lāṭa|diṇḍino nām' âite n' âtibhinnāḥ piśācebhyaḥ. kutaḥ? sarvo hi Lāṭaḥ—

> nagnaḥ snāti mahājane 'mbhasi sadā,
>   nenekti vāsaḥ svayaṃ,
> keśān ākulayaty, a|dhauta|caraṇaḥ
>   śayyāṃ samākrāmati,
> yat tad bhakṣayati, vrajann api pathā
>   dhatte paṭaṃ pāṭitaṃ,
> chidre c' âpi sakṛt prahṛtya sahasā
>   Lāṭaś ciraṃ katthate.

sarvathā kṛtam anena sva|deś'|āupayikam. mā tāvad bhoḥ!

avicintya phalaṃ vallyās tvayā puṣpa|vadhaḥ kṛtaḥ.

1.115 kiṃ bravīṣi? «katham?» iti.

idaṃ hi rajasā dhvastam uttarīyaṃ vilokyatām!

I'll chat with him. Bhatti Makha·varman, why do you make your friends pine for you with your prolonged daytime pleasures? Fair enough, may I be honored by your presence at least for a minute? 1.110

Here he comes, smiling, his disorderly garment covering his right shoulder as he pants forth 'Welcome!,' hands folded in salutation. Ah! How come he could have sex with Pushpa·dasi when he told me today that she was menstruating? *(reflecting)* These Lata cynics are not very different from goblins. Why? For every Lata—

Always bathes naked in public,
washes his clothes himself, musses up his hair,
goes to bed without washing his feet,
eats anything,
wears a torn garment
even when he walks on the street.
And, once a Lata has brutally hit one's weak point
he boasts for a long time.

Undeniably, he has done what comes naturally in his country. This is unacceptable!

Heedless of the fruit you have destroyed the flower*
of the vine.

What are you saying? "How so?" 1.115

Just take a look at this cloak of yours, soiled by
menstrual discharge!

kiṃ bravīṣi? «śayy" | ânt' | âvalambitaṃ tāmbūl' | âvasiktam etad avagacchāmi» iti.

mā tāvat! idaṃ kṣudra|muktāphal' | âvakīrṇam iva lalāṭaṃ sveda|bindubhiḥ kim iti vakṣyati?

eṣa pārśvam avadhāy' ôccaiḥ prahasitaḥ.

1.120 haṇḍe jaghanya|kāmuka, katham anayā chalitaḥ? kiṃ bravīṣi? «kaś chalito nāma? nanv anugṛhīto 'smi! śrūyatām! sā hi—

vipulatara|lalāṭā
samyat'|âgr'|âlakatvād,
racita|jaghana|bhārā
vāsas" ârdha|ūrukeṇa,
vivṛta|tanur apoḍha|
prāg|alaṃkāra|bhārā
kathaya katham agamyā
puṣpitā strī|latā syāt?

api ca śrotum arhati bhavān

What are you saying? "I draped it over the end of the bed and I guess it got spattered with betel *pan*."

Not so fast! What does this forehead of yours tell us, bedecked with drops of sweat as if with tiny pearls?

He bursts out laughing, holding his sides.

Hey you wretched lecher, how did she dupe you? What are 1.120
you saying? "Who's been duped at all? Surely I've been favored! Listen! For she—

Draws back her front locks
making her forehead seem wider;
her heavy hips are veiled with a garment
reaching to mid-thigh;
her figure is exposed
since the encumbrance
of her frontal ornaments
has been removed:
tell me,
why shouldn't I have sex
with a blossoming* vine-like woman?

Furthermore please listen to the following, sir:

pārśv'|āvartita|locanā nakha|padāny
ālokayantī mayā
dṛṣṭā c' ēṣad avāṅ|mukhī sva|bhavana|
pratyātape 'vasthitā
saṃgṛhy' âtha kara|dvayena kaṭhināv
utkampamānau stanau
prāviśy' ântar|agāram argalavatā
dvāraṃ kareṇ' āvṛṇot.

tato 'ham anudrutaṃ praviśya

1.125 kaca|nigraha|dīrgha|locanāṃ
rabhas'|āvartita|valgita|stanīm
kim as' îti na h' îti vādinīṃ
samacumbaṃ sahasā vilāsinīm.» iti

bhoḥ, citraḥ khalu prastāvaḥ. pṛcchāmas tāvad enām. tatas tataḥ?

kiṃ bravīṣi? «atha sakhe—

samupasthitasya jaghanaṃ
raśanā|tyāgād viviktatara|bimbam
pāṇibhyāṃ vrīḍitayā
nimīlite me 'nayā nayane.» iti

dhik tvām astu! a|vikatthana udvejanīyo hy asi nindyaś c' ārya|janasya saṃvṛttaḥ.

When I spied her standing
 in the portico of her house
her eyes turned sideways,
as she examined her nail-marks,
gently lowering her head,
then she clutched her firm,
trembling breasts with both hands,
went indoors and grasping the bolt
she slammed the door.

Then I pursued her inside.

Her eyes were stretched long 1.125
 as I pulled her hair,
her breasts bounced when I rolled them,
while she said 'What are you...? Stop!'
I passionately kissed that coquette."

Well, a curious prelude indeed. I'll ask her about it. And then?

What are you saying? "Then, my friend,

When I fell upon her hips,
the orb of which was fully exposed
 freed of her girdle,
she bashfully covered my eyes
 with her hands."

Shame on you! If you are not bragging then you've truly become an object of fear and loathing for civilized people.

1.130 kiṃ bravīṣi? «evam apy anugṛhīto 'smi. na tvayā Mahā|bhārate śruta|pūrvam?

‹yasy' âmitrā na bahavo
yasmān n' ôdvijate janaḥ
yaṃ sametya na nindanti
sa Pārtha puruṣ'|âdhamaḥ.› » iti

bho, etat khalu ḍiṇḍitvaṃ nāma. tath" âpi sādhu bhoḥ, prīto 'smi bhavato 'nena ḍiṇḍitvena. sarvathā viṭeṣv ādhirājyam arhasi. ayam idānīm āśīr|vādaḥ.

kiṃ bravīṣi? «avahito 'smi» iti. śrūyatām:

prabhātam avagamya pṛṣṭham
upagūhya suptasya te
pragalbham adhiruhya pārśvam
apavāsas" âik'|ōruṇā
tath" âiva hi kaca|graheṇa
parivartya vaktr'|âmbujaṃ
pibatv atha ca pāyayatv a-
dharam ātmanas tvāṃ priyā.

1.135 eṣa khalv anugṛhīto 'sm' îty uktvā palāyate. namo 'stu bhagavate. sādhayāmas tāvat.

(parikramya) aye kā nu khalv eṣā sva|bhavan'|âvalokanam apsarā vimānam iv' âlaṃkaroti? eṣā hi sā Kāśīnāṃ vāra|mukhyā Parākramikā nāma sukha|matiḥ piñcholayā

What are you saying? "Be that as it may, I thank you kindly. 1.130
Have you never heard the following in the Maha·bhárata:*

'He who does not have many enemies,
whom people do not fear,
whom they do not unite to censure:
that man, O Partha,
is the vilest human being.'"

Oh, this is exactly what is called cynicism. Nevertheless, well done, sir, I'm impressed by your cynicism. By all means you are worthy of sovereignty among pimps. Now here is my benediction.

What are you saying? "I am all ears." Listen:

When she notices that the day is dawning,
and embraces your back as you sleep
and boldly surmounts your side
  with one uncovered thigh,
may your beloved turn round your lotus-face
  pulling your hair, as you did,
and drink your mouth,
and make you drink her own lower lip.

He says "I'm obliged" and vanishes. Thank God. I'm moving on now. 1.135

(walks about) Hey, who is this woman who bedizens the terrace of her house as an *ápsaras* does her flying palace? This must be the hetaera from Kashi called Ms Amazon. She seduces the eye with the flirtatious movements of

krīḍantī rūpa|lāvaṇya|vibhramair locanam anugṛhṇāti. āścaryam!

viracita|kuca|bhārā
hema|vaikakṣyakeṇa
sphuṭa|vivṛta|nitambā
vāsas" ârdh'|ōrukeṇa
vicarati calayantī
kāminām cittam eṣā
kisalayam iva lolā
cañcalaṃ veśa|vallyāḥ.

api ca,

gaṇḍ'|ânt'|āgalit'|âika|kuṇḍala|maṇi|
cchāy"|ânulipt'|ānanām
anvabhyastatayā hi|kāra|piśunaiḥ
śvāsair avāk|tālubhiḥ
piñcholām adhare niveśya madhurām
āvādayantīm imāṃ
maṇḍūka|svana|śaṅkito gṛha|śikhī
paryeti vakr'|ānanaḥ.

1.140 kiṃ nu khalv asyā udavasitād Indrasvāmino rahasya|sacivo Hiraṇyagarbhako niṣpaty' êta ev' âbhivartate? kim atr' āścaryam? Indrasvāmī Hiraṇyagarbhako veśa iti saṃhitam idaṃ taptaṃ tapten' êti. eṣa mām añjalin" ôpasar-

her ravishing body as she jauntily plays the flute. Wonderful!

Her heavy breasts supported
   by a golden cross-band,
her buttocks clearly exposed
   by her garment reaching mid-thigh,
she saunters about and stirs the hearts
   of gallants,
swinging like a swaying sprout
   on the vine of the courtesans' quarter.

Furthermore,

Her face tinted by the gleam
   of the jewel in the one earring
   that hangs upon her cheek,
as she puts the mellifluous flute
   to her lower lip and plays it expertly
   with breaths like amorous sighs*
exhaled through her lowered palate,
the pet peacock suspects it to be the croaking
   of a frog,
   screws up its face and
   walks around her.

What in the world! Indra·svamin's* private counselor Hiránya·gárbhaka rushes out of her house and is headed right this way! But is this really surprising? Indra·svamin, Hiránya·gárbhaka, the brothel quarter: hot stuff is melded here with hot stuff. He approaches me respectfully folding his hands. Hey Hiránya·gárbhaka, why are 1.140

pati. haṇḍe Hiraṇyagarbhaka, kim idaṃ veśa|dev'|āyatanam Aparānta|piśācair vidhvaṃsayitum iṣyate?

kiṃ bravīṣi? «eṣa khalu svāmino 'smi videśa|rāgeṇ' âivaṃ dhuri niyuktaḥ. eṣā hi pūrvaṃ pañca|suvarṇa|śatāni gaṇayati, adhunā sahasreṇ' âpy upanimantrit" âpi mātr" âpi viniyujyamānā n' âiva śakyate tīrtham avatārayitum. tad arhasi tvam api tāvad enāṃ gamayitum» iti. atyārjavaḥ khalv asi. na hi śata|sahasreṇ' âpi prāṇā labhyante.

kiṃ bravīṣi? «kiṃ c' âsyāḥ prāṇa|saṃdehe kāraṇam asmāsu paśyasi?» iti. āviṣkṛtaṃ hi tatra|bhavatyā bhartṛ|svāminaś cāmara|grāhiṇyāḥ Kuṭaṅgadāsyāḥ svāminaḥ saṃsargāt tathā|bhūtaṃ vyasanam anubhūtam.

kiṃ bravīṣi? «ālabhasva tāvad idaṃ me śarīram! satyam ev' êdam?» iti. a|satyena na svāminam evaṃ brūyāt.

kiṃ bravīṣi? «cir'|âbhyastam ev' êdam asmat|svāmi|pādānām iti.» ata eva na śakyam anyathā kārayitum. na c' âitad evam. paśyatu bhavān:

goblins from Aparánta trying to ruin this temple of the courtesans' quarter?

What are you saying? "Actually I am on a mission from my master, since he adores exotic countries. She used to charge five hundred gold pieces, but now even if she is invited for as much as a thousand, and even if her mother solicits her, I cannot make her condescend to my respectable master. Therefore could you please also try and encourage her?" You really are naive! For even a hundred thousand cannot buy someone's vital breaths.

What are you saying? "What makes you think that we are a source of danger to her life?" Since it is widely known that such a calamity befell the respectable Kutánga·dasi, his lordship's chowrie-bearer, as a result of her liaison with her master.*

What are you saying? "Now swear upon my body here! Is this really true?" She wouldn't say such things about her master if they were untrue.

What are you saying? "This is indeed an ingrained habit of our honorable master." And for this reason it cannot be remedied. But that is not the case. Observe, sir:

1.145 kāvye gāndharve nṛtta|śāstre vidhijñaṃ
dakṣaṃ dātāraṃ dakṣiṇaṃ Dākṣiṇātyam
veśyā kā n' êcchet svāminaṃ Koṅkaṇānāṃ
syāc ced asya strīṣv ārjavāt saṃnipātaḥ?

api ca,

saṃcārayan kalabhakaṃ gaja|nartakaṃ vā
veśy"|âṅgaṇeṣu Bhagadatta iv' Êndradattaḥ
udvīkṣyate stana|niviṣṭa|kar'|âmbujābhir
vyāghro mṛgībhir iva vāra|vilāsinībhiḥ.

api c' âiṣā bhartur no 'dhirājasya syālaṃ pāraśavaṃ Kauśikaṃ Siṃhavarmāṇaṃ mitram apadiśantī sarvān kāminaḥ pratyākhyānena vrīḍayati.

kiṃ bravīṣi? «kiṃ ca tasy' âiṣ" âtikāmitay" âvamanyate» iti. yuṣmad|deś'|āupayikam eva kila satatam atisevanam.

1.150 kiṃ bravīṣi? «deś'|āupayikam a|deś'|āupayikam iti n' âvagacchāmi. vispaṣṭam abhidhīyatām!» iti. evam anugṛhītaḥ kathaṃ na kathayiṣyāmi? śrūyatām:

He is an expert in poetry, 1.145
music and choreography, he is intelligent,
generous, courteous,
and a man from the South:
is there any courtesan
who would not desire the lord of the Kónkanas
  if he were more forthright in his liaisons with
    women?

Furthermore,

When Indra·datta,
  as if he were Bhaga·datta,*
parades a young elephant
  or an elephant trained to dance
in the courtyards of courtesans,
the coquettes eyeball him as does eye a tiger,
placing their lotus-hands on their breasts.

What's more, she shames all her suitors by spurning them when she intimates that the bastard Káushika Simha·varman, our sovereign's brother-in-law, is her friend.

What are you saying? "So she despises him because of his insatiable passion?" People say that continuous extreme sex is normal in your country.

What are you saying? "'Befits a country—does not befit a 1.150
country:' I don't understand your point. Speak clearly!" Why should I not tell you when you petition me so kindly? Listen:

śravaṇa|nikaṭa|jair nakh'|âvapātair
vana|gaja|damya iv' âṅkitaḥ pratodaiḥ
vivṛta|jaghana|bhūṣaṇāṃ vivastrāṃ
vṛṣa iva vatsatarīm ih' ôpayāti.

kiṃ bravīṣi? «tena hy anen' âiv' ôpāyanen' âinam upasthāsyāmi» iti. yady evam Indrasvāmī vijñāpyaḥ:

daśana|maṇḍala|citra|kakundarāṃ
dayita|mālya|nivāsita|mekhalām
tvad|aparaṃ prati sā jaghana|sthalīṃ
na vivṛṇoti vṛt" âpi śataṃ|śataiḥ.

svasti bhavate, sādhayāmas tāvat.

1.155 *(parikramya)* aye ko nu khalv eṣa Śaurpakārikāyā Rāmadāsyā bhavanān niṣpatya ḍiṇḍi|gaṇa|parivṛto veśam āviṣkaroti? *(vilokya)* etaj jaṅgamaṃ viṭa|tīrtham udīcyānāṃ Bālhikānāṃ Kārūśa|Maladānāṃ c' ēśvaro mahā|pratīhāro Bhadrāyudhaḥ. eṣaḥ

viracita|kuntala|mauliḥ
śravaṇ'|ârpita|kāṣṭha|vipula|sita|kalaśaḥ×
janam ālapañ jakārair
unnāṭayat' îva Lāṭānām.

In this land one approaches a woman
who is naked, revealing the ornament of her buttocks,
like a bull approaches a young cow:
with nail-wounds around one's ear,
just as a forest elephant
that needs to be tamed is scarred by goads.

What are you saying? "Then I shall approach him with this advice." If so then tell Indra·svamin the following:

Even if she is rewarded with many thousands,
she will not reveal the surface of her buttocks,
girded with her lover's garland,
to anyone else but you,
their hollows dimpled with round tooth-marks.*

All the best to you, sir, I must go.

(walks about) Hey! Who is this man rushing from the house 1.155
of Rama·dasi of Shurpáraka* and who, surrounded by a group of cynics, personifies the brothel quarter? *(looking)* This is Bhadráyudha,* a moving sacred site for the veneration of pimps, the chief door-keeper, the lord of the northern Bactrians, Kárushas and Máladas.* He,

With coiffed hair,
with enormous, white, wooden jugs* affixed to his ears,
accosting people with "ja" sounds,
he seems to be mocking the Latas.*

kā ca tāvad asya Lāṭeṣu sādhu|dṛṣṭiḥ! etāvat sarvo hi Lāṭaḥ:

saṃveṣṭya dvāv uttarīyeṇa bāhū
rajjvā madhyaṃ vāsasā saṃnibadhya
pratyudgacchan saṃmukhīnam śakāraiḥ
pād'|āpātair aṃsa|kubjaḥ prayāti.

api ca,

1.160 urasi kṛta|kapotakaḥ karābhyāṃ
vadati jaj' êti yakāra|hīnam uccaiḥ
sama|yugala|nibaddha|madhya|deśo
vrajati ca paṅkam iva spṛśan kar'|âgraiḥ.

sarvathā n' âsty a|piśācam aiśvaryam. athav" âsy' âiv' âikasya deś'|ântara|vihāro yuktaḥ. kutaḥ?

yen' Âparānta|Śaka|Mālava|bhūpatīnāṃ
kṛtvā śiraḥsu caraṇau caratā yath"|êṣṭam
kāle 'bhyupetya jananīṃ jananīṃ ca Gaṅgām
āviṣkṛtā Magadha|rāja|kulasya lakṣmīḥ.

api ca,

And he really does have a perceptive eye for Latas! For in fact every Lata

Wraps up both his arms in his cloak,
girds his waist with a piece of cloth using a rope,
assaults everyone he meets with "sha" sounds*
and then rushes on with hunched shoulders.

Furthermore,

Placing his hands on his chest in the 1.160
"pigeon-gesture,"*
yelling "jaja" without "ya" sounds,
his waist girt with a pair of smooth cloths,
he promenades as if he were touching mud
with his fingers.

Without doubt, there could be nothing divine if there were not the demonic. Or rather, he is is uniquely suited to sojourning in foreign countries. Why?

He roamed wherever he pleased
placing his feet on the heads of the kings of
Aparánta,* the Shakas and the Málavas;*
and in time he betook himself to his mother
and mother Ganges,
and made manifest the glory
of the Mágadha* dynasty.*

Furthermore,

vel”|ânilair mṛdubhir ākulit’|âlak’|ântā
gāyanti yasya caritāny Aparānta|kāntāḥ
utkaṇṭhitāḥ samavalambya latās tarūṇām
hintāla|māliṣu taṭeṣu mah”|ârṇavasya.

1.165 kiṃ tad gītam?

«u hi māṇuso tti Bhaḍḍā-
uheṇa ṇavi ko vi licchaï āuhe
ṇa soṇṇāri tassa kamma|siddhiṃ
viḍā hi khalu bhuñjanti sokara|siddhiṃ.»

(parikramya) eṣa khalu Pradyumna|dev’|āyatanasya vaijayantīm abhilikhati. etad ḍiṇḍitvaṃ nāma bhoḥ! ḍiṇḍino hi nām’ âite n’ âtiviprakṛṣṭā vānarebhyaḥ. bhoḥ kiṃ ca tāvad asya ḍiṇḍikeṣu priyatvam! ḍiṇḍino hi nāma

ālekhyam ātma|lipibhir gamayanti nāśaṃ,
saudheṣu kūrcaka|maṣīmalam arpayanti,
ādāya tīkṣṇatara|dhāram ayo|vikāraṃ
prāsāda|bhūmiṣu ghuṇa|kriyayā caranti.

kiṃ ca tāvad ayaṃ likhati? *(vilokya)* «Nirapekṣaḥ» iti. sthāne khalv asy’ êdaṃ nāma. suṣṭhu khalv idam ucyate: «arthaṃ nāma śīlasy’ ôpaharati» iti. tathā hy eṣa dhāntras tāṃ naḥ priya|sakhīm[×] anapekṣayā veśa|tāpasī|vratena karśayati. sā hi tapasvinī

The beauties of Aparánta,
  their locks tousled by the gentle coastal breezes,
sing his deeds as they passionately embrace
the lianas of the trees on the ocean's shore
  wreathed by date palms.*

How does that song go? 1.165

"What a man!" they think,
and no one wants to take up arms against
  Bhadráyudha.
Heroes do not benefit from his manliness,
for the pimps exploit him with ease."*

(walks about) I see someone scribbling on the banner of this Pradyúmna temple.* Now this is staggering cynicism! For these cynics are indeed not very far removed from monkeys. And what's more, he* must be a favorite among the cynics! For the cynics

Vandalize frescoes with their own graffiti,
splotch ink with brushes on whitewashed
  mansions,
and putting on sharp-edged metal blades
  they walk on the floors of temples
  acting like woodworms.

Now what is he writing? *(looking)* "Blasé." He has an apt name. It is indeed rightly said: "One's name betrays one's character."* That is why this fellow ravages my dear friend* with his apathy, forcing her to live like an ascetic in the courtesans' quarter. For that poor woman,

1.170 netr'|âmbu pakṣmabhir arāla|ghan'|âsit'|âgrair
netr'|âmbu|dhauta|valayena kareṇa vaktram
śokaṃ guruṃ ca hṛdayena samaṃ bibharti
trīṇi tridhā tri|vali|jihmita|roma|rājiḥ.

tad upālapsye tāvad enam. bho bhagavan Nirapekṣa, karuṇ'|ātmakasya bhavato maitrīm ādāya vartamānasya tvayi muditāyāṃ yoṣiti yuktam upekṣā|vihāritvam?

kiṃ bravīṣi? «gṛhīto vañcitakasy' ârthaḥ. spṛṣṭo 'smy upāsakatvena. īdṛśaḥ saṃsāra|dharma ity uktaṃ Tathāgatena» iti. mā tāvad bhoḥ! tasyām eva bhagavatas Tathāgatasya vacanaṃ pramāṇaṃ n' ânyatra?

kiṃ bravīṣi? «kutra vā kadā vā mama Tathāgatasya vacanam apramāṇam?» iti. iyaṃ pratijñā?

kiṃ bravīṣi? «kutaḥ saṃdehaḥ?» iti. bhadra|mukha, śrūyatām:

1.175 śrama|niḥsṛta|jihvam unmukhaṃ
hṛdi niḥsaṅga|nikhāta|sāyakam
samavekṣya mṛgaṃ tath"|āgataṃ
smarasi tvaṃ na mṛgaṃ Tathāgatam?

Whose line of abdominal hair is rippled 1.170
by the three folds above her navel,
holds at the same time three things in three ways:
tears on her eyelashes with thick black, curved tips,
her face on her hands,
their bracelets washed by tears,
and deep sorrow in her heart.

I will reprimand him. Ho! Venerable Blasé! You are compassionate and practice loving-kindness: so is it appropriate that you practice indifference towards a woman who feels altruistic joy for you?*

What are you saying? "I know what you are insinuating. I am blessed with being a lay disciple of the Buddha. As the Tathágata has said: 'Such is the way of the world.'" Now wait a sec! The words of the blessed Tathágata apply only to that woman, and not anyone else?

What are you saying? "Where or when have the Tathágata's words not been authoritative for me?" Is that what you assert?

What are you saying? "Why would anyone doubt it?" Listen, gentle sir:

When you see a deer, 1.175
its tongue hanging out from exhaustion,
raising its head,
and its heart pierced by a freely flying arrow,
don't you recall the Tathágata
who was once a deer in the same condition?

eṣa prahasitaḥ. kiṃ bravīṣi? «na khalu Tathāgata|śāsanaṃ śaṅkitavyam. anyadd hi śāstram, anyā puruṣa|prakṛtiḥ. na vayaṃ vītarāgāḥ» iti. yady evam arhati bhavāṃs tatra|bhavatīṃ Rādhikāṃ tathā|bhūtām śoka|sāgarād uddhartum.

kiṃ bravīṣi? «yad ājñāpayati vayasyaḥ. ayam añjaliḥ. sādhu mucyeyam» iti. sarvathā durlabhas te mokṣaḥ. kiṃ tv iyam āśīḥ pratigṛhyatām:

viproṣy' āgata utsukām avanatām
utsaṅgam āropaya,
skandhe vaktram upopadhāya rudatīṃ
bhūyaḥ samāśvāsaya,
ābaddhāṃ mahiṣī|viṣāṇa|viṣamām
unmucya veṇīṃ tato
lambaṃ locana|toya|śauṇḍam alakaṃ
chindhi priyāyāḥ svayam.

eṣa prahasya gataḥ. ito vayam. *(parikramya)* aye ko nu khalv eṣa ita ev' âbhivartate?

1.180 duścīvar'|âvayava|saṃvṛta|guhya|deśo
bast'|ānanaḥ kapila|romaśa|pīvar'|âṃsaḥ
āyāti mūlakam adan kapi|piṅgal'|âkṣo
Dāśerako yadi na nūnam ayaṃ piśācaḥ.

He is laughing. What are you saying? "The Tathágata's teaching must never be questioned. Theory is indeed one thing, and another thing is human nature. I'm not devoid of passion." If so then please, sir, rescue lady Rádhika, who is in such a sorry state, from the ocean of grief.

What are you saying? "As you command, my friend. I pay my respects, may I be released now?" Release is hardly attainable for you. Still, take this blessing:

When you return from abroad
and the woman who desires you bows down,
take her on your lap, rest her face again and again
  on your shoulder and console her when she cries.
Then may you let down her woven braid,
  rugged as a cow-buffalo's horn,
and may you cut your beloved's long locks,
  which are drunk with tears, yourself.

He goes away, laughing. I'm off. *(walks about)* Hey! Who's that, coming this way?

His private parts are covered with a piece of tattered 1.180
  cloth,
he is goat-faced,
  with red hair on his bulky shoulders
  and eyes tawny like a monkey,
he comes munching a radish:
if he is not a Dashéraka then he must be a goblin.

bhavatu, dṛṣṭam. eṣa khalu bhrātur athavā vayasyasya tatra|bhavato Dāśerak'|âdhipater apatya|ratnasya Guptakulasy' āvāse dṛṣṭa|pūrvaḥ. tat kim asy' êha prayojanam? eṣa māṃ kṛt'|âñjalir upasarpati.

kiṃ bravīṣi? ⌜«Gupta|kuleṇa pekkhasi ovārida v(p)aṇap(v)añcadiccu gaṇikā (kāvi?) kide psayadi tahṇā, ṇaṃ poravīthīe aṣeṣaāyitaṃ puṃṇi (puṇṇi) kāvi gaṇikā ṇa dīṣai tahammi taṣṣa adīye (ādīye), teṇayyuṃ samaṃ khelanto ṇiyyudiṣṣaye, ambā hi me ṣāvitā tuyyaṃ atthakeṇa dāṇi gaṇikā kāmuppūlida aṣṣeṇa kulonthiṃtheṇe(a)va kāmā ṇa yaṣṣe (aṃṣe), jai gacchāmi viṣikkha(h?)e daṇḍituṃ homi diṣuvaśoviṣu eka evaṃ» ti.⌟[×] aho deśa|veṣa|bhāṣā|dākṣiṇya|sampad|upeto Guptakulasya yuva|rājasya madana|dūtaḥ! veśa eva vartamāno veśam āpaṇ'|âbhidhānena pṛcchati. tan na śakyam īdṛśaṃ *ratnam* avabodhya vināśayitum. īdṛśa ev' âstu. evaṃ tāvad enaṃ vakṣye: bhadra, rāja|vīthyāṃ *lāvaṇik'/āpaṇeṣu* mṛgyatāṃ gaṇikā. eṣa praharṣāt praṇipatya gataḥ. ito vayam.

(parikramya) kva nu khalv idānīṃ Dāśeraka|darśan'|âvadhūtaṃ cakṣuḥ prakṣālayeyam? *(vilokya)* bhavatu, dṛṣṭam. etadd hi tad asmākaṃ pūrva|praṇayinyāḥ Śūrasenasundaryā niveśanam. katham! apāvṛta|pakṣa|dvāram eva. yāvad etat praviśāmi. *(praviṣṭakena)* kva nu khalv imaṃ pāda|pracāra|śramam apanayeyam? bhavatu, dṛṣṭam. iyaṃ khalu priyaṅgu|vīthikā priy" êv' ôtsaṅgena śilā|talena mām upanimantrayate. yāvad atr' ôpaviśāmi. *(vilokya)* kim ih' âbhilikhitam? *(vācayati)*

All right, I see. Of course I've seen him before in the house of the honorable Gupta·kula, the excellent son of the lord the Dashérakas, my brother, or rather, my friend. Well, what is he up to here? He folds his hands and approaches me.

What are you saying? "....................."* Oh! How sophisticated in attire, diction, and the gallantry of his native land is the love-courier of crown prince Gupta·kula! Though he is already in the courtesans' quarter, he inquires about it calling it a "shop." It would be unbecoming to ruin such a *gift : precious man* with information. Let him go on as he is. This is what I tell him: My friend, look for a courtesan in the *shops of salt-dealers : beauty shops : brothels* along the high street.* He bows with joy and rushes off. I move on.

(walks about) Where can I cleanse my eyes now that they have become defiled by the sight of a Dashéraka? *(looking)* All right, I see. This is indeed the house of Shura·sena·súndari,* my ex-beloved. Strange! The side door is open. Well, I'll enter. *(mimes entering)* Where can I relieve the fatigue of my promenade? All right, I see. This *priyángu* terrace invites me with its stone slab, like a beloved woman with her lap. Well, let's sit down. *(looking)* What's written here? *(reads aloud)*

«sakhi, prathama|saṃgame
na kalah'|āspadaṃ vidyate
na c' âsya vimanaskatām
aśṛṇavaṃ na v" âkalyatām.
yuvānam abhisṛtya taṃ
cira|manoratha|prārthitaṃ
kim asy amṛdit'|âṅga|rā-
ga|racanā tath" âiv' āgatā?»

1.185 iti. *(vicintya)* kasyāś cit khalv iyaṃ ken' âpi pratyākhyāta|praṇayāyā daurbhāgya|ghoṣaṇā ghuṣyate. tat kaṃ nu khalu pṛccheyam? *(karṇaṃ dattvā)* aye iyaṃ caraṇ'|ābharaṇa|śabda|sūcitā Śūrasenasundar" îta ev' âbhivartate. y" âiṣā

ālamby' âikena kāntaṃ kisalaya|mṛdunā
pāṇinā chattra|daṇḍaṃ
saṃgṛhy' âikena nīvīṃ cala|maṇi|raśanāṃ
bhraśyamān'|âṃśuk'|ântā
āyāty abhyutsmayantī jvalitatara|vapur
bhūṣaṇānāṃ prabhābhiḥ
sajyotiṣkā sacandrā savihaga|virutā
Śarvarī|devat" êva.

bhoḥ! yat satyam abhyutthāpayat' îva mām apy asyās tejasvitā. eṣā māṃ kapotaken' ôpasarpati. alam asmān upacāreṇa pratyādeṣṭum.

kim āha bhavatī? «cirād api tāvat svāminām upagatānām upacāreṇa tāvad ayaṃ jana ātmānam anugṛhṇīyāt» iti. alam alam atyupālambhena! idam ucitam utsaṅg'|āsanam anugṛhyatām. eṣā me «śirasā pratigṛhītam» ity uk-

"My friend,
there is no call for a quarrel on a first date,
nor did I hear that he was depressed or sick.
You went to meet that young man
whom you had passionately entreated for long,
so why have you returned in such a state,
the makeup on your body untouched?"

(reflecting) This sounds like a proclamation of a spurned woman's ill fate. Whom shall I ask about it? *(listening)* Oho! Here comes Shura·sena·súndari, the sound of her anklets betrays her. She 1.185

Holds with one hand, delicate as a sprout,
the beautiful handle of her parasol,
and with the other she gathers up her skirt,
its bejeweled girdle swaying,
while the end of her garment is slipping off.
She comes towards me with a smile,
her body even more radiant
with the luster of her ornaments,
as if she were the goddess Night
invested with stars, moon, and bird-calls.

Well, I say! Her splendor makes even me get up. She approaches me with her hands in the pigeon-position. Please do not put me to shame with etiquette.

What are you saying, my lady? "Please allow this person to do herself a favor now by revering your lordship who has visited me, though after a long time." Pray do not reproach me so excessively. Please take this convenient seat beside me.* She replies: "Much obliged," and sits

tvā śilā|tal'|ârdham śroṇī|bimben'ˣākṣipant" îv' ôpaviśati. aye na khalv atr' ôpaveṣṭavyam.

kim āha bhavatī? «kim|artham?» iti. nanv idaṃ kasy' âpiˣ caritaṃ ken' âpi pratyākhyāta|praṇayāyāḥ śloka|saṃjñakam ayaśo 'smābhir dṛṣṭam. katham! hastābhyāṃ pramārṣṭi. cori, na śakyam idaṃ pramārṣṭum. idaṃ hi me hṛdi likhitam. eṣā kiṃ vārayati?

1.190 kim āha bhavatī? «jānīta ev' âsmat|svāmī yath" âsmat|sakhyāḥ Kusumāvatikāyāḥ priya|vayasyaṃ citr'|ācāryam Śivasvāminaṃ prati mahān madan'|ônmādaḥ» iti. suṣṭhu jānīmaḥ. kiṃ ca tatra|bhavatyā Kusumāvatikayā tatra|bhavān abhigamanen' ânugṛhītaḥ.

kim āha bhavatī? «madana|viklavasya strī|hṛdayasy' âyaṃ svabhāvaḥ. kṛtam anayā strī|cāpalyam» iti. citraḥ khalu prastāvaḥ. pṛcchāmas tāvad enām. bhavati, visrambhaḥ pṛcchati na para|rahasya|kutūhalatā. tat katham anayoś cir'|âbhilaṣita|samāgam'|ôtsavo nirvṛtto 'bhūt?

kim āha bhavatī? «śrūyatām» iti. avahito 'smi.

kim āha bhavatī? «tasyāṃ kila vāruṇī|mada|lakṣyeṇa tatra|bhavantam anugṛhītavatyāṃ tatra|bhavato vayasyasya

down, eclipsing, so to say, half of the stone slab with her spherical buttocks.* Wait! Do not sit here!

What are you saying, my lady? "Why not?" Surely I see here someone's work,* the versified disgrace of a woman whose love has been rejected by some man. What! She wipes it with both hands. Thief, you cannot efface it completely! For it is written in my heart. What is she concealing?

What are you saying, my lady? "My lord surely knows that 1.190
my friend Kusumávatika has fallen madly in love with your dear friend Shiva·svamin, the teacher of pictorial art." Of course I know this. What's more, the honorable Kusumávatika has favored the honorable gentleman by paying him a visit.

What are you saying, my lady? "Such is the nature of a woman's heart perturbed by love. She has committed a rash act characteristic of women." This overture is really curious. Well, let me ask her. My lady, it is trust that asks you, not inquisitiveness about other people's secrets. So how did the festival of their long-desired rendezvous conclude?

What are you saying, my lady? "Listen." I am all ears.

What are you saying, my lady? "They say that when she paid her respects to the honorable gentleman under the pretext of inebriety, your honorable friend

gataḥ pūrvo yāmaḥ
śruti|virasayā malla|kathayā,
dvitīyo vikṣiptaḥ
palala|guḍa|bāhya|vyatikaraiḥ,
tṛtīyo gātrāṇām
upacaya|kathābhir vigalitas.
tatas tan|nirvṛttaṃ
kathayitum alaṃ tvayy api yadi.»

1.195 iti. sundari, kutas tvay" âitad upalabdham?

kim āha bhavatī? «tasy' âiva sakhyur udavasitād āgatāt pratihāra|Padmapālād upalabdha|vṛttāntayā may" âiṣa ślokaḥ sukha|prāśnika|hasten' ânupreṣitaḥ. tataḥ sā ten' âiva paricārakeṇa saha mām upasthitā lajjā|vilakṣam upahasant" îva mām uktavatī: ‹na ca rahasy'|ânākhyānena bhavatīm avakṣeptum arhāmi. śrūyatām idam apūrvam› iti. tato 'nayā yathā|vṛttaṃ sarvaṃ mahyam ākhyātam. tena hi tvam apy anena śrotr'|âmṛtena saṃvibhaktum arhasi» iti. eṣā sa|tala|ghātaṃ prahasya kathayati.

sundari, kiṃ bravīṣi? «śrūyatām idānīṃ yan mama priya|sakhyā kathitam. sā hi mām uktavatī: ‹priya|sakhi, sa hi mayā

Spent the first watch of the night
    relating insipid stories about wrestlers,
wasted the second watch
    casually exchanging sweets,
and let the third slip away
    talking about the growth of limbs.
I wonder if I can tell even you
    what he achieved after that."

Where have you learnt this, my beauty? 1.195

What are you saying, my lady? "When I heard this story from the door-keeper Padma·pala who had come from your friend's house, I sent someone to pay her a courtesy visit and give her this verse. Then she called on me together with that servant, and told me with an embarrassed smile: 'I shouldn't insult you, milady, with keeping things back. Listen to this snorter!' Then she related to me everything as it had happened. Therefore you must also share in this audible nectar." She laughs, clapping her hands, as she recounts the story.

What are you saying, my beauty? "Hear now what my dear friend told me. For she said to me: 'My dear friend, when I

āliṅgito 'pi bahudhā paricumbito 'pi
  śroṇy|arpito 'pi karajair upacodito 'pi
khinn" âsmi dārv iva yadā na sa mām upaiti
  śayy"|âṅgam ekam upagūhya tato 'smi suptā.›

iti. tato may" ôktā: ‹kṛcchraṃ bat' ânubhūtavaty asi. kim etan n' âvagacchāmi› iti. tato niḥśvasya mām uktavatī:

1.200 ‹yadā sarv'|ôpāyaiś
    caṭubhir upayāto 'pi sa mayā
  na yatnaṃ kurvāṇo
    mayi manasij'|êcchām alabhata
tatas tasmin sarva|
    pratihata|vidhān" âsmi sahasā
  sva|daurbhāgyaṃ matvā
    stana|taṭa|vikampaṃ praruditā.

tataḥ sa māṃ rudatīm utsaṅgam āropya muhur muhur vyarthaiś cumbana|pariṣvaṅgair āśvāsayan nāma dṛḍham ātmānam āyāsitavān. uktaṃ ca mayā: ‹kiṃ te mayā pāṇibhyāṃ spṛṣṭayā durbhagayā?› iti. tato vrīḍ"|ârjita|sādhvasa|sveda|vepathuḥ śuṣyat" êva mukhena nātipragalbh'|âkṣaram uktavān:

Embraced and kissed him again and again,
even sat him on my lap and poked him with my
  nails,
he did not respond to me,
as if he were a piece of wood:
then I became exhausted and fell asleep,
clutching one side of the bed.'

Then I told her: 'It seems you were indeed experiencing some difficulties. I don't understand what this is all about.' Then she sighed and said to me:

'When I approached him with all my devices
  and honeyed words
and yet he did not feel lust for me,
  no matter how he tried, then,
as all my skills failed with him,
I thought I was not desirable
and broke out into sobs
  until the slopes of my breasts shook.

Then, as I was weeping, he took me on his lap and did his utmost to console me again and again with futile kisses and embraces. I asked him: 'What's the use of touching me with your hands, repulsive as I am?' Then, perspiring and trembling with panicked shame, his mouth parched, he said in a feeble voice:

‹na ninditum anindite
subhagatāṃ nijām arhasi,
cyutaṃ hi mama cakṣur e-
tad abhito nidhiṃ paśyataḥ.
vadhāya kila medaso
yad apibaṃ purā gulgulum
tad etad upahanti me
vyatikar'|âmṛtaṃ tvad|gatam.›

iti. tato mayā cintitam:

‹medaḥ kṣayāya pīto
yadi gulgulur indriya|kṣayaṃ kurute
dhūp'|ârtho 'pi na kāryo
gulgulunā kāmayayamānena iti.›

1.205 iti. evam āvayoś cira|prārthitam apārthakaṃ samāgamanaṃ prāpta|kālam icchatoḥ

rajanī|vyapayāna|sūcako
nṛpater dundubhi|pāripārśvikaḥ
apaṭhat stuti|maṅgalāny alaṃ
sakhi ghaṇṭām abhihatya ghāṇṭikaḥ.

tatas ten' âiva dakṣiṇen' êva suhṛdā tasmāt saṃkaṭāt parimocitā kāminā savrīḍaṃ muhūrtam anugamya preṣitā svagṛham āgatā ca tvayā ca sukha|prāśnik'|âbhidhānen' ôpahasit" âsmi. tad etat te sarvam aśeṣataḥ kathitam. aham idānīṃ mithyā|prajāgaraṃ divā|svapnen' âpaneṣyāmi›

'Impeccable woman,
please do not belittle your own allure,
for my eyes popped out
when I saw such bounty all around.
The fact is that I had drunk guggul
in order to get rid of my fat,
and that is what has ruined for me
the nectar of enjoying sex with you.'

Then I pondered over this problem:
'If guggul drunk to reduce fat
reduces one's senses,
then a man who wants to have sex
must not use guggul even as perfume.'

And so, my friend, as we hungered in vain for our long-desired, opportune union, 1.205

The watchman with his drum as his maidservant,
announced the end of the night
as he loudly recited auspicious eulogies
for the king and struck the gong.

Then, when I had been rescued from that fix by that very man, as if by an amiable friend, my gallant, feeling ashamed, accompanied me for a while and then dismissed me. I came home, and then you made fun of me through the words of that person whom you sent to inquire about my health. So I've told you everything unreservedly. Now I shall recover from my pointless vigil with a daytime nap.' She said this and departed with my leave. Your lordship, for your part, came right after she

ity uktvā may" ânujñātā gatā. tad|anantar'|āgatena svāmin" âpy etac chrutam» iti. tena hy anen' âiva parihāsa|plavena tatra|bhavataḥ Śivadattasya putram Śivasvāminaṃ puruṣa|dambha|gambhīra|kīrti|sāgaram avagāhiṣye. paśyatu bhavatī:

yo gulgulum pibati medasi sampravṛddhe
  tasya kṣayaṃ vrajati caṇḍy acireṇa medaḥ.
strīṇāṃ bhavaty atha sa yauvana|śālinīnām
  ālekhya|yakṣa iva darśana|mātra|ramyaḥ.

eṣā prahasy' ôtthitā yāsyām' îti. bhavatu, alam añjalinā. ito vayam.

1.210 *(parikramya)* kiṃ nu khalv imāny uddaṇḍa|puṇḍarīka|vana|ṣaṇḍa|śobh"|ânukāriṇy udgrīva|vadana|puṇḍarīkāṇi vismaya|vitat'|âkṣi|mālā|śabalāny urasi nihita|kara|pallavāny anyonya|saṃjñā|parivartakāni nivṛtta|kanduka|piñcholā|kṛtaka|putraka|duhitṛkā|krīḍanakāni veśa|rathyāyāṃ pratibhavana|cchāyāsu veśa|kanyakā|vṛndakāny avalokayanti? aye kiṃ nu khalv idam?

arañjaram idaṃ luṭhaty
  atha dṛtiḥ samākṛṣyate?
kabandham idam utthitaṃ
  vrajati? kiṃ kusūlo nv ayam?×
bhavet kim idam adbhutaṃ?

had left, and have now heard it." Then I shall sail into the deep notoriety-ocean of human hypocrisy, that is Shiva·svamin, the honorable Shiva·datta's son, with the following joke-boat. Look, my lady:

He who drinks guggul
  because he has become too fat,
his marrow will be gone in no time,
  my haughty lady.
Then, to youthful women, he will become
like a painted *yaksha*:
only their eyes can be amused by him.

She laughs and gets up saying: "I'm going." All right, don't bother with formalities. I'm off.

(walks about) What are these throngs of courtesan girls gawking at, standing in the shade of every house along the courtesans' street, forgetting their amusements with balls, flutes, male and female dolls? They match the beauty of clusters* of straight-stemmed lotuses as they raise their lotus-faces, dappled with garlands in the form of their eyes wide open with astonishment. They place their sprout-like hands on their bosoms and exchange signs among each other. Good heavens! What on earth is this? 1.210

Can it be a rolling water-jug,*
or a water-bag that is being dragged along?
An upright barrel that is moving?
Might it be a granary?
What can this marvel be?
Aha, I see now:

bhavatu, sāṃpratam lakṣitaṃ:
tad etad Upagupta|saṃ-
jñam udaraṃ samutsarpati.

bhoḥ suṣṭhu khalv idam ucyate dhūrta|pariṣatsu:

«karabho 'gaur Gupta|galo,
Hari|kṛṣṇaḥ kṛṣṇa eva vana|mahiṣaḥ,
go|mahiṣo Hari|bhūtir,
dṛtir Upagupto 'nil'|ādhmātaḥ.»

iti. kathaṃ ca tāvad imaṃ sā tapasvinī Gaṅgā|Yamunayoś cāmara|grāhiṇī pustaka|vācikā Madayantī priya|vayasyaṃ nas tatra|bhavantaṃ traividya|vṛddhaṃ pustaka|vācakam utsṛjy' Ôpaguptam anuraktā? tathā c' âsya komalābhyāṃ bhujābhyāṃ pariṣvajyate. athavā na tasyāḥ pariṣvaṅgena prayojanam. sā hi tapasvinī nivṛtta|kāma|tantrā rajo|'parodhāt kevalaṃ kuṭumba|tantr'|ârtham śabda|kāmam anuvartate. gamyaś c' âyam asyāḥ: «apumāñ śabda|kāmaḥ» iti Dāttakīyāḥ.

1.215 *(vilokya)* kiṃ ca tāvad ayam āvigna iva? ā jñātam! tasyā eva mātrā paṇ'|ârtham adhikaraṇāy' ākṛṣyata iti veśe may" ôpalabdham. tataḥ śvaśrvā saha kṛta|vivāden' ânena bhavitavyam. mahad idaṃ parihāsa|vastu. na śakyam asy' âtikramaṇād ātmānaṃ vañcayitum. yāvad enam upasarpāmi.

it is the belly called Upagúpta
that is trundling this way.

Oh, it is rightly said in the rakes' circles:

"Gupta·gala is a camel, not an ox,*
Hari·krishna is in fact a black forest-buffalo,
Hari·bhuti is a domestic buffalo,*
Upagúpta is a leather-bag
inflated by the wind."

Now how could that poor Mádayanti, the chowrie-bearer of Ganga and Yámuna, the reciter of scriptures,* dump my dear friend, an honorable reciter of scriptures who is an expert in the three Vedas, and fall in love with Upagúpta? And so she is embraced by his soft arms. Or rather, she has no use of embraces. For that poor woman has put aside the art of erotics because menstruation prevents her, and engages only in verbal sex in order to manage her household. He is accessible to her: "A eunuch is desirous of words," as Dáttaka's followers* teach.

(looking) Now why does he seem to be somewhat upset? 1.215
Aha! I know! I've heard in the courtesans' quarter that her mother* has summoned him to extort payment from him. He must have had a debate with his mother-in-law. This is an eminent target for ridicule. I cannot cheat myself by ignoring him. Let's go closer.

(upetya) haṇḍe veśa|vīthī|yakṣa, kuto bhavān? eṣa pāda|cāra|khedāt kāk'|ôcchvāsa|śrama|viṣamit'|âkṣaram «ayam añjalir ity» uktvā sthitaḥ. svasti bhavate.

kiṃ bravīṣi? «eṣa khalu tayā vṛddha|puṃścalyā saha vivād'|ârthaṃ gatvā kumār'|âmāty'|âdhikaraṇād āgacchāmi» iti. katham! bhavantaṃ jayena vardhayāmaḥ, ut' āhosvid daṇḍa|sāhāyyena saṃbhāvayāmaḥ?

kim āha bhavān? «kuto jaya|daṇḍābhyāṃ saha saṃyogaḥ? kevalaṃ kleśo 'nubhūyate» iti. kasmāt? kiṃ bravīṣi?

«pradhyāti Viṣṇudāso,
bhrātrā kila tarjito 'smi Koṅkena,
ḍāken' âbhihato 'haṃ
krośati Viṣṇuḥ svapiti c' âtra.

1.220 api ca,

mṛgayante tad|adhikṛtā,
mṛgayante pusta|pāla|kāyasthāḥ,
kāṣṭhaka|mahattarair api
vidhṛto 'smi ciraṃ mṛgayamānaiḥ.

api ca tato may" âvadhṛtam:

gaṇikāyāḥ kāyasthān
kāyasthebhyaś ca vimṛśato gaṇikāḥ
gaṇikāyai dātavyaṃ,
ratir api tāvad bhavaty asyām.»

(approaches) Hey there, *yaksha* of the courtesans' street, where are you coming from? Spluttering with the exertion of his crow-like wheezing due to the travail of moving his feet he stops, saying: "Here is my greeting." All the best to you.

What are you saying? "I am coming from the office of the prince's minister,* I went there to quarrel with that old prostitute." What! May I felicitate you on your victory, or do I perhaps have to assist you with your fine?

What are you saying, sir? "What do victory or fines have to do with it? It is just a nuisance." Why? What are you saying?

> "Vishnu·dasa was immersed in meditation.
> A man from Kónkana, apparently his brother,*
> threatened me.
> The thug* hit me.
> Vishnu yelled and fell asleep.

What's more, 1.220

> His clerks interrogated me,
> record-keepers and scribes interrogated me,
> even the senior officers* detained me
> with their endless interrogation.

What's more, I then understood:

> One who wavers between paying off
> prostitutes or scribes
> or scribes rather than prostitutes
> should buy the prostitute:
> at least one finds pleasure in her."

iti. diṣṭyā kāyastha|vāgur'|âtītaṃ bhavantam akṣataṃ paśyāmi. sarvathā pratibuddho 'si. idānīm iyam āśīḥ:

1.225 kala|madhura|rakta|kaṇṭhī
śayane madir"|âlasā samadanā ca
vaktr'|âparavaktrābhyām
upatiṣṭhatu vāra|mukhyā tvām.

eṣa satala|ghātaṃ prahasya prasthitaḥ. ito vayam. *(parikramya)* aye ayam aparaḥ

srasteṣv aṅgeṣv āḍhakāī×Lāṭa|bhaktyā
dattvā citrān ko 'yam āyāti mattaḥ?
vibhrānt'|âkṣo gaṇḍa|vichinna|hāso
veśa|svargaṃ kiṃ|kṛte 'yaṃ praviṣṭaḥ?

bhavatu, vijñātam:

Śarkarapālasya gṛhe
jātaḥ Kīreṇa carma|kāreṇa
eṣa khalu Koṅka|ceṭyāṃ
piśācikāyāṃ Tṛṇapiśācaḥ.

1.230 api ca,

Śarkarapālaṃ pitaraṃ
vyapadiśati bhrātaraṃ ca Nirapekṣam.
prāyeṇa dauṣkuleyāḥ
sah' âiva dambhena jāyante.

I'm happy to see that your honor has escaped unhurt from the snares of the bureaucrats. You really have seen the light. And now a benediction:

May the odalisque, languid with wine, 1.225
passionate, and with a voice that is soft,
  sweet, and enchanting
approach you on the bed
  with verses in *vaktra* and *ápara·vaktra* meters.

He laughs, clapping his hands, and goes his way. I'm off. *(walks about)* Hey! Here comes someone else!

Who is this drunken fellow?
He has put streaks of fragrant earth*
on his slack limbs in the manner of the Latas,
his eyes roll and he laughs from ear to ear
—why has he invaded the heaven
  of the courtesans' quarter?

All right, I know:

This must be Trina·pishácha,*
born in the house of Shárkara·pala,*
begotten by a Kira* cobbler
  with a maid from Kónkana, a goblin woman.

Moreover, 1.230

He claims that Shárkara·pala is his father
and Mr Blasé is his brother.
People of low parentage
  are often born hypocrites.

(parikramya) bhoḥ kaṃ nu khalu pṛccheyaṃ kim asya veśa|praveśe prayojanam iti? aye ayaṃ jarad|viṭo Bhaṭṭi|Ravidatta ita ev' âbhivartate. yāvad enaṃ pṛcchāmi. aṃgho Bhaṭṭi|Ravidatta, kac|cij jānīte bhavān asya puruṣa|vetālasya veśa|praveśa|prayojanam?

kiṃ bravīṣi? «bhavān eva jānīte» iti. tad gacchatu bhavān. *(parikramya)* kva nu khalv idaṃ puruṣa|kāntār'|âvagāhana|śrāntaṃ mano vinodayeyam?× bhavatu, dṛṣṭam!

idam aparaṃ priya|suhṛdaḥ
suhṛd|bhayād arpit'|ârgalaṃ bhavanam
veśyā|surata|vimardeṣv
akṛta|virāmasya Rāmasya.

1.235 tat kathaṃ praviśāmi? *(karṇaṃ dattvā)*

yathā kāñcī|śabdaś
carati vikalo nūpura|ravair
yathā muṣṭy|āghātaḥ
patati valay'|ôdghāta|piśunaḥ
yathā niḥśūtkāram
śvasitam api c' ântar|gṛha|gataṃ
dhruvaṃ rāmā Rāmaṃ
yuvati|viparītaṃ ramayati.

tad alam iha praviṣṭakena. kaḥ surata|rath'|âkṣa|bhaṅgaṃ kariṣyati? ito vayam. *(parikramya)* aye ayam aparaḥ kaḥ?×

(walks about) Whom can I ask why he has come to the brothel quarter? Oho! Here comes Bhatti Ravi·datta, that old pimp. Let me ask him. Say, Bhatti Ravi·datta, you must know for what purpose this human zombie has come to the brothel quarter.

What are you saying? "But you are the one who knows!"* Please just go away, sir. *(walks about)* Where shall I divert* my soul now, exhausted by penetrating into this human jungle? All right, I see!

> This house here belongs to my dear friend, Rama.
> He never stops his sex-battles with courtesans,
> and, afraid of his friends, he has bolted the door.

So how shall I enter? *(listening)* 1.235

> Since the sound of girdle, blended with the noise of
> anklets, spreads,
> since punches fall betraying thrashing with
> bracelets,
> and since heaving without hissing*
> also comes from the inner chamber,
> I'm sure that a lovely woman
> is having sex with Rama in a manner unusual for a
> young girl.

So I cannot enter here. Who would break the axle of a love-chariot? I'm off. *(walks about)* Hey! Who is this other fellow?

dagdhaḥ śālmali|vṛkṣaḥ
katipaya|viṭap'|âgra|śeṣa|tanu|śākhaḥ
kṛṣṇaḥ kṛśo viṭa|bako
veśa|nalinyā maru|piśācaḥ.

bhavatu, vijñātam! eṣa hi Sauparas Tauṇḍikokiḥ Sūryanāgaḥ. tataḥ kim ih' âsya prayojanam? katham! eṣa māṃ dṛṣṭv" âiv' ôttarīy'|âvakuṇṭhanena mukham apavārya Kāma|dev'|āyatanam apasavyaṃ kṛtvā prasthitaḥ. bho yadā tāvad adya tṛtīye 'hani bahiḥ|śivike kuṭaṅk'|âgāra|niketanābhiḥ patākā|veśyābhiḥ saṃprayukto mlecch'|âśva|bandhakair vyavahār'|ârtham śrāvaṇikair adhikaraṇam upanīyamānaḥ Skandakīrtinā bala|darśakena svāmino me Viṣṇoḥ syālī|patir iti kṛtvā kṛcchrāt pramocita iti vayasya|Viṣṇunā me kathitam, tat kim ayam idānīm asmād veśa|saṃsargād vrīḍita iv' ātmānaṃ pariharati?

1.240 *(vicintya)* āḥ, pārthiva|kumāra|saṃnikarṣa enam anayā pravṛttyā vrīḍayati. āścaryam. guṇavān khalu guṇavatāṃ saṃnikarṣaḥ, yad ayam api nām' âivaṃ guṇ'|âbhimukhaḥ. tan na śakyam enam a|pratyabhijñānena sa|kāmaṃ kartum. yāvad aham apy āyatanaṃ pradakṣiṇī|kurvan nāma saṃmukhīnam enaṃ parihās'|âvaskandena hanmi.

A burnt silk-cotton tree
with only the tips of a few twigs left intact
  on its thin branches,
a black, lean pimp-crane
in the lotus-pond of the courtesans' quarter,
a desert-goblin.

All right, I know! For this is Taundi·koki Surya·naga from Súpara.* Now what is he up to here? What! As soon as he notices me he hides his face with his upper garment as a veil and steals away, keeping the temple of Kama to his left. Hey! When my pal Vishnu·naga told me that two days ago in the suburbs,* while Surya·naga was in the company of "banner-courtesans"* who live in thatched huts, he was taken to court by interrogators* in a matter concerning his lawsuit with barbarian stablemen, general Skanda·kirti* recalled that he was the husband of his master's, Vishnu's, sister-in-law and rescued him with great difficulty, then why is he skulking away now, as if he were now ashamed of being associated with the courtesans' quarter?

(reflecting) Aha! His familiarity with the king's son makes 1.240
him feel ashamed of this conduct. How wonderful! Familiarity with the virtuous clearly has its virtue, since in this way even he has turned towards virtues. So I cannot possibly give him the satisfaction of not being recognized. I'll also circumambulate the temple keeping it on my right and swoop down on him with ridicule when we meet face to face.

(parikramya) eṣa māṃ pratimukham ev' âvalokya prahasitaḥ. haṇḍe Sūryanāga, kim ayaṃ veśa|nav'|âvatāro 'ndhakāra|nṛttam iva suhṛd|avakṣepeṇa viphalī|kriyate?

kiṃ bravīṣi? «ka iva mam' êh' ârthaḥ? ahaṃ hi kārāyām avaruddhasya mātulasya Maudgalyasya pāraśavasya Hari|dattasya pūrva|praṇayinīm akalya|rūpām adya vārttāṃ praṣṭuṃ ten' âiva prahito 'smi. tvaṃ tu māṃ katham apy avagacchasi» iti. āścaryam idaṃ hi bhavataḥ suhṛd|vyāpāreṣu sthairyaṃ tasyāś ca vāra|mukhyāyāḥ pūrva|praṇayiṣv āpad|gateṣv api pratipattiś ca. ataś c' âinām—

varṇ'|ânurūp'|ôjjvala|cāru|veṣāṃ
   Lakṣmīm iv' ālekhya|paṭe niviṣṭām
s'|âpahnavāṃ kāmiṣu kāmavanto
   'rūpāṃ virūpām api kāmayante.

api ca, atiduṣkara|kāriṇīṃ c' âinām avagacchāmi. kutaḥ? asaṃśayaṃ hi sā

1.245 kārā|nirodhād avikāra|gauraṃ
   dev'|ârcanā|jāta|kiṇaṃ lalāṭe
āsyaṃ bṛhac|chmaśru|vitāna|naddhaṃ
   tālv|asthi|nirbhugnam iv' âvaleḍhi.

(walks about) He has noticed me coming straight towards him and bursts out laughing. Hullo Surya·naga, why do you make this fresh descent to the brothel quarter as pointless as dancing in the dark by shaking off your pal?

What are you saying? "You mean, why am I here? My uncle, the Párashava* Maudgálya Hari·datta, who is detained in prison, asked me to inquire about his former mistress today as she feels unwell. But you can hardly understand me." Your honor's constancy in your friends' affairs and the respect that courtesan shows towards her former lovers, even when they are in a fix, is truly marvelous. And thus

Infatuated men can adore
even a shapeless or misshapen woman who is tactful
with her lovers, as if she were Lakshmi depicted on
a canvas
in a brilliant and beautiful garment
that suits her complexion.*

What's more, I consider her to be performing an extremely difficult feat. Why? For doubtlessly she

Kisses his face which is 1.245
unrelentingly pallid
because of his imprisonment,
callous on the forehead
due to his worship of the Gods,
covered with a long, bushy beard,
and seems to have a deformed hard palate.*

kim āha bhavān? «ata ev' âsyām asmākam ādaraḥ» iti. bhavatv evam suhṛd|anuraktaṃ bhavantaṃ khyāpayāmo vayam. eṣa khalu «prasīdatu svāmī» iti pāda|mūlayor upagṛhṇāti.

kiṃ bravīṣi? «n' ârhati svāmī mam' âivaṃ veśa|praveśaṃ kva cid api prakāśī|kartum» iti. bho vayasya, kaś candr'|ôdayaṃ prakāśayati? nanu yad" âiva bhavāṃs tatra|bhavatyā Rūpadāsyāḥ paricārikāṃ kubjāṃ prati baddha|madan'|ânurāgas tad" âiv' âitasmin pradeśa udaka|taila|bindu|vṛttyā vikasitaṃ yaśaḥ. mā tāvad bhoḥ!

parịsvaktā vakṣaḥ
　　kṣipati gaḍunā y" âtibṛhatā,
trike bhugnā n' ēṣṭe
　　jaghanam upadhātuṃ sa|madanā,
sa|rūpā ṭiṭṭibhyā
　　bhavati śayitā yā ca śayane
kathaṃ tāṃ tvaṃ kubjām
　　avanata|mukh'|âbjāṃ ramayasi?

kiṃ bravīṣi? «śāntaṃ pāpam śāntaṃ pāpam. pratihatam aniṣṭam. svāgatam anvākhyānāya. paśyatu bhavān:

What are you saying, sir? "That is exactly why I hold her in high esteem." All right, I shall let everyone know that your honor is so attached to his friends. He says "Have mercy, my lord!" and grasps my ankles.

What are you saying? "Please, my lord, do not ever publicize that I've come to the brothel quarter!" Why, my friend, who would advertize that the moon has risen? Surely your fame has spread in this region, like a drop of oil does on water, the very moment you fell in love with that hunchback attendant of the honorable Rupa·dasi.* But hold on!

When embraced she thrusts ahead her bosom
  because of her enormous hump,
bent into a triangle, she cannot move her hips closer
  when impassioned,
and she resembles a female lapwing*
  when she lies on her bed:
how do you make love to that hunchback girl
  whose lotus-face is bent down?

What are you saying? "Heaven forbid, heaven forbid! May evil be repelled! A detailed explanation is welcome. Observe, sir:

1.250 sa|vibhrāntair yātaiḥ
karabha|lalitaṃ yā prakurute,
muhur vikṣiptābhyāṃ
jalam iva bhujābhyāṃ tarati yā,
mukhasy' ôttānatvād
gagana iva tārā gaṇayati
spṛśet kas tāṃ prājñaḥ
kṛmi|janita|rogām iva latām?»

iti. aho dhik kaṣṭam. evaṃ dharma|jñasya bhavato na yuktam upayukta|strī|nindāṃ kartum. api ca,

yady api vayasya kubjā
nāḍī|nalikā|kṛśā ca gaḍulā ca
asatām iva saṃprītir
mukha|ramaṇīyā bhavati tāvat.[×]

na c' êyaṃ tābhyo 'raṇya|vāsinībhyaḥ patākā|veśyābhyaḥ pāpīyasī. kiṃ bravīṣi? «kābhyaḥ?» iti. katham! na jānīṣe?

yās tvaṃ mattāḥ kākiṇī|mātra|paṇyā
nīcair gamyāḥ s'|ôpacārair niyamyāḥ
lokaiś channaṃ kāmam icchan prakāmaṃ
kām'|ôdrekāt kāminīr yāsy araṇye.

What intelligent man would touch a woman 1.250
who manages the charm of a camel
with her staggering gait,
who seems to be swimming
with her arms thrown about again and again,
and with her face stretched upwards
looks as if counting the stars in the sky?
She is like a vine diseased with worms."

I'm disappointed in you! You are conversant with law, you should not revile in this manner a woman you've enjoyed! What's more,

Though she is a hunchback, my friend,
as thin as the tube of a vein and humped,
she still has a *pretty face*,*
just as friendly relations with the wicked
are *pleasant only in the beginning.*

And she is not worse than those "banner-courtesans" who live in the wilderness. What are you saying? "Than who?" What! Don't you know

Those passionate women, available for just a penny,
approachable by the lowborn,
who can be controlled by kindliness,
whom you frequent in the wild
as your mistresses when your sexual urge swells up
and you seek love of your own accord,
hidden from the world?

1.255 kiṃ bravīṣi? «kutas tvay" âitad upalabdham?» iti. sahasra|cakṣuṣo hi vayam īdṛśeṣu prayojaneṣu. api ca padāt padam ārokṣyati bhavān:

tyaktvā rūp'|ājīvāṃ
yas tvaṃ kubjāṃ vayasya kāmayase
kubjām api hi tyaktvā
gant" âsi svāminīm asyāḥ.

eṣa prahasya prasthitaḥ. ito vayaṃ sādhayāmaḥ.

(parikramya) aye ayam aparaḥ kaḥ Siṃhalikāyā Mayūrasenāyā gṛhān niṣpatya skandha|vinyasta|nivasano vimala|kuṭil'|âsi|pāṇibhir dākṣiṇātyaiḥ parivṛto bhadr'|âṅkaṃ viralam uttarīyam ākarṣann Āndhrakaṃ kārṣṇ'|âyasaṃ nivasitaḥ kuṅkum'|ânurakta|cchavis tāmbūla|samādāna|vyagra|pāṇir ita ev' âbhivartate? bhavatu, dṛṣṭam! eṣa hi Vidarbha|vāsī tala|varo Hariśūdraḥ. bho yadā tāvad ayaṃ tāṃ Kāverikām anurakta iti mam' âiva samakṣaṃ sa|pāda|parigraham anunayann apy uktas tayā:

«tām ehi! kiṃ tava mayā?
jyotsnā yadi ka iva dīpa|śikhay" ârthaḥ?
virama saha saṃgrahītuṃ
bilva|dvayam eka|hastena.»

What are you saying? "How do you know this?" I have a thousand eyes in such affairs. Moreover, you will ascend step by step, sir: 1.255

You have dumped a common prostitute
and love a hunchback woman, my friend:
you will also dump the hunchback
and go to her mistress.

He laughs and goes off. I'm moving on from here.

(walks about) Hey! Who is this other fellow who rushes out of the Ceylonese Mayúra·sena's house with his garment thrown on his shoulder? Surrounded by Southerners holding spotless, curved swords he gathers up his beautifully ornamented, thin cloak. He is coming right this way, wearing Andhran iron armor, his complexion reddened by saffron, and his hands busy with holding betel. All right, I see! This is indeed the guard Hari·shudra who lives in Vidárbha. Well, even though he tried to conciliate her by clasping her feet, she believes that he is in love with that Kavérika and told him before my very eyes:

"Go to her! What do you need me for?
What is the use of lamplight
when the moon is shining?
Stop holding two wood-apples
in one hand."

1.260 iti. tat katham anen' êyam anunītā bhaviṣyati? kim ayam anuraktām api tyaktv" ânyāṃ prakāśaṃ kāmayata iti veśa | pratyakṣam ātmano daurbhāgyam ayaśasyam iti svayam eva prasannā? āho|svit kāmyamānaṃ kāmayante striya iti strī|svabhāvād asyāḥ saṃgharṣa utpannaḥ? utāho parivyay' | ârtha | karśitayā mātr" âiv' ânuniyuktā bhaviṣyati? sarvathā prakṣyāmas tāvad enam. *(upasṛtaken' âñjaliṃ kṛtvā)*

tāṃ sundarīṃ darīm iva
  siṃhasya manuṣya|siṃha Siṃhalikām
yuktaṃ bhavatā moktuṃ
  Dramiḷī|surat'|âbhilāṣeṇa?

kiṃ bravīṣi? «anunītā mayā Mayūrasenā. eṣa tasyā eva gṛhād āgacchāmi» iti. kathaya kathaya katham avaśīrṇa| prāyaḥ saṃdhir anuṣṭhitaḥ?

kiṃ bravīṣi? «adya tṛtīye 'hany aham api veśy"|âdhyakṣa|pratihāra|Drauṇilaka|gṛhe prekṣāyām upanimantritaḥ. tatra ca Mayūrasenāyā lāsya|vāro buddhi|pūrvaka ity avagacchāmi. tataḥ prasāriteṣv ātodyeṣu devatā|maṅgalaṃ pūrvam upohya prastute gītake pranṛttāyāṃ nartakyāṃ prathama|vastuny eva Mayūrasenāyāḥ khalu nṛtte prayoga|doṣā gṛhītāḥ» iti. mā tāvad bhoḥ! Mayūrasenāyāḥ

Then how could he conciliate her? Has she calmed down by herself, considering the disgrace if the news spreads in the courtesans' quarter that she is not desirable, since he has dumped her, though she was infatuated with him, and now openly loves another woman? Or has she perhaps become jealous, for this is the nature of women: they love a man who is already loved? Or perhaps it was her mother, impoverished as she is due to her expenses, who persuaded her? I absolutely must ask him. *(mimes approaching, folding his hands)* 1.260

Lion among men,
is it proper that you ditch that Ceylonese beauty,
as a lion abandons its lair,
because you itch for sex
with a Tamil girl?

What are you saying? "I have conciliated Mayúra·sena. I am actually coming from her house." Tell me, tell me, how did you restore your alliance that had almost disintegrated?

What are you saying? "Two days ago I was also invited to a show in the house of Draunílaka, the doorkeeper and superintendent of courtesans. There I learnt that it had been decided that it was Mayúra·sena's turn to dance. Then, after the instruments had been tuned, first they offered a prayer to the deity, and when the song began and the danseuse started to perform, one could clearly detect faults in the performance of Mayúra·sena's dance right from the first sequence." Impossible! Faults

khalu nṛtte prayoga|doṣā gṛhyante? kasy' âyam ataṭa|prapātaḥ?

kiṃ bravīṣi? «bhagavatyā Vāruṇyāḥ» iti. yuktaṃ nitya|saṃnihitā bhagavatī Surā|devī pratihāra|gṛhe. atha kam antarī|kṛty' âyaṃ surā|vibhramaḥ?

1.265 kiṃ bravīṣi? «vayasyam eva te lāsakam Upacandrakam» iti. upapannam āyatanaṃ hi sa īdṛśānām. api tu sa viṣayas tasy' âiva! tatas tataḥ?

kiṃ bravīṣi? «tata Upacandra|pakṣe sarva|sāmājika|janaḥ. may" âpi Mayūrasenāyāḥ pakṣaḥ parigṛhītaḥ» iti. sādhu vayasya, deśa|kāl'|âupayikam anuṣṭhitam. tatas tataḥ?

kiṃ bravīṣi? «tato na teṣāṃ buddhiṃ paribhavāmi. aparibhūtāyām eva sadasy āgama|pradhānatayā mama prāśnik'|ânumate pratiṣṭhitaḥ pakṣaḥ» iti. sādhu vayasya, an|anya|sādhāraṇena paṇyena krītā tatra|bhavatī. tatas tataḥ?

kiṃ bravīṣi? «tataḥ sarva|gaṇikā|jana|pratyakṣaṃ datte pāritoṣike Mayūrasenāyāḥ smita|puraḥsareṇ' âpāṅga|pātinā kaṭākṣeṇa prasādita iv' âsmi. Kāverikāyās tu punar asūyā|piśunam utthāya gacchantyā ākāreṇa bah'|ûpālabdha iv' âsmi. tayoś ca kopa|prasādayoḥ pratyakṣatay" ôbhaya|taṭa|bhraṣṭa iva saṃdeha|srotasā hriyamāṇas tasmāt

were clearly detected in a dance performance by Mayúra·sena? To what can we ascribe such an extraordinary fiasco?

What are you saying? "To the blessed Goddess of Wine." It is appropriate that the Goddess of Spirits is always present in the doorkeeper's house. Now whom did this alcohol-induced debacle involve?

What are you saying? "None other than your friend, the 1.265
dancer Upachándraka." He is indeed a likely candidate in such matters. But even so! That he should be involved in such an affair! What happened then?

What are you saying? "Then the audience was unanimously on Upachándra's side. As for me, I took Mayúra·sena's side." Well done, my friend, you did what befitted the place and the occasion. And then?

What are you saying? "Then I couldn't overcome their opinion. Even though the spectators remained unconvinced, my position was upheld with the approval of the arbiters because they deemed me an aloof man of Scripture."* Well done, my friend, you purchased that honorable woman for a price unattainable to others. And then?

What are you saying? "Then Mayúra·sena was given the prize in front of all the hetaeras, and she seemed to favor me with a smile followed by a flirtatious glance from the corner of her eye. Kavérika, however, seemed to reproach me severely with her demeanor as she stood up and left in a way that betrayed her jealousy. And as both anger and grace were within sight, I drifted away from

saṃkaṭāt kathaṃ cid gṛhān āgata upaviṣṭaś ca k" ânayoḥ kiṃ pratipatsyata iti vitarka|ḍolāṃ vāhayāmi. tataḥ sahas" âiva me priyayā sametya netre nimīlite. tato vihasya may" ôktā:

‹netra|nimīlana|nipuṇe
kiṃ te hasitena cori gūḍhena?
sūcayati tvā pāṇyor
ananya|sādhāraṇaḥ sparśaḥ.›

1.270 evam uktay" ânayā surabhita|niḥśvāsa|sūcita|mada|skhalit'|âkṣaram abhihito 'ham: ‹ācakṣva mā k" âham› iti. tato may" ôktā:

‹romāñca|karkaśābhyāṃ
pratyukt" âsi nanu me kapolābhyām.
yad vadasi punar mugdhe
svayam ev' ācakṣva s" âham iti.›

tata unmīlya mām uktavatī: ‹anen' âiva romāñca|saṃjñakena kaitaven' âyaṃ jana ākṛṣyate.› ity uktvā mā kapole cumbitvā prasthitā. tato may" ôktā:

‹cumbiten' êdam ādāya
hṛdayaṃ kva gamiṣyasi?
cori pādāv imau mūrdhnā
dhṛtau me, sthīyatāṃ nanu.›

both shores so to say, and, carried by a stream of doubt, I could hardly escape from that predicament and make it home. There I sat down and gave myself up to a swinging vacillation, pondering which of the two girls would do what. Then all of a sudden my beloved came to me and covered my eyes. Then I laughed and said to her:

'You thief, skilled in covering one's eyes!
Why do you bother to muffle your laughter?
The incomparable touch of your hands
gives you away.'

Thus addressed she said to me, stammering with a tipsiness 1.270
that was betrayed by her fragrant breath: 'Tell me who I am!' Then I said to her:

'Surely my cheeks, rough with goosebumps,
speak to you.
But say that thing you say, innocent girl,
admit it yourself: 'It's me!''

Then she uncovered my eyes and said: 'It is a trick called "goosebumps" that wins over this woman here.' Then she kissed me on the cheek and was about to go. Then I said:

'Thief! Where are you going,
stealing this heart with your kiss?
I've put your feet on my head,
you must stay!'

evaṃ c' ôktā śayanam upagamy' ôpaviṣṭā. tato may" âsyāḥ svayaṃ pādau prakṣālitau. anayā c' âsmy uktaḥ: ‹gṛhītaṃ pādyam. eh' îdānīm. kitavaḥ khalv asi› iti. tato vikośa|mukula|jālaken' êva mālatī|latā|vihasiten'[×] âikahasten'[×] âvalambita|saraśana|nivasanā paryaṅk'|āveṣṭana|dvi|guṇa|madhya|bāhu|mṛṇālikā|trika|parivartana|sācī|kṛta|darśanīyatarā tadānīṃ veṣṭamāna|madhya|viṣama|vali|pranaṣṭa|nābhi|maṇḍala|viṣamī|kṛta|roma|rājir eka|stan'|âvagalita|hār'|âpāśrit'|êtara|stana|kalaśa|pārśv" âvagalita|kapola|paryasta|kuṇḍala|makar'|âdhiṣṭhita|viśeṣaka|kāntataren' âṃsa|parāvarta|śobhin" âvasthānena lajj"|âdvitīyā Ratir iva rūpiṇī samutthit'|âika|bhrū|latikena kuvalaya|śabalaṃ jalam iv' ākirantī dṛṣṭi|vikṣepeṇa mām uktavatī: ‹yat te rocate› iti.

1.275 tato 'ham āsannam ālekhya|varṇaka|pātraṃ gavākṣād ākṣipya caraṇa|nalina|rāgāy' ôpasthitaḥ. atha vayasya, alaktaka|vinyāsa|vinyasta|cakṣur utkṣipta|pārṣṇi|gulpha|nūpur'|âdhiṣṭhita|jaṅghā|kāṇḍāyās tasyā a|saṃbhuktatvād an|ūru|grāhiṇo marmarasy' ôpasaṃhāra|bhaṅg'|ābhog'|ânukāriṇaḥ kauśeyasy' âsaṃyatatvād gaja|kalabha|daśana|cchad'|ântaram iva kadalī|garbham iva c' ântar|ūrum

Thus addressed she went to the bed and sat down. Then I washed her feet myself. She said to me: 'I am done with the foot wash. Come here now. You really are a cheat.' Then she caught hold of her girdled garment with one hand that, resembling a lattice of full-blown buds, belittled a blossoming jasmine-vine. She appeared even more beautiful when her waist doubled over while she sat cross-legged, her arms tender like lotus-fibers, bending aside as she turned her back. Her twisting waist stretched her stomach-folds, hid the circle of her navel and ruffled the line of hair on her belly; her necklace had slipped down from one breast and rested on the side of her other pot-like breast; her *mákara*-shaped earring slipped down and, hanging over her cheek, it covered the patterns on her face: this made her posture even more charming, though it was already attractive with the twisting of her shoulders. She had no rival in bashfulness and was as shapely as Rati. She raised one of her vine-like eyebrows, and with a glance seemed to sprinkle me with water mixed with blue lilies, and said: 'Do as you please.'

Then I took a cosmetics box from the window nearby and 1.275
approached to color her lotus-feet. Well, my friend, as I directed my eyes to the application of lac and she raised her heel and ankle so that her anklets slipped up on her shank, I caught sight of the inside of her thighs because her rustling silk underskirt, being brand new, did not cling to her thighs, hung loose and followed her bends and curves as she tried to gather it up. They were like the

īkṣe. īkṣamāṇaṃ c' âpohy' âvinīta|cakṣur as' îty uktvā pādam ākṣipy' ôrasi mā tāḍitavatī.

tato romāñca|kavaca|karkaśa|tvacā may" ôktā: ‹sundari, n' ârhasi mām *a/samāpta/rāgam* avakṣeptum› iti. tatas tay" âham uktaḥ: ‹sādhu khalu nimīlit'|âkṣaḥ samāpay' âinam› iti.

tatas tasyā lākṣā|rasaṃ nimīlit'|âkṣo 'rpayāmi caraṇābhyāṃ. sa|kaca|graham adhar'|âuṣṭhe gṛhīto 'smi. tatas tath" âiva vivṛta|romāñcaṃ mā samabhivīkṣya ‹aśoka|sama|dohalo 'si. namo 'stu te śāṭhyāya› iti māṃ pariṣvajya śayanam upagatā. tataḥ paraṃ devānāṃ|priya eva jñāsyati» iti. yady evam arhati bhavān api Tauṇḍikoki|Viṣṇunāga|prāyaścitt'|ârthaṃ saṃnipatitān viṭān upasthātum.

kiṃ bravīṣi? «śāntam! etat punar api yadi śiro me tasyāś caraṇa|kamala|tāḍanen' ânugṛhyeta tad eva me prāyaścittam» iti. yady evaṃ Yamunā|hrada|nilayo Yadu|pati|caraṇ'|âṅkita|lalāṭo nāgaḥ Kāliya iva Vainateyasy' âvadhya idānīṃ sarva|viṭānām asi. eṣa vihasy' âyam añjalir iti prasthitaḥ. yāvad aham api viṭa|samājaṃ gacchāmi. aho nu khalu suhṛt|kathā|vyagrair asmābhir atītam apy aho na vijñātam. saṃprati hi

inside of a young elephant's lips or the pith of a plantain tree. As I was peeping she pushed me away saying: 'You have insolent eyes!,' swung her foot and kicked me on my chest.

Then I said, my skin rough with an armor of goosebumps: 'My fair one, please do not dismiss me until I finish the *coloring : making love.*' Then she said to me: 'Fine, finish it with your eyes closed!'

Then I applied lacquer to her feet with my eyes closed. She grabbed my hair and kissed my lower lip. Then, ascertaining that my hair was visibly bristling, she embraced me saying 'Your desires are like those of the *ashóka* tree.* I appreciate your guile,' and lay down. What happened then, O favorite of the gods, you know it yourself." If this is what happened, then you should present yourself in front of the pimps who are assembling to decide on a propitiatory ritual for Taundi·koki Vishnu·naga.

What are you saying? "Heaven forbid! If my head were favored with another kick of her lotus-foot, that in itself would be a propitiatory ritual for me!" If that is so then no pimp will hurt you now, just as Gáruda will not kill the serpent Káliya who lives in the waters of the Yámuna because his forehead was marked by Krishna's foot. He laughs and sets off saying goodbye. Well, as for me I shall go to the pimps' council. Oh dear, I was so engrossed in conversations with my friends I did not even realize that the day has passed. For now

s'|ôtkaṇṭhair iva gacchat' îti kamalair
mīladbhir ālokitaḥ
pracchāyair adhiruhya veśma|śikharāṇy
utsāryamāṇ'|ātapaḥ
taiḥ spṛṣṭvā ciram unmukhīṣu kiraṇair
udyāna|śākhāsv asau
yāty astaṃ valabhī|kapota|nayanair
ākṣipta|rāgo raviḥ.

1.280 api c' êdānīm

prākār'|âgre gavākṣaiḥ patati khaga|rutaiḥ
sūcyamāno biḍālaḥ;
prāsādebhyo nivṛtto vrajati samucitāṃ
vāsa|yaṣṭiṃ mayūraḥ;
sāṃdhyaṃ puṣp'|ôpahāraṃ pariharati mṛgaḥ
sthaṇḍile svaptu|kāmas;
toyād uttīrya c' âsau bhavana|kamalinī|
vedikāṃ yāti haṃsaḥ.

(parikramya)

ete prayānti ghanatāṃ valabhīṣu dhūpā
vaiḍūrya|reṇava iv' ôtpatitā gavākṣaiḥ;
rathyāsu c' âitam avagāḍham udagram etya
snān'|ôdak'|âugham anu ṣaṭ|caraṇā bhramanti.

The sun is setting,
gazed after by closing lotuses
that seem to mourn its departure;
it climbs the turrets of the houses,
its heat lessened by the dense shade;
it lingers to stroke with its rays
the uplifted branches in the groves,
its red glow reflected in the eyes of doves
in the eaves.

What's more, now 1.280

A cat jumps on to a wall:
the bird-cries from the windows betray it;
the peacock returns from the lofty terraces
and makes for his familiar perch;
a deer that wants to sleep on the ground
avoids the evening flower-offering;
here a wild goose emerges from the water
and goes to the verandah by the house's
lotus-pond.

(walks about)

The smoke of incense,
wafting through the lattice windows
like particles of cat's-eye, gathers thickly
around the gables;
bees are buzzing up and down the streets,
following the streams of bath water.

aho nu khalv idānīm asya saṃmṛṣṭa|sikt'|âvakīrṇa|kusuma| pradvār'|âjirasya prādoṣik'|ôpacāra|vyagra|paricāraka|janasya deśa|vayo|vibhav'|ânurūp'|âlaṃkāra|vyāpṛta|vāramukhyā|janasya pracarita|madana|dūtī|saṃcāra|ramaṇīyasya pravṛtta|matta|viṭa|vidagdha|parihāsa|ras'|ântarasya snāt'|ânulipta|pīta|pratīta|taruṇa|jan'|âvakīrṇa|catuṣpatha|śṛṅgāṭakasya veśa|mahā|pathasya parā srīḥ! iha hi

1.285 eṣā rauty upaveśitā gaja|vadhūr
āruhyamāṇā śanair;
etat kambala|vāhyakaṃ pramadayā
dvāḥ|sthaṃ samāruhyate;
śiñjan|nūpura|mekhalām upavahan
veśyāṃ calat|kuṇḍalāṃ
śroṇī|bhāram apārayann iva hayo
gacchaty asau dhauritam.

api c' âsminn imāḥ

Ah! How magnificent the high street of the courtesans' quarter is! The forecourts have been swept, sprinkled with water and strewn with flowers; servants are busy with their evening duties; hetaeras are engaged in ornamenting themselves as befits their country, age and financial situation. The street is delightful with the bustle of love-messengers sent on errands, it is suffused with the exuberance of the gleeful jests of the inebriated pimps, and young people crowd the crossroads and carrefours: they have bathed, anointed themselves, drunk and are now merry. Here

An elephant cow has been made to sit down 1.285
and now trumpets as she is being
carefully mounted;
here a coquette climbs into a blanketed carriage
that waits at the door;
here a horse carries a courtesan
with jingling anklets and girdle
and swinging earrings,
trotting as if it could not cope
with the burden of her hips.

Moreover here these

pradīpa|kara|vallarī|
jaṭila|cāru|vātāyanā,
mayūra|gala|mecakair
anusṛtās tamobhiḥ kva cit
vibhānti gṛha|bhittayo
nava|sudh"|âvadāt'|ântarās
tamāla|haritāla|paṅ-
ka|kṛta|pattra|lekhā iva.

(parikramya) sarvathā ramaṇīyas tāvad ayam udbhidyamāna|candra|sa|nātha utsavaḥ pradoṣa|saṃjñako jīva|lokasya. saṃprati hy eṣa bhagavāṃś cakṣuṣāṃ sādhāraṇaṃ rasāyanaṃ hasitam iva kumuda|vāpīnām udayati śīta|raśmiḥ. ya eṣaḥ

«kiṃ nīl'|ôtpala|pattra|cakra|vivarair
abhyeṣi mā cumbituṃ?
na tvāṃ paśyati Rohiṇī? kathaya me!
saṃtyajyatāṃ vepathuḥ!»
mattānāṃ madhu|bhājaneṣv iti|kathāḥ
śrotuṃ sa|hāsā iva
strīṇāṃ kuṇḍala|koṭi|bhinna|kiraṇaś
candraḥ samuttiṣṭhati.

1.290 *(parikramya)*

gāyaty eṣā valgu|kānta|dvitīyā,
suprakvāṇā spṛśyate 'sau vipañcī,
baddhvā goṣṭhīṃ pīyate pānam etadd
harmy'|âgreṣu prāpta|candr'|ôdayeṣu.

House-walls are sumptuous
with stylish windows crested
by the burgeoning rays of lamps;
in part they are suffused with shadow,
dark blue as a peacock's neck,
with their interstices white with fresh stucco,
they seem to bear ornamental patterns
of black and yellow paint.

(walks about) This world-festival called "evening," presided over by the emerging moon, is delightful in every respect. For now the blessed cool-rayed moon is rising, an elixir for everyone's eyes, a veritable smile of the lily ponds. Now,

The moon,
its rays refracted by the edges of their earrings,
is taking form in the wine-cups
of inebriated women
as if to eavesdrop on their pillow talk:
"Why do you come to kiss me
through the gaps in the bands of blue lily leaves?*
Won't your wife Róhini see you?
Tell me! Stop shivering!"

(walks about) 1.290

Here a girl is singing in the company
of her handsome lover,
here someone plays a sweet-sounding lute,
here people party and drink,
while the moon has risen to the rooftops
of the palaces.

api c' êdānīm eṣa bhagavān

viracayati mayūkhair
dīrghik"|âmbhaḥsu setuṃ,
visṛjati kadalīṣu
svāḥ prabhā|daṇḍa|rājīḥ,
punar api ca *sudhābhir*
varṇayan saudha|mālāḥ
kṣarati kisalayebhyo
mauktikān' îva candraḥ.

(parikramya) aho nu khalu kṣīr'|ôden' êv' ôdvela|pravṛtta|vikīryamāṇa|vīci|rāśinā jyotsnā|saṃjñakena payasā prasarpat" ânugṛhīta iva jīva|lokaḥ. saṃprati hi

1.295 ete vrajanti turagaiś ca kareṇubhiś ca
karṇī|rathair api ca kambala|vāhyakaiś ca
āliṅgitā yuvatibhir mṛditā yuvāno
gandharva|siddha|mithunāni vihāyas' îva.

(parikramya)

What's more, the blessed

Moon
fashions a bridge over the water of the ponds
with its rays,
radiates rows of rods of light
into the plantain groves,
and as it repaints the ranks of stuccoed mansions
with its *plaster : nectar*
it seems to drip pearls from the tips of branches.

(walks about) Ah, the world appears as if bedecked with streaming milk called moonlight,—a milk-ocean with massive waves spilling over its shore and spreading all around. For now,

These young men, 1.295
embraced and squeezed by young women,
process on horses and elephants,
in rickshaws and carriages
covered with blankets
as if they were couples of *gandhárvas*
and *siddhas* in heaven.

(walks about)

asāv anvārūḍho
　　mada|lalita|ceṣṭaḥ pramadayā
parịṣvaktaḥ pṛṣṭhe
　　nibiḍatara|nikṣipta|kucayā
parāvṛttaś cumban
　　vrajati dayitāṃ yasya turago
gṛhān eṣo 'bhyāsād
　　anupatati n' ôtkrāmati pathaḥ.

kaś ca tāvad ayam asmiṃś candr'|ātape 'py andhakāra iva vartamāno veśa|rathyāyāṃ garbha|gṛha|bhogena tiṣṭhan nairlajyam āviṣkaroti? ā jñātam! eṣa Saurāṣṭrikaḥ Śaka|kumāro Jayanandaka imāṃ ghaṭa|dāsīṃ barbarikām anuraktaḥ. kiṃ ca tāvad anen' âiva tasmāt sarva|veśyā|pattanād veśa|barbaryā guṇavattvam avalokitam? yadā tāvat

adhidevat" êva tamasaḥ
　　kṛṣṇā śuklā dvijeṣu c' âkṣṇoś ca
asakala|śaśāṅka|lekhe-
　　va śarvarī barbarī bhāti.

1.300 athavā Saurāṣṭrikā vānarā barbarā ity eko rāsiḥ. kim atr' āścaryam? tathā hi:

gavala|pratimāyām api
　　barbaryāṃ sakta|cakṣuṣo hy asya
alasa/sakaṣāya/dṛṣṭer
　　jyotsn" âp' îyaṃ tamisr" êva.

There goes a mounted man,
his gestures playful with rapture,
he is embraced by a passionate woman sitting
behind him,
crushing her breasts tightly against his back.
As he turns around while kissing his beloved,
his horse finds its way home
out of habit and does not stray
from the path.

Now who is this, displaying his shamelessness by enjoying the pleasures of the bedroom on the main street of the brothel quarter lit by moonlight, as if he were in the dark? Ah! I know! It is Jaya·nándaka, the Shaka prince from Surat, who is infatuated with this barbarian water-bearer woman. Now how is it that he of all people believes that that barbarian courtesan is the most meritorious in the whole town of courtesans? Since,

Like the presiding deity of darkness,
her teeth white and her eyes dark,*
a barbarian woman shines like the night
with the thin streak of the moon.

Or rather—men of Surat, monkeys or barbarians: it makes 1.300
no difference. What is there to be surprised at? For:

His eyes are riveted to this barbarian girl,
though she resembles a buffalo:
for him this moonlight
might as well be darkness,
since his
eyes are dull and dim : attitude is lazy and lustful.

tad alam, ayam asya panthāḥ. ito vayam. *(parikramya)* iyam aparā kā?

karṇa|dvay'|âvanata|kāñcana|tāla|pattrā
veṇy|anta|lambi|maṇi|mauktika|hema|gucchā
kūrpāsak'|ôtkavacita|stana|bāhu|mūlā
Lāṭī nitamba|parivṛtta|daś"|ânta|nīvī.

(vicārya) bhavatu, vijñātam. eṣā hi sā Rākā rājñaḥ syālam Ābhīrakaṃ Mayūra|kumāraṃ mayūram iva nṛtyantam āliṅgantī candra|śāl"|âgre veśa|vīthyām ātmanaḥ saubhāgyaṃ prakāśayati. ayam api c' ārjaven' ânayā tapasvī krīta iva.

1.305 api ca Mayūrakumāraṃ
gaurī kṛṣṇam atidurbalaṃ sthūlā
svam iva pracchāy'|âgrakam
urasi vilagnaṃ vahaty eṣā.

(parikramya) iyam aparā kā? *(vicārya)* iyaṃ hi sā tatra|bhavataḥ sugṛhīta|nāmnaḥ Śārdūlavarmaṇaḥ putrasya naḥ priya|vayasyasya Varāhadāsasya[×] priyatamā Yavanī Karpūraturiṣṭhā nāma. praticandr'|âbhimukhaṃ madhunaḥ kāṃsyam aṅguli|trayeṇa dhārayantī kapola|tala|skhalita|bimbam avalambya kuṇḍalaṃ kiraṇaiḥ preṅkholitam aṃsa|deśe śaśinam iv' ôdvahantī yā eṣā

Enough of this, that is his path, this is mine. *(walks about)* Who is this other woman?

> Golden palm-leaf-shaped ornaments
> droop from her ears, bunches of gems,
> pearls and gold dangle from the end of her braid,
> her breasts and upper arms are reinforced with
> a bodice:
> she is a Lata girl, her petticoat tied
> around her hips with its loose ends.

(musing) All right, I know! She must be Raka. She advertises her sensual felicity on the street of the courtesans' quarter by embracing Mayúra·kumára,* the king's Abhíra brother-in-law, who dances like a peacock, in the forepart of the moon-apartment.* She has bought, so to say, even that poor wretch with her forthrightness.*

> What's more, she, the fair, plump woman, 1.305
> clasps the scrawny, black Mayúra·kumára
> to her bosom,
> as if he were the mere tip of her huge shadow
> clinging to her chest.

(walks about) Who is this other woman? *(reflecting)* She is that Greek girl called Karpúra·turíshta, the darling of my dear friend Varáha·dasa,* the son of the honorable Shardúla·varman of blessed name. This Greek girl is holding on to an earring, the reflection of which is quivering on her cheek, and thus she appears to be exhibiting the moon, coruscating with beams of light, on her shoulders. With three fingers she holds up a brass

cakora|cikur'|ēkṣaṇā
madhuni vīkṣamāṇā mukhaṃ
vikīrya Yavanī nakhair
alaka|vallarīm āyatām
madhūka|kusum'|âvadā-
ta|sukumārayor gaṇḍayoḥ
pramārṣṭi mada|rāgam ut-
thitam alaktak'|āśaṅkayā.

api ca Yavanī gaṇikā vānarī nartakī Mālavaḥ kāmuko gardabho gāyaka iti guṇataḥ sādhāraṇam avagacchāmi. sarvathā sadṛśa|yogeṣu nipuṇaḥ khalu Prajāpatiḥ. tathā hi:

khadira|tarum ātmaguptā
paṭola|vallī samāśritā nimbam
śliṣṭo bata saṃyogo
yadi Yavanī Mālave saktā.

1.310 tat kāmam iyam api me sakhī, na tv enām abhibhāṣiṣye. ko hi nāma tāni vānarī|niṣkūjit'|ôpamāni sītkāra|bhūyiṣṭhāny apratyabhijñeya|vyañjanāni kiṃcit|kāraṇ'|ântarāṇi pradeśinī|lālana|mātra|sūcitāni svayaṃ veśa|yavanī|kathitāni śroṣyati? tad alam anayā.

goblet to this mock moon, and,

She, squint-eyed like a partridge,*
observes her face in the wine,
dishevels the rampant liana of her locks
with her nails, and, mistaking it for lac,
she tries to wipe off the drunken blush
on her cheeks,
which are white and delicate
like the flowers of the butter tree.

Furthermore, I deem a Greek hetaera monkey danseuse to be a fair match for a Málavan popinjay donkey-singer. Clearly the Creator is skilled in making harmonious pairs. For,

Firm indeed is the bond
when the cowage
climbs on the catechu tree,
the cucumber-vine climbs on the neem tree:
when a Greek girl
clings to a man from Málava.

She may be also a friend of mine, but I shall not address her. 1.310
For who would willingly listen to the prattle of a Greek girl of the brothel quarter? It sounds like the whining of a she-monkey, is full hissing, its consonants are unrecognizable, is punctuated simply by finger-wagging and indiscriminately interrupted. So enough of her.

(parikramya) ayam aparaḥ kaḥ?

pratimukha|pavanair vegād
utkṣipt'|âgr'|âlak'|ôttarīy'|ântām
kāntāṃ harati kareṇvā
Vāsavadattām iv' Ôdayanaḥ.

(vicārya) ā viditam! eṣa sa ibhya|putro Viṭa|pravāla iti ḍiṇḍibhir abhyasta|nāmā surata|raṇa|paṭa|kaṭy|ambarāṇām adhipatis tāṃ veśa|sundarīm asmad|bālikāṃ madana|para|vaśaḥ pitur mātuś ca śāsanam upekṣy' ânurakta eva. tat kāmam atiḍiṇḍī khalv ayaṃ, śvaśura|śabd'|âvaguṇṭhanās tu vayam. tad alam anen' âbhibhāṣitena. ayam asy' âñjaliḥ. itas tāvad vayam.

(parikramya) yāvad aham api viṭa|samājam eva gacchāmi.

1.315 eṣo 'smi bhoḥ suvṛth"|âtivāhite veśa|mahā|pathe viṭa|mahattarasya Bhaṭṭi|Jīmūtasya samantāt saṃnipātita|viṭa|jana|vāhana|sahasra|saṃbādha|pradvār'|âṅgaṇam utkṣipta|rajata|kalaśa|pādya|paricārak'|ôpasthita|toraṇaṃ bhavanam anuprāptaḥ. suṣṭhu khalv idam ucyate: «mahāntaḥ khalu mahatām ārambhāḥ» iti. sāṃprataṃ hy etad daś'|ârdha|varṇaṃ puṣpam utkīryate muktam āsajyate

(walks about) Who is this other man?

He carries away his beloved on an elephant,
as once Údayana eloped with Vásava·datta,
the headwind of their headlong rush
lifts the tips of her locks
and the hem of her garment.

(reflecting) I know! This must be that rich man's son acclaimed as "the budding pimp" by the cynics, the commander of underwear—the war flag for the battle of love. He is in love with the beauty of the courtesans' quarter—my daughter—and, overcome by passion, he gives no heed to his parents' orders. So, even though he is clearly a supercynic, I am encumbered by the title "father-in-law." So I won't speak to him. Here I fold my hands to greet him and move on now.

(walks about) Well then, I too shall go straight to the council of pimps.

After nonchalantly idling along the high street of the cour- 1.315
tesans' quarter I have at last reached the mansion of Bhatti Jimúta, the prime pimp. The courtyard before its gate is congested with thousands of vehicles of the pimps who have been assembled from far and wide, and the portal is staffed by servants with water for washing the feet in raised silver jars. It is indeed rightly said: "The undertakings of the great are truly grandiose." For now flowers of five colors are scattered in the air and arranged

grathitam; saṃcāryante dhūpāḥ; prajvālyante dīpāḥ; ucyate svāgatam; mucyate yānam; dṛśyate vibhramaḥ; upagīyate gītam; upavādyate vādyam; dīyate hastaḥ; kathyate ślakṣṇam; āliṅgyate snigdham; avalambyate sa|praṇayam; avanamyate sa|vinayam; spṛśyate pṛṣṭham ānatasya; gamyate sa|bhrū|kṣepam; āghrāyate śiraḥ; sthīyate sa|vibhramam; upaviśyate sa|līlam; viśrāṇyate candanam; ālipyate varṇakam; vinyasyate vilepanam; utkīryate cūrṇaḥ; parihāsyate viṭaiḥ; pratigṛhyate vilāsinībhir iti kiṃ bahunā?

puṣpeṣv ete jānu|daghneṣu lagnāḥ
 kṛcchrāt pādā vāmanair uddhriyante;
vibhrānt'|âkṣyaḥ ketakīnāṃ palāśān
 sīt|kurvāṇāḥ pāda|lagnān haranti.

api c' âite viṭa|mukhyāḥ

śrīmantaḥ sakhibhir alaṃkṛt'|āsan'|ārdhāḥ
 kurvantaś caturam a|marma|vedhi narma
veśyābhiḥ samupagatāḥ samaṃ samantād
 ukṣāṇo vraja iva bhānti s'|ôpasaryāḥ.

api c' âiṣām etat sadaḥ

in bouquets; incense is wafted around; lamps are lit; people are welcomed; a vehicle is sent off; one can see elegant gestures; there is singing and music; a helping hand is given; there is genteel talk and warm embraces; people affectionately hold on to one another, politely bow to each other and touch the back of those who bow; someone passes by raising his eyebrows; another is kissed on the head; some gracefully loiter, others sit down elegantly; sandal is circulated; some apply make-up; ointments are distributed; aromatic powder is scattered in the air; pimps joke around and coquettes riposte—but enough of details!

These dwarves
can hardly lift their feet
  stuck in the knee-deep flowers;
panting, they roll their eyes
  and drag along *kétaki* blossoms*
  stuck to their feet.

Moreover these eminent pimps,

Fortunate to share their seats
  with their friends,
playing clever jokes that do not cut to the quick,
  crowded by courtesans from all sides
they are as attractive as bulls in their herds
  with their cows waiting to be approached.

What's more, their assembly here,

1.320 nabha iva śata|candraṃ
yoṣitāṃ vaktra|cakraiḥ,×
kṛta|śabala|dig|antaṃ
saṃpatadbhiḥ kaṭākṣaiḥ,
sa|parighamˣ iva yūnāṃ
bāhubhiḥ saṃprahārair
nicitam iva śilābhiś
candan'|ārdrair urobhiḥ.

api c' âsmin

ete vibhānti gaṇikā|jana|kalpa|vṛkṣās
tādātvikāś ca khalu mūla|harāś ca vīrāḥ
bālye 'pi kāṣṭha|kalahān kathayanti yeṣāṃ
vṛddhāḥ Suyodhana|Vṛkodarayor iv' ôccaiḥ.

tad etāvad aham api suhṛn|nideśa|veṣṭane śirasi bhagavate Citteśvarāy' âñjaliṃ kṛtvā suhṛn|nideśād imam adhikāraṃ puras|kṛtya prāyaścitt'|ârthaṃ tatra|bhavatas Tauṇḍikoker Viṣṇu|nāgasya ghoṣaṇā|pūrvakaṃ viṭān vijñāpayāmi.

(parikramya) bho bhoḥ! sakala|kṣiti|tala|samāgatāḥ priya|kalahāḥ kalahānāṃ ca niveditāro dhūrta|miśrāḥ, śṛṇvantu śṛṇvantu bhavantaḥ!

With the women's thronging faces* 1.320
  is like a sky filled with a hundred moons;
it streaks the horizon with side-glances cast around;
it seems to be barricaded by the clashing arms of
  young men
and seems walled off with boulders
  in the form of breasts moist with sandal.

Moreover here

These heroes
  who squander both income and patrimony*
  are glorious trees of plenty for the courtesans;
while they were still children,
  old folks loudly acclaimed their club-fights
  as those of Duryódhana and Bhima.

Now I too pay reverence to the blessed Lord of Hearts, folding my hands above my head that is crowned with the turban of my friends' command. Then, in the matter of the present case, in compliance with my friends' command, after making my proclamation I shall request the pimps to find a propitiatory ritual for the honorable Taundi·koki Vishnu·naga.

(walks about) Sirs! Gentle-rogues who have gathered here from all over the world, disputation-enthusiasts and proponents of disputes, may I have your attention!

1.325 Kāmas tapasviṣu jayaty adhikāra|kāmo
viśvasya citta|vibhur indriya|vājy|adhīśaḥ
bhūtāni bibhrati mahānty api yasya śiṣṭiṃ
vyāvṛtta|mauli|maṇi|raśmibhir uttamāṅgaiḥ.

(parikramya)

atha jayati mado vilāsinīnāṃ
sphuṭa|hasita|pravikīrṇa|karṇa|pūraḥ
skhalita|gatir adhīra|dṛṣṭi|pātas;
tad|anu ca yauvana|vibhramā jayanti.

tad evaṃ vāra|mukhyā|jana|caraṇa|rajaḥ|pavitrī|kṛtena śirasā dhūrta|miśrān praṇipatya vijñāpayāmi. kiṃ c' âitad vijñāpyam iti śrūyatām:

nāgavad Viṣṇu|nāgo 'sāv
urasā veṣṭate kṣitau.
prāyaścitt'|ârtham udvignaṃ
tam enaṃ trātum arhatha.

1.330 kiṃ māṃ pṛcchanti bhavantaḥ? «ko 'sy' âpanayaḥ?» iti. śrūyatām:

Kama, who desires authority, 1.325
is triumphant among ascetics.
He rules everyone's hearts and
governs the steeds of the senses.
Even the great bear his commands on their heads,
the radiance of their crest-jewels dimmed.

(walks about)

Similarly victorious
is the coquettes' inebriety:
it disarranges their ear-ornaments
with boisterous laughter,
makes them stumble and cast unsteady glances;
and as a consequence
the courting of the youths
is crowned with success.

After bowing before the gentle rogues in this way with my head purified by the foot-dust of odalisques, I shall make a proclamation. What is it that I must announce? Listen!

Like a snake,
Vishnu·naga squirms
with his chest on the ground.
He is anxious for a propitiatory ritual:
please deliver him!

What are you asking me, gentlemen? "What is his predica- 1.330
ment?" Listen:

utkṣipy' âlakam×īkṣaṇ'|ânta|galitaṃ
kop'|âñcit'|ânta|bhruvā
daṣṭ'|ârdh'|oṣṭham adhīra|danta|kiraṇaṃ
protkampayantyā mukham
śiñjan|nūpurayā vikṛṣya vigalad|
rakt'|âṃśukaṃ pāṇinā
mūrdhany asya sa|nūpuraḥ sa|madayā
pādo 'rpitaḥ kāntayā.

kiṃ kiṃ vadanti bhavantaḥ? «kasyāḥ punar idam avijñāta|puruṣ'|ântarāyāḥ pramāda|saṃjñakam a|yaśo vistīryate?» iti. nanu tatra|bhavatyāḥ Saurāṣṭrikāyā Madanasenikāyāḥ.

ete viṭā «diṣṭyā n' êha kaś cid» iti saṃbhrāntā iva. ya ete

nirdhūta|hastā vinigūḍha|hāsā
dhig|vādino dhīra|mukhāni baddhvā
dhyāyanti saṃprekṣya parasparasya
jāt'|ânukampā iva nāma dhūrtāḥ.

1.335 eteṣāṃ tāvad āsīnānāṃ niyukto dhuri×viṭa|mahattaro Bhaṭṭi|Jīmūtaḥ kṛpayā nāma paraṃ vaiklavyam upagataḥ, ya eṣaḥ

Tossing up a curl that had slid
  to the corner of her eye,
bending the ends of her brows in anger,
biting her lower lip and
making her mouth with its scintillating teeth
  quiver,
her anklets jingling as she pulled up
  her slipping red garment with her hand,
his inebriated, passionate mistress
  planted her ankleted foot on his head.

What? What are you saying, gentlemen? "But who is this woman, ignorant of a man's heart, whose disgrace called 'negligence' you are making public?" Who else but her ladyship Mádana·sénika from Surat.

The pimps seem to be agitated: "Thank heavens it's not someone among us!" These

Rogues,
  shaking their hands,
  choking their laughter,
  voicing dismay with grave faces,
look at each other,
become pensive,
and seem filled with pity.

Among those seated it is Bhatti Jimúta, the prime pimp, ap- 1.335
pointed as their head, who seems most anguished with pity. For,

kaṣṭaṃ kaṣṭam iti śvāsān
muñcan klānta iva dvipaḥ
jīmūta iva Jīmūto
netrābhyāṃ vāri varṣati.

eṣa mām āhvayati. ayam āgato 'smi. kim ājñāpayati bhaṭṭiḥ? «sruta|pūrvaṃ mayā bhūyo 'pi vadasi. evaṃ prāyascitt'|ârthaṃ brāhmaṇ'|ôpagamanam, tasmād ev' âham upaviṣṭaḥ. tat samaya|pūrvakam upagṛhyantām atra|bhavanto× viṭāḥ» iti. yad ājñāpayati bhaṭṭiḥ. bho bhoḥ śṛṇvantu śṛṇvantu bhavantaḥ!

dyūteṣu mā sma vijayiṣṭa paṇaṃ kadā cin,
mātuḥ śṛṇotu, pitaraṃ vinayena yātu,
kṣīram śṛtaṃ pibatu, modakam attu mohād,
vyūḍhā|patir bhavatu yo 'tra vaded ayuktam.

api ca,

1.340 paricaratu gurūn, apaitu goṣṭhyā,
bhavatu ca vṛddha|samo yuvā vinītaḥ,
palitam abhisamīkṣya yātu śāntiṃ
ya idam ayuktam udāharen niṣaṇṇaḥ.

Jimúta heaves: "Alas, alas!"
like an exhausted elephant, and,
like a cloud,
he rains water from his eyes.

He is calling me. Here I am! What is your command, master? "You corroborate what I have already been appraised about. He approached the brahmins in the same way for a propitiation, and therefore I am in session here. Make sure these honorable pimps are held in check by a pledge." As your lordship commands. Attention please! Listen to me, gentlemen!

He who speaks improperly in this matter,
may he never win the stakes at gambling,
may he obey his mother,
may he obediently approach his father,
may he drink boiled milk,
may he eat confectionary by mistake,
may he become a married man.

Furthermore,

He who says something inappropriate 1.340
while sitting here—
may he attend his elders
may he stay away from parties,
may he become a youth
as disciplined as an old man,
may he adopt quietism
when he notices his first grey hair.

(vivṛty' âvalokya) eṣa Dhārayakir Anantakathaḥ sahas" ôtthāya mām āhvayati.

kiṃ bravīṣi? «tasyā ev' êdam avijñāta|praṇayāyāḥ pātakaṃ n' âtra|bhavataḥ. śrotum arhati bhavān.

aśokaṃ sparśena
drumam asamaye puṣpayati yaḥ,
svayaṃ yasmin Kāmo
vitata|śara|cāpo nivasati
sa pādo vinyastaḥ
paśu|śirasi mohād iva yayā
nanu prāyaścittaṃ
caratu suciraṃ s" âiva capalā.»

iti. samyag bhavān āha. tayā hi

1.345 upavīṇita eṣa gardabhaḥ
samupaślokita eṣa vānaraḥ
payasi śṛta eṣa māhiṣe
sahakārasya raso nipātitaḥ.

api tv ārt'|ânupātāni prāyaścittāni nāma. ārtaś c' âyam upāgatas, tad anugrahītum arhanti bhavantaḥ.

tat kiṃ nu khalv eṣāṃ Gogla|naptā mada|rabhasa|calita|maulim eka|hastena pratisamābadhya kṣudra|mukt'|âvakīrṇam iva sveda|bindubhir lalāṭa|deśaṃ pradeśinyā parimṛjya «śrūyatām asya prāyaścittam» iti mām āhvayati.

(turns around and looks) Dharáyaki Anánta·katha* has suddenly risen to his feet and now he is calling me.

What are you saying? "The blame lies with that woman alone, not with this gentleman, since she failed to establish his capacity for love. Please hear me out, sir:

She unwittingly planted her foot
on the head of a brute—
a foot which makes the *ashóka* tree
blossom out of season by its touch
and in which Kama himself dwells
with his bow strung—
surely it is the careless woman
who must be penitent
for a very long time."

Well spoken, sir. For

She has accompanied a donkey on the lute, 1.345
sung paeans in praise of a monkey,
she has adulterated mango-juice
with boiled buffalo-milk.

But in fact, propitiations are pursued by the injured party. And an injured person has presented himself, so please show him some consideration.

Now isn't that Gogla's grandson in their midst? He secures with one hand his coiffure that has slipped out of place in the furor of his euphoria, dabs with his index finger his brow that is dappled with drops of perspiration as if with tiny pearls, and yells out to me: "Let his propitiation be heard!"

yāvad upasarpāmi. ete viṭāḥ «kaś ca tāvad ayaṃ viṭa|bhāva|dūṣit'|ākāraḥ prathamataro viṭo viṭa|pariṣady utthāya prāyaścittam upadiśati» iti kupitāḥ. haṇḍe Mallasvāmin, śrutam? evam āhur atra|bhavantaḥ.

kiṃ bravīṣi? «mā tāvad bhoḥ! ucyantām× atra|bhavantaḥ:

1.350 tāte pañcatvaṃ pañca|rātre prayāte
mitreṣv ārteṣu vyākule bandhu|varge
ekaṃ krośantaṃ bālam ādhāya putraṃ
dāsy" âhaṃ× sārdhaṃ pītavān asmi madyam.

katham aham a|viṭaḥ?» iti. evaṃ cet tvām anujānanti viṭa|mukhyo 's' îti. āsyatām.

kiṃ bravīṣi? «dīyatām madya|prāyaścittam»× iti. bāḍham. bhūyaḥ śrāvayāmi. tat kiṃ nu khalv eṣa× Śaibyaḥ kavir Āryarakṣito vāyu|vaiṣamya|nipīḍit'|âkṣaro mām āhvayan «na khalu na khalv idaṃ prāyaścittam!» iti pratiṣedhati? ×ativiṭaś c' âiṣa dhāntraḥ. kutaḥ?

vikrīṇāti hi kāvyaṃ
śrotriya|bhavaneṣu madya|caṣakeṇa
yaḥ Śibi|kule prasūto
Bhartṛ|sthāne jarāṃ yātaḥ.

I shall step up to him. The pimps here are indignant: "Now who might this be, whose appearance brings disrepute to pimp-kind?* He stands up as an eminent pimp in the assembly and dictates that there should be a propitiation!" Well now, Malla·svamin, have you heard? These gentlemen are speaking like this.

What are you saying? "How absurd! Please inform these honorable gentlemen:

Five days after the death of my father, 1.350
while my friends grieved
  and my relatives were anguished,
I dumped my crying only baby son
and drank wine
  with a maidservant.

How could I not be a pimp?" If this is how it is then they will acknowledge you as a paragon of a pimp. Please take your seat.

What are you saying? "Let him be purified by wine."* Very well, let me repeat this. Wait, isn't that the Shibi poet Arya·rákshita calling me, his words muffled by his spasmodic wheezing? He dissents: "That is no propitiation at all!" And this fellow is a super-pimp. Why?

For he hawks his poetry
for a cup of wine in the houses of priests—
he who was born in the family of Shibis
  and grew old in Bhartri·sthana.*

api ca

1.355 krīṇanti kavaya evaṃ×
kāvyāni hi madya|caṣakena×
Kāśiṣu ca Kosaleṣu ca
Bhargeṣu Niṣāda|nagareṣu.

yāvad enam upasarpāmi. sakhe, ayam asmi. kiṃ bravīṣi?

«dhṛto gaṇḍ'|ābhoge
kamala iva baddho madhu|karo×
vilāsinyā mukto
bakula|tarum āpuṣpayati yaḥ
vilāso netrāṇāṃ
taruṇa|sahakāra|priya|sakhaḥ
sa gaṇḍūṣaḥ sīdhuḥ×
katham iva śiraḥ prāpsyati paśoḥ?»

iti. ayam aparo Bhavakīrtir baddha|karaḥ prāyaścitt'|ârthaṃ mām āhvayati. ativiṭaś c' âiṣa māṇavakaḥ. kutaḥ?

muṇḍāṃ vṛddhāṃ jīrṇa|kāṣāya|vastrāṃ
bhikṣā|hetor nirviśaṅkaṃ praviṣṭām
bhūmāv ārtāṃ pātayitvā sphurantīṃ
yo 'yaṃ kāmī kāma|kāraṃ karoti.

What's more,

For "poets" can buy poetry 1.355
for just a cup of wine*
in Banaras,
among the Kósalas,
Bhargas,
and in the towns of the Nishádas.

I'll go up to him. Here I am, my friend. What are you saying?

"Can it really be possible
that this mouthful of liquor,
detained in her curving cheek
like a bee enclosed in a lotus flower,
which makes the *bákula* tree* blossom
when the coquette releases it,
a seducer of the eyes,
a beloved companion of the young mango tree,
should come in contact with
the head of such a brute?"*

Here someone else, namely Bhava·kirti is folding his hands and summons me in concerning the propitiation. And this lad is a super pimp. Why?

He is the one who floored
a shaven-headed old woman,
in tattered, red robes,
who had entered unsuspectingly for alms,
and, aroused, he did whatever he wanted
with that trembling, wretched woman.

1.360 yāvad enam upasarpāmi. kiṃ bravīṣi? «idam asya prāyaścittam:

badhyatāṃ mekhalā|dāmnā
samākṛṣya kaca|grahaiḥ
atha tasyāḥ prasuptāyāḥ
pādau saṃvāhayatv ayam.»

iti. bho etad api pratihatam. eṣa ibhya|putraś ceṭa|putrair abhyasta|nāmā Gāndharvasenako hastam udyamya mām āhvayati. yasy' âiṣa hastaḥ

vādyeṣu tri|vidheṣv aneka|karaṇaiḥ
saṃcārit'|âgr'|âṅgulis
tāmr'|âmbhoruha|pattra|vṛṣṭir iva yas
tantrīṣu paryasyate;
kolamb'|ânugatena yena dadhatā
śroṇī|taṭe vallakīm
ibhy'|ântaḥ|pura|sundarī|kara|ruha|
kṣepāḥ samāsvāditāḥ.

yāvad enam upasarpāmi. kiṃ bravīṣi?

1.365 «jaghana|ratha|nitamba|vaijayantī
surata|raṇa|vyatiṣaṅga|yoga|vīṇā
kva ca maṇi|raśanā var'|âṅganānāṃ
kva ca caraṇāv aśubhasya gardabhasya?»

I shall go up to him. What are you saying? "Here is a propitiation for him: 1.360

Let her bind him with her girdle
and drag him by his hair;
then let him massage her feet
while she sleeps."

Sir, that too is contested. Here is Gandhárva·sénaka, the son of a rich man, whose name is a byword among the sons of servants. He raises his hand and calls me. That hand of his,

Its fingertips astir,
with numerous *kárana* strokes,*
descends upon the strings
of three kinds
of musical instruments*
like a shower of rosy lotus petals;
by placing it, as it cradles the lute's body,
on their hips,
it savors
the nail strokes inflicted on the beauties
in a rich man's seraglio.

I shall go up to him. *(approaches)* What are you saying?

"How can there be any congruity 1.365
between the jeweled girdles of exquisite women
—the buttock-banners
on their loin-chariots,
magical lutes in the duel
of the battle of love—

iti. *(parivartakena)* ayam idānīṃ dākṣiṇātyaḥ kavir Āryakaḥ prāyaścittam upadiśati. kiṃ bravīṣi?

«vibhram'|āceṣṭiten' âiva
dṛṣṭi|kṣepeṇa bhūyasā
śiraḥ karṇ'|ôtpalen' âsya
tāḍyatāṃ mattayā tayā.»

iti. etad api pratihatam anena Gāndhārakeṇa Hasti|mūrkheṇa. kim idam ucyate bhavatā?

«nakha|vilikhitaṃ karṇe nāryā
niveśita|bandhanaṃ
khacita|śabalaṃ dṛṣṭi|kṣepair
apāṅga|vilambibhiḥ
yadi nara|paśor asy' êdaṃ bhoḥ
śirasy abhipātyate
surabhi|rajasā prāyaścittaṃ
kim asya bhaviṣyati?»

1.370 iti. «bāḍham, evam etad» iti pratipannā viṭa|mukhyāḥ. *(parivartakena)* imāv aparau māṃ āhvayataḥ

and the feet of a vile donkey?"*

(changing the subject) Now Áryaka, the poet from the South suggests a propitiation. What are you saying?

"Let her in her intoxication
repeatedly
beat his head
with the lotus flower
that adorns her ear,
while casting coquettish glances at him."

That too is disputed by this Hasti·murkha* from Gandhára.* What are you saying, sir?

"It has been incised by her nails,
she placed its stem behind her ear,
it has been suffused and dappled
by glances shot from the corner of her eye:
Good lord! Can it be a propitiation
for this human beast,
if this flower with fragrant pollen
is whacked over his head?"

"True, it is as you say", the head pimps concur. *(with a* 1.370
change of subject) Two others call out to me:

Gupta|Maheśvaradattau
 suhṛdāv ek'|āsana|sthitāv etau
upagata|kāvya|pratibhau
 Vararuci|kāvy'|ânusāreṇa.

yāvad upasarpāmi. *(upasṛtya)* haṇḍe Gupta | Romaśa, kim āha bhavān?

«pāda|prakṣālanen' âsyāḥ
 śiraḥ prakṣālyatām iti.»

katham? etad api pratiṣiddhaṃ traividya|vṛddhair atisuhṛdbhir anugṛhīta|nāmnā Maheśvaradattena:

1.375 «pāda|prakṣālanaṃ tasyāḥ
 pātum apy eṣa n' ârhati.»

iti. ayam aparo 'smat|suhṛt Sauvīrako vṛddha|viṭaḥ svacchanda|smit'|ôdagrayā vācā mantrayate. kim āha bhavān?

«nirbhūṣaṇ'|âvayava|cārutar'|âṅga|yaṣṭiṃ
 snān'|ārdra|mukta|jaghana|sthita|keśa|hastām
tām ānayāmy aham, ayaṃ tu dadhātu tasyā
 netra|prabhā|śabala|maṇḍalam ātma|darśam.»

iti. idam api pratiṣiddham anena kavinā Dāśerakeṇa Rudravarmaṇā. kiṃ bravīṣi?

Gupta* and Mahéshvara·datta,
two friends sharing one seat,
who became poetically inspired*
  by studying Vara·ruchi's poem.*

I shall approach. *(goes closer)* Hello, Gupta Rómasha, what are you saying, sir?

"Let his head be cleansed
  with the water she washed her feet in."*

What? That too is vetoed by Mahéshvara·datta, whose name is celebrated by his bosom friends who are eminent scholars of the three Vedas:

"He is not worthy 1.375
of even drinking her foot-water."

Here another friend of mine, the old pimp Sauvíraka, speaks with a voice animated by a spontaneous smile. What are you saying, sir?

"I shall summon her,
her slender body even more beautiful
  without jewelry,
her plentiful hair wet from bathing,
  unbraided, falling to her hip,
and he should hold up a mirror for her,
its disc a kaleidoscope for her flickering eyes."

That too is ruled out by this Dashéraka poet Rudra·varman. What are you saying?

«vidvān ayaṃ mahati Koki|kule prasūto
mantr'|âdhikāra|sacivo nṛpa|sattamasya
veśy"|âṅganā|caraṇa|pāta|rajo|'vadhūtān
keśān na dhārayitum arhati: muṇḍyatāṃ saḥ!»

1.380 iti. eṣa khalv anugṛhīto 'sm' îty uktvā Viṣṇunāgo vijñāpayati: «kiṃ kila sad"|ānamitam× idaṃ dāsī|pada|nyāsa|dharṣitam śiro vicchinnam icchāmi, prāg eva tu śiro|ruhāṇi.» iti. katham! etad apy asya pratihatam anena viṭa|mahattareṇa Bhaṭṭi|Jīmūtena. kim āha bhavān?

«skhalita|valaya|śabdair
añcita|bhrū|latānāṃ
khacita|nakha|mayūkhair
aṅgulīya|prabhābhiḥ
kisalaya|sukumāraiḥ
pāṇibhiḥ sundarīṇāṃ
suciram anabhimṛṣṭān
dhārayatv eṣa keśān.

api c' êdam asya prāyaścittam śrūyatām:

tasyā mad'|âlasa|vighūrṇita|locanāyāḥ
śroṇy|arpit'|âika|kara|saṃhata|mekhalāyāḥ
s'|ālaktakena caraṇena sa|nūpureṇa
paśyatv ayam śirasi mām anugṛhyamāṇam!»

"This scholar,
born in the great Koki* family,
a ministerial counselor of His Royal Highness,
he ought not to wear such locks
as have been polluted by the dust
from the kick of a courtesan:
he must be shaved!"

Vishnu·naga says: "Much obliged," and announces: 1.380
"Surely,* I wish to have my head, which is forever abased, cut off, as it has been violated by the step of a slave girl, but even before that, my hair!" What! The prime pimp, Bhatti Jimúta forbids him even this. What are you saying, sir?

"He must wear his hair for a long time
unstroked by the hands of beautiful women
with curved eyebrows—
hands delicate as tender shoots,
the luster of their nails
inlaid by the rays of rings,
stammering with the sound of their bracelets.

Furthermore, listen to the following propitiation for him:

Let him look on
as she favors my head with her foot
dyed with lac
and adorned with anklets,
while her eyes,
languid with tipsiness, are rolling,
and she holds together her girdle
with one hand put on her hip!"

iti. ete viṭāḥ sādhu|vād'|ânuyātrā «etad eva prāyaścittam» iti vādinaḥ sabhājayanti viṭa|mahattaraṃ Bhaṭṭi|Jīmūtam. eṣa «sarvath" ânugṛhīto 'smi» ity uktvā prasthitas Tauṇḍikokir Viṣṇunāgaḥ. eṣa mām āhvayati viṭa|mahattaro Bhaṭṭi|Jīmūtaḥ. ayam asmi, kim āha bhavān?

1.385 «anuṣṭhitam idam. kiṃ te bhūyaḥ priyam upaharāmi?» iti. bhoḥ śrūyatām:

kuṭṭinyaś catura|kathā bhavantv arogā,
dhūrtānām adhika|śatāḥ paṇā bhavantu,
bhūyāsuḥ priya|viṭa|saṃgamāḥ pure 'smin
vāra|strī|praṇaya|mah"|ôtsavāḥ pradoṣāḥ.

niṣkrānto viṭaḥ.

iti kaver udīcyasya Viśveśvaradatta|putrasy' ārya|Śyāmilakasya kṛtiḥ «Pādatāḍitakaṃ» nāma bhāṇaḥ samāptaḥ.

The pimps here celebrate Bhatti Jimúta, the prime pimp, saying "bravo" and "this alone is the propitiation." Now Taundi·koki Vishnu·naga says: "I am profoundly grateful," and sets off. Bhatti Jimúta, the prime pimp, is calling out to me now. Here I am, what are you saying, sir?

"This has been settled. In what other way can I please you?" 1.385
Well, listen:

May the silver-tongued bawds
be in good health,
may the rogues have hundreds of coins,
may the nights in this town,
when the pimps like to party,
be fabulous festivals of love with courtesans.

Exit the Pimp.

The end of the Causerie "The Kick" by the noble Shyámilaka from the North, the son of Vishvéshvara·datta.

UBHAYĀBHISĀRIKĀ

THE MUTUAL ELOPEMENT

2.1 *nāndy|ante tataḥ praviśati* SŪTRA|DHĀRAḤ

SŪTRA|DHĀRAḤ:

«ko 'si tvaṃ me kā v" âhaṃ te?
visṛja śaṭha mama nivasanaṃ.
mukhaṃ kim apekṣase?
na vyagr" âhaṃ! jāne hī hī
tava subhaga daśana|vasanaṃ
priyā|daśan'|âṅkitam.
yā te ruṣṭā sā te n' âhaṃ.
vraja capala hṛdaya|nilayāṃ
prasādaya kāminīm.»
ity evaṃ vaḥ kandarp'|ārtāḥ
praṇaya|kṛta|kalaha|kupitā
vadantu vara|striyaḥ.

evam ārya|miśrān vijñāpayāmi... aye, kiṃ nu khalu? mayi vijñāpana|vyagre śabda iva śrūyate. aṅga paśyāmi...

NEPATHYE:

vasanta|pramukhe kāle
lodhra|vṛkṣo gata|prabhaḥ
mitra|kāryeṇa sambhrānto
dīno viṭa iva sthitaḥ.

2.5 *niṣkrāntaḥ.*

Then, at the end of the benediction, enter the DIRECTOR. 2.1

DIRECTOR:

"What are you to me, or rather, what am I to you?
Let go of my dress, villain!
Why are you gawking at my face?
Not that I care! Ah me, I know very well,
you flirt, that your lips are scarred
by the teeth of your lover.
It is not I who is that lady who is angry at you.
Begone, you cheat, and make up
with that passionate woman who dwells
in your heart."
Thus may exquisite women
tormented by Love, incensed by love-quarrels,
accost you!

Esteemed audience, let me announce to you... What on earth! A disturbance as I am trying to make an announcement. Let me see what it is...

BEHIND THE SCENES:

In early spring the *lodh* tree
endures, bereft of elegance,
... like the poor pimp who toils
on his friend's behalf.*

Exits. 2.5

sthāpanā

tataḥ praviśati VIṬAḤ.

VIṬAḤ: aho vasanta|samṛddhiḥ ! kutaḥ?

parabhṛta|cūt'|âśokā
  dolā|vara|vāruṇī|śaś'|âṅkaś× ca
madhu|guṇa|viracita|śobhā×
  Madanam api sa|vibhramaṃ kuryuḥ.

2.10 aho paraspara|vyalīkaṃ sahate kāmi|janaḥ! aho apratihata|śāsano bhramati dūtī|janaḥ ! aho ṛtu|kāla|prādhānyaṃ pravāla|muktā|maṇi|raśanā|dukūla|pelav'|âṃśuka|hāra|hari|candan'|ādīnām vardhate saubhāgyam.

sarva|jana|madana|janane loka|kānte vasanta evaṃ vijṛmbhamāṇe Sāgaradatta|śreṣṭhi|putrasya Kuberadattasya Nārāyaṇadattāyāś ca kaś cit kalah'|âbhiniveśaḥ saṃvṛttaḥ. etat|kāraṇāt Kuberadatten' ātmanaḥ paricārakaḥ Sahakārako nāma māṃ prati preṣitaḥ:

«atha× bhagavato Nārāyaṇasya bhavane Madanasenayā samadanayā× Madan'|ārādhane saṃgītake yathā|rasam abhinīyamāne× ‹mām atītya sā tvayā praśastā› iti tat|saṃkrānta|madan'|ânurāga|śaṅkayā parikupitā Nārāyaṇadattā caraṇa|patanam apy anavekṣya sva|bhavanam eva gatā.

End of the Prologue

Then enter the PIMP.

PIMP: Ah, the bounty of spring! What do I mean?

> Cuckoos, mango and *ashóka* trees,
> swings, exquisite wines, the hare-marked moon
> —their beauty arrayed* by the skill of spring,
> they could stir up even the god of love himself.

Ah! Lovers are cheating on each other! Oh! Go-between girls rush about with pressing errands! Ah! The intensity of the season increases the sensuality of girdles wrought from corals, pearls and gems, of garments of silk and smooth *dukúla* fabric,* of pearl-necklaces, of pale sandal and the like. 2.10

Now that spring, loved by all, is so potent, impassioning everyone, Kubéra·datta, the son of guild-master Ságara·datta, and Ms Naráyana·datta have fallen out with each other for some reason. That is why Kubéra·datta sent to me his servant, Saha·káraka by name, with the following petition:

"In the temple of the Blessed Naráyana* the impassioned Ms Mádana·sena was performing a recital* in harmony with the aesthetic sentiment, to worship the god of love. Ms Naráyana·datta took umbrage: 'You've slighted me and praised her,' and suspecting that my love had gone over to that girl she went home straight away in a huff, paying no heed even to my falling at her feet.

tad|gata|madan'|ânurāga|tapta|hṛdayasya yathā mam' êyaṃ rajanī rajanī|sahasravan na vyatigacchet tath" âsya nagarasya sarva|kāla|vasanta|bhūtena bhāva|Vaiśikācalena kṛtaṃ sandhim icchāmi» iti.

śrutv" âiva tad|vacanam—abhijñātatayā madana|duḥkhasy' âprasahyasya—pradoṣa ev' âbhiprasthitaḥ sann, asmad|vayaḥ|pariṇāmam agaṇayanty" ātma|yauvan'|âvasthām eva cintayanty" âsmad|gehiny" ânyathā|śaṅkamānayā nivārito 'smi. eṣa idānīṃ tasyāḥ kopa|vināśane kṛta|pratijño gamiṣyāmi. athavā kim atra mayā pratijñātavyam? kutaḥ?

2.15 madhuraiḥ kokil'|ālāpaiś
cūt'|âṅkura|vibodhitaiḥ
vasantaḥ kalah'|âvasthāṃ
kāminīm anuneṣyati.

api ca,

kāntaṃ rūpaṃ yauvanaṃ cāru|śīlam
dānaṃ dākṣiṇyaṃ vāk ca sām'|ôpapannā:
yaṃ prāpy' âite sad|guṇā bhānti sarve
loke kāminyaḥ kena tasya prasādyāḥ?

(parikramya) aho Kusumapura|rāja|mārgasya parā śrīḥ! iha hi su|sikta|saṃmṛṣṭ'|ôcc'|âvaca|kusum'|ôpahārā anya|gṛhāṇāṃ vāsa|gṛhāyante rathyāḥ. nānā|vidhānāṃ paṇya|samudāyānāṃ kraya|vikraya|vyāpṛta|janena śobhante

I am longing for a reconciliation, to be arranged by the honorable Vaishikáchala,* the everlasting spring of this city, so that I may not spend this night like a thousand nights, my heart tormented with maddening love* for her."

Upon hearing his words, I, being familiar with the pain caused by love—which can be unbearable—, was about to set out that very evening, but my wife, who did not take into account my declining years and was only aware of her own youth, held me back, suspecting something else. I will go now, determined to bring an end to that girl's pique. Or rather, why need I even make a resolve in this matter? For—

With its sweet cooing of cuckoos, 2.15
elicited by mango-shoots,
spring will mollify
the sulking woman.

Anyway,

A fine figure, youth, charm,
generosity, courtesy, and conciliatory words:
if all these virtues become a man's ornaments
why need anyone reconcile him
with enamored women?

(walks about) Oh! How exquisitely beautiful is the high street of Pátali·putra! For here, with their gaudy flower-decorations, the washed and swept roadways are veritable bed-chambers compared to other rooms. The gateways to the central market are graced with people busily buying and selling a surfeit of goods. A file of palaces

'ntarāpaṇa|mukhāni. brahm'|ôdāharaṇa|saṃgīta|dhanur|jyā|ghoṣair anyonyam abhivyāharant' îva Daśa|mukha|vadanān' îva prāsāda|paṅktayaḥ.

kva cid udghāṭita|gavākṣeṣu rucira|prāsāda|megheṣu rathy'|âvalokana|kutūhalāḥ śobhante pramadā|vidyutaḥ Kailāsa|parvat'|ântara|gatā iv' âpsarasaḥ. api ca pravara|haya|gaja|ratha|gatā itas tataḥ paricalantaḥ śobhante mahā|mātra|mukhyāḥ. taruṇa|jana|nayana|mano|haraṇa|samarthāś cāru|līlāḥ sthāna|vinyasta|bhūṣaṇāḥ Sura|vara|nagara|yuvati|śriyam apahasantyaḥ paricaranti preṣya|yuvatayaḥ. sarva|jana|nayana|bhramarair āpīyamāna|mukha|kamala|śobhā rathy'|ânugrah'|ârtham iva pāda|pracāra|līlām anubhavanti gaṇikā|dārikāḥ. kiṃ bahunā?

2.20 sarvair vīta|bhayaiḥ prahṛṣṭa|vadanair
nity'|ôtsava|vyāpṛtaiḥ
śrīmad|ratna|vibhūṣaṇ'|âṅga|racanaiḥ
srag|gandha|vastr'|ôjjvalaiḥ
krīḍā|saukhya|parāyaṇair viracita|
prakhyāta|nānā|guṇaiḥ
bhūmiḥ Pāṭaliputra|cāru|tilakā
svargāyate sāṃpratam.

seems to chat with one another with Veda-recitation, music, and twanging bow-strings—as if they were the mouths of Ravana, the ten-faced demon.

Here and there gleam flashes of women-lightning in the open circular windows of the magnificent palace-clouds, eager to cast glimpses on the highway,* like *ápsaras*es on Mount Kailása. What's more, senior high dignitaries parade up and down majestically on exquisite horses, elephants, and in carriages. Go-between girls, fit to captivate the eyes and hearts of young men, do their rounds, and with graceful coquetry and neatly arranged ornaments they mock the charms of the girls in Indra's heaven. Young hetaeras luxuriate in sauntering about, as if to favor the roadway, while their beautiful lotus-faces are being drunk in by the eye-bees of all onlookers. Enough said!

The earth, adorned with Pátali·putra 2.20
as its beautiful head-ornament, is like heaven—*
everyone enjoys security;
with delighted faces they are engaged
in ceaseless festivities;
they wear precious gems, jewelry, and ornaments,
are resplendent with garlands and perfumes,
and *haute couture*;
they abandon themselves to pleasant recreations,
and they are endowed with all esteemed
refinements.*

(parikramya) aye! iyaṃ khalu Cāraṇa|dāsyā duhit" Ânaṅga|dattā nāma surata|pariśrama|khed'|âlasā catura|mṛdu|pada|vinyāsā nayan'|âmṛtāyamāna|rūp" êta ev' âbhivartate. avaśyam anayā priya|jana|nirday'|ôpabhuktayā bhavitavyam! kutaḥ?

daśana|pada|cihnit'|oṣṭhaṃ
  nidr"|âlasa|lola|locanaṃ vadanam,
jaghanaṃ ca surata|vibhrama|
  vilulita|raśanā|guṇa|parītam.

bhoḥ! asyā darśana|mātram eva ca naḥ kārya|siddhi|nimittam. aye mām anavekṣy' âiva gatā. abhibhāṣiṣye tāvad enām. hanta svayam eva pratinivṛttā.

(upagamya) vāsu, kathaṃ n' âbhivādayasi?

2.25 kiṃ bravīṣi? «cireṇa vijñāt" âsmi bhavantam. abhivādayāmi» iti.

śrūyatām iyam āśīḥ:

prathama|vayasaṃ sva|tantraṃ
  dātāraṃ cāru|rūpam arth'|āḍhyam
bhadre labhasva bhadraṃ
  kuśalaṃ kāntaṃ rati|paraṃ ca.

vāsu, sarvaṃ tāvat tiṣṭhatu.

vidheyo manmathas tasya,
  saphalaṃ tasya jīvitam
veśa|lakṣmyā tvayā sārdhaṃ
  yasy' êyaṃ rajanī gatā.

(walks about) Well well! Here comes Anánga·datta,* the daughter of Chárana·dasi. Languid by the fatigue caused by sexual gymnastics, she approaches with deft and gentle steps—her figure is nectar to the eye. She must have been mercilessly enjoyed by her lover! Why?

Her lips are scarred by tooth-marks
her eyes are languid and unsteady with drowsiness,
and her hips are girt with girdle-strings
  disordered by vehement love-making.

Ah! The mere sight of this woman is a good omen that foretells the success of my business. Ay! She has gone without even looking at me. Let me address her. Oh! She has turned back by herself.

(approaches) Darling, why don't you say hello?

What are you saying? "It took me a while to recognize you.* 2.25
Good morning."

Listen to this blessing:

My dear girl, may you obtain a kind lover
who is in the prime of his youth,
who is independent, generous, handsome,
a man of substance, skilled,
and always ready to make love.

But never mind all that, darling.

Kama obeys him, his life is fruitful
he who spent this night with you,
the glory of the courtesans' quarter.*

2.30 kiṃ bravīṣi? «mahā|mātra|putrasya Nāgadattasy' ôdavasitād āgacchāmi» iti.

bhadre, bhūta|pūrva|vibhavaḥ khalv eṣaḥ. vyaktaṃ tvayā mātur apriyam utpāditam. katham? vrīḍ"|âvanata|vadanay" ânayā hasitam. hanta saphalo naḥ pratarkaḥ. sundari, mā m" âivam. kutaḥ?

mātur lobham apāsya yad rati|sukheṣv
āsakta|cittā satī
tyaktvā vaiśika|śāsanaṃ bahu|phalaṃ
veśy"|âṅganā|dustyajam
gatvā kānta|niveśanaṃ bahu|rasaṃ
prāpt" âsi kām'|ôtsavam
ten' âyaṃ gaṇikā|janas tava guṇair
nikṣipta|pādaḥ kṛtaḥ.

aho sthāne khalu te vrīḍā. kiṃ śapathena? gṛham āgaty' ânuneṣyāmi te mātaram. tvayā tu veśy"|ôpacāra|viruddhaṃ kṛtam. gacchatu bhavatī.

kiṃ bravīṣi? «abhivādayāmi» iti.

2.35 subhage, śrūyatām iyam āśīḥ.

sva|guṇāḥ sad|guṇāḥ sarve
na stotavyāḥ sthitās tvayi.
loka|locana|kāntaṃ te
sthirī|bhavatu yauvanam.

What are you saying? "I am coming from the house of Naga·datta, the son of a high dignitary." 2.30

My dear girl, his fortune is surely a thing of the past. What you have done is clearly not to your mother's liking. What? She bashfully lowers her head and smiles. Oh, I've guessed right! Pretty girl, this is no good. For,

> Spurning the greed of your mother,
> your heart addicted to the pleasures of love,
> renouncing the principles of harlotry
> which yield a good profit and cannot be forgone
> by courtesans,
> you have gone to the house of your lover
> and enjoyed a delicious love-festival—
> thus the hetaeras have been trampled on
> by your virtues.*

Ah, your bashfulness is indeed appropriate. Must I swear an oath? I shall come to your house and set your mother's heart at rest. But you have infringed the mores of the courtesans. You may go, my lady.

What are you saying? "Goodbye!"

Lovely woman, listen to this blessing: 2.35

> All your qualities are good qualities,
> I need not praise them as long as you have them.*
> May your youth which delights people's eyes
> be everlasting.

gat" âiṣā. vayam api gacchāmaḥ. *(parikramya)* aye eṣā khalu Viṣṇudattāyā duhitā Mādhavasenā nāma, anapekṣita|parijan'|ânusaraṇā vyāghr'|ânusāra|vitrasta|mṛga|potik" êva tvaritatara|pada|vinyās" êta ev' âbhivartate. vyaktam idānīṃ jananī|lobha|doṣād aniṣṭa|jana|saṃbhoga|parikliṣṭay" ânayā bhavitavyam. tathā hi

na glānaṃ vadanaṃ, na keśa|racanā
prabhraṣṭa|puṣpa|dyutir,
dant'|ākrānta|nipīta|komala|rucir
n' âiv' âdhar'|oṣṭhaḥ kṛtaḥ,
gāḍh'|āliṅgana|varjitau stana|taṭāv
akliṣṭa|cūrṇa|śriyau,
śroṇyāṃ rāga|rati|prabandha|śithilā
na vyākulā mekhalā.

aye aniṣṭa|jana|saṃbhoga|janita|santrāsā mām an|avekṣy' âiv' âtikrāntā. bhavatu. enām anusṛtya nirveda|kāraṇaṃ jñāsyāmahe. hanta svayam eva pratinivṛttā.

2.40 kiṃ bravīṣi? «na mayā bhāvo 'lakṣyata» iti.

vāsu,× n' âsti doṣaḥ. parikliṣṭatayā vyākulita|cittānāṃ buddhayo hi sa|saṃbhramā bhavanti.×

She's gone. I shall also set off. *(walks about)* Well well! This is indeed the daughter of Vishnu·datta, Mádhava·sena by name. Paying no regard to the escort of her attendants she is coming right this way, apace as a fawn alarmed by a chasing tiger. It is clear now: due to the vicious avarice of her mother she must have been forced to be with a man she did not like. For,

> Her face is not languid,
> her headdress has not lost its splendor of flowers,
> her lower lip is not pale:
> it has not been worked on by teeth and drunk up,
> the beauty of her powder is not spoiled on her
> breasts:
> they have escaped close embraces,
> and the girdle on her hips is not disordered:
> it has not been slackened
> in the course of passionate love-making.

Oh, she passes by without even looking at me, so upset is she about this union with a despised man. Fine, I will follow her and find out more about her depression. Ah! She has turned back by herself.

What are you saying? "I did not notice you." 2.40

I take no offense, darling, for the minds of those whose hearts are troubled with discomfiture are prone to confusion.*

kiṃ bravīṣi? «abhivādayāmi› iti.

pratigṛhyatām ayam āśīr|vādo :

ādhyās te dayitāḥ santu,
vipriyāḥ santu nir|dhanāḥ,
mātur lobhāt kadā cit syān
n' âpriyair api saṅgamaḥ

2.45 vāsu, kuta āgamyate?

kiṃ bravīṣi? «Dhanadatta|sārtha|vāha|putrasya Samudradattasy' ôdavasitād āgacchāmi» iti.

aho prāptaṃ kṛtam! adya|kāla|Vaiśravaṇaḥ khalv esaḥ. kiṃ dīrgh'|ôṣṇa|śvāsa|vikampit'|âdhara|kisalayaṃ bhrukuṭī|vijihmita|nayanaṃ vyāvartitam ev' ânayā vadana|kamalam? hanta, ath' âvitatha|pratarkāḥ smaḥ. kutaḥ?

kṛcchrād datt'|oṣṭha|biṃbaṃ
virala|mṛdu|kathaṃ hāsa|līlā|viyuktam
jṛmbh'|ôṣṇa|śvāsa|miśraṃ
pariśithila|bhuj'|āliṅganaṃ vīta|rāgam
duḥkhād āśritya śayyāṃ
kṛtaka|rati|vidhau ceṣṭitaṃ bhāva|hīnam
vyaktaṃ bāle 'kṛthās tvaṃ
niśi divasa|karasy' ôdayaṃ cintayantī.

What are you saying? "Good morning."

Please accept this benediction:

> May rich people be your lovers,
> may those whom you dislike be penniless,
> may you never have to be with men
> you do not like because of your mother's avarice.

Where are you coming from, darling? 2.45

What are you saying? "I am coming from the house of Samúdra·datta, the son of the merchant Dhana·datta."

Well done, indeed! He is undoubtedly the Kubéra of our times. Why does she avert her lotus-face, with her sprout-like lower lip quivering from long, hot sighs, and her eyes narrowed by frowning? Well, my guess was not wrong after all. For,

> You forced yourself to bed without passion,
> listlessly giving your lips, red like a *bimba* fruit,
> with sparse and faint words,
> without jokes or love-games,
> now yawning, now heaving hot sighs,
> with very loose embraces;
> and then, sweetie, you clearly moved your body
> following the rules of artificial love-making
> but without feeling, all night long,
> with the sunrise in your mind.

vāsu, alam alaṃ viṣādena. rūp'|âvaro 'pi dhanavān gamyeṣv abhihita eva. śrūyatām:

2.50 sarvathā rāgam utpādya
vipriyasya priyasya vā
arthasy' âiv' ârjanaṃ kāryam
iti śāstra|viniścayaḥ.

kiṃ bravīṣi? «bhāvasy' âpi khalu me jananyāḥ samo niścayaḥ» iti.

bhavati, mā m" âivam. asty etat|kāraṇam. gacchatu bhavatī. tvad|gṛham ev' āgatya śāstra|tattvataś śrutiṃ grāhayiṣyāmi.

aho upadeśa|doṣād an|abhivādy' âiva gatā. aho tapasvinyā udvegaḥ! vayam api sādhayāmas tāvat. *(parikramya)*

aye eṣā khalu Vilāsakauṇḍinī nāma parivrājikā sa|lalita|mṛdu|pada|vinyāsā nayan'|âmṛtāyamāna|rūp" êta ev' âbhivartate. asyāḥ paṭa|vāsa|gandh'|ônmatta|bhramara|ganāś cūta|śikharāṇy api tyaktvā parivrajanti khalv enām. abhibhāṣiṣye tāvad enām, yato nayana|śravaṇa|kutūhalam apaneṣyāmi.

2.55 bhagavati, Vaiśikācalo 'ham abhivādaye.

kiṃ bravīṣi? «na vaiśik'|âcalena prayojanaṃ, bhaved vaiśeṣik'|âcalena» iti.

Don't be depressed, darling. A rich man, even if not handsome, is indeed named among those fit for sex. Listen,

> Rousing by any means the passions of a man, 2.50
> whether she likes or dislikes him,
> she just has to earn money
> —such is the ruling of the textbooks.

What are you saying? "Even your verdict, sir, is the same as my mother's."

Do not say so, my lady. There is a reason for this. You may go, my lady. I shall come to your house and make you understand the purport of the textbooks.

Darn! I've made the mistake of moralizing, so she left without even saying goodbye. How distressed the poor girl must be! I shall also go now. *(walks about)*

Well well! Here comes the wandering mendicant woman called Vilása·káundini. She is headed this way with playful and soft steps, her figure nectar for the eyes. Swarms of bees, drunk with the perfume of her petticoat, abandon even the mango-shoots and become her fellow wanderers. I shall speak to her, to satisfy my eager eyes and ears.

Venerable lady, I, Vaishikáchala bid you a good morning! 2.55

What are you saying? "I have no use of a 'mountain of harlotry,' though I might have need of a 'mountain of Vaishéshika'."

asty etat|kāraṇam. kutaḥ?

dṛṣṭis te 'ti|viśāla|cāru|rucirā
n' âikatra saṃtiṣṭhate,
glānyā kāntataraṃ rati|śrama|yutaṃ
śūn'|âdhar'|oṣṭhaṃ mukham,
ācaṣṭe surat'|ôtsava|prakaraṇaṃ
khed'|âlasā te gatir:
vyaktaṃ te kathitaṃ priyeṇa subhage
raty|artha|vaiśeṣikam.

kiṃ bravīṣi? «aho dāsen' ātma|sadṛśam abhihitam» iti.

2.60 dhanyā bhavanti subhage
dāsās te caraṇa|kamala|yugalasya.
asmad|vidhasya vara|tanu
kuto 'sti tat kṣīṇa|puṇyasya?

kiṃ bravīṣi? «ṣaṭ|padārtha|bahiṣ|kṛtaiḥ saha sambhāṣaṇam asmākaṃ gurubhiḥ pratiṣiddham» iti.

bhagavati, yuktam ev' âitat. kutaḥ?

There is a reason for this. For,

Your very large, lovely, bright eyes
do not remain fixed on one thing;
your face with its swollen lower lip
is fatigued by love-making
and is made even more charming by its
exhaustion;
your gait, lazy with weariness,
speaks about a prolonged sex-festival:
lovely lady, your lover has clearly imparted to you
the "distinctions"*
pertaining to the category love-making.

What are you saying? "Spoken like a true slave."

Lovely lady, blessed are the slaves of your lotus-feet. 2.60
Fine woman,
how could such a lot fall to such as me,
whose merit-rewards have been consumed?

What are you saying? "Our guru has forbidden conversation with those who are not included among the six categories."*

This is indeed proper, venerable lady! For,

dravyaṃ te tanur, āyat'|âkṣi, dayitā
rūpādayas te guṇāḥ,
sāmānyaṃ tava yauvanaṃ, yuva|janaḥ
saṃstauti karmāṇi te,
tvayy ārye samavāyam icchati jano,
yasmād viśeṣo 'sti te,
yogas te taruṇair mano|bhilaṣitair,
mokṣo 'py an|iṣṭāj janāt.

aye prahāsa eva naḥ prativacanam. hanta, saphalo naḥ pratarkaḥ.

2.65 kiṃ bravīṣi? «sāṃkhyam asmābhir jñāyate: *alepako nirguṇaḥ kṣetra|jñaḥ puruṣaḥ*» iti.

hanta *niruttarāḥ* smaḥ. asmat|kathā|prasaṅgena s'|ôtkaṇṭh" êva bhavatī dṛśyate. taruṇa|jana|surata|vighno 'py asmābhiḥ parihartavyaḥ. sādhayatu bhagavatī.[×] gat" âiṣā. gacchāmas tāvat.

(parikramya) aye kiṃ nu khalv eṣā Cāraṇadāsyā mātā Rāmasenā nāma vayaḥ|prakarṣe 'pi vartamānā vilāsa|viprekṣita|gati|hasitair yuvati|jana|līlāṃ viḍambayant" îta ev' âbhivartate. aho vismayanīyā khalv eṣā!

Your body is your "Substance," long-eyed lady,
your "Qualities"
are your precious figure and the like,
and your "Universal Property" is youth.
Young men praise your "Actions,"
and people wish for "Inherence" in you, milady,
since you are endowed with "Specialty."
Your "Union" takes place with juveniles who appeal
to you,
and you have "Freedom" from those whom you
dislike.*

Oho, laughter is the only answer to my words. Ah, I've guessed right!

What are you saying? "I am conversant with Sankhya: *the Soul is stainless, without Qualities, and the Knower of the field of experiences*: *This person uses no cosmetics, has no merits, he is a plowman.*"* 2.65

Alas! *I've been silenced*: *I am second to none.* As a consequence of our conversation you look prurient, madam. I must not stand in the way of young people's lovemaking. You may move on, venerable lady. She's gone. Let's go then.

(walks about) Well, lo and behold! This is Chárana·dasi's mother, called Rama·sena, coming right this way. Though she is well on in years, with her playful glances, gait, and smile she mocks the coquetry of young women. Ah, she is truly a wonder!

bhuktvā bhogān īpsitān kāmi|dattān,
kṛtvā saktān svair guṇaiḥ pīta|sārān,
bhūtvā yūnāṃ vaira|saṃgharṣa|yoniḥ
nūnaṃ dogdhuṃ yāti kāntaṃ sutāyāḥ.

hanta kāmi|jana|mṛtyu|bhūtāyā ā|deha|pāta|līlām anubhavāmas tāvad asyāḥ. namo 'stv asyai kāmuka|jana|mah"|âśanaye. bāle Rāmasene, duhitṛ|saṅkrānta|yauvana|saubhāgye kasya kāminaḥ kul'|ôtsādan'|ârtham abhiprasthitā bhavatī? bhoḥ kardane śapatha eva naḥ prativacanam?

2.70 kiṃ bravīṣi? «tvac|chīlam eva tvām ākrośayati» iti.

alam atra bahu|bhāṣitvena. tvad|gamanam eva tāvad ucyatām.

kiṃ bravīṣi? «duhitā me Cāraṇadāsī vyatīte 'hani gatā dhanik'|ôdavasitam. enāṃ saṅgītaka|vyapadeśen' ākarṣitum abhiprasthit" âsmi» iti.

aho Cāraṇadāsyāḥ pramādaḥ! kutaḥ? kāmuka|jana|sarvasva|haraṇa|kuśalāyā niṣpīta|sāra|parityāga|sāmarthya|yuktāyās tav' âpi nāma duhitā bhūtvā śāstr'|ôpadeś'|âgrahaṇena śocyā khalu sā tapasvinī. kutaḥ?

She enjoyed the pleasures she sought for,
given by her lovers;
with the help of her inherent virtues she bled dry
the men she had enthralled;
she was a source of feuds and rivalries
among young men:
and now she is going to milk
the sweetheart of her daughter.

Alas, now I must endure a flirtation unto death with this woman, who is death incarnate for gallants. Homage to her, the great thunderbolt for gallants! Rama·sena, my little girl, now that you have transferred your youth and attractiveness to your daughter, who is that gallant whose family you have set out to ruin? Hey! A curse while farting is my only answer?*

What are you saying? "It is just your personality that makes me find you so repulsive." 2.70

Let's not waste time prattling! Just tell me where are you going.

What are you saying? "My daughter, Chárana·dasi, went to the house of a rich man yesterday. I'm on my way to draw her away* on the pretext of a concert."

How careless is Chárana·dasi! Why? The poor girl is clearly to be pitied. She did not comprehend the import of the treatises, even though she had become the daughter of yours, and you are skilled in cleaning out gallants and adept at dumping those you have sucked dry. For,

labdhvā gamyaṃ prāpya c' ârthaṃ yathāvat
jñātvā samyaṅ|nirdhanatvaṃ ca tasya
rāgāt saktaṃ vipramoktuṃ na vetti
mithyā tasyāḥ śāstra|tattv'|ôpadeśaḥ.

2.75 kiṃ bravīṣi? «saṅgītaka|vyapadeśena tāṃ gṛham ānayiṣyāmi. tvay" âpi pratyāgatena tatr' āgamya śāstra|tattvataḥ śrutir grāhayitavyā» iti.

evam astu. kiṃ tu tvar"|ânuṣṭheyaṃ mitra|kāryam asti. tat samānīya bhavatyāḥ kāryam api sādhyiṣyāmi. gacchatu bhavatī. sādhayāmas tāvat.

aho aviśvasanīyāni khalu gaṇikā|janasya hṛdayāni. kutaḥ?

snigdhaiḥ praśliṣṭaiḥ krīḍanair lālayitvā
hṛtvā sarvasvaṃ nirghṛṇāḥ kāmukānām
lubdhā veśyās tān *anya|saṃrañjan'|ârtham*
dehān *vairāgyād* dehivat saṃtyajanti.

aho gaṇikā|mātaro nāma kāmuka|janasya niṣpratīkārā ītayaḥ. sarvathā svasty astu kāmukebhyaḥ. vināśo 'stu kāmuka|jana|sarvasva|haraṇa|kuśalābhyo gaṇikā|jana|mātṛbhyo gaṇik"|âmogh'|âstra|sarga|nipuṇābhyaḥ.

A woman who obtains a suitable lover,
in due course gets all his money,
sees that he is completely penniless,
but then out of affection
cannot leave the man who is attached to her:
she has been taught in vain
the principles of the doctrine.

What are you saying? "I shall bring* her home on the pretext of a concert. As for you, when you return, please come there and make her understand the scriptures according to their true import." 2.75

All right. But I have to attend to an urgent business of a friend of mine. After settling that I shall see to your business, too. You may go, madam. I am moving on now.

Ah! The hearts of hetaeras are truly fickle. For,

The greedy harlots caress their lovers
with affectionate embraces and petting,
then clean them out mercilessly,
and then, *indifferent*,
they quit them to please others,
just as souls quit bodies
out of detachment,
in order to be gratified in other bodies.

Upon my word, the madams are an incurable plague for gallants. In any case, may the gallants fare well, and may the madams perish, skilled as they are in cleaning out gallants, and masterful in hurling the unerring weapon: the courtesan.

2.80 *(parikramya)* aye rāja|mārgasya kaliḥ Sukumārikā nāma tṛtīyā prakṛtir ita ev' âbhivartate. aho amaṅgala|darśan" âiṣā. bhavatu. anabhibhāṣy' âināṃ vastram antarīkṛty' âtikramiṣyāmas tāvat. *(tathā kurvan)* aye anudhāvaty eva mām. k" êdānīṃ me gatiḥ? aho balavān kṛtāntaḥ. tasmāt priyam abhibhāṣy' âināṃ vyāghra|mukhād iv' ātmānaṃ mocayiṣyāmi.

kiṃ bravīṣi? «abhivādayāmi» iti.

vāsu, avidhavā bahu|putrā bhava. atha ca

bhrū|kṣep'|âkṣi|vicāraṇ'|oṣṭha|calanair
bāhvoś ca vikṣepaṇaiḥ
gatyā cārukayā vilāsa|hasitaiḥ
strī|vibhramā nirjitāḥ.
vispaṣṭ'|ākula|lola|lambi|raśanā
śroṇī viśāl'|āyatā.
kasy' āyāsi ratair atṛpta|hṛdayā
gehād viśāl'|ēkṣaṇe?

kiṃ bravīṣi? «rāja|syālasya Rāmasenasya gṛhād āgacchāmi» iti.

2.85 aho sa|phalaṃ jīvitaṃ tasya. subhage, kim idānīṃ cakravāka|mithunasy' êva viyogaḥ saṃvṛttaḥ?

(walks about) Oh no! The transvestite* called Miss Delicate, the demon of discord embodied on the High Street, is coming right this way. Good god! Seeing her is not auspicious. I must cover myself with my garment and pass her without a word. *(He does so.)* Oh no! She is running after me. How can I escape now? Fate is truly mighty. Well, I'll be nice to her and so rescue myself, as if from the jaws of a tiger. 2.80

What are you saying? "Good day to you."

My dear girl, may you never be widowed and have many sons. What's more,

Feminine coquetry is vanquished*
by your dancing eyebrows,
roving eyes and pouting lips,
waving arms, lovely gait and playful smiles.
Your broad hips sport a striking girdle,
tangled as it jumps and slips down.
Whose house are you coming from,
large-eyed girl,
with your heart unsatisfied by lovemaking?

What are you saying? "I am coming from the house of Mr Rama·sena, the king's brother-in-law."*

Oh, his life has born fruit. Lascivious girl, you were like a couple of Brahminy shelducks: why are you apart? 2.85

kiṃ bravīṣi? «rāj'|âvasthānaṃ gacchantyā gaṇikā|paricārikayā Ratilatikayā catura|madhura|hasita|rati|ceṣṭayā sa|sneha|lalita|kaṭākṣa|vikṣep'|âmbubhir abhiṣicyamāna|hṛdayaḥ samudgata|romāñca|nivedyamāna|madan'|ânurāgaḥ sa tasyās taṃ madan'|ânurāgaṃ śiraḥ|praṇāmena pratigṛhītavān. tatas tat pratyakṣa|vyalīkam asahamānayā mayā pratyādiṣṭaḥ san pādayor me patitaḥ.

tath" âpi ca may" ērṣy"|âbhibhūta|hṛdayayā n' âiv' âsya prasādaḥ kṛtaḥ. tato mām asau balāt|kāreṇa gṛham ānīya paryaṅka|talam āropya mayā sah' āsitaḥ. sa puno māṃ madan'|ākrānto rajanyāṃ madana|vega|kheda|suptāṃ parityajya tasyā eva gṛhaṃ gatv" âdya katipayāny ahāni n' âiva gṛham āgacchati. punaḥ s" âham anunayam agṛhītvā paścāt|tāpena dahyamānā bhāva|samīpam upāgatā yadṛcchayā bhāvaṃ samāsādit" âsmi. tad bhāvaḥ prāṇa|samena me bhartā saha sandhānaṃ kartum arhati» iti.

vāsu, aho Rāmasenasya pramādaḥ! kutaḥ?

vyākṣepaṃ kurutaḥ stanau na surate
gāḍh'|ôpagūḍhasya te,
rāga|ghnas tava māsi māsi subhage
n' âiv' ārtavasy' āgamaḥ,
rūpa|śrī|nava|yauvan'|ôdaya|ripur
garbho 'pi n' âiv' âsti te.
hy evaṃ tvāṃ suguṇāṃ vihāsyati sa ced
raty|utsavaṃ tyakṣyati.

What are you saying? "When, on her way to the palace, Rati·látika, the maid of the courtesans, sprinkled his heart with the waters of her loving, playful glances, with lovely, sweet smiles and amorous gestures,* he accepted her passionate affection with a bow of his head, his goosebumps betraying his own passion. I could not put up with such a blatant insult, and reprehended him: then he fell at my feet.

Still, I did not pardon him, since my heart was overwhelmed with jealousy. Then he forced me to his home, laid me on the bed, and had me. Then, at night, overcome by concupiscence, he left me, while I, exhausted by passion, was asleep. He went straight to her house, and did not come home for some days, until today. Once more I did not accept his attempts at conciliation, and then, burning with remorse, was about to visit your honor when I chanced upon you. So please, sir, unite me with my lord, who is as dear to me as my life."

Darling, how unthinking is Rama·sena! For,

> Your breasts do not set a bar against lovemaking
>   when he embraces you tightly;
> sensual girl, you have no period
>   to kill passion every month;
> you will never become pregnant
>   which would militate against the perfection
>   of your figure, beauty, and youth;
> in fact, if he dumps you
>   who are thus equipped with virtues,
> he will give up the festival of love.

2.90 bhavatv idānīm. mānini, tasy' âiv' ôdavasite māṃ pratipālaya. asti tāvan mama mitra|kāryaṃ kiṃ cit tvar'|ânuṣṭheyam. tat samānīya taṃ bhaginī|saubhāgya|garvitaṃ sukumāra|hṛdayānāṃ tvad|vidhānāṃ yuvatīnāṃ bhāva|bahiṣ|kṛtaṃ gṛham āgatya caraṇayos te pātayiṣyāmi. gacchatu bhavatī. sādhayāmy aham.

aho kṛcchreṇa khalv asmābhiḥ prākṛta|janād ātmā mocitaḥ. aham apy asmat|kāryam anuṣṭhāsyāmi.

(parikramya) aye ko nu khalv ayam abhigamya abhivādayati? svasti bhavate. ciren' êdānīṃ mayā saṃlakṣito 'si. Pārthaka|sārtha|vāha|putro Dhanamitro nanu bhavān. atha bhadra|mukha, bhṛty'|ârthi|saṃbandhi|suhṛj|janānāṃ dāridrya|tamo|apaharaṇasya yuvati|jana|hṛdaya|kumuda|vibodhana|karasya Kusumapura|gagana|pūrṇa|candrasya katham ayaṃ te vyasan'|ôparāgaḥ saṃvṛttaḥ? kim ati|lābha|kāṃkṣayā kuṭumba|sarvasvena saṃgṛhīta|bhāṇḍo deś'|ântaram abhigacchann antare corair abhyāsādito bhavān? āho svid rājño 'pathyaṃ samācaratas te rājñ" âpahṛtaṃ sarvasvam? athav" âik'|âkṣa|pāta|mātreṇa Dhanadasy' âpi vibhava|haraṇa|samarthena dyūtena kṣapito bhavān? kiṃ bahunā?

That's enough for now. Sulky woman, wait for me in his house. Now I have to attend to an urgent business of a friend of mine. After settling that I shall visit that man—proud of the amatory success of his sister, and clueless about the feelings of tenderhearted young women like you—at his home and make him fall at your feet. You may go, madam. I am moving on now. 2.90

Oh, I could barely save myself from this Neanderthal. I shall deal with my own business now.

(walks about) Oho! Who is this approaching and greeting me? Hail, milord. It's a long time since I saw you. Surely you are Mr Money's Friend, the son of Mr Kinglet, the merchant. Tell me now, gentle sir: you are the full moon in the sky of Kúsuma·pura, dispelling the darkness of poverty for servants, petitioners, relatives and friends, and opening up the lotus-hearts of young women—how has such an eclipse of misfortune befallen you? Did you use your family fortune to procure merchandise in the hope of a handsome profit, and were you then attacked by bandits on your travels abroad? Or did the king confiscate your property because you were scheming against him? Or have you been fleeced by a single throw of the dice, which is able to despoil even the generous Kubéra? But enough of this prattle!

saṃrūḍha|dīrgha|nakha|roma|mal'|ācit'|âṅgo
dhyān'|âbhibhūta|paripāṇḍura|śuṣka|vaktraḥ
aślakṣṇa|jīrṇa|mala|kīrṇa|viśīrṇa|vastro
n' ābhāsi divya|muni|śāpa|hato yath" âiva.

kiṃ bravīṣi? «yathā Rāmasenāyā duhitari Ratisenāyāṃ paramo me madan'|ânurāgaḥ saṃvṛttaḥ. tasyāś ca mayi tathā. sarvam etad viditaṃ bhāvasya. ato mātur lobha|vikāraṃ jñātv" âpi sā māṃ na saṃtyakṣyat' îti suhṛj|janena nivāryamāṇen' âpi mayā kuṭumba|sarvasvaṃ tasyai yugapad ev' ôpanītam. tatas tad gṛhītvā katipayeṣv ev' âhaḥsu gateṣu snāna|vyapadeśena snānīya|śāṭikāṃ paridhāpya mām aśoka|vanikā|dīrghikāṃ praveśya dvāre c' âpihite aśoka|vanikā|rakṣibhir vidita|paramārthaiḥ puruṣaiś chidra|dvāreṇa niṣkrāmito 'ham. tato 'sminn eva nagare ūrjitam uṣitvā katham idānīṃ bahūny ahāni dīna|vāsaṃ paśyām' îti araṇyam abhiprasthitena mayā yadṛcchayā bhāva ev' āsāditaḥ. suguhyam apy etad bhāvasya niveditam. tad idānīṃ bhāven' ânujñātaḥ sv'|ātma|niḥśreyasaṃ cintayiṣyāmi» iti.

2.95 aho lobh'|âbhiniveśo veśasya! aho kuṭila|svabhāvatā ca veśy"|âṅganānām! ehi bhoḥ pariṣvajāmahe tāvad bhavantam. diṣṭyā jīvantaṃ tvāṃ paśyāmi. kutas?

Your nails and hair have grown long,
your body is dirty,
your face is brooding,
is very pale and shriveled,
your clothes are rough, ratty, drab and ragged:
you look miserable,
as if struck by the curse of a divine sage.

What are you saying? "It's because I fell desperately in love with Rama·sena's daughter, Rati·sena, and she requited my love. You know all about this, sir. Even though I knew how morbidly greedy her mother was, I thought she would not leave me, and so, despite the protest of my friends, I transferred to her at once my family's entire property. Then, laying her hands on it, just a few days later, she made me put on a bathing suit under the pretext of going to the baths, and made me enter a pool in the *ashóka* park. When the gate was closed some men who were park-keepers, who were in on the matter, threw me out through a hole. Then I thought to myself: how could I now live out day after day in penury in the very city where I had lived in luxury? So I was about go to the forest, when I stumbled upon your honor. This is strictly confidential, but I've let you in on it nevertheless. Now, with your honor's permission, I shall think out the best solution for myself."

Wow, the brothel is indeed obsessively avaricious! And how 2.95
deceitful the courtesans are! Come on, let me embrace you, sir. It is lucky that I see you alive. For,

śāntiṃ yāti śanair mah"|âuṣadhi|balād
    āśī|viṣāṇāṃ viṣaṃ,
  śakyo mocayituṃ mad'|ôtkaṭa|kaṭād
    ātmā gaj'|êndrād vane,
grāhasy' âpi mukhān mah"|ârṇava|jale
    mokṣaḥ kadā cid bhaved,
  veśa|strī|baḍabā|mukh'|ânala|gato
    n' âiv' ôtthito dṛśyate.

atha bhadra|mukha, bhavato nirvedasya kāraṇaṃ Ratisenā, āho svid asyā jananī?

kiṃ bravīṣi? «kim atr' ânṛtam× abhidhāsyāmi? Ratisenā māṃ prati sa|sneh" âiva. mātṛ|doṣeṇ' âiv' êdaṃ saṃvṛttam. yadi tāvad bhāvaḥ svalpam api tasyā mātur aviditam eva me samāgamaṃ prati yatnaṃ kuryāt tato me prāṇāḥ pratyānītā bhaveyuḥ» iti.

jāne tasyās tvayy anurāgam anyasmād api janād mayā× śrutam. hā roditi.× alam alaṃ viṣādena. mam' êdānīṃ kiṃ cit tvar'|ânuṣṭheyaṃ mitra|kāryam asti. tat sampādya punar āgamya tav' âpi kāryaṃ sādhayāmi. gacchatu bhavān.

2.100 aho nipuṇatā veśy"|âṅganānām! kutaḥ?

Powerful herbs can eventually neutralize
snake-poison;
it is possible to run away
from a mighty elephant in the forest,
his temples dripping with ichor;
perhaps one could even extricate oneself
from the jaws of a mighty sea-monster—
not a single man who entered
the hetaera's submarine fire*
has ever been seen to escape.

Now, my good fellow, is Rati·sena the cause of your despondence, or her mother?

What are you saying? "Why should I lie to you about this? Rati·sena loves me, that is beyond question. This has happened through the malice of her mother alone. If your honor could make just a small effort so that I could meet her without her mother's knowledge, I would be restored to life."

I am aware of her affection for you, others have told me of it too. Oh dear, he cries. Don't be dejected! Now I have to attend to an urgent matter for a friend of mine. After settling that I shall come back and put things straight for you, too. You may go, sir.

How cunning the courtesans are! For, 2.100

yathā nar'|êndrāḥ kuṭila|svabhāvāḥ
svaṃ duṣkṛtaṃ mantriṣu pātayanti,
tath" âiva veśyāḥ śaṭha|dhūrta|bhāvāḥ
svaṃ duṣkṛtaṃ mātṛṣu pātayanti.

aho gata eva tapasvī khala|jan'|ôpādhyāyaḥ. vayam api sādhayāmas tāvat.

(parikramya) aye vasanta|vana|kokil'|ânukāriṇā snigdha|madhureṇa svareṇa kayā nu khalv asman|nāmadhey'|âbhivyaktiḥ kriyate? *(vilokya)* aye Priyaṅgusenā! ayi Priyaṅgusene ayam aham āgacchāmi.

kiṃ bravīṣi? «abhivādayāmi» iti.

2.105 vāsu, pratigṛhyatām iyam āśīḥ :

ramaṇaṃ nivārayantī
komala|kara|caraṇa|tāḍanaiḥ śayane
tad|ati|rati|rabhasa|vimṛdita|
suvipula|jaghanā sukham upehi.

vāsu, rati|pariśrānta|jaghan'|āpyāyana|karasya nānā|gandh'|âdhivāsitasya surabhi|gandhino gandha|tailasy' ātm'|âṅga|sparśa|pradānena kim anugrahaḥ kriyate? bhadra|mukhi, avatārita|ghaṇṭā|graiveyaka|kakṣāyā rāj'|ā-upavāhya|kareṇor iv' âvamukt'|âlaṅkārāyā nirvyāja|ma-

Just as monarchs, devious by nature,
shift the blame for their own misdeeds
to their ministers,
in the same way courtesans,
these villains and deceivers,
shift the blame for their own misdeeds
to their mothers.

Oh! The wretched master of knaves has gone. Let's move on now.

(walks about) Hey! Who is calling me by my name with a voice as soft and sweet as the koel's in the spring forest? Aha! It's Priyángu·sena! Wait, Priyángu·sena, here I come!

What are you saying? "Good morning."

Darling, please accept this blessing: 2.105

May you find delight
when you are holding back your lover
with slaps and kicks
of your tender hands and feet,
while your broad hips are being crushed
in his violent lovemaking.

Darling, why do you confer the favor of touching your body to the fragrant aromatic oil, which is scented with many perfumes and soothes your hips wearied by sex? Lucky girl, a man would clearly be deceived if he did not see your stunningly beautiful body, naturally attractive with your ornaments taken off, just as the body of the king's

nohara|rūpāyāś cāru|śobhaṃ te vapur yo na paśyati sa khalu vañcitaḥ syāt. kutaḥ?

mukt'|âlaṅkāra|veṣāṃ×
nakhara|pada|citāṃ gandha|tail'|âṅga|rāgām
īṣat|tāmr'|ânta|netrāṃ
prahasita|vadanāṃ yauvan'|ôṣṇa|stan'|āḍhyām×
su|ślakṣṇ'|ârddh'|ōru|vastrāṃ
vyapagata|raśanāṃ vyāyata|śroṇi|biṃbāṃ
dṛṣṭvā tvāṃ cāru|rūpāṃ
pravicalita|dhṛtir Manmatho 'py āturaḥ syāt.

kiṃ bravīṣi? «priya|vacanam idaṃ× bhāvasya» iti.

2.110 bhoḥ! kim ayaṃ sevā|vādaḥ? alaṃ vrīḍām utpādya. āhvāna|prayojanaṃ tāvad ucyatām.

kiṃ bravīṣi? «śrūyatām» iti.

vāsu, avahito 'smi.

kiṃ bravīṣi? «bhagavato 'pratihata|śāsanasya Kusumapura|Purandarasya× bhavane Purandara|vijayaṃ nāma saṅgītakaṃ yathā|ras'|âbhinayam abhinetavyam iti Devadattayā saha me paṇitaṃ saṃvṛttam.× atra mam' âbhyudayasya bhāva eva× kāraṇam» iti.

riding elephant with its bells, neck-ornament and girth removed. For,

> Even Kama would suffer, his firmness gone,
> if he saw your ravishing body
> without ornaments and clothes,
> covered with nail-marks,
> rubbed with scented oil and cosmetics,
> with eyes reddish at the corner and smiling face,
> well-endowed with breasts warm with youth,
> your silky petticoat reaching to the middle of your thighs,
> with the girdle removed
> and the orbs of your hips exposed.

What are you saying? "You are blandishing me, sir."

Now really! These are supposed to be words of flattery? But I shall not embarrass you. Just tell me why I've been summoned. 2.110

What are you saying? "Please listen."

I am all ears, my dear.

What are you saying? "I have made a bet with Deva·datta that the lay called 'Puran·dara's Victory' will be staged with a performance expressing the aesthetic sentiment in the abode of Pátali·putra's Blessed Puran·dara,* whose commands are irresistible. You alone, sir, can make me triumphant in this matter."

mā m" âivam. sakala|śaśāṅka|vimalāyāṃ rajanyāṃ n' âsti dīpa|prayojanam. api ca balavato n' âsti sahāya|sampat|prayojanam. bhavaty ev' âtra kāraṇam. asminn ev' ârthe tvad|arpita|madan'|ânurāga|hṛdayena Rāmasenen' âbhyarthito 'smi.

2.115 katham! sa|bhrū|vilāsa|vikṣepam īṣat|kuñcita|nayana|kapola|nivedyamān'|ântar|gata|praharṣaṃ pracalit'|âdhara|kisalayaṃ mukha|kamalaṃ parivartya parijanam avalokayanty" ânayā hasitam. hanta prāptaṃ sevā|phalaṃ Rāmasenena. Priyaṅgusene, aho Devadattāyā akuśalatā, yā tvayā saha saṃgharṣaṃ kurute, yasyās tāvat prathamaṃ rūpa|śrī|nava|yauvana|dyuti|kānty|ādīnāṃ guṇānāṃ sampat, caturvidh'|âbhinaya|prasiddhiḥ, dvātriṃśad|vidho hasta|pracāraḥ, aṣṭādaśa|vidhaṃ nirīkṣaṇaṃ, ṣaṭ sthānāni, gati|dvayam, aṣṭau rasāḥ, trayo gīta|vāditra|layā ity evam|ādīni nṛtt'|âṅgāni tvad|āśrayeṇ' âlaṃkṛtāni. athavā anen' âpi veṣeṇa dev'|âsura|maharṣi|mano|nayana|haraṇa|samarthānām apsarogaṇānām api laṃghana|samarth" êti tvāṃ paśyāmi. api ca,

pratinartayase nityaṃ
  jana|nayana|manāṃsi ceṣṭitair lalitaiḥ.
kiṃ nartanena, su|bhage?
  paryāptā cāru|līl" âiva.

Do not say so! There is no need for a lamp on a night floodlit by the full moon. Moreover, a man of means does not need his friend's resources. You alone are the instrument. Mr Rama·sena, whose heart is full of passionate love for you, has called upon my help precisely in this matter.

What! She smiles, looks at her attendants, with her lotus-face turned away, eyebrows playfully knit, her inner joy betrayed by her cheeks and slightly squint eyes, and the sprout of her lower lip trembles. Oh, Rama·sena has reaped the reward of his services. Priyángu·sena! How ill-advised Deva·datta is, entering into a competition with you who, first of all, abound in such qualities as a good figure, grace, fresh youth, radiance, and splendor, you who are accomplished in the four kinds of acting,* the thirty-two kinds of hand-gestures,* eighteen* ways of looking, six postures,* two kinds of gait,* eight aesthetic sentiments,* three times* of vocal and instrumental music—these and the other constituents of dancing become beautiful with you as their locus. Or rather I see you capable of humiliating, even in the clothes you are wearing now, no less than the bevies of nymphs who are able to captivate the hearts and eyes of gods, demons, and great sages. Moreover, 2.115

You incessantly make the eyes and hearts of men
dance before you with your playful gestures.
Why dance at all, sensual girl?
Your graceful coquetry alone is sufficient.

aye vrīḍitā. hanta anen' âiva vrīḍ"|âlaṅkāreṇa visarjitāḥ smaḥ. gacchāmas tāvat.

(parikramya) aye kiṃ nu khalu! eṣā Nārāyaṇadattāyāś ceṭikā Kanakalatā nāma cūrṇ'|āmodita|karkaśa|stana|yugalā vividha|kusum'|âlaṃkṛta|keśa|hastā kim api khalu prahṛṣṭa|vadanā mada|vilāsa|skhalita|pada|vinyās" êta ev' âbhivartate. abhibhāṣiṣye tāvad enām. katham? antikam upetya mām abhivādayati.

vāsu, kiṃ bravīṣi? «abhivādayāmi» iti.

2.120 vāsu, priyasya dayitā bhava. bhavati, caraṇa|kamala|vinyāsena kim ayaṃ mārg'|ânugrahaḥ kriyate?

kiṃ bravīṣi? «priya|vādī khalu bhāvaḥ» iti.

n' âiṣa saṃstavaḥ.

kiṃ bravīṣi? «anugṛhīt" âsmi» iti.

sarvaṃ tāvat tiṣṭhatu. kim idānīṃ cakravāka|mithunasy' êva viyogas saṃvṛttaḥ?

2.125 kiṃ bravīṣi? «īrṣy"|âbhibūta|hṛdayāyāṃ parityakta|snāna|bhojana|śayan'|âlaṅkāra|kathāyām aśoka|vanikāyām aśoka|bāla|vṛkṣa|saṃśrite śilā|tala upaviṣṭāyām īṣat|paryāpta|candra|maṇḍala|darśanen' ânibhṛta|madhukara|raveṇa vasanta|kusuma|gandh'|āmoda|karkaśena dakṣiṇa|pavanena ca parivardhita|santāpāyāṃ sakhī|jana|madhura|vacanair āśvāsyamānāyām asmad|ajjukāyām aśoka|vanik"|âbhyāśe ko 'pi khalu puruṣaḥ saṃdiṣṭa iva Ma-

Oh! She blushed. Well, I have been dismissed with this very ornament of shyness. I am moving on now.

(walks about) Hey, what on earth! Naráyana·datta's maid, Kánaka·lata by name, is coming right this way, her firm breasts perfumed with powder, her braid decorated with colorful flowers, her face beaming with joy, stumbling with wanton rapture. I will speak to her. What? She comes here to greet me.

What are you saying, darling? "Good morning."

May your lover cherish you, darling. Why are you gracing the road with the steps of your lotus-feet? 2.120

What are you saying? "Your honor is indeed a complimenter."

This is no flattery.

What are you saying? "Thank you."

That's all right now. Why have they, who seemed like a couple of Brahminy shelducks, parted company?

What are you saying? "My mistress, her heart engulfed by jealousy, had given up even the talk about bathing, eating, sleeping, and ornaments, and sat down in the *ashóka* grove on a boulder next to a young *ashóka* tree. There her anguish was heightened by the sight of the nearly full moon's disc,* the noisy buzzing of the bees, and the southern breeze, cruel with the fragrant perfume of spring flowers. When her friends were heartening her with sweet words, some man passed by the *ashóka* grove, as if commissioned by the Love God, tuned his lute to 2.125

danen' âvyakta|kākalī|racanā|mūrchanām× vīṇāṃ kṛtv"
ême vaktr'|âpara|vaktre gāyann atikrāntaḥ:

‹niṣphalaṃ yauvanaṃ tasya
  rūpaṃ ca vibhavaś c' âiva×
yo janaḥ priya|saṃsakto
  na krīḍati vasante 'smin.×

api ca:

śaśinam abhisamīkṣya nirmalam
  para|bhṛta|ramya|ravaṃ niśamya vā
anunayati na yaḥ priyaṃ janam
  viphala|taraṃ bhuvi tasya jīvitam.›

iti. tatas tena gītakena śithilī|kṛta|māna|parigrah" âsmad|ajjukā yuṣmad|āgamanam apy apratipālayantī mām ev' āhūya pāda|cāreṇ' âiv' âsmad|bhartṛ|dāraka|gṛham abhiprasthitā. tath" âiv' âsmad|bhartṛ|dārako 'pi vasant'|ākrānta|śithilī|kṛta|dhṛtir bhūtvā saha ken' âpy asmad|ajjukām anunetum āgacchan vīṇ"|ācāryasya Viśvāvasudattasy' ôdavasita|dvāry asmad|ajjukāṃ samāsāditavān. tatas tau kiṃ cid apratipadyamānau dṛṣṭvā yadṛcchayā nirgatena Viśvāvasudatten' ātmana udavasitam eva praveśitau. tataḥ prabhāte 'smad|ajjukay" âham abhihitā ‹bhāva|Vaiśik'|âcalaṃ gṛhītv" āgaccha› iti. tad āgamyatām» iti.

2.130 aho śruti|sukhaṃ niveditaṃ bhavatyā. kim anyāṃ te prītim utpādayiṣyāmi? pratigṛhyatām ayam āśīrvādaḥ:×

a scale with faint blue notes and sang these two *vaktra* and *ápara·vaktra* verses:

'Fruitless are the youth, beauty, and wealth
of every one who does not have a good time
together with a loved one
in this spring season.

What's more,

Completely futile is the earthly life
of those who do not conciliate their dear ones
when they have seen the spotless moon
and heard the lovely song of the cuckoo.'

Then my mistress, her sulking mitigated by that ditty, could no longer wait for your arrival* but called me and set out on foot to the house of my master. In the same way my master, too, his firmness alleviated by spring's attack, was coming with someone to conciliate my mistress when he met my mistress in the doorway of the house of Vishva·vasu·datta, the lute teacher. Then Vishva·vasu·datta, coming out by chance and seeing that they were a bit confused, took them right inside his house. Then, in the morning, my mistress told me: 'Find the honorable Váishikachala and bring him here.' So please come."

Excellent! Your words are music to my ears, milady. Shall 2.130
I gladden you with something else? Please accept this blessing:

tava bhavatu yauvana|srīḥ,
priyasya satataṃ bhava priyatamā tvam.
anavaratam ucitam abhimatam
upabhoga|sukhaṃ ca te bhavatu.

gacch' âgrataḥ. *(parikramya)*

kim āha Kanaka|latā? «etad|gṛhān praviśāvaḥ» iti.×

bāḍhaṃ. praviśāvas× tāvat.

2.135 *(praviśya)* alam alaṃ saṃbhrameṇa! āstām āstāṃ kāmi|yugalam.

ātma|guṇena vasanto
yath" âdya yuvayoḥ samāgamam akārṣīt
ṛtavas tath" âiva sarve
kurvantu samāgamaṃ kalahe.

ātma|guṇa|garvitena vasanten' âham api vañcito yato yuvayoḥ samāgama|bahiṣ|kṛtaḥ. kim idānīm abhidhāsyāmi? athavā n' âsty atr' âparādho vasantasya. kutas?

udyānāni niśāś ca candra|sahitā
vīṇāś ca rakta|svarāḥ
goṣṭhī dūti|jano vicitra|vacano
nānā|vidhāś ca' rtavaḥ:
n' âitat kāmi|janasya saṃgama|vidhau
samjāyate kāraṇaṃ
hy anyo 'nyasya guṇ'|ôdbhavair akṛtakai
rāg'|ôcchrayaḥ kāraṇam.

May the glory of youth be yours,
may you always be your lover's favorite,
and may the pleasure of your enjoyment be
uninterrupted, appropriate and agreeable.

Please lead on. *(walks about)*

What are you saying, Kánaka·lata? "Let's enter this house."

OK. Let's enter then.

(entering) Please do not trouble yourself! The pair of lovers should remain at ease. 2.135

As spring has now brought you together,
by its virtues,
so may all the seasons bring you together
when you quarrel.

I have also been cheated by spring, who is proud of his own virtues,* since I've been kept in the dark of your reconciliation. What can I say now? Or rather, spring is not to blame in this case. For,

Gardens, moonlit nights,
the passionate sounds of lutes, parties,
honey-tongued go-betweens,
and the various seasons:
all this cannot effect the union of lovers,
for they are brought together
by intense passion manifested
by each other's natural virtues.

tasmād anya|jana|durlabhena paraspara|guṇ'|âtiśaya|niciten' ātma|guṇ'|ôpanītena Madana|tantra|sāreṇa Kusuma|pura|prakāśena yuvayor eva rāgeṇa vañcitāḥ smaḥ.

2.140 kiṃ brūthaḥ? «āvayor rāgo 'pi bhāvasy' âiva prayatna|janitaḥ. tena bhāva eva samāgama|kāraṇam. kṛtsnam idānīṃ Pāṭaliputraṃ yasya vacana|līlām anubhavati sa kathaṃ kāmi|jana|viśeṣair atiśayito bhavet» iti?

kathā|prasaṅgena surata|tṛṣitasya kāmi|yugalasya rati|vyākṣepaḥ parihartavyaḥ. tad anujñāto gantum icchāmi.

bharatavākyam:

vyākoc'|âmbhoja|kāntaṃ mada|mṛdu|kathitaṃ
cāru|vistīrṇa|śobham
jātas tvaṃ prīti|yuktaḥ priya|yuvati|mukhaṃ
vīkṣamāṇo yath" âdya,
evaṃ sasya'|rddhi|yuktāṃ jala|nidhi|raśanāṃ
Meru|Vindhya|stan'|āḍhyām
prītiṃ prāpnotu sarvāṃ kṣitim adhika|guṇāṃ
pālayan no nar'|êndraḥ.

Therefore I have been cheated by your passion alone, unobtainable for others, which has been intensified by the eminence of your virtues, realized about by your own qualities, and which is the essence of *ars amatoria*, celebrated in Pátali·putra.

What are you saying? "Our love has also been effected by the good offices of none other than your honor. So your honor alone is the cause of our union. How could the excellences of lovers outdo someone whose playful words the whole of Pátali·putra enjoys these days?" 2.140

One must not interrupt with too much talk the lovemaking of a pair of lovers thirsty for sex. So, by your favor, I should like to leave.

The actor's verse:

Just as you have become delighted today
looking at your youthful beloved's face,
lovely as a blown lotus, talking softly with passion,
and radiating charming beauty,
so may our majesty take delight in cherishing the
whole, most excellent earth, rich in crops,
girdled by the ocean,
and well-endowed with breasts:
the Meru and the Vindhya mountains.

iti niṣkrānto viṭaḥ.

2.145 *iti śrīmad|Vararuci|muni|kṛtir «Ubhayābhisārikā» nāma bhāṇaḥ samāptaḥ.*[×]

The pimp exits.

Thus ends the causerie "The Mutual Elopement," 2.145
the work of the illustrious sage Vara·ruchi.

PADMAPRĀBHṚTAKA

THE LOTUS GIFT

3.1 *nāndy|ante tataḥ praviśati* SŪTRA|DHĀRAḤ.

SŪTRA|DHĀRAḤ:

jayati bhagavān sa Rudraḥ
kopād atha v" âpy anugrahād yena
strīṇāṃ vilāsa|mūrtiḥ
kāntatara|vapuḥ kṛtaḥ Kāmaḥ.

api ca,

puṣpa|samujjvalāḥ kuravakā
nadati parabhṛtaḥ,
kāntam aśoka|puṣpa|sahitaṃ
calati kisalayam,
cūta|sugandhayaś ca pavanā
bhramara|ruta|vahāḥ;
saṃprati kānaneṣu sadhanur
vicarati Madanaḥ.

3.5 kiṃ c' ânyat,

ātodyam pakṣi|saṃghās, taru|rasa|muditāḥ
kokilā gānti gītaṃ,
vāt'|ācāry'|ôpadeśād abhinayati latā
kānan'|ântaḥ|pura|strī,
tāṃ vṛkṣāḥ sādhayanti sva|kusuma|hṛṣitāḥ
pallav'|âgr'|âṅgulībhiḥ,
śrīmān prāpto vasantas, tvaritam apagato
hāra|gauras tuṣāraḥ.

Then, at the end of the benediction, enter the DIRECTOR. 3.1

DIRECTOR:

Triumphant is the blessed Rudra,
who in anger—nay as a kindly favor—
gave Cupid a more dazzling* body,
the coquetry of women.

Moreover,

The *kúrabaka*s gleam with blossoms,
the cuckoo calls,
a delicate shoot,
laden with *ashóka* flowers
beckons, the mango-perfumed breeze
transports the humming of bees;
now the God of love,
bow in hand,
roams the woodlands.

What's more, 3.5

The flocks form an orchestra,
the koel,
thrilled with fresh tree-sap, sing the chorus,
the vine,
mistress of the forest-seraglio,
dances, guided by the wind-professor,
the trees, bristling with flowers,
applaud her with shoot-fingers,
illustrious spring arrives,
and frost, pale as a pearl necklace,
quickly slips away.

mūlād api madhyād api
viṭapād apy aṅkurād aśokasya
piśuna|stham iva rahasyaṃ
samantato niṣkasati puṣpam.

aho ayam

sa|saṃbhrama|parabhṛta|rutaḥ
sa|sinduvāraḥ sa|kunda|sahakāraḥ×
sa|mada|madanaḥ sa|pavanaḥ×
sa|yauvana|jana|priyaḥ kālaḥ.

3.10 *niṣkrāntaḥ.*

sthāpanā

tataḥ praviśati VIṬAḤ.

VIṬAḤ: sādhu bhoḥ. ramaṇīyaṃ khalu tāvad idaṃ. śiśira|jarā|jarjarasya saṃvatsara|viṭasya hima|rasāyan'|ôpayogāt punar āvṛttaṃ vasanta|kaiśorakam upohyate. saṃprati hi

Flowers burst forth all around,
even from the root,
the trunk,
the boughs,
the twigs of the *ashóka* tree,
like secrets entrusted to an informer.

Ah!

This is the time melodious with busy cuckoos,
with chaste tree flowers,*
with mango trees supporting jasmine,
intoxicated with bees,
cooled by breezes, dear to the young.

Exits. 3.10

End of the Prologue

Then enter the PIMP.

PIMP: Good good! This truly is delightful. For this year-pimp, withered by winter-senescence, returning spring-juvenility shows itself by virtue of the application of the *elixir vitae:* cool mist. For now,

pracala|kisalay'|âgra|
pranṛtta|drumaṃ yauvanasthāyate
phulla|vallī|pinaddhaṃ vanaṃ,×
tilaka|śirasi keśa|
pāśāyate kokilaḥ, kunda|puṣpe sthitaḥ
strī|kaṭākṣāyate ṣaṭ|padaḥ,
kva cid acira|virūḍha|
bāla|stanī kanyak" êv' ôdgataiḥ śyāmalaiḥ
kuḍmalaiḥ padminī śobhate,
vara|yuvati|rati|śrama|
svinna|pīna|stana|sparśa|dhūrtāyitā
vānti vāsantikā vāyavaḥ.

3.15 itthaṃ ca Madana|śara|saṃtāpa|karkaśo balavān ṛtur ayam,× yad Devadattā|surata|suprativihita|yauvan'|ôtsavasy' âpi ×Karṇīputrasy' ônmucyamāna|bāla|bhāva|yauvan'|âvatāra|komalāṃ madana|mañjarikāṃ Devasenā|cūta|yaṣṭim atilaṅghayate madana|bhramaraḥ. athavā kim iva Karṇīputrasy' âtikramiṣyati? sa|madhu|sarpiṣkaṃ hi param annaṃ sopadaṃśam āsvādyataraṃ bhavati. ataḥ śanke Devadattā|surata|madhu|pān'|ôpadaṃśa|bhūtaṃ caṇḍālik"|āśrayaṃ bāla|bhāva|nirupaskṛt'|ôpacāra|hasita|lalita|ramaṇīyaṃ dārikā|sundarī|rati|ras'|ântaram

This grove acts like a youth,
garlanded with blossoming vines,
its trees dancing with agile hand-gestures
—quivering shoots;
the cuckoo acts like a hair-tuft
on the head formed by the *tílaka* tree;
the bee, resting in a jasmine flower,
enacts the side-glances of a damsel;
over here the lotus-pond
with upright dark buds
is as beautiful as a girl
whose tender breasts have just recently grown;
the spring breezes blow,
misbehaving like rogues fondling
the swollen breasts of exquisite women,
glistening with the exhaustion of love-making.

To elucidate: mighty is this season, harsh with the torment 3.15
of Cupid's arrows, since the passion-bee of Karni·putra,* who has partied away his youth enjoying Ms Gods'-Gift, flits over to Ms Gods'-Army, a mango-stalk swarming with passion-blossoms. She is delicate with the advent of adolescence that barely leaves behind childhood. But hold! Will Karni·putra really go that far? Even an exquisite rice-pudding mixed with honey and ghee becomes more delectable when blended with condiments. So methinks he hankers after a different flavor: intimacy with a young beauty, embodied in a *chandála* girl, delightful with merrymaking, jokes, and the straightforward hospitality of youth—a flavor which is the condiment to reveling in the wine of making love to Ms

abhiprārthayata iti. *(parikramya)* aho nu khalv ayaṃ laghu|rūpo 'pi balavān madana|vyādhiḥ, yen' âneka|śāstr'|âdhigata|niṣpanna|buddhiḥ sarva|kalā|jñāna|vicakṣaṇo vyutpanna|yuvati|kāma|tantra|sūtra|dhāraḥ Karṇīputro 'pi nām' âitām avasthām upanītaḥ. sa hi

unnidr"|âdhika|tānta|tāmra|nayanaḥ
pratyūṣa|candr'|ānanaḥ
dhyāna|glāna|tanur vijṛmbhaṇa|paraḥ
saṃtapta|sarv'|êndriyaḥ
ramyaiś candra|vasanta|mālya|racanā|
gāndharva|gandh'|âdibhir
yair eva pramukh'|āgataiḥ sa ramate,
tair eva saṃtapyate.

athavā Devasenām uddiśy' êti n' âitad āścaryam. kutaḥ? ślāghyaṃ Manmatha|manoratha|kṣetraṃ hi sā dārikā, arhaty asyā rūpa|yauvana|lāvaṇyaṃ Karṇīputrasy' ônmādaṃ janayitum. tasyā hi

vibhrānt'|ēkṣaṇam akṣat'|oṣṭha|rucakaṃ
prāpīna|gaṇḍaṃ mukhaṃ
pratyagr'|ôtpatita|stan'|âṅkuram uro
bāhū latā|komalau
avyakt'|ôtthita|roma|rekham udaraṃ
śroṇī kuto 'py āgatā
bhāvaś c' ânibhṛtaḥ sva|bhāva|madhuraḥ
kaṃ nāma n' ônmādayet?

Gods'-Gift. *(walks about)* How strange! This malady of Love indeed is flighty yet serious. Whereby even Karni·putra, who achieved intellectual brilliance by studying many sciences, is an expert in all the fine arts, and who is a professor of the *ars amatoria* with professionally trained girls, has been reduced to this state. For,

His eyes bleary, utterly strained with insomnia,
his face washed-out like a dawn-moon,
his body enfeebled with brooding,
ever yawning, all his senses aflame,
the very pleasures that normally delight him
—moon, spring, garlandry, music, perfumes etc.—
now scorch him.

Rather, as far as Ms Gods'-Army is concerned this is to be expected. How so? For this girl is Cupid's worthy lust-field, the grace of her figure and her youth are easily able to drive Karni·putra crazy. For,

Her face with darting eyes,
radiant with unkissed lips,
chubby-cheeked,
her chest budding with freshly risen breasts,
her arms, tender like vines,
her belly with an indistinctly rising hair-line,
her buttocks which have grown plump
all of a sudden,
her unrestrained temperament,
naturally sweet—
whom would these not drive crazy?

(parikramya) sa idāniṃ Devasenā|samutthaṃ madan'|āmayam ativyāyāma|kṛta|jvaram uddiśya hāra|tāla|vṛnta|candan'|ôpanīyamāna|dāha|pratīkāras tat|samāgam'|āśā|kṛta|prāṇa|dhāraṇaḥ śayana|parāyanaḥ kathaṃ cid vartate. adya tu prāg|ahar eva Puṣpāñjaliko nāma Devadattāyāḥ paricārikaḥ s'|ôpacāram upagamya Karṇīputram uktavān: «ārya|putra, vijñāpayaty ajjā Devadattā, ‹na khalu me hyastane 'hany anāgamanād bahu|māna|madhyasthatām avagantum arhaty ārya|putraḥ. iyaṃ hi me bhaginikā caṇḍālikā kim apy asvastha|rūpā, tad|anukampayā paryuṣit" âsmi. iyaṃ tu sāṃpratam āgacchāmi› iti.» tatas tad|ukta|datta|prativacanaḥ pratiprasthāpya Puṣpāñjalikaṃ Karṇīputraḥ s'|ôpagraham iva mām uktavān, «sakhe Śaśa, tvay" âpi nāma śrutam, ‹sāṃpratam ih' āgacchāmi› iti. tad eṣa idānīm avasaraḥ sukha|praśn'|âbhigamanena vivikta|visrambhāṃ Devasenām avagāhya saṃtāpa|kāraṇam asyāḥ parijñātum. tad eṣo 'ñjaliḥ. sarv'|ôpāyair arhati devānām|priyo 'smākaṃ Devasenā|samutthaṃ hṛdaya|gatam āpuṅkha|nikhātaṃ madana|śara|śalyaṃ samuddhartum» iti.

3.20 tataḥ sasmit'|ânuyātram ukto mayā, «bhavatu dhūrt'|âcārya, kim idaṃ tvayā divā dīpa|prajvālanaṃ kriyate? kiṃ n' âbhijño 'haṃ yuvayor anyonya|manoratha|mūka|dūtakānāṃ nayana|saṃgatakānām? api ca sa ev' âsmi Mū-

(walks about) He now languishes with difficulty on a bed, love sick on account of Ms Gods'-Army, enduring a fever brought on by excessive exertion, while he is supplied with remedies for inflammation—pearl necklaces, palm fans and sandal paste,—his vital breaths sustained by the hope of her arrival. But today in the morning an errand boy of Ms Gods'-Gift called Pushpánjalika approached politely, and said to Karni·putra: "Venerable sir, my mistress Ms Gods'-Gift informs you: 'Venerable sir, on no account must you believe that my esteem for you has lessened because I did not come yesterday. My sister, the *chandála* girl, was somewhat unwell, and I took pity on her and spent the night with her. But now I will come.'" Then, after entrusting a reply to Pushpánjalika and dismissing him, Karni·putra, seemingly improving, said to me: "My friend, Mr Rabbit, you heard it yourself, 'I will come today.' Now is the proper occasion, approaching with queries about her well-being, to fathom the reason for Ms Gods'-Army's affliction: she will confide it in private. I am folding my hands with respect: using every means possible, you, beloved of the Gods, must pull out the barb of Cupid's arrow that has darted from Ms Gods'-Army and buried itself in my heart up to the fletching."

Then I said to him smilingly: "Very well, master rogue, why 3.20
are you lighting a lamp during the day? Am I not well aware of the meetings of your glances, the silent messengers of your desire? Moreover, I am none other than Mr Rabbit, the buddy of Mula·deva.* I shall not return

ladeva|sakhaḥ Śaśo 'ham. n' âinām apratāry' āgamiṣyāmi» ity uktvā prasthito 'smi. tat kiṃ tu rāja|mārge suhṛt|praśna|saṃkathābhiḥ kālaṃ kṣapayatā tathā gantavyaṃ yathā Devadattā|virahitāṃ Caṇḍālikām āsādayeyam. *(parikramya)* aho nu khalu vasuṃdharā|vadhū|jambū|dvīpa|vadana|kapola|pattra|lekhāyā nānā|bhāṇḍa|samṛddhāyā Avanti|sundaryā Ujjayinyāḥ parā śrīḥ! iha hi

puṇyās tāvad Ved'|âbhyāsāḥ,
dvi|rada|ratha|turaga|ninadāḥ,
dhanur|guṇa|nisvanāḥ,
dṛśyaṃ, śrāvyaṃ, vidvad|vādāḥ,
catur|udadhi|samudaya|phalaiḥ
kṛtā vipaṇi|kriyāḥ,
gītaṃ, vādyaṃ, dyūtaṃ, hāsyaṃ
kva cid api ca viṭa|jana|kathāḥ,
kva cit sakalāḥ kalāḥ,
krīḍā|pakṣi|kṣubdhāś c' êmāḥ
pracuratara|valaya|raśanā|
svanā gṛha|paṅktayaḥ.

(parikramya) ap' îdānīm abhimata|kārya|niṣpatti|sūcakaṃ kiṃ cin nimittaṃ paśyeyam!

until I have seduced her." After I said this I set off. Now I must proceed in such a manner that I waste time by telling tales and asking questions from my friends on the main street so that I come upon the *chandála* girl without Ms Gods'-Gift. *(walks about)* Oh the supreme glory of the city of Ujjáyini, the belle of the land of Avánti, opulent with all kinds of accoutrements, the ornamental cosmetic painting on the cheek of the Jambu-continent face of the Earth! For here,

> Sanctifying Veda recitations,
> the sounds of elephants, chariots and horses,
> the hum of bow-strings,
> things worth seeing,
> things worth hearing,
> the debate of the learned,
> commerce involving the accumulated products of the four oceans,
> song, music, gambling, jests,
> here, what's more, the chatting of pimps,
> there all the arts,
> and these lines of houses,
> alive with pet birds,
> resounding with an abundance of bracelets and girdles.

(walks about) If only I perceived some sort of an omen indicating a successful completion of my desired undertaking!

(vilokya) aye× ayaṃ tāvat kāvya|vyasanī Kātyāyana|gotraḥ Śāradvatī|putraḥ Sārasvata|bhadraḥ sva|gṛha|dvāra|koṣṭhake śveta|varṇa|vyagr'|âgra|hastaś cintit'|ôpasthit'|āsvāditān kāvya|rasān× akṣi|bhrū|vikārair abhinayann iva cakra|pīḍaka|krīḍām anubhavati. tat kāmam asmin kāle pravṛtta|pratibhā|sroto|vighātinaṃ su|priyam api suhṛdam abhyasūyante kavayaḥ. kiṃ tu na śakyaṃ× sarasvatī|latā|prabhavānāṃ vāk|puṣpakāṇāṃ karṇa|pūram akṛtv" âtikramitum. vañcitam iv' ātmānaṃ manye. yāvad enam upasarpāmi.

(upetya) sakhe Kātyāyana, kim idam ākāśa|romanthanaṃ kriyate?

3.25 kiṃ bravīṣi? «sa eva mā kāvya|piśāco vāhayati» iti. mā tāvad bhoḥ! aṃgho× purāṇa|kāvya|pada|ccheda|grathana|carma|kāra, kim idaṃ naṣṭa|go|yūtha iva go|pālako *nava/padāny* anveṣase? atha sakhe, kiṃ vastu parigṛhya kṛtaḥ ślokaḥ?

kiṃ bravīṣi? «nanu khalv imam eva vartamāna|ramaṇīyaṃ vasanta|samayam āśritya kṛtaḥ ślokaḥ» iti. atha śakyaṃ śrotum?

kiṃ bravīṣi? «nanv eṣa bhitti|gato vācyatām» iti. kv' âsau? *(vilokya)* aye ayam

(looking) Oho, here, in fact, is the son of Sharádvati, the honorable Sarásvata from the lineage of Katyáyana, who is addicted to poetry. He is playing with a yo-yo* in the porch of his house, his fingers busy with a piece of chalk, as if miming with the grimaces of his eyes and brows the poetic flavors he relishes when they present themselves after reflection. No doubt, in such moments poets do not tolerate even a dear friend to block the gushing torrent of inspiration, but it is impossible to pass by without adorning my ears with the flowers of his words blossoming on the vine of eloquence. I would feel myself cheated. I'll approach him.

(approaching) My friend, Katyáyana, why are you chewing over the air?

What are you saying? "The demon of poetry himself im- 3.25
pels me." Not so fast, you cobbler who stitches together verse-patches from old poems, why are you now seeking *new verses*, as a cowherd who has lost his herd searches for *fresh footprints*? Well, my friend, what subject have you versified?

What are you saying? "But this is obvious: I have made a verse about this current, delightful spring season." May I hear it?

What are you saying? "Surely, read it out, it's here on the wall." *(looking)* Where is it? Ah, here we go,

puṣpa|spaṣṭ'|âṭṭahāsaḥ sa|mada|madhu|karaḥ
  kokil'|ālāpa|mūḍhaḥ
śrīmat|sved'|âvatāra|prasubhaga|pavanaḥ
  karkaś'|ôddāma|kāmaḥ
bālām apy apragalbhāṃ vara|tanum avaśāṃ
  kāmine saṃpradātuṃ
kālo 'yaṃ tat kariṣyaty anunaya|nipuṇaṃ
  yan na dūtī|sahasram.

sādhu bhoḥ! kalyāṇaṃ khalu tāvan nimittam. vayasya, sat|putra|lābha iva yaśas|karaḥ śloko 'yam astu. api ca Vāk|puro|bhāgānām abhāgī bhava. aye ken' âitadd hasitam? *(vilokya)* aye Dardarakaḥ pīṭha|mardo 'py atra! aṃgho Dardaraka, kim atra hāsya|sthānam?

3.30 kiṃ bravīṣi? «idaṃ khalu bhavatā samudr'|âbhyukṣaṇaṃ kriyate yad vāg|īśvaraṃ vāgbhir arcayasi» iti. mā tāvad aloka|jña, kiṃ vasanta|māso na puṣp'|ôpahāram arhati? api ca na tvayā śruta|pūrvam?

sūryaṃ yajanti dīpaiḥ
  samudram adbhir vasantam api puṣpaiḥ.
arciṣyāma bhavantaṃ
  vayam api vāg|īśvaraṃ vāgbhiḥ.

This time of year,
when the laughter of flowers bursts forth
and bees are drunken,
bewildering with the chattering of koels,
when breezes are graced
with the descent of blessed sweat
and desire is harsh and violent,
will accomplish what a thousand go-betweens,
skilled in reconciliation, would not:
handing over even a young,
shy girl of choice body
helplessly to her lover.

Bravo! This augurs well. My friend, may this verse bring you fame, as does the birth of a good son. And what's more, may you never have a share in the resentment of Goddess Speech. Hey, who is laughing at this? *(looking)* Oho, the toady Dardáraka is also here. Hey Dardáraka, what is so funny about this?

What are you saying? "Sir, you are clearly besprinkling 3.30
the ocean when you worship the Lord of Words with words." Don't say so, you ignoramus. Does not the spring season deserve an offering of flowers? And furthermore, haven't you heard before?

People offer lamps to the sun,
water to the sea, and flowers to spring.
We, for our part, shall worship
the Honorable Lord of Words
with words.

bhavatu. darśitas te pīṭha|marda|sva|bhāvaḥ: sevito 'tra|bhavān. atha vā vasanta|kālo×'yam acchalaḥ para|bhṛta|pralāpānām: īdṛśa ev' âstu bhavān. sādhayāmy aham.

(parikramya vilokya) aye ayam aparo *Vipul"|âmātyaḥ* Kāmadattaḥ× prākṛta|kāvya|pratiṣṭhāna|bhūto vaiśika|vṛtty" âdhomukhaḥ× prasthitaḥ. ā gṛhītam. eṣa Devadattā|saubhāgya | saṃkrānte Mūladeve Vipul" | âvamānād ātmānam avadhīritam avagacchati.× praṇaya|kruddhaḥ khalv eṣa dhāntraḥ. bhavatu. parihāsa|plaven' âinam avagāhiṣye. *(nirdiśya)* bhoḥ suhṛt, kumudāny anavabodhayan divā|candra|līlay" âtikrāmasi. pṛcchāmas tāvat kiṃ cit.

kalā|vijñāna|saṃpannā
  garv'|âika|vrata|śālinī
na khalv atyanta|dhīrā sā
  khinnā te *vipulā matiḥ?*

3.35 kiṃ bravīṣi? «gṛhīto vañcitakasy' ârthaḥ. kitav'|ācāryaḥ× Mūladevo na jñāyate?» iti. mā m" âivam. Devadattā|surata|saṃkrāntasy' âpi Vipulā|gatam eva hṛdayam.

Fine. You have revealed yourself a parasite: this gentleman has been rendered a service. Or rather, this spring time is free from the prattle of cuckoos: conform yourself to this, sir. I am off.

(He walks about and looks.) Oho, here is someone else, Mr Cupid's-Gift, *advisor in irregular meters : counselor of Ms Big*, the very foundation of Prakrit poetry. He has set out somewhere, with eyes downcast, as it is usual in the courtesans' quarter. I know! He thinks himself slighted because Ms Big has been treated with disrespect when Mula·deva was won over by the charms of Ms Gods'-Gift. This fellow is clearly jealous. All right, I shall drown him in a flood of jokes. *(He points.)* Hello, my friend, you are passing by, miming the grace of the daytime moon, without waking up the water-lilies. Let me ask you something.

That extremely solid, broad intellect of yours :
That extremely solid heart of your Ms Big,
endowed with the knowledge of the arts
and devoted to pride alone, is surely not anguished?

What are you saying? "I have grasped the meaning of your riddle. Don't you know Mula·deva, the master of swindlers?" Oh no, don't say so. Even though he has gone over to the love-sports of Ms God's Gift, his heart is with Ms Big alone. 3.35

kiṃ bravīṣi? «etad api mūladevīyaṃ śāṭhyam» iti. āma. bhavān khalu saty'|ārjavaḥ. kim idānīṃ sva|śiṣyāṃ Vipulāṃ n' ôpālabhate, yayā praṇaya|kop'|ânunay'|ârtham abhigataḥ Karṇīputraḥ?

prāpta iva śarat|kālaḥ
  prāvṛṭ|kaluṣāṃ nadīṃ prasādayitum,
kṣiptaḥ kadarthayitvā
  hemante tāla|vṛnta iva.

kiṃ bravīṣi? «kadā? katham?» iti. sakhe, śrūyatām. nanu katipay'|âham iv' âdya mad|dvitīyaḥ Karṇīputro Vipulām anunetum abhigataḥ. atha dvāra|koṣṭhaka|sthen' ânena krodh'|âgādha|parīkṣ"|ârtham aham āditaḥ s'|ôpagrahaṃ kalpitaḥ. so 'haṃ priya|vacan'|ôpanyāsen' âbhigataś c' âinām. s" âpi c' ērṣyā|doṣa|dūṣita|lāvaṇyā dṛṣṭv" âiva māṃ «kuto 'yam āyāsaḥ?» ity uktvā parāṅ|mukhī saṃvṛttā. tataḥ sa|parihāsam uktā mayā:

«kim uktā kena tvaṃ?
  prativaca idaṃ kasya vacasaḥ?
tad āvṛttā bhūtvā
  vada vadana|candreṇa vanite.
prasannāṃ tvāṃ dṛṣṭvā
  bhavati hi mama prītir atulā,
bhujaṃg" îva kruddhā
  bhru|kuṭir iyam udvejayati mām.»

What do you say? "This is also a lie typical of Mula·deva." So be it. No doubt, you are genuinely sincere, sir. Why don't you scold now your pupil, Ms Big, who was approached by Karni·putra in order to appease her love-born anger?

> He came as autumn comes
> to settle the river troubled by the monsoon rains
> —he was deemed useless and thrown out
> like a fan in winter.

What are you saying? "When? How?" Listen, my friend. Surely, recently Karni·putra, accompanied by myself, set off to conciliate Ms Big. Then he, taking up his position in the porch, pushed me forward imploringly, in order to examine the abyss of her anger. And then I approached her, speaking kind words. But she, her beauty spoiled by the blemish of jealousy, as soon as she saw me, said: "Why this exertion?," and turned away. Then I told her jokingly:

> "Who told you what? To whose words is this
> a retort?
> So turn back your moon-like face, madam,
> and speak.
> For I shall be incomparably delighted
> as soon as I see that you are amicable.
> This knitting of your brows terrifies me
> as would an angry snake."

3.40 iti. tad|anantaram Avantisundaryā sakhy" âbhihitā:

«kiṃ kṛtvā bhru|kuṭī|taraṅga|viṣamaṃ
roṣ'|ôparaktaṃ mukhaṃ
niśvāsa|jvarit'|âdharaṃ priya|sakhaṃ
prāptaṃ na saṃbhāṣase?
saubhāgyena hi śatru|karma kuruṣe,
strī|garva|medhāvini.×
mānaṃ mānini muñca. sarvam acirād
atyāyataṃ chidyate.»

iti. atha «guṇa|vatī pariṣad» iti kṛtvā Karṇīputro 'py abhigataḥ. sa c' ânayā praṇipāt'|âvanataḥ saroṣam avadhūy' âbhihitaḥ:

«kṛtvā vigraham āgato 'si niyataṃ,
nirvāsito vā tayā
kānt"|âlābha|vinodane kila vayaṃ
viśrāma|bhūmis tava.×
kiṃ nairāśya|nirutsukasya manasaḥ
saṃdhukṣaṇair me punaḥ?
pīten' âtra kim auṣadhena kaṭunā?
su|svāgataṃ. gamyatām.» iti.

kiṃ bravīṣi? «yadi evaṃ tām ev' âvinītāṃ tāvad eṣa upālabdhuṃ× gacchāmi» iti. chandataḥ. tayā gṛhīta|vākyo bhavān astu. sādhayāmas tāvat.

Right after that her friend, Avánti·súndari told her: 3.40

"Your face is distorted with the waves
of frowning and red with anger,
your lips are scorched by your sighs
—why don't you speak to your dear friend
who has come to you?
Expert with feminine guile,
you fight against your good fortune.
Give up your anger, you peevish woman.
Everything breaks quickly when stretched too much."

Then, Karni·putra showed up, saying, "What delightful company!" And she, shaking him off with anger as he bowed before her, said to him :

"Without doubt you come
because you have quarreled,
or maybe because she threw you out.
I am just here for you to while away your time
when you cannot get your beloved.
Why rekindle my heart
that is indifferent with hopelessness?
Why drink bitter medicine?
Welcome. Please go."

What are you saying? "If that is so then I will go to rebuke that ill-behaved woman." As you please. May she heed your counsel. Let's go.

3.45 *(parikramya)* hā dhik aparaṃ mūrtimad gamana|vighnam upasthitam. eṣa hi pāṇinīya|pūrvako Dandaśūka|putro Dattakalaśir nāma vaiyākaraṇaḥ pratimukham ev' ôpasthito 'smān. ap' îdānīm avighnen' âsya vāg|vāgurām uttareyam. saṃrabdham iv' âinaṃ paśyāmi. ā vāda|vighaṭṭiten' ânena bhavitavyam. tathā hy asya kalaha|kaṇḍurā vāg īṣad api spṛṣṭā deva|kula|ghaṇṭ" êv' ânusvanati. priya|gaṇikaś c' âiṣo dhāntraḥ. tāṃ kila Nūpurasenāyā duhitaraṃ Raśanāvatikāṃ nāma vyapadiśati. bhoḥ kaṣṭam. karabha|kaṇṭh'|âvasaktāṃ vallakīm iva śocāmi tāṃ tapasvinīṃ Raśanāvatikām. eṣa udyamy' âgra|hastam abhibhāṣata ev' âsmān.

kim āha bhavān? «api sukham aśayiṣṭhāḥ?» iti. kā gatiḥ? bhavatu, sabhājayiṣyāmy enam. svāgatam akṣara|koṣṭh'|āgārāya. vayasya Dattakalaśe, saṃrabdham iva tvāṃ paśyāmi. kaccit kuśalam?

kiṃ bhavān āha? «eṣo 'smi bali|bhugbhir iva *saṃghāta|balibhiḥ* Kātantrikair avaskanditaḥ.» iti. hanta pravṛttaṃ kāk'|ôlūkam. sakhe, diṣṭyā tvām *alūna|pakṣaṃ* paśyāmi.

kiṃ bravīṣi? «kā c' êdānīṃ mama vaiyākaraṇa|pāraśaveṣu kātantrikeṣv āsthā?» iti. yathā|tath" âstu bhavataḥ. sādhayāmy aham.

(walks about) Alas! Another embodied obstacle to our progress has arrived. For here is the son of Danda·shuka, the eminent grammarian Datta·kálashi, whose prefix is "Paninian," coming right towards me. I hope I can escape his net of words without complications. He seems distraught. Ah! He must have been crushed in a debate. Consequently his voice, itching for a fight, resonates like a temple bell, no matter how lightly touched. And this fellow is fond of courtesans. He has designs on Rashanávatika, the daughter of Ms Army-of-anklets. Oh dear, I pity poor Rashanávatika like a garland hung from a donkey's neck. He stretches forth his hand and accosts me. 3.45

What are you saying? "Art thou hale?" Good grief! Never mind, I will socialize with him. Welcome, O storehouse of words. My friend Datta·kálashi, you seem distraught. Are you well?

What are you saying? "I have been assaulted by the crow-like Katantrika grammarians,* who are strong in *battle : compounds.*" Alas, a strife of crows and owls! My friend, luckily I see you *with your wings unshorn : with your theses intact.*

What are you saying? "What now is my standing among the bastard Katántrika grammarians?" Just as is theirs for you.* I'm off.

kiṃ bravīṣi? «kva saṃcicariṣuḥ? tiṣṭha tāvat. kim asi dudrūṣuḥ?» iti. hā dhik prasīdatu bhavān. n' ârhaty asmān evaṃ|vidhaiḥ kaṣṭa|prahāra|niṣṭhurair vāg|aśanibhir abhihantum. sādhu vyāvahārikayā vāc" ācaratv asmān. abhājanaṃ hi vayam īdṛśānāṃ śarabh'|ôdgāra|durbhagānāṃ śrotra|viṣa|niṣeka|bhūtānāṃ vaiyākaraṇa|vāg|vyasanānām.

3.50 kiṃ bravīṣi? «katham aham idānīm aneka|vāvadūka|vādi|vṛṣabha|vighaṭṭan'|ôpārjitām aneka|dhātu|śata|ghnīṃ vācam utsṛjya strī|śarīram iva mādhurya|komalāṃ kariṣyāmi?» iti. hā dhik, upahataḥ syām. aho anāthaḥ khalv asi. kutaḥ?

svair'|ālāpe strī|vayasy'|ôpacāre
  kāry'|ārambhe loka|vād'|āśraye ca
kaḥ saṃśleṣaḥ kaṣṭa|śabd'|âkṣarāṇāṃ
  puṣp'|āpīḍe kaṇṭakānāṃ yath" âiva?

kim āha bhavān? «asthāne sā puṃścalī śabda|śībharam ābhāṣitā ruṣṭā.» iti. tat k" êyaṃ puṃścal" îti?

kiṃ bravīṣi? «priyā|nāma ken' ôcyate?» iti. *(vimṛśya)* ā viditam. Raśanāvatikā. etac c' ârhati. n' âtaś ca bhūyaḥ kaṣṭa|taraṃ yā sā pracura|cūta|pādap'|ântara|cāriṇ" îva kokilā sva|bhāva|kharaṃ bilva|pādapam āśritā. kaṣṭaṃ bhoḥ! mahad idaṃ parihāsa|vastu. āsvādayiṣyāmas tāvat.

What are you saying? "Whither art thou desirous of precipitating thyself? Rest awhile. Why art thou put to flight?" Ah! Have mercy! Please do not strike me with such word-thunderbolts, harsh with painful blows.* Speak to me in plain language. I am not *au fait* with the speech vice of you grammarians, a dose of poison for the ears, vile like the bellowing of a camel.

What are you saying? "How could I renounce now a style of 3.50
speech, a hundred-killer war-machine with its countless verbal bases, which I mastered as a result of clashing with the bulls among garrulous disputants? And how could I make my diction as sweet and soft as a woman's body?" Ouch! I think I've been hit!* Oh how helpless you are. Why?

In an uninhibited chat,
when attending to women and friends,
when a new task is begun,
when talking to ordinary people
what pertinence have hard words and syllables
or what pertinence have thorns in a flower chaplet?

What are you saying? "Inappropriately that wanton woman spoke a rain of words in anger." Now who is this "wanton woman?"

What are you saying? "Who would call her 'beloved'?" *(reflecting)* Aha! I know. Rasanávatika. And this is proper. Nothing is more distressing than this that she who is like a cuckoo who moves amidst bountiful mango trees should resort to an inherently harsh wood-apple tree.

vayasya Dattakalaśe, evaṃ sva|bhāva|dakṣiṇasya bhavataḥ kathaṃ kāminī virakt" êti paraṃ me kutūhalaṃ śrotum. tad ucyatāṃ tāvad vistarataḥ.

kim āha bhavān? «sādhu. sā puṃścalī pūrve|dyuḥ parva|kāle veśa|koṣṭhakam upetya riraṃsayā māṃ havir juhūṣantaṃ jighṛkṣat" îv' ôpāsīdat. tato 'ham enām avocam: ‹vṛṣali, havir juhūṣantaṃ mā mā sprākṣīḥ.› iti.» hanta idaṃ tad uṣṭra|gāndharvaṃ× nāma. sukumāraḥ khalu kāminī|saṃparigrahaḥ. kalaho 'yam upacāro nu? mā tāvad alokajña! na yuktaṃ nāma tvayā praṇay'|âbhigatāṃ kāminīṃ virāgayitum. strī|jano 'pi tvayā kaṣṭa|śabda|niṣṭhurābhir vyākaraṇa|visphuliṅgābhir vāgbhir uttrāsayitavyo bhavati. idam api na tvayā śruta|pūrvam?

3.55 raty|arthinīṃ rahasi yaḥ sukumāra|cittāṃ
kāntāṃ sva|bhāva|madhur'|âkṣara|lālanīyām
vāg|arciṣā spṛśati karṇa|viśoṣaṇena×
raktāṃ sa vādayati vallakim ulmukena.

What a pity! This is a great joke. Let me relish it. Friend Datta·kálashi, I am eager to hear more about how your mistress lost interest in you who are so spontaneously courteous. Tell me in detail.

What are you saying? "All right. Yesterday, on the ritual occasion as the moon passed through its node, the 'wanton woman' came to the wall of the courtesans' quarter,* and, itching for sex, approached me as if to embrace me as I was about to make a ritual offering of ghee. Then I said to her: "Thou cinderwench, mayest thou not touch me as I am about to make an offering!" Alas! This is precisely that camel music. A passionate woman must be tenderly received. Is this affection or a quarrel? This will not do you ignoramus! It is not appropriate for you to alienate a passionate woman who comes to you affectionately. Moreover you terrify women-folk with your speeches, sparking with grammar, intolerable with difficult words. Have you not heard this before?

He who in private touches 3.55
his impassioned beloved
who is intent on love,
whose feelings are most tender,
who needs to be engaged
with inherently sweet syllables,
with the flame of speech that desiccates the ear, he plays a lute with a firebrand.

sarvathā duṣkara|kāriṇī khalu Raśanāvatikā, yā bhaktam anena kalpayati. athavā tu tasyāḥ śāpaḥ. vayasya Dattakalaśe, śrutaṃ śrotr'|âvatarpaṇam. svasti bhavate. sādhayāmy aham.

(parikramya) idam aparaṃ manuṣya|kāntāram upasthitam. eṣa hi dharm'|āsanika|putraḥ Pavitrako nāma pracchanna|puṃścalīko 'caukṣaś caukṣa|vādiko rāja|mārge 'vidita|jana|saṃsparśaṃ pariharann iva saṃgṛhīt'|ārdra|nivasanaḥ saṃkucita|sarv'|âṅgo nāsikām aṅgulī|dvayena pidhāya catvara|Śiva|pīṭhikām āśritya sthitaḥ. hāsyaḥ khalv eṣa tapasvī. yathā tāvad ayaṃ Mattakāśinyā duhitaraṃ Vāruṇikāṃ nāma bandhakīm anurakta iti śrūyate. tad idānīṃ kim ayam āma|kumbhaṃ vahati? idam asy' âvinaya|pracāra|pustaka|bhāṇḍam udghāṭyate. aṃgho Pavitraka, kim idam uṣṇa|sthalī|kūrma|līlayā sthīyate?

kiṃ bravīṣi? «rāja|mārge sulabham avidita|jana|saṃsparśaṃ pariharāmi» iti. aho avijñāta|jana|saṃsparśo nāma parihriyate bhavatā? tad idānīṃ Vāruṇī|jaghana|pātraṃ Jāhnavī|tīrtham iva parama|pavitram nanu.

kiṃ bravīṣi? «n' âitad asti» iti. bhadraka, kim idaṃ gopāla|kule takra|vikrayaḥ kriyate? kitaveṣv api nāma kaitavam ārabhyate?

Rashanávatika has really set herself a formidable task in hobnobbing with this man.* Or rather he is her curse. My friend Datta·kálashi, you have heard the ear-medicine. Good day to you, I'm off.

(walks about) Here comes another human jungle. For this son of the Lord Justice, Mr Filter by name, a secret whores-man, an impure fellow who is an adherent of the Pure Vaishnavas' doctrine, gathering up his wet clothes and contracting all his limbs as if avoiding the touch of strangers on the High Street, he leans against the base of a Shiva-pedestal at the crossroads, covering his nostrils with two fingers. This wretch is so ridiculous, since, to begin with, he is said to be in love with a harlot called Ms Liquor, the daughter of Ms Boozy-Looking. So why is he now carrying a water-jar? Now the book of his wanton conduct will be opened. Hey, Mr Filter, why are you standing there like a turtle on the hot ground?

What are you saying? "I am avoiding the touch of strangers who are easily met on the High Street." Oho, so you say you are avoiding the touch of strangers? But then the vessel of Ms Liquor's buttocks is surely as extremely pure as a ghat of the Ganges.

What are you saying? "It's not like that." My good fellow, why are you selling now butter-milk in a household of cowherds? Does one start cheating among cheaters?

3.60 kiṃ bravīṣi? «sādhu, marṣayatu bhavān, nipuṇaḥ khalu te cāraḥ» iti. kasya cāraḥ kutaś cāraḥ? na sūryo dīpen' ândhakāraṃ praviśati. na hi mama cāra|kṛtyam asti, sahasra|cakṣuṣo hi vayam īdṛśeṣu prayojaneṣu. tad apanaya śaṭha|pracāra|kañcukam. ākṛti|mātra|bhadrako bhavān, mithy"|ācāra|vinīto hi asi. aṃgho saj|jana|sa|brahmacārin, viṭa|pāraśava! caukṣya|piśāco veśyā|prasaṅgaś c' êty ācāra|viruddham etad viruddh'|âśanam iva māṃ pratibhāti. api ca caukṣ'|ôpacāra|yantritas tām upagṛhṇan saṃdaṃśena nava|mālikām apacinoṣi.

kiṃ bravīṣi? «sarvathā nivṛtto 'smi vibhramāt» iti. vāyas'|ôpavāsam iva ka etac chraddhāsyati?

kiṃ bravīṣi? «yady evaṃ suprasanno 'si śiṣyatve niṣpādayatu māṃ bhavān» iti. diṣṭyā bhavān sat|patham ārūḍhaḥ. yadi ca viṭatve kṛto niścayaḥ śīghram eva veśa|yuvati|praṇaya|parigha|bhūtaṃ mithy"|ācāra|kañcukam udghāṭyatām. ghuṣyatāṃ viṭa|śabdaḥ!

kim āha bhavān? «praṇato 'smi» iti. hanta, idānīṃ dattaḥ pradeyakaḥ. svairam ayantritaś ca cara. ayam idānīm āśīr|vādaḥ.

What are you saying? "All right, please forgive me, Sir, your spy is apparently clever." Whose spy? A spy: what for? The sun does not enter darkness with a lamp. I have no need of spies at all, since I have a thousand eyes for such purposes. So take off the cuirass of dishonest behavior. You, sir, are a good man only from the outside, for you are well-trained in hypocrisy. O you fellow student of the virtuous, bastard of pimps! Demonical purity and addiction to harlots: this contradictory conduct appears to me as eating ill-matched food. And what's more, when you approach her so constricted by pure demeanor, you are seizing a jasmine flower with a pair of tongs. 3.60

What are you saying? "I have completely renounced flirtation." It is like the fasting of crows: who will believe it?

What are you saying? "If you are so sympathetic, sir, please admit me as your pupil." Congratulations, sir, you have entered the right path. And if you have decided to become a pimp, you must immediately peel off the cuirass of hypocrisy that seals you from the love of courtesans. Proclaim aloud your name: a pimp!

What are you saying? "I bow to you." Well, now you have given me a small present. Walk freely, without constraints. Here is my benediction:

ākṣipta|srasta|vastrāṃ praśithila|raśanāṃ
mukta|nīvīṃ vihastāṃ
hasta|vyatyāsa|gupta|stana|vivara|valī|
madhya|nābhi|pradeśām
lajjā|līn'|ôpaviṣṭāṃ na hi na hi visṛj' êty
evam ākrandamānāṃ
śayyām āropya kāntāṃ surata|samudayasy'
âgra|sasyaṃ gṛhāṇa.

3.65 kiṃ bravīṣi? «upaskāritaṃ śreyaḥ, cikitsito 'smi.» yady evam ācārya|dakṣiṇ" êdānīm eṣṭavyā.

kiṃ bravīṣi? «nanv ayam añjaliḥ» iti. bho nanv ayam ativyayaḥ. bhavatu, idānīṃ niṣpanna|śiṣyāḥ smo vayam. bhavān idānīm ācāryaḥ saṃvṛtto na śiṣyaḥ. gaccha svairam ayantritaś ca. sādhayāmy aham.

(parikramya) hī hī sādhu bhoḥ! nānā|kusuma|samavāya|saṃvardhitena vasanta|madhy'|âhna|sved'|âvatāra|sparśa|subhagena pratyudgamya pratihārita iv' âhaṃ māly'|āpaṇa|prāsāda|saṃbādha|viniḥsṛtena vipaṇi|vāyunā nūnam upasthito 'smi. *(puṣpa|vīthīṃ vilokya)* mūrtimat" îva nānā|kusuma|samavāy'|âṅga|pratyaṅgā vasanta|vadhūḥ. iyaṃ hi

May you gather the first harvest of love's growth
when you lay your powerless beloved on the bed,
her clothes ripped off
and strewn about, her girdle about to drop,
the knot of her petticoat undone,
her hands hiding by turns the hollow of her breasts,
her belly-folds, her waist, and her navel,
sitting down melted by shame,
and crying 'No, don't, let me go.'

What are you saying? "My ultimate bliss is secured, I am 3.65
cured." If so, now you should arrange the tuition fee.

What are you saying? "But look, I am folding my hands with respect." Ha, this generosity is surely prodigal. Fine, now I have an accomplished pupil. Now you have become a master, sir, not a mere pupil. Walk freely, without constraints. I am going.

(walks about) Wow! Great! Now the wind in the market—nourished by the heaps of various flowers, blessed with the touch of sweat that appears at this spring midday, blowing from among the garland-shops and mansions standing shoulder to shoulder—has approached me indeed, coming forth and blocking my way, so to say. *(looking at the flower-market)* Mrs Spring appears as if embodied: the collection of various flowers form her bigger and smaller limbs. For she—

padm'|ôtphulla|śrīmad|vaktrā
sita|kusuma|mukula|daśanā
nav'|ôtpala|locanā
rakt'|âśoka|praspand'|oṣṭhī
bhramara|ruta|madhura|kathitā
vara|stabaka|stanī
puṣp'|āpīḍ'|âlaṃkār'|āḍhyā
grathita|śubha|kusuma|vasanā
srag|ujjvala|mekhalā
puṣpa|nyastaṃ nārī|rūpaṃ
vahati khalu kusuma|vipaṇir
vasanta|kuṭumbinī.

bhoḥ sarvathā nānā|kusuma|samavāya|gandha|hṛta|hṛdayo duṣkaraṃ khalu karomy enām atikrāman. *(parikramya)* aye idam aparaṃ parihāsa|pattanam upasthitam. eṣa hi Mṛdaṅgavāsulako nāma purāṇa|nāṭaka|viṭo Bhāva|Jarad|gava iti gaṇikā|jan'|ôpapādita|dvitīya|nāmadheyaḥ su|kumāra|gāyakasy' ārya|Nāgadattasy' ôdavasitān nirgacchati. suṣṭhu tāvad anena nīlī|karma|snān'|ânulepana|parispandena jarā|kaupīna|pracchādanam anuṣṭhitam. sarva|sakhaś c' âiṣo dhāntraḥ. na śakyam imam anabhibhāṣy' âtikramitum. parihasiṣyāmy enam. *(nirdiśya)* Bhāva|Jarad|gava, *api subhikṣam anayā jarasā?*

Her beautiful face is a full-blown lotus,
her teeth: buds of white blossoms,
her eyes are fresh lilies,
her trembling lips: red *ashókas*,
her sweet voice is the hum of bees,
her breasts: two exquisite bouquets,
she is adorned with a chaplet
  and ornaments of flowers,
her dress is made of bright blossoms
  strung together,
her shining girdle: a garland
—this flower-market, the wife of spring,
has the form of a woman entrusted to flowers.

Ah, I find it hard indeed to pass her by when my heart is completely enraptured by the fragrance of the multitude of flowers. *(walks about)* Oho, here comes another market-town of ridicule. For here is a pimp of obsolete dramas called Mridánga·vásulaka, who was renamed by the courtesans as the Venerable Old Bull. He is coming out of the house of the handsome young singer, Sir Dragons'-Gift. Bravo! He has managed to hide the pudenda of old age by the trappings of hair-dye, bathing, and unguents. And this fellow is everybody's pal. One cannot pass by without speaking to him. I shall make fun of him. *(pointing)* Venerable Old Bull, *do you have abundant provisions in view of your digestion: could you beg enough in view of your decrepitude?*

3.70 kim āha bhavān? «eṣo *bhavato nirvedāj jarad|bhujaṃga* iva jarā|tvacam utsṛjāmi» iti. prāṇaiḥ sah' êti paśyāmaḥ. punar yuv" âiva bhāvaḥ saṃvṛttaḥ. siddhaṃ hi te māyayā yauvana|karma. tava hi

rāg'|ôtpādita|yauvana|pratinidhi|
channa|vyalīkaṃ śiraḥ,
saṃdaṃś'|âpacit'|ôttar'|oṣṭha|palitaṃ
nirmuṇḍa|gaṇḍaṃ mukham,
yatnen' āracitā mṛjā, guṇabalen'
ânena c' âṅgasya te
lepen' êva purāṇa|jarjara|gṛhasy'
āyojitaṃ yauvanam.

kiṃ bravīṣi? «madanīyaṃ khalu purāṇa|madhu» iti. manoratha eṣa bhāvasya. sarvathā triphalā|gokṣura|loha|cūrṇa|samṛddhir astu bhavataḥ. sādhayāmy aham.

(parikramya) aye ayam idānīṃ sahas" ôpasthite mayi dyūta|sabh"|âlinda|nataḥ śilā|staṃbhen' ātmānam āvṛtya sthitaḥ. *(vilokya)* bhavatu. vijñātam. Śaiṣilako 'yam. kiṃ nu khalv asy' âsmad|darśana|parihāreṇa prayojanam? ā tasya Mālatikā|dūtī|svayaṃ|grah'|âvinaya ātma|śaṅkām utpādayati. bhavatu. parihāsa|plaven' âinam avagāhiṣye.

What do you say, Sir? "*Due to your loathing* ⁝ *Since you fail to interest me*, Sir, now I am sloughing off the skin of senescence as an *old snake* ⁝ *old gallant*." Along with your vital breaths, as I see. Your Honor has indeed become young again. You have been truly successful in rejuvenescence through magic. For 3.70

The ugliness of your head has been concealed
by a substitute for youth made by hair-dye,
grey hair has been weeded out
 with a pair of pincers from your upper lip,
your cheeks are close-shaven,
with great effort you have achieved
 a clear complexion,
and with these merits of your body
you have made it young,
as one rejuvenates an old, crumbling house
 by plastering.

What are you saying? "Old wine, as we know, is inebriating." That is your honor's wishful thinking. May you have abundant medicines of *tri·phala, go·kshura*, and iron filings.* I'm moving on.

(walks about) Oho, this guy here has ducked on the terrace of the casino when I showed up unexpectedly, and now he is concealing himself behind a stone pillar. *(looking)* All right, I know. This is Shaishílaka. What can be his motivation for avoiding my sight? I see! The brutality of assaulting Malátika's confidante has filled him with alarm. All right, I shall inundate him with the flood of mockery. *(pointing)* Hello, brahmin's baby-boy, why do

(nirdiśya) bho dvija|kumāraka, kim idam ātma|pracchādanena suhṛt|samāgamaś chattreṇa candr'|ātapa iva pratiṣidhyate? eṣo niḥsṛtya prahasitaḥ.

kiṃ bravīṣi? «svāgataṃ suhṛt|karṇa|dhārāya» iti. bhadra, kuto me suhṛt|karṇa|dhāratā yo 'haṃ tasmād dvandva|rati|praṇaya|sāhasād bahiṣkṛtaḥ? kiṃ bravīṣi? «n' âitad asti» iti. ayi surat'|ôñcha|vṛtte, mā m" âivam! prakāśaṃ khalv etad yathā Śaiṣilakasya gṛhe śākya|bhikṣukī prativasat' îti. sā kila tvayi utpanna|kāmayā Mālākāra|dārikayā Mālatikayā tvat|sakāśaṃ dautyen' ânupreṣitā. tasyāś ca tvayā nirupaskṛta|bhadrakaṃ rūpa|yauvana|lāvaṇyam āmiṣa|bhūtam uddiśya tadātvam ev' âpekṣitaṃ, n' āyatikam.

3.75 kiṃ bravīṣi? «sakhe, yat|satyam anāgata|sukh'|āśayā pratyupasthita|sukha|tyāgo na puruṣ'|ârthaḥ. na dīpen' âgni|mārgaṇaṃ kriyate» iti. bhoḥ suṣṭhu kṛtam. vañcitaṃ khalu rahasyaṃ yad' îdaṃ na vistarato brūyāḥ. vistarata idāniṃ śrotavyam.

kim āha bhavān? «ka idānīm avinaya|prapañcam ātmanaḥ prakāśayati? kiṃ tu samāsataḥ śrūyatām. tayā hi pragalbham ākrāntay" âbhihito 'ham:

you avoid meeting with a friend by hiding yourself, as one might repel moonshine with a parasol? He steps forward and laughs.

What are you saying? "Welcome, pilot of pals." Good fellow, how could I be a pilot of pals when I've been excluded from the violent affection of a couple's love-making? What are you saying? "There's nothing like that!" Hey you sex-gleaner, do not say so! It's public knowledge that a Buddhist nun lives in Shaishílaka's house. She, as I've heard, was sent on a mission to you by Malátika, Malákara's daughter, who had fallen in love with you. And you, aiming at the no-frills but pleasing charms of the nun's figure and youth as if at a prey, cared only for the present, not the future.

What are you saying? "My friend, it is a recognized fact 3.75
that giving up present happiness in the hope of future pleasure is not among the goals of human life. One does not search for fire with a lamp." Ah, very well done. You could clearly keep the secret if you did not give me a detailed account. Give me now the particulars.

What are you saying, sir? "Who would disclose now the details of his own brutishness? But listen, I give you a resume. When I assaulted her she said to me bravely:

‹saṃpāten' âtibhūmiṃ pratarasi śaṭha he,
 mānyāḥ khalu vayam.
dautyen' âbhyāgatāyāś capala na sadṛśaṃ
 yat te vyavasitam.
kṛcchr'|ārūḍh" âsmi jātā para|gṛha|vasatiṃ
 saṃprāpya vijane.
mā m" âivaṃ hā prasīda priya visṛja purā
 kaś cit praviśati!› iti.»

sādhu bho amṛdaṅgo nāṭak'|âṅkaḥ saṃvṛttaḥ. anena surata|saṃdhi|chedena sthirī|kṛto Vasiṣṭha|putreṇa viṭa|śabdaḥ. vayasya, subhago bhava. sādhayāmy aham.

(parikramya) hanta bho ete smaḥ surata|sarv'|âtithi|saṃniveśaṃ veśam anuprāptāḥ. yo 'yam

3.80 kām'|āveśaḥ kaitavasy' ôpadeśo
 māyā|kośo vañcanā|saṃniveśo
nirdravyāṇām aprasiddha|praveśo
 ramya|kleśaḥ supraveśo 'stu veśaḥ.

'With your rush you overstep the bounds.
Hey, you rogue, I am a respectable woman!
Foolhardy man, what you have undertaken
against me who had come to you
on a mission is not proper.
I ran into trouble
when I came to the home of another man,
with no witnesses around.
No, don't, compose yourself, my dear,
let me go before somebody comes in!'"

Bravo! An act in a play has taken place, without drums. The son of Vasíshtha consolidated the word 'pimp' with this sexual break-in. My friend, may women love you. I'm moving on.

(walks about) By George! I have arrived at the Courtesans' Quarter, the gathering place of all the guests of lovemaking. Which is

Absorption in Love, 3.80
instruction in imposture,
the treasury of illusion,
the headquarters of cheating,
not to be entered by the penniless,
where pains are sweet
—may this quarter of the courtesans be easy of access!

(parikramya) ka eṣa malina|prāvār'|âvaguṇṭhita|śarīraḥ saṃkucita|sarv'|âṅgo veśy"|âṅganād drutataram abhiniṣkrāmati? aye ayaṃ saṃbhramād bhraṣṭaṃ kāṣāy'|ântam upalakṣaye. ā sa eṣa Dharm'|âraṇya|nivāsī Saṃghilako nāma duṣṭa|śākya|bhikṣuḥ. aho *s'|âriṣṭatā* Buddha|śāsanasya, yad evaṃ|vidhair api vṛthā|muṇḍair asad|bhikṣubhir upahanyamānaṃ pratyaham abhipūjyata eva. athavā na vāyas'|ôcchiṣṭaṃ tīrtha|jalam upahatam bhavati. eṣa tiraskṛty' ātmānaṃ dṛṣṭv" âiv' âsmān abhiprasthitaḥ. bhavatu. mama vāk|śara|gocarād akṣato na yāsyati. abhibhāṣiṣye tāvat. *(nirdiśya)* aṃgho *vihāra*|vetāla, kv' êdānīm ulūka iva divā|śaṅkitaś carasi?

kiṃ bravīṣi? «sāṃprataṃ *vihārād* āgacchāmi» iti. bhūt'|ârthaṃ jāne *vihāra|śīlatāṃ* bhadantasya. dhāntra, kv' êdānīṃ veśa|vīthī|dīrghikā|gato baka iva śaṅkitaś carasi? nanu surata|piṇḍa|pātam anuṣṭhīyate.

kiṃ bravīṣi? «mātṛ|vyāpatti|duḥkhitāṃ Saṃghadāsikāṃ Buddha|vacanaiḥ paryavasthāpayitum āgato 'smi» iti. hanta vinaṣṭaṃ tvan|mukhād Buddha|vacanaṃ mada|bhramād iv' ôpasparśaṃ paśyāmaḥ. bhoḥ kaṣṭam!

(walks about) Who is this fellow stepping out hastily from the courtyard of a courtesan, his body wrapped in a dirty shawl, his limbs all drawn in? Oho! I can see the edge of his red robe slipped down in his hurry. Aha! He is that corrupt Buddhist monk called Sánghilaka,* who lives in the Forest of Dharma.* Lo and behold, the Buddha's teaching is indeed *proof against damage ⁝ shows the signs of approaching death*, since it is still being reverenced day after day, in spite of being defiled by such vainly shaved bogus monks. Or rather, the water of a sacred place does not become polluted because crows drink from it. This fellow has covered himself and set off as soon as he noticed me. All right, he will not leave the range of my word-arrows unhurt. Let's speak to him first. *(pointing)* Hey you, zombie of *the monastery ⁝ enjoyments*, where are you going now, afraid of daylight as an owl?

What are you saying? "I have just come from *the monastery ⁝ a bacchanalia*." I know that your reverend's *monastic discipline ⁝ fondness of revelry* is a solid fact. You fool, why are you walking in the street of the courtesans so distrustfully as a crane in a pond? Surely the alms of sex are being distributed.

What are you saying? "I have come to raise the spirits of Ms Maid-of-the-Sangha, who is dejected because of her mother's death, with the Buddha's teaching." Ah, in my eyes the Buddha's teaching from your mouth is as defiled as the ritual rinsing of the mouth when made with liquor by mistake. Fie, for shame!

veśy"|âṅgaṇaṃ praviṣṭo
mohād bhikṣur yadṛcchayā v" âpi
na bhrājate prayukto
Dattaka|sūtreṣv iv' oṃkāraḥ.

3.85 kiṃ bravīṣi? «marṣayatu bhavān. nanu sarva|sattveṣu prasanna|cittena bhavitavyam» iti. sthāne *nitya/prasanno* bhadantas *tṛṣṇā/chedena parinirvāṇaṃ prāpsyasi.* eṣo 'ñjali|pragrahaṃ karoti.

kiṃ bravīṣi? «sādhu, mucyeyam» iti. bhavatu. alaṃ vṛthā|śrameṇa. sarvathā durlabhaḥ khalu te mokṣaḥ.

kiṃ bravīṣi? «gacchāmy aham. akāla|bhojanam api parihāryam» iti. hī hī sarvaṃ kṛtam. etad avaśiṣṭam, askhalita|pañca|śikṣā|padasya bhikṣoḥ kāla|bhojanam atikrāmati. dhvaṃsasva vṛthā|muṇḍa, na śvitrī dadruṇ"[×] âpatrapate. gaccha, *Buddho* hy asi. hanta dhvasta eṣa dur|ātmā. tat kva nu khalv idāniṃ duṣṭa|śākya|bhikṣu|darśan'|ôpahataṃ cakṣuḥ prakṣālayeyam?

A monk who enters
the courtyard of a courtesan by error or,
even worse, willfully,
looses his luster
just as does the OṂ when used to introduce
Dáttaka's manual on erotics.*

What are you saying? "Show mercy, sir. Surely one should be kindly disposed towards all beings." Truly, your reverend, *you are constantly kind, and so you will achieve final Nirvana through cutting your desires : you always drink booze and so, thanks to the quenching of your thirst, you will completely zonk out.* Now he offers his cupped hands. 3.85

What are you saying? "OK, may I be released now?" All right, enough of this futile exertion. In any case, release is hard to get for you.

What are you saying? "I am going now. One should also avoid eating at the wrong time." Ha ha, that does it. That's all that is wanting: the scheduled mealtime of this monk, who has never transgressed the Buddha's five moral precepts, is about to run out. Scram, you useless shaveling, a leper is not ashamed of herpes. Go, you are indeed *a Buddha : clever.* At last, this profligate has buzzed off. So now where shall I rinse my eyes, defiled by the sight of a debauched Buddhist monk?

(parikramya) sādhu bhoḥ! idaṃ viṭa|jana|nayana|pāvanam upasthitam. eṣā hi Vasantavatyā duhitā Vanarājikā nāma vana|rājik" êva rūpavatī kusuma|samājam iva śarīre saṃniveśya yath"|ôcitaṃ pūjā|puraskāram upanīya Kāma|dev'|āyatanād avatarati. yadā sarv'|ādara|gṛhīta|puṣpa|maṇḍan'|āṭopā śaṅke priya|jana|sakāśaṃ prasthitay" ânayā bhavitavyam. yāvad enāṃ priya|vacan'|ôpanyāsen' ôpasarpāmi. *(nirdiśya)* vāsu Vanarājike, kim idaṃ vasanta|kusum'|āgrayaṇaṃ kurvantyā bhavatyā na khalv atithi|lopaḥ kṛtaḥ?

kim āha bhavatī? «svāgatam āryāya. ayam añjaliḥ» iti. pratigṛhīta eṣa dākṣiṇya|pallavaḥ. api c' âcirād āgatas tāvad vasantas tava śarīre saṃniviṣṭo nanu.

3.90 kim āha bhavatī? «katham iva?» iti. śrūyatāṃ tāvat.

vāsantī|kunda|miśraiḥ kuravaka|kusumaiḥ
    pūritaḥ keśa|hastaḥ,
lagn'|âśokaḥ śikh"|ântaḥ, stana|taṭa|racitaḥ
    sinduvār'|ôpahāraḥ,
pratyagraiś cūta|puṣpaiḥ pracala|kisalayaiḥ
    kalpitaḥ karṇa|pūraḥ:
puṣpa|vyagr'|âgrahaste vahasi su|vadane
    mūrtimantaṃ vasantam.

(walks about) Excellent! I've chanced upon an eye cleaner for pimps. For here comes Ms Vernal's daughter, Ms Forest-Alley by name, comely as a forest alley, combining a configuration of flowers, so to say, into her body, descending from the Kama-temple after properly accomplishing the arrangements of the worship. Since she proudly exhibits the flower-ornaments put on with all her care, I presume she must have set off to visit her lover. Well then, I'll approach her saying some affable words. *(pointing)* My dear Ms Forest-Alley, by making this offering of the first flowers of spring have you not lost a guest?

What are you saying, miss? "Welcome sir. I am folding my hands with respect." I appreciate this bud of courtesy. Surely spring, not long since it has arrived has entered into your body.

What are you saying, miss? "How so?" Listen then. 3.90

Your hair is filled with *kúravaka* flowers
    mixed with spring jasmine,
your topknot is crowned with *áshoka* blossoms,
sinduvára adorns the slopes of your breasts,
you have made earrings from fresh mango-blossoms
    with dangling fronds,
your fingers are preoccupied with flowers:
fair-faced one, you bear the embodiment of spring.

kiṃ bravīṣi? «eṣa te pradeyakaḥ» iti. bhavatu. tvayy eva tāvat tiṣṭhatu nyāsaḥ. kālen' ôpapādayiṣyāmaḥ. sukhaṃ bhavatyai. prasthito 'smi. *(parikramya)* aye idam Irima|kāminyās Tāmbūlasenāyā gṛham. nitya|saṃnihitaś c' âiṣa dhāntraḥ. kiṃ nu praviśāmi? *(vicārya)* na śakyam anabhibhāṣy' âtikramitum. yāvat praviśāmi.

(praviśya) asti ko 'pi bhoḥ suhṛd|gṛhe Śaśaṃ pratipālayati?

aye iyaṃ Tāmbūlasen" âsmad|bahumānād avilambita|tvarita|pada|vinyāsā saṃbhramād bhraṣṭam uttarīyam ākarṣantī pradvāra eva pratyudgatā. atyupacāraḥ khalv eṣaḥ. śaṅke na māṃ praviśantam icchat' îti, tad eṣā bahir eva prayojayituṃ nirgatā. yath" âsyāḥ pratyagra|surata|cihnāny upalakṣaye sadyaḥ|surata|bhukta|muktay" ânayā bhavitavyam. nūnaṃ divā|surata|saṃmardam anubhūtavān Irimaḥ. aho surata|lolupaḥ khalu dhāntraḥ. bhavatu. parihasiṣyāmy enām. Tāmbūlasene, kim idaṃ dākṣiṇy'|âtivyayaḥ kriyate? kathaṃ? surata|pariśrama|śvāsa|vicchinn'|âkṣaraṃ «svāgataṃ priya|vayasyāya» ity āha. aviraktike, tāla|vṛntaṃ tāvad ānaya. kṛta|vyāyāmā khalu Tāmbūlasenā. cori, api balaṃ vardhate?

What are you saying? "Here is a little gift for you." Very well. Let it remain in your custody. I will reclaim it in due time. I wish you happiness! I'm off. *(walks about)* Oho! This is the house of Ms Betel-Army, Mr Hermes' beloved. And this fellow always hangs around. Shall I enter? *(musing)* One cannot pass by without speaking to her. Well, I'll enter then.

(entering) Hey, is there anyone in the house of my friend to take care of Mr Rabbit?

Oho! Ms Betel-Army has come to meet me already before the entrance, out of respect for me, with not leisurely but rapid steps, dragging behind her overgarment that has slipped down in her hurry. This is indeed an extreme case of courtesy. I suspect she does not want me to enter, that's why she came out, to settle things outside. As I see the signs of fresh lovemaking on her, she must just have been allowed to get up from her sexual delicacies. Mr Hermes is clearly enjoying a sexual gymnastics by daytime. Ah, that fellow is indeed a sex maniac. All right, I shall make fun of her. Ms Betel-Army, why are you lavishing your courtesy? What? She says with words faltering by her panting due to sexual sport: "Welcome, my dear friend." Impassioned girl, bring a fan first. Ms Betel-Army was clearly doing exercises. My thief, are you regaining your strength?

3.95 kiṃ bravīṣi? «na khalv avagacchāmi» iti. etat priya|jana|pariṣvaṅga|saṃkrānta|kālīyakaṃ stana|taṭa|dvayam. pṛcchāmi tāvat. asaṃtuṣṭe, anavarata|niśā|vihārasy' Êrimasya div" âpi nāma tvayā na deyo viśramaḥ? nanu sāyam|prāto homo vartate.

kiṃ bravīṣi? «sad" âpi nāma para|pakṣa|parihāsa|priyo bhāvaḥ» iti. n' âitad asti. api dur|vidagdhe, na tvayā śruta|pūrvam ākāra|saṃvaraṇam apy ākāra ev' êti?

kiṃ bravīṣi? «kathaṃ jānīṣe?» iti. cori, katham idaṃ na jñāsyāmi? yathā,

vikhaṇḍita|viśeṣakaṃ mṛdita|
rocanā|bindukaṃ
kapola|tala|lagna|keśam apa-
viddha|karṇ'|ôtpalam
mukhaṃ vraṇita|pāṭal'|oṣṭam ala-
sāyamān'|ēkṣaṇaṃ
prakāśayati te divā|surata|
lolupaṃ kāminam.

kiṃ bravīṣi? «sadyaḥ|supt'|ôtthit" âham. kim apy āśaṅkase? iti.» bhavatu. saṃjñaptāḥ smaḥ. na hi te sūkṣmam api kiṃ cid agrāhyaṃ paśyāmi. kiṃ tu

What are you saying? "I don't quite follow you." Sandal powder* has been smeared off from this pair of breasts of yours when you were embracing your lover. Let me ask you something. Insatiable woman, Mr Hermes was sporting all night, without rest: can't you leave him in peace at least by daytime? Surely sacrifice is performed in the morning and in the evening. 3.95

What are you saying? "You've always been fond of joking at the expense of others." That's not true. Haven't you heard before, sly woman, that concealing one's features is nevertheless also a feature?

What are you saying? "How do you know?" My thief, how come could I not know it? Look,

Your face-painting is blurred,
the yellow paint of your *bindu* is smudged,
tresses stick to your cheeks,
the lilies, your ear-ornaments,
  have been removed,
your pale-red lips are wounded,
your eyes are languid:
your face reveals that your lover
  is covetous of daytime sex.

What are you saying? "I've just woken up. Do you suspect something else?" Fine, I am convinced. For I don't see anything about you, however subtle it might be, that could not be fathomed. Nevertheless,

3.100 svapn'|ânte nakha|danta|vikṣatam idaṃ
śaṅke śarīraṃ tava.
prīyantāṃ pitaraḥ, svadh" âstu subhage,
vāso 'pasavyaṃ hi te.
kiṃ c' ânyat tvarayā na lakṣitam idaṃ:
dhik tasya duḥ|śilpinaḥ
mohād yena tav' ôbhayoś caraṇayoḥ
savye kṛte pāduke.

cori, sah'|ōḍh" âbhigṛhītā kv' êdānīṃ yāsyasi? eṣā hi praviśy' ântar|gṛham uccaiḥ prahasitā saha ramaṇena. *(karṇam dattvā)* eṣa Irimo vyāharati: «nanu bho dhūrt'|ācārya, praviśyatām» iti. sakhe, kaḥ surata|ratha|dhuryayor yoktra|cchedaṃ kariṣyati? evam ev' âvirata|surat'|ôtsavo 'stu. Gārgī|putra, sādhayāmy aham.

(parikramya) aye k" êyam idānīṃ bāhya|dvāra|koṣṭhake devatābhyo balim upaharati?

nibhṛta|vadanā śoka|glānā
nirañjana|locanā
malina|vasanā sneha|tyakta|
pralamba|ghan'|âlakā
śithila|valayā puṣp'|ôtkṣepaiś
cyut'|âṅguli|veṣṭanā
taruṇa|yuvatis tanvī bhūyas
tanutvam upāgatā.

I guess your body was wounded 3.100
by nails and teeth at the end of your sleep.
May the ancestors be satisfied, blessed woman,
let there be offering for them,
for your garment covers your right shoulder.
And another thing
that you haven't noticed in your hurry:
fie on that botcher who was so deranged
as to make two left-foot sandals for you.

My thief, where are you going now once you've been caught with hot goods? Well, she's gone inside and burst out laughing with her lover. *(listening)* This is Mr Hermes speaking, "Why hello, master of rogues, come on in!" My friend, who would cut the rope that ties two horses to the carriage of love-making? May the uninterrupted festival of sex go on in the same way. Son of Gargi, I am moving on.

(walks about) Oho, who is this girl offering food to the deities at the porch of the outer door?

She is languid with sadness,
with motionless face and eyes without mascara,
her clothes are dirty,
her long, thick tresses lack hair-oil,
her bracelets are loose
and her ring has slipped off
because of the strewing of flowers:
this delicate, gracile maiden
has become even more slender.

ā s" âiṣā Bhāṇḍīra|senāyā duhitā Kumudvatī nāma. bhoḥ kaṣṭam. apratyabhijñeyā khalv iyaṃ tapasvinī saṃvṛttā. tat kasy' êyaṃ veśa|vāsa|viruddhaṃ viraha|yogya|vrataṃ carati? ā vijñātam. tam eṣā Maurya|kumāraṃ Candrodayam anurakt" êti śrūyate. sa ca subhagaḥ sāmanta|praśaman'|ârthaṃ daṇḍen' ôdyataḥ. hanta bho upapadyate Candrodaya|virahāt Kumudvatī niḥśrīkā saṃvṛtt" êti. bhoḥ pratyādeśaḥ khalv ayam kula|vadhūnām. api c' âiṣā sva|bhavana|valabhī|puṭa|sthaṃ vikṣipta|bali|praṇay'|ôpasthitaṃ svāgata|vyāhāreṇ' âbhinandati vāyasam:

3.105 «bhadraṃ te valabhī|gavākṣa|tilaka
śrāddh"|ôpahār'|âtithe!
jīvantyāṃ mayi kaccid eṣyati sa me
nitya|prayāsī priyaḥ?
yady āgacchati gaccha tāvad itara|
dvār'|āśritaṃ toraṇaṃ,
niḥśokā hi sametya me priyatamaṃ
dāsyāmi dadhy|odanam.»

iti. aho nu khalu niṣkaitavo 'nurāgaḥ. an|apahāsa|kṣamam etad rāja|yautakam. mahiṣy" âvaguṇṭhana|bhāginī bhavatv eṣā. ito vayam ek'|ântena gacchāmaḥ.

I see, she is the daughter of Ms Bhandira-Army,* called Ms Lily-Pond. Oh my, this poor girl has become quite unrecognizable. So for whose sake is she observing this vow, suitable when a wife is separated from her husband, but inconsistent with life in the courtesans' quarter? I know! It is rumored that she is in love with that Maurya prince Moonrise. And that fortunate man has risen up in arms to bring his vassals to heel. By George, it is proper that Ms Lily-Pond has lost her beauty separated from Prince Moonrise. I say, she clearly puts to shame the women of noble families. And what's more, she is greeting with welcoming words the crow that has come out of desire for the scattered offering and is now standing in a niche on the roof of her house:

"Good luck to you, head-ornament 3.105
of the gable-niche,
guest for the Sraddha-offering.
Will he return in my life,
my love who is always on the road?
If he comes back,
go now to the arch above another door,
for once I've come together with my lover
and become free from sorrow
I shall give you curd and rice."

Why, her passion is indeed immune from deceit. This royal dowry is not fit for mockery. May her head be veiled by the first queen. I shall take my leave discreetly.

(parikramya) aye ayam idānīm dakṣiṇena vṛkṣa|vāṭikāṃ bhūṣaṇa|praṇādāt saṃbhrānta|vihaga|saṃkulaḥ śabda iva śrūyate. bhavatu. apāvṛta|dvār" êyaṃ vṛkṣa|vāṭikā. yāvad avalokayāmi.

(vilokya) hī hī nanu nayan'|ôtsavaḥ khalv iha vartate. tathā hi Pāñcāladāsyā duhitā Priyaṃguyaṣṭikā nāma jaghan'|ôtsek'|ôtpādit'|âhaṃkāreṇa nava|yauvana|rājyakena vilobhyamānā nānā|vilāsa|bhāva|hāva|dākṣiṇya|samuditā sakhī|jana|parivṛtā kanduka|krīḍām anubhavati. y" âiṣā

pravāla|lol'|âṅgulinā kareṇa
manaḥ|śilaṃ kandukam udvahantī
sva|pallav'|âgr'|âbhihat'|âika|puṣpā
nat'|ônnatā nīpa|lat" êva bhāti.

3.110 kāmam asyāḥ saṃdarśanam ev' ânargho lābho bhavatu. saṃtuṣṭasy' âpi janasya na tv amṛte paryāptir asti. ato 'bhibhāṣiṣye tāvad enām. *(upagamya)* vāsu Priyaṃguyaṣṭike, kim idaṃ kanduka|krīḍā|vyājena nṛtta|kauśalaṃ pratyādiśyate sakhī|janasya? kathaṃ? smita|mātra|datta|prativacanā krīḍaty eva. ā yathā kanduk'|ôtpātān gaṇayanty asyāḥ paricārikāḥ, śaṅke paṇitam anayā sakhībhiḥ sah' ôpanibaddham iti. aho paṇita|prītiḥ! sarvathā nat'|ônnat'|āvartan'|ôtpatan'|âpasarpaṇa|pradhāvana|citra|pracāra|manoharaṃ yadṛcchayā dṛśyam āsāditaṃ khalv

(walks about) Oho! I thought I heard a noise on the right side of the orchard, confused with the chirrup of birds startled by the jingling of jewels. Fine, the door of this orchard is open. Let's see now.

(looking) Ha ha! There is a veritable feast for my eyes here. For the daughter of Ms Panchála·dasi, Ms Priyángu-Stalk by name, is enjoying a ball game surrounded by her friends. Her pride, aroused by the swelling of her hips and governing her fresh youth, entices her, and she is well supplied with skill in all kinds of coquetry, sport and dalliance.

Lifting up the ball of realgar
with her hand with fingers like mobile coral,
she is as beautiful as a winding *nipa* vine*
striking a single flower with its twigs.

Granted, her sight is a priceless gain, but even a satisfied 3.110
person cannot drink his fill of nectar. Therefore I will speak to her. *(approaches)* My dear Ms Priyángu-Stalk, why are you demonstrating your skill as a dancer to your friends under the pretext of playing with a ball? What? She answers merely by smiling and continues to play. Aha! Here friends are counting her ball throws, I fear there is a wager between her and her friends. Ah, the joy of betting! By all means, I have clearly chanced upon something worthy of watching, delightful with various movements of bowing, stretching, spinning, leaping, retreating and running. Why say more? I think even the wind, eager to enter into her garment blown up by her turning around, turning back, and leaping, runs after

asmābhiḥ. kiṃ bahunā? śaṅke parivartana|nivartan'|ôdvartana|paryādhmāta|vasan'|ântara|praveśa|kutūhalo vāyur apy enām abhikāmo 'nubhramat' îti. yat|satyaṃ sva|bhāva|dur|balatvād eka|pāṇi|grāhyasya yauvana|pīṭha|payodhara|bhāra|namitasya bibhemy aham asyā madhya|visaṃvādanasya. na śakṣyāmy enām upekṣitum. abhibhāṣiṣye tāvat. ayi yauvan'|ônmatte, sva|saukumārya|viruddhaḥ khalv ayam āraṃbhaḥ kriyate. virama virama tāvat. aye tvāṃ khalu bravīmi. katham upārohaty ev' âsyāḥ praharṣaḥ. hanta idānīm āśāsye.

prenkholat|kuṇḍalāyā
balavad anibhṛte kanduk'|ônmāditāyāś
cañcad|bāhu|dvayāyāḥ
pravikaca|visṛt'|ôdgīrṇa|puṣp'|âlakāyāḥ
āvart'|ôdbhrānta|vega|
praṇaya|vilasita|kṣubdha|kāñcī|guṇāyāḥ
madhyasy' āvalgamāna|
stana|bhara|namitasy' âsya te kṣemam astu.

eṣā pūrṇaṃ śatam iti vyavasthitā. vāsu Priyaṃguyaṣṭike, sakhī|jana|paṇita|vijayena diṣṭyā vardhase.

kiṃ bravīṣi? «svāgatam āryāya. hanta vijay'|ârghaṃ gṛhyatām» iti. vāsu, tvad|darśanam ev' ânargho lābhaḥ. smartavyāḥ smaḥ. sādhayāmo vayam.

her infatuatedly. Truly, because of it's inherent weakness, I fear for her the false promise of her waist, that can be seized with a single hand, that is bowed down by the burden of her breasts which are the seat of her youth. I cannot ignore her. Let me talk to her. Hey, you who are drunk with youth, you are engaged in exertions opposed to your delicacy. Stop, please stop! Hey! I'm talking to you. What, this just increases her mirth. Ah! I will teach her.

Your earrings are swinging
as you are carried away in your obsession with
the ball,
your two arms are astir,
your locks shower fullblown flowers all around,
the strings of your girdle spring when you turn,
and thanks to the speed they glitter and swing
—may your waist be unharmed,
as it bends down
with the burden of your bouncing breasts.

She has managed a full one hundred throws and now stops. My dear Ms Priyángu-Stalk, by great good luck you have won the wager with your friends.

What are you saying? "Welcome sir. Please accept my welcome gift of victory." My dear, just seeing you is a priceless gain. I am to be remembered. I'm off.

(parikramya) aye idam aparaṃ suhṛd | vinodan' | āyatanam upasthitam. idaṃ hi Candradhara | kāminyā Nāgarikāyā duhituḥ Śoṇadāsyā gṛham. eṣa praviśāmi. na śakyam anabhibhāṣy' âtikramitum. *(praviṣṭaken' âvalokya)* aye iyaṃ Śoṇadāsī kim api cintayantī dvāra|koṣṭhaka ev' ôpaviṣṭā. tat kim idānīṃ nirmukta|bhūṣaṇatayā vivikta|śarīra | lāvaṇyā malina | prāvār' | ârdha | saṃvṛta | śarīrā rakta|candan'|ânulipta|lalāṭā sita|dukūla|paṭṭikā|veṣṭita|śīrṣ" âvanata | vadana | candra | maṇḍal" âṅk' | âdhirūḍhāṃ vallakīm īṣat kara|ruhair avaghaṭṭayantī kākalī|manda|madhureṇa svareṇa kaiśik'|āśrayam ākūjantī tiṣṭhati. utkaṇṭhitay" ânayā bhavitavyam. kaiśik' | āśrayaṃ hi gānaṃ paryāya | śabdo ruditasya. kiṃ nu khalv idam? aśruta | pūrvaṃ mayā Candradharād eva praṇaya|kalaha|kṛtaṃ vyāharaṇam anayoḥ. priya|nirodhāt paścāt|tāpa|gṛhītay" ânayā bhavitavyam. bhavatu. parihasiṣyāmy enām. vāsu Śoṇadāsi, kim idaṃ veśa|tāpasī|veṣaḥ parigṛhyate? vāsu, na khalv ayam aparāddhaś Candradharaḥ? katham? te 'śru|mokṣaḥ prativacanam. nigṛhyatāṃ bāṣpaḥ. kathyatāṃ tāvat.

3.115 kiṃ bravīṣi? «mān' | âika | grāha | kuśalena vyāpādit" âsmi sakhī|janena» iti. nanu sarva|jan' | âdhikā te sakhī, Śonadāsi, tvām utthāpayati?

(walks about) Oho! Another pleasurable sanctuary for a friend has appeared. For this is the house of Shona·dasi,* the daughter of Ms Urbane and the beloved of Chandra·dhara.* I will enter. I cannot pass by without speaking to her. *(mimes entering and looks around)* Oho! Here is Shona·dasi seated in the gate-chamber mulling something over. Now why is she here, the beauty of her body departed since she is without ornaments, her body half wrapped in a dirty cloak, her forehead smeared with red sandal paste, her head wrapped in a turban of fine white cloth, the moon of her face bent down, lightly plucking a lute on her lap with her fingernails, humming a Káishika composition with blue notes that are sweet and slow? She must be longing for someone. For a Káishika song is synonymous with crying. What could this be? I have never heard them being talked about because of a love-quarrel due to Chandra·dhara.* She must be feeling remorse because she frustrated her lover. Very well. I will make fun of her. My dear Shona·dasi, why are you wearing the garb of an ascetic of the brothel quarter? My dear, surely Chandra·dhara has not committed an offense? What? You release tears as my answer. Restrain your tears. Tell me about it.

What are you saying? "I am ruined by my confidante who is only skilled in haughtiness." Surely Shona·dasi, your friend is more important to you than anyone else, yet she upsets you? 3.115

kiṃ bravīṣi? «tasyā eva dur|mantritair āpadam imām udvahāmi» iti. apaṇḍitā khalv asi. nanu sā tvay" âivaṃ vaktavyā—

prāyaḥ śīt" âparāddhā,
kṣaṇam api na punar dūti māna|kṣam" âhaṃ.
tuṣṭ" êdānīm anārye
bhava madana|tulāṃ mām ih' āropya ghorām.
mān'|âika|grāha|vākyair
anunaya|vidhurais tāvakais tat kṛtaṃ me
pāṇibhyāṃ yena saṃpraty
anucita|śithilāṃ mekhalām udvahāmi.

kiṃ bravīṣi? «parājita idānīṃ madanena mānaḥ. kiṃ tu saubhāgya|kṛt'|âvalepas te vayasyaḥ stabdhaḥ» iti. tataḥ kim idāniṃ n' âbhisāryate? sundari, alam alaṃ vrīdayā.

niśvasy' âdho|mukhī kiṃ
vicarasi manasā bāṣpa|paryākul'|âkṣī?
śaithilyaṃ bhūṣaṇānāṃ
svayam api subhage sādhv avekṣasva tāvat.
hitvā kūla|stha|vākyāny
anunaya ramaṇam. kiṃ vṛthā|dhīra|hastaiḥ?
saṃrūḍhasy' âtimūḍhe
praṇaya|samudayasy' âbhimāno 'vamānaḥ.

What are you saying? "Because of her bad advice I bear this misfortune." You are naive. Your should speak to her like this—

When I mostly remained cold I offended him,
but now I cannot bear haughtiness even for
a moment,
O go-between.
Take satisfaction now, you ignoble woman,
having placed me here on the terrible scales
of love.
With your advice to resort to haughtiness alone,
avoiding conciliation,
you have brought me to the state
where I must lift up
my unaccustomed slack girdle with my hands.

What are you saying? "Now pride is vanquished by love. But your friend, his haughtiness produced by amatory triumphs, is obstinate." Then why don't you go to him? Fair one, put aside your bashfulness.

Why are you deliberating,
your face turned down and sighing,
your eyes filled with tears?
Lovely woman,
see for yourself the slackness of your ornaments.
Conciliate your lover with agreeable words.
Why bother with vainly steadying your hands?
Haughtiness, O innocent woman,
is contempt for a stable reunion.

3.120 kiṃ bravīṣi? «striyā nāma puruṣo 'nuneyo nanu śauṇḍīryam» iti. mā tāvat. atimanasvini, kiṃ na Gaṅgā sāgaram abhiyāti? alam alaṃ vrīḍayā. athavā sakām" âstu bhavatī. aham eva Candradharam anunayāmi. kiṃ bahunā? ady' âiva te cira|viraha|samāropitasya madan'|âgni|hotrasya punar|ādhānaṃ karomi. katham? anavasita|bāṣpay" âiva smitam anayā. idaṃ khalu varṣa'|rtu|jyotsnā|darśanam. sundari, alam alaṃ ruditena. pratyupasthitaṃ kalyāṇam.

kiṃ bravīṣi? «satya|pratijñen' êdānīṃ bhāvena bhavitavyam» iti. prabhāte jñāsyasi. katham? uparato bāṣpaḥ. sādhayāmy aham.

(parikramya) aho idam aparaṃ śṛṅgāra|prakaraṇam upasthitam. eṣā hi Nāgarikā|duhitā gaṇikā Magadhasundarī nāma śarad|amala|śaśi|sadṛśa|vadan" âsita|mṛdu|kuñcita|snigdha|surabhi|śirasi|ruhā vikasita|kuvalaya|dala|lola|locana|yugalā vidruma|cārutara|tāmr'|âdhara|saṃparka|paripāṭala|daśana|mayūkhā kunda|kusuma|mukula|dhavala|sama|sahita|śikhara|datī pīna|kapola|stan'|ōru|jaghana|cakrā bāhya|dvāra|kavāṭ'|ârdha|saṃvṛta|śarīrā dakṣiṇa|hast'|âṅguli|dvayena tiraskariṇy|eka|deśam avalambamānā vāma|caraṇa|kamal'|âika|deśena bhūtale tālam abhisaṃyojya rakta|svara|madhura|tāra|saṃyuktām asaṃkīrṇa|varṇām avaghuṣṭ'|âlaṃkār'|âlaṃkṛtāṃ

What are you saying? "But surely it is effrontery if a man is conciliated by a woman?" Nonsense! Learned woman, does not the Ganges approach the ocean? Have done with your bashfulness. Or rather, may your wish be granted. I myself will conciliate Chandra·dhara. Why say more? This very day I will rekindle love's fire sacrifice that has been deposited in separation for a long time. What? She smiles without interrupting her tears. Verily an image of the moonlight of the rainy season. Fair one, enough of these tears. Good fortune is at hand. 3.120

What are you saying? "You must now be true to your promise." You will know in the morning. What? The tears have ceased. I take my leave.

(walks about) Oho! Another living textbook of erotics approaches. Here is the courtesan Ms Belle-of-Magadha, the daughter of Ms Urbane, awaiting the arrival of some gallant. Her face resembles the clear autumnal moon; her hair is black, soft, curled, glossy and fragrant; her flighty eyes are a pair of blooming lily petals; the rays shooting from her teeth are reddened by contact with her ruddy lips more exquisite than coral; her teeth are like buds of jasmine flowers: white, equal, dense and pointed; the curves of her cheeks, breasts, thighs and buttocks are generous, her body is half concealed by the panel of the exterior door, she holds with two fingers of the right hand one side of the curtain and beats a rhythm on the ground with a part of her left foot lotus as she coos a *Vállabha* quatrain in the Shadja scale,* entrancing

śrotra|manoharāṃ ṣaḍja|grām'|āśrayāṃ vallabhāṃ nāma catuṣ|padām ākūjamānā netra|bhrū|kṣepaiḥ saṃkalpitān bhāvān abhinayantī kasy' âpi subhagasy' āgamanaṃ pratīkṣamāṇā tiṣṭhati. bhoḥ ko nu khalv ayaṃ Mahendra iva surata|yajñāy' āhūyate? bhavatu. pṛcchāmy enām. bhavati veśa|megha|vidyul|late, pṛcchāmas tāvat—

śukl'|âsit'|ânta|raktā
  s'|āpāṅg'|âvekṣiṇī vikasit" êyam
dhanyasya kasya hetoś
  candra|mukhi bahir|mukhī dṛṣṭiḥ?

hā dhik! vitrasta|mṛga|potik" êva saṃtrastayā dṛṣṭyā māṃ nirīkṣate. pratyāgata|cittay" ânayā bhavitavyam.

3.125 kiṃ bravīṣi? «mā maivam. brahmacāriṇī khalv ahaṃ vasantam upavasāmi» iti. śraddheyam etat. ayam idānīṃ te sarasa|danta|kṣat'|âdhar'|oṣṭhaḥ kim iti vakṣyati?

kiṃ bravīṣi? «s'|âvaśeṣa|tuṣāra|paruṣasya vasanta|vāyoḥ padāny etāni» iti. bhavatu tāvat. saṃjñaptāḥ smaḥ.

danta|pada|jarjar'|oṣṭhī
  yathā ca niyamaṃ tvam ātmano vadasi
su|vyaktam a|vrata|ghnaṃ
  cumbita|cāndrāyaṇaṃ carasi.

to the ear, adorned with clearly articulated musical ornaments, its syllables not slurred, in a most sweet register with impassioned notes, while she enacts the evoked sentiments with eye and brow movements. Wow! Who can it be that is summoned like great Indra to a love-sacrifice? Very well. I will ask her. Madam, gracile lightning of the cloud-brothel, I ask—

For the benefit of what lucky man,
o moon-faced girl,
are you peeping outside with your eyes
white, black and red at the ends,
casting sidelong glances?

Oh dear! She looks at me fearfully like a startled young deer. She must have come back down to earth.

What are you saying? "Nothing like that! As an ascetic I am honoring spring." A likely story. Now what does your lower lip, scarred with fresh bite marks tell me? 3.125

What are you saying? "These are the marks of the spring breeze, still somewhat harsh with ice." Never mind. I understand.

Considering your lips
scarred by teeth-marks
and the fact that you say you are retrained,
it is evident that you are observing
a lunar kissing fast*
that does not impinge upon your vow.

eṣā saṃvṛtya kavāṭena mukhaṃ prahasitā. tapo|vṛddhir astu bhavatyai. sādhayāmy aham.

(parikramya) hanta bhoḥ kathaṃ cid veśa|yuvati|pralāpa|śṛṅkhalam unmucya prāpto 'smi Devadattāyā gṛham. ap' îdānīṃ Devadattā gatā syāt. kaṃ[×] nu khalu pṛccheyam? *(vilokya)* ā ayaṃ tāvad vṛkṣa|vāṭikā|pakṣa|dvāreṇ' âtikrāmati bhāva|Gandharvadattasya nāṭak'|ācāryasy' ântevāsī Dardurako nāma nāṭerakaḥ. yāvad enaṃ pṛcchāmi. *(nirdiśya)* aṃgho Darduraka, kutas tvam āgacchasi? api jānīṣe kiṃ Devadattā karot' îti?

3.130 kim āha bhavān? «gatā khalu Devadattā sukha|praśn'|ârtham ārya|Mūladevaṃ draṣṭum. ahaṃ tu Devasenāṃ draṣṭum ācāryeṇa preṣito 'smi» iti. atha kena kāraneṇa?

kiṃ bravīṣi? «Kumudvatī|bhūmikā|prakaraṇaṃ pattram upanay' êti» iti. ath' ôpanītaṃ pattrakaṃ gṛhītaṃ ca tayā?

kiṃ bravīṣi? «ācārya|gauravāt pratigṛhītaṃ tat pattrakaṃ tayā, pārśva|sthāyās tu sakhyā haste nyastam. api ca Kumudvatyai namaskṛty' ôktavatī ‹asvasthā tāvad asmi› iti» iti. hanta prasiddha|tarkāḥ smaḥ. etad asyāḥ kām'|âikatānatāṃ sūcayati. aṃgho Darduraka, kim idaṃ pattrake 'bhilikhitam?

kiṃ bravīṣi? «vācayasva» iti. *(gṛhītvā vācayati)*

She laughs, averting her face behind the door panel. May your asceticism prosper. I take my leave.

(walks about) At last! I have burst the shackles of the courtesans' prattle and arrived at Ms Gods'-Gift's house. Perhaps she has gone out already. Whom shall I ask? *(looking)* Ah, here is the young son of a danseuse, Mr Frog, pupil of the dance teacher Mr Gandharva's-Gift, passing through a private door in the enclosed grove. I will ask him. *(pointing)* Hey, Mr Frog, where are you coming from? Do you know what Ms Gods'-Gift is up to?

What are you saying, sir? "Ms Gods'-Gift has gone to ask 3.130
Mula·deva how he is doing. I was sent by my teacher to see Ms Gods'-Army." For what reason?

What are you saying? "I was told: 'Bring her the letter with a play containing Kumúdvati's part!'"* And you brought it and she took it?

What are you saying? "Out of respect for the teacher she took the letter, but she handed it to a friend who stood beside her. Then she saluted Kumúdvati and said: 'I am quite unwell.'" Ah, my suspicions are confirmed. This betrays her singleminded devotion to love. Mr Frog, what was written in this letter.

What are you saying? "Read it." *(takes it and reads)*

kāntaṃ Kandarpa|puṣpaṃ stana|taṭa|śaśinaṃ
  rāga|vṛkṣa|pravālaṃ
śayyā|yuddh'|âbhighātaṃ surata|ratha|raṇa|
  śrānta|dhurya|pratodam
unmeṣaṃ vibhramāṇāṃ karaja|pada|mayaṃ
  guhya|sambhoga|cihnaṃ
rāg'|ākrāntā vahantām jaghana|nipatitaṃ
  karkaśāḥ strī|kiśoryaḥ.

3.135 sādhu bhoḥ karkaśa|strī|kiśorī|pratāraṇāy' âbhiprasthitasya me mahad idaṃ maṅgalam artha|siddhiṃ sūcayati. aṃgho Darduraka, api jāṇīṣe kutra|sthā Devasen" êti?

kiṃ bravīṣi? «vṛkṣa|vāṭikāṃ gatā» iti. hanta madana|karm'|ânta|bhūmau vartate. sādhu. gacchatu bhavān. praviśāmas tāvat. *(praviśya)* aye iyam iyaṃ Devasenā

kṛśā vivarṇā paripāṇḍu|niṣprabhā
  prabhāta|doṣ'|ôpahat" êva candrikā
vahaty asādhāraṇa|gūḍha|vedanaṃ
  manomayaṃ vyādhim a|dāruṇ'|âuṣadham.

ā yath" âivaṃ sarva|guhya|dhāriṇyā sneh'|âtisṛṣṭa|sakhī|bhāvayā Priyavādinikayā nāma paricārikayā saha parivarjit'|ânya|janā vāyuṃ paryupāste. bhavatu. etad apy asyā ekatānatāṃ sūcayati. sarvo 'pi vivikta|kāmaḥ kāmī bhavati.

May tough women-fillies,
overcome by love,
carry the lovely flower of Cupid,
  the crescent upon their breast-mountain-slopes,
  the shoot of the tree of passion,
  the blow in the battle of the bed,
  the goad for the exhausted horse
    in the chariot battle of love,
  the unfolding of coquetry
—the mark of secret enjoyment
    consisting of nail-marks
  fallen upon their buttocks.

Exquisite! This magnificent benediction augurs success for me who have set forth to seduce a tough woman-filly. Mr Frog, do you know where Ms Gods'-Army is? 3.135

What are you saying? "She has gone to the enclosed grove." Ah, she is in the grounds where matters of love are brought to completion. Good, please go. I will enter. *(enters)* Oho here is Ms Gods'-Army,

Emaciated, wan, lusterless and pale,
like moonlight afflicted by the dawn
she endures an uncommon secret anguish,
a mental ailment requiring a mild medicine.

Aha, so that's why she is enjoying the breeze alone, only with a confidant called Ms Dear-speaker who knows all her secrets and whose friendship is heightened by affection. Indeed, this too betrays her single-mindedness. Those in love all love solitude. She is in my sphere.

asmad|viṣaya|gat" êyam. yāvad enām upasarpāmi. *(upetya)* vāsu Devasene, visrambh'|ālāpa|viccheda|kāriṇo na khalu vayam asūyitavyāḥ.

kiṃ bravīṣi? «svāgataṃ bhāvāya. abhivādayāmi» iti. bhavatu, pratigṛhītaḥ samudācāraḥ. alam alaṃ pratyutthāna|yantraṇayā.

3.140 kim āha bhavatī? «upaviśa, idam āsanam» iti. bāḍham upaviṣṭo 'smi. vāsu, kim idaṃ *bandhu/jana/santāpaḥ* kriyate? ko nām' âyam a|cakṣur|grāhyo gūḍha|vedanaḥ svayaṃ|grāhyaḥ prāk|kevalo vyādhiḥ?

kiṃ bravīṣi? «na khalu kiṃ cit» iti. ayi paṇḍita|mānini, alam asmān vikṣipya. sad" âpi nāma tvam asmākaṃ bāla|krīḍanak'|ânveṣaṇ'|ādiṣu praṇayavatī. api ca, sa ev' âhaṃ Mūladeva|sakhaḥ Śaśaḥ. tad ucyatāṃ sad|bhāvaḥ. kim|āśrayo 'yaṃ santāpaḥ? tava hi

a|vyādhi|glānam aṅgaṃ,
kara|tala|kamal'|âpāśritaṃ gaṇḍa|pārśvaṃ,
dṛṣṭir dhyān'|âikatānā,
jaḍam iva hṛdayaṃ, jṛmbhaṇā, varṇa|bhedaḥ
niśvās'|āyāsa|kartā
na ca na rati|karas tāpanaś c' êndriyāṇām
eka/dravy'/âbhilāṣī
pratinava iva te, cori, ko 'yaṃ vikāraḥ?

So let's approach her. *(approaches)* My dear Ms Gods'-Army, you must bear me no malice for interrupting your private talk.

What are you saying? "Welcome sir, I greet you." Very well, I accept your polite greeting. Please don't bother to get up.

What are you saying, miss? "Please sit, here is a seat." Sure, 3.140
I'll sit down. My dear, *why are you causing pain to your*
friends : why are you aching for a friend? What is this
self-inflicted, invisible ailment with hidden pain, which
had no preliminary symptoms?

What are you saying? "It is nothing." So! You fancy yourself clever! Don't try to brush me off! You were always fond of me when I was looking for your toys, for example. What's more, I am that very Mr Rabbit, Mula·deva's friend. Now tell me what is really the matter. What is the reason for this pain? For,

> Your body is languid without disease,
> the side of your cheek rests in your palm-lotus,
> your eyes are steadily focussed in meditation,
> your heart seems inert,
> yawning, paleness
> —thief, what is this new,
> evil transformation of yours?
> It fatigues you with sighs,
> yet it does give you delight—
> an inflamer of the senses,
> *that craves only one thing : that requires only*
> *one medicine.*

katham? niśvasitam anayā. hanta saṃdhukṣate madan'|âgniḥ. bhavatu. idānīm ātma|gataṃ bhāvam asyā jñāsyāmaḥ. yadi vayam a|pātrī|bhūtā visraṃbhānām arog" âstu bhavatī. sādhayāmy aham.

kiṃ bravīṣi? «capalaḥ khalu bhāvaḥ» iti. hanta pratijñātam. eṣ" âpi marma vakṣyati. vāsu, kuto me dhṛtis tav' ēdṛśena śarīr'|ôdantena? api ca dīrgha|sūtratā nāma kāry'|ântaram utpādayati. tad ucyatāṃ saṃtāpa|kāraṇam.

3.145 kiṃ bravīṣi? «na khalu me bhāvaṃ prati guhyam asti. ayaṃ tu vasanta|sva|bhāvo yan me guru|jana|yantraṇayā nibhṛtasy' âpi manasaḥ kim apy akāraṇen' āutsukyam utpādayati» iti. sādhu bho n' âyaṃ vyādhi|vyapadeśaḥ. cori, etad api jānīṣe sādhu yuvatī khalu Devasenā saṃvṛtt" êti. vāsu, yady evam alam alam anubandhena. ṛtu|pariṇāmena svasthā bhaviṣyasi. katham? vrīḍitam anayā. Priyavādinike, kim idaṃ tāla|pattrake 'bhilikhitam?

kiṃ bravīṣi? «nāṭaka|bhūmikā» iti. paśyāmas tāvat. *(gṛhītvā vācayati)* «Kumudvatī|prakaraṇe Śūrpaka|saktāṃ rāja|dārikāṃ dhātrī rahasy upālabhate.

What? She sighs. Alas the fire of love has flared up. So be it. Now I will get to know her inner feelings. If you will not take me into your confidence, then may you fare well. I must take my leave.

What are you saying? "You are indeed fickle, sir." Oho, she admitted it! Now she will tell me her weak spot.* My dear, how could I show fortitude when your body is in such a condition? And long-windedness brings to mind another business.* Please tell me the cause of your affliction.

What are you saying? "I could clearly not hide anything 3.145
from your honor. But such is the nature of spring that, even in my heart that is guarded by the restraints placed upon me by my elders, something evokes a spontaneous longing." Very well, that is not the name of a disease. You thief, you too know this well, Ms Gods'-Army has become a young woman. My dear, if this is how it is then enough of these symptoms. You will become well with a change of season. What? She is being coy. Ms Dear-speaker, what is written on this palm-leaf?

What are you saying? "A role for a play." Let me see it. *(takes and reads)* "In the play Kumúdvati: the nurse maid in private admonishes the princess who is infatuated with Shúrpaka:

unmatte, n' âiva tāvat stana|viṣamam uraḥ,
n' ôdgatā roma|rājiḥ,
na vyutpann" âsi ca tvaṃ. vyapanaya yuvatī|
dohalaṃ, dur|vidagdhe.
vyutpannābhiḥ sakhībhiḥ satatam avinaya|
grantham adhyāpyase tvaṃ.
ken' êdaṃ, bāla|pakve, manasija|kadanaṃ
kartum abhyudyat" âsi?»

kim āha Devasenā? «etat tāvan may" âiva na śrutam asti» iti. hanta eṣa udgīrṇaḥ sva|bhāvaḥ. ittham aham api kāmayām' îty uktaṃ bhavati.

kim āha Devasenā? «chala|grāhī bhāvaḥ» iti. vāsu, alam alam asmān vikṣipya. megh'|âvagūḍham api candra|masaṃ kumudvatī|prabodhaḥ sūcayati. gaccha puruṣa|dveṣini. āpann" êdānīm asi.

You crazy girl,
your chest is not yet uneven with breasts,
the down running to your navel
has not yet appeared,
you are not yet accomplished.
Give up this craving of young maidens,
you wrongheaded girl.
You are always being made
  to study the book of misbehavior
  by your accomplished friends.
Why are you poised, barely ripe girl,
to do what slaughters love?"

What does Ms Gods'-Army say? "I had not heard that part yet." Ha! You have blurted out your true state. You might as well have said: "I too am in love."

What does Ms Gods'-Army say? "You tend to detect pretense, sir." My dear, please stop brushing me off. Though he be hidden by clouds the opening of the night-lily heralds the moon. Go, you misandrist. Now you are unlucky.

3.150 n' âiv' âhaṃ kāmayām' îty asakṛd abhihitaṃ
yat tvayā, gūḍha|bhāve,
sā tvaṃ tanvī|svabhāvāt kathaya tanu|tarā,
cori, ken' âsi jātā?
hasta|pratyasta|gaṇḍe, praśithila|valaye,
bhinna|niśvāsa|vaktre,
vyādhi|kliṣṭo jano 'yaṃ kim idam, atiśaṭhe,
vāhyate dhīra|haste?

kim āha Priyavādinikā? «sati pravṛtte *kāma/tantra/prakaraṇe* diṣṭy" êdānīm asmat|svāminī puruṣa|viśeṣam anuraktā na pṛthag|janam» iti. tat kasy' âyam Avanti|nagaryāṃ puruṣa|viśeṣa|śabdaḥ pracarati?

kim āha bhavatī? «kasya tāvat tvay" âbhyupagamyate?» iti. kasy' ânyasya? nanu Karṇīputrasya. sa hi—

kule prasūtaḥ śrutavān avismitaḥ
smit'|âbhibhāṣī caturo vimatsaraḥ
priyaṃ|vado rūpa|vayo|guṇ'|ânvitaḥ
śarīravān Kāma iv' âdhanur|dharaḥ.

More than once you have said, 3.150
    hiding your feelings: "I am not in love."
Then tell me, you thief,
why have you become even thinner
    than your usual slenderness?
Your cheek is consigned into your hands,
your bangles hang loose,
your mouth is parted with sighs.*
This person is afflicted with an ailment,
you rogue, how is this endured,
you who have such steady hands?*

What does Ms Dear-speaker say? "Now that *a play on erotics has been produced: an opportunity for the art of love has arisen,* by great good fortune our mistress is attached to an exceptional man, not a yokel." Then for whom in Avánti's city is this term "exceptional man" in use?

What are you saying, miss? "Who do you think?" Who else, it must be Karni·putra. For he—

Born in a noble family,
is learned, not arrogant,
smiles when he speaks,
is skilled, not envious, speaks kindly,
is handsome, virtuous and in his prime,
is like an embodiment of Cupid
    without his bow.

kim adho|mukhī Devasenā saṃvṛttā? alam alam, ati-nibhṛte, dukūla|daś"|ânt'|ôdveṣṭanena. kathyatāṃ tāvat. api ca yadi vayaṃ bhājanī|bhaviṣyāmaḥ! sa|maunam ev' āste. athavā lajjā nāma vilāsa|yautakaṃ pramadā|janasya viśeṣataś c' âprauḍha|kāminīnām. tad eṣā katham iva svayaṃ vakṣyati? tat kāmaṃ puruṣa|viśeṣa ity asādhāraṇa eva śabdaḥ Karṇīputre prativasati, tath" âpi nāma tv alabdha|gāmbhīryo dhṛtim upayāta enāṃ vyāhārayāmi. vāsu Devasene, kim asmākaṃ para|rahasya|śravaṇena? udāsīnāḥ khalu vayam. tad āmantraye bhavatīm. Karṇīputro 'pi Pāṭalīputra|virahāt sva|jana|darśan'|ôtsuko bhṛśam asvasthaḥ. sa eṣo 'dya śvo vā prasthāsyate. punar draṣṭ" âsmi bhavatīm. kiṃ tu svastha|rūpayā tvayā bhavitavyam. smartavyāḥ smo vayam.

3.155 *(utthāya prasthitaḥ. satvaraṃ nivṛttya)* aye ken' âitad uktaṃ «hanta vyāpann" êdānīm» iti. ā Devasenā roditi. vāsu, kim idam? alam alaṃ ruditena. bhavatu, gṛhītam. diṣṭyā pātra|gato manorathaḥ. Karṇīputrasy' âpi tvan|maya eva vyādhiḥ. tad itar'|êtarasy' āuṣadhatvena kalpayitavyam.

kiṃ bravīṣi? «kim uccaiḥ kathayasi? duḥkha|śīlaḥ khalu bhāvaḥ» iti. alam alaṃ yantraṇayā.

What? Ms Gods'-Army is staring at the ground. You are too shy, there is no need to hide yourself with the hem of your robe. Tell me about it. I wish I could win her confidence! She remains silent. Or rather, coyness in fact belongs to women's dowry of coquetry, and especially so in the case of immature passionate women. So how could she speak herself? Clearly the uncommon expression "exceptional man" befits Karni·putra. Nevertheless, insignificant as I am, I shall brace myself and sound her out. My dear Ms Gods'-Army, what will it profit me if I listen to someone else's secret? It's clearly none of my business. So I say goodbye to you, miss. As for Karni·putra, he is homesick for Pátali·putra and, yearning to see his own people, is seriously unwell. He may depart today or tomorrow. I will see you again. But you must get well. Don't forget me.

(stands up to go, turns back suddenly) Oh no! Who just said: 3.155
"Alas! Now I am dead!" Ah, Ms Gods'-Army weeps. My dear, why this? Enough tears. All right, I understand. Fortunately your longing has reached a fit receptacle. Karni·putra's illness too is on your behalf. You can become each other's medicine.

What are you saying? "Why are you shouting? You truly are ready to cause pain." Stop holding back.

Dakṣ'|ātmajāḥ, sundari, yoga|tārāḥ
kiṃ n' âika|jātāḥ śaśinaṃ bhajante?
āruhyate vā sahakāra|vṛkṣaḥ
kiṃ n' âika|mūlena latā|dvayena?

kiṃ bravīṣi? «tath" êdānīṃ saṃpradhāryatāṃ yath" ôbhayaṃ rakṣyate» iti. atha kim? saṃpradhāritam ev' âitat. śvaḥ kila te bhaginī yath"|ôcitam ācārya|gṛhaṃ nṛtta|vāreṇa yāsyati. tato labdh'|ântara|visrambhā, subhage, sukha|praśna|vyāhāra|vyājena tvaṃ vā tatra yāsyasi sa v" êh' āgamiṣyati. kim iyaṃ vimarśa|dolā vāhyate?

kim āha Priyavādinikā? «na mam' êh' ārya|putrasy' āgamanaṃ rocate yath" âtra|bhavatyās tatra gamanam. gaṇikā|jano nāma paiśunya|prābhṛt" âiṣā jātiḥ. tasmād aham ev' âsyā× yath"|ôcitaṃ yojayiṣyāmi yathā nṛtta|vārāt prasthit" âjjā× Devadattā svayam eva mama svāminīṃ sukha|praśn'|âbhigamanen' ārya|Mūladeva|sakāśam anuneṣyati» iti. sādhu Priyavādinike, idānīṃ khalu te yath"|ârtha|nāmatā.× ucitaṃ c' âsyās tatra gamanam. kiṃ tu svastha|rūpay" ânayā bhavitavyam.

3.160 kim aha Devasenā? «nanu bhāva|darśanāt svasth" âiv' âham» iti. priyaṃ me. kṛtaṃ madana|karma. Karṇīputra|prāṇa|dhāraṇ'|ârthaṃ kiṃ cit smaraṇīyaṃ dātum arhasi.

Are the chief stars, fair one,
though born together
as the daughters of Daksha,
not all devoted to the moon?
Is the mango tree not climbed
by two vines from a single root?

What are you saying? "Now then it must be resolved to protect both." Why, certainly! It is resolved. Tomorrow in fact your sister, as usual, will go to the house of the teacher for her dance lesson. Then you, lovely girl, regaining your confidence, will go to him under the pretext of asking about his health, or he will come here. Why is her head spinning?

What does Ms Dear-speaker say? "I do not like the idea of the gentleman coming here as much as I do her going there. The caste of courtesans gives slander as gift. Therefore I myself will arrange for her that mistress Gods'-Gift, returning from her dance lesson, will herself lead my mistress to the noble Mula·deva to ask about his health." Excellent Ms Dear-speaker, now you bear your name rightly. It is appropriate for her to go there. But she must look healthy.

What does Ms Gods'-Army say? "Surely I am already feeling 3.160
better because I have seen you." Why thank you. The transaction of love is completed. You must please give me a souvenir to support the life of Karni·putra.

kiṃ bravīṣi? «kiṃ dāsyāmi?» iti. kiṃ nāma vicāryate? idaṃ khalu

īṣal|līl"|âbhidaṣṭaṃ stana|taṭa|mṛditaṃ
pattra|lekh"|ânuviddhaṃ
khinnaṃ niśvāsa|vātair malaya|taru|rasa|
kliṣṭa|kiñjalka|varṇam
prātar|nirmālya|bhūtaṃ surata|samudaya|
prābhṛtaṃ preṣay' âsmai
padmaṃ, padm'|âvadāte, kara|tala|yugala|
bhrāmaṇa|kliṣṭa|nālam.

katham? kaṭākṣa|pāten' âitad anujñātam anayā. hanta pratigṛhītaṃ prābhṛtaṃ surata|satyaṃ|kārasya. yāvad anen' âuṣadhena Karṇīputraṃ saṃjīvayāmi. *(gṛhītv" ôtthāya sthitvā)* prasthito 'smi. sukham bhavatyai. subhage, gṛhyatām āśīḥ:

What are you saying? "What shall I give?" What is there to wonder about? It's clear!

You are as unblemished
  as a lotus—
send him this lotus,
lightly and playfully bitten,
rubbed against your sloping breasts,
inlaid with your body paint pattern,
withered by your sighs,
its filaments discolored
  with the juice of sandal tree,
a sacred offering remaining
  from the early morning,
a gift for felicity in love,
its stalk blemished
  by twirling it in your hands.

What? She assents with a side-glance. Ah, I have received the gift that is an earnest promise of love. With this medicine I will revive Karni·putra. *(takes it and stands up)* I must go. Fare well, miss. Lovely girl, receive my blessing:

bhaya|drutam asūyitaṃ×
pracala|mekhalā|nūpuraṃ
sa|śaṅka|śithil'|ôpagū-
ham avamukta|nīvī|patham
svayaṃ samabhivāhayatv
ayam udātta|rāg'|āyudhas
tava prathama|corikā|
surata|sāhasaṃ Manmathaḥ.

3.165 *iti niṣkrānto viṭaḥ.*

iti śrī|Śūdraka|viracitaḥ «Padmaprābhṛtakaṃ» nāma bhāṇaḥ samāptaḥ.

May the Love God himself,
with ardent passion as his weapon,
grant the success of your temerity when,
for the first time, you stealthily make love,
flustered with fear and jealous,
your girdle and anklets swinging,
when fear makes embraces weak,
when undergarments slip and give way.

Exit the Pimp. 3.165

Thus ends the causerie called "The Lotus Gift"
composed by the illustrious Shúdraka.

DHŪRTAVIṬASAṂVĀDAḤ

ROGUE AND PIMP CONFER

4.1 *nāndy|ante tataḥ praviśati* SŪTRA|DHĀRAḤ

SŪTRA|DHĀRAḤ:

vidyayā khyāpitā khyātiḥ,
  sajjan'|ārādhanaṃ dhanam,
teṣāṃ prītyā bhaved dharma:
  ity asmākam upakramaḥ.

tasmād ārya|jana|manaḥ|prīty|arthaṃ× kiṃ cin nāṭakam ārabhāmahe. ārye, sa|dhana|jana|prīti|varddhana|karāyām a|dhanānāṃ yauvan'|ôtpīḍita|manda|bhāgyānāṃ cintā|parāyaṇānāṃ śoka|vardhana|karāyāṃ kumuda|kuvalaya|kalhāra|kamala|nicula|ketakī|kakubha|kandalī|ṣaṇḍa|maṇḍitāyām asyāṃ prāvṛṣi hṛdaya|prīti|jananaṃ× kiṃ cid gītaṃ gīyatām. ayaṃ khalu tāvat kālaḥ—

jala|dhara|nīl'|ālepas
  taḍit|samālabhana|vijvalad|gātraḥ×
vikasita|kuṭaja|nivasano
  viṭo yathā bhāti ghana|samayaḥ.

4.5 *niṣkrāntaḥ.*

sthāpanā

Then, at the end of the benediction, enter the DIRECTOR. 4.1

DIRECTOR:

Fame is spread through erudition,*
wealth is the propitiating of worthy persons,
when they are pleased religious merit
  accrues:*
this is our mission.*

Therefore, in order to delight the hearts of these gentlefolk, we shall stage some play.* Madam, we need a song* that will delight the heart in this season of rains that is made beautiful with clusters of white and blue water-lilies, white and pink lotuses, *níchulas*, *kétakis*, *kákubhas* and plantains, that brings joy to the wealthy and increases the sorrow of the wretched, those hapless individuals oppressed by youth and engrossed in anxiety. Now, this above all is the time—

Darkened by the hair-dye of rain-clouds,
limbs shining with the unguent of lightning,
decked out in finery of full-blown *kútaja* flowers
—this rainy season presents itself
just like a pimp.

Exits. 4.5

End of the Prologue

tataḥ praviśati VIṬAḤ.

VIṬAḤ: sādhv|abhihitam etat.

śrīmad|veśma|mṛdaṅga|vādya|kuśalā
dhārāḥ sṛjanty ambudāḥ,
kruddha|strī|bhrukuṭī|taraṅga|kuṭilā
vidyud|latā dyotate,
gāḍh'|āliṅgana|hetavaḥ pracalitāḥ
śītāḥ payod'|ânilāḥ,
Kāmaḥ kāmi|manaḥsu muñcati dṛḍhān
ā|karṇa|pūrṇān iṣūn.

4.10 api ca:

«te dagdhāḥ pravasanti ye samadanā
n' āyānti vā proṣitā;
mugdhās te 'nunayanti ye na kupitāḥ
kupyanti v" âtyāyatam;
dhanyās te khalu ye priyā|vaśa|gatā
yeṣāṃ priyā vā vaśe.»
kālaḥ kārayat' îva megha|paṭahair
evaṃ jagad|ghoṣaṇām.

Then enter the PIMP.

PIMP: Well said.

Clouds,
deft at drumming upon the mansions of the wealthy,
pour forth torrents;
a lightning streak,
rippling like a wave in the brows of angry women,
flashes forth;
cold wet winds,
coercing tight embraces, blow;
Kama lets fly his unfailing arrows,
drawn right back to his ear,
into the hearts of lovers.

Moreover: 4.10

"The impassioned who depart abroad
or who cannot return from abroad,
are scorched;
those who do not conciliate angry women
or who carry anger to far, are simpletons;
those who are enthralled by their lovers
or who hold their lovers in thrall,
are indeed fortunate."
In this way the season seems
to make a public proclamation
announced by cloud-drums.

aho nu khalu jalada|kālasya lalita|jana|mano|grāhiṇī bahu|vṛttāntatā! samprati hi *sa/jala/jalad'/âvaruddha/dinakara/karāḥ s'/ôpasnehā bhūmi/bhāgā* bahu|divasa|sadṛśa|vṛttāntatayā saukumāryam iv' ôpagatā divasāḥ. kuṭaja|gandh'|āvartita|madhukarāṇi pravṛtta|nṛtta|barhiṇāni śīt'|âmbuvanti vihāra|kṣamāṇy araṇyāni. pracalit' êndragopakā nava|harita|tṛṇ'|âṅkurāḥ s'|ālaktaka|yuvati|caraṇa|vinyāsa|yogyā vana|bhūmayaḥ. *kaluṣa/salila/vāhinyo* 'vibhāvanīya|tīrthāḥ śaṭhā iva nāryo dur|avagāhā nadyaḥ. api ca,

kadamba|gandham ādāya
  van'|ântara|viniḥsṛtaḥ
āyāti dhārā|śiśiraḥ
  sa|prābhṛta iv' ânilaḥ.

tad ramaṇīyo 'yaṃ kālo. na c' âsminn autsukyaṃ na bhavati. kutaḥ?

4.15 bhrānta|pavaneṣu samprati
  sukhino 'pi kadamba|vāsita|vaneṣu
autsukyaṃ vahati mano
  jala|dhara|malineṣu divaseṣu.

Ah! The rainy season's bustling excitement, thrilling the hearts of jovial people! For now *the rays of the sun are occluded by clouds laden with water, patches of the ground are wet: the hands of Mr Daymaker are overwhelmed by perspiring breasts, the sides of Ms Earth are moist with sweat,* the days seem lovely with the bustle of many days rolled into one. The forests are ready for recreation, with bees lured by the scent of *kútaja*s, with dancing peacocks, with cool waters. The forest soil, astir with fire-flies, with fresh tawny grass shoots, invites the lac-reddened feet of maidens to tread upon it. The rivers, *flowing with turbid water,* their fords imperceptible, are as difficult to cross as cheating women *who are menstruating* are impossible to catch out. What's more,

A breeze draws near,
laden with the fragrance of *kadámba*s,
coming from deep inside the forest,
cooled by showers,
as if it carried gifts.

That is why this time is so delightful. It is inconceivable that there should be no yearning in it. For—

Now in these days, 4.15
turbid with clouds,
when forests are scented
with *kadámaba* flowers
and breezes roam,
even the heart of a happy person
is filled with longing.

tatra dvividham autsukyaṃ bhavati—kāraṇād akāraṇāc ca. tatra kāraṇ'|ôdbhūtasy' âutsukyasya śakyā pratikriyā kartum. yat tv akāraṇād utpadyate tat kumbhadāsī|kṛtaka|ruditam iva duścikitsaṃ bhavati. vayaṃ ca kāni cid imāny ahāni durdiṇa|doṣād alpa|pada|pracāratvāc ca bhṛśataram unmanasaḥ saṃvṛttāḥ. kuṭumbinyāś ca naḥ kaṇṭha|mādhuryeṇa ten' āpyāyita|manaso 'py apayānam eva bahu manyāmahe.

(vilokya) diṣṭy" êdānīṃ api tāvat su|dinaṃ saṃvṛttam. saṃprati hi—nivṛtta|saṅgīta|mṛdaṅga|sannibhāḥ praśānta|ravā meghāḥ. durdina|doṣa|cakitaḥ prāsādam āruhya pakṣau vitatya virauti gṛha|mayūraḥ. saṃdaṣṭ'|ôpavīṇā|viyukta|virala|tantrī śīta|vāta|vepit" êva kāminī bāl'|ātapam āsevate vīṇā. niṣṭhīvant' îva vimala|muktā|dāma|saṃnibhān praṇālī|mukhais toy'|āvaśeṣān harmya|sthalāni. durdina|doṣān niṣprabhāḥ pramṛjyante darpaṇāḥ. api ca—

And that longing is of two kinds—that arising from a cause and that which has no cause. Of these two, that which arises from a cause is amenable to a cure. But that which arises without a cause, is as incurable as are the fake tears of a harlot.* These last few days I have become bored to death, and the blame lies with the bad weather and the hindrances to my constitutional. Although my heart is satiated by the sweet cadences of my dear wife, I would prefer to make my escape.

(looks about) Excellent! At least for now, the weather has cleared. For now, the clouds, their thunder stilled, resemble drums at the end of a concert. The tame peacock, alarmed through the fault of the bad weather, mounts the terrace, spreads its wings and cries.* A lute, its slack strings detached and its bindings pinched,* warms itself in the morning sunlight, like an impassioned woman shivering in the cool wind. The palace-terraces seem to sputter forth the remaining water, resembling immaculate pearl necklaces, through the mouths of the spouts. The mirrors, dimmed by the damp weather, are being polished. Moreover,

pravara|gṛha|nirodha|khed'|âlasā
yānti vātāyanāny aṅganā.
jalada|samaya|doṣa|gāḍh'|ârpaṇā
hema|kāñcī punar yojyate;
upavana|gamanāya saṃtvaryate×
vāra|mukhyo janaḥ kāmibhis;
taruṇa|tṛṇa|sakheṣu lākṣā|rasaḥ pātyate
pāda|padmeṣv anaṅg'|āvahaḥ.

tat kva nu khalv idam autsukyaṃ vinodayeyam? kiṃ nu dyūta | sabhāyām āhosvid veśa | vāṭe? *(vicārya)* namo 's-tu dyūtāya. eka | śāṭikā | mātr' | âvaśiṣṭo hi naḥ paricchadaḥ, akṣāś ca nām' ânabhijāt'|ēśvarā iva na sarva|kāla|sumukhā bhavanti. tato veśam eva yāsyāmaḥ. tatra hi—

4.20 kāntāny ardha|nirīkṣitāni, madhurā
hās'|ôpadaṃśāḥ kathāḥ,
pīna|śroṇi|niruddha|śeṣam atula|
sparśaṃ tad ardh'|āsanam,
sneha|vyakti|karān kara|vyatikarāṃs
tāṃs tāñ ca ramyān guṇān
veśyābhyaḥ praṇayād ṛte 'pi labhate
jñāt'|ôpacāro janaḥ.

Women, listless with the weariness of being
confined in their fine houses,
go to the windows.
The golden girdle,
a tight fit after the tribulations of the rainy
season, is put on again.
Arch-courtesans are hurried to the groves
by their lovers.
Lac-juice, which arouses passion,
is applied to lotus-feet
—friends to tender grass.

So where now can I quell this saudade? In the casino or in the brothel quarter? *(after some reflection)* With all due respect to gambling, but I'm down to this last piece of cloth to cover me. And dice, like parvenus, are not always benign. So off to the bordello! For there—

The captivating half-glances, 4.20
the sweet chatter spiced with giggles,
the shared seat—incomparable to the touch
—half taken up by her full thighs,
hands intertwined, betraying affection,
and all those delicious pleasures
can be won from courtesans by a man with
savoir faire,
even if he is not their favorite.

(nirīkṣya) saṃvriyatāṃ dvāraṃ. kim āha bhavatī? «valmīkam iva bahu|dvāraṃ te gṛham» iti. yady apy anyo 'sti nagara|ghaṭṭakānāṃ praveśāya mārgas tath" âpi tair anya|gṛha|paricayād dvāra eva lakṣyaṃ gṛhyate. api ca, alam alam uttar'|ôttareṇa. hā dhvasto 'smi. *(parikramya)* sthāne khalu Kusumapurasy' ân|anya|nagara|sadṛśī Nagaram ity aviśeṣa|grāhiṇī pṛthivyāṃ sthitā kīrtiḥ. bahūni khalv asya purasya gṛhāṇy ucchrāyavanti. paṇya|samudāyāj jana|bāhulyāc ca tāṃs tān samṛddhi|viśeṣān dṛṣṭvā vismayate janaḥ. tatra ko vismayaḥ? santi hy anyāny api samṛddhimanti purāṇi. ye tv asya niḥsādhāraṇā guṇās tān vakṣyāmaḥ. tathā hi,

dātāraḥ sulabhāḥ, kalā bahu/matā,
dākṣiṇya/bhogyāḥ striyo,
n' ônmattā dhanino, na matsara/yutā
vidyā/vihīnā narāḥ,
sarvaḥ śiṣṭa/kathaḥ, paraspara/guṇa/
grāhī kṛta/jño janaḥ.
śakyaṃ bho Nagare surair api divaṃ
santyajya labdhuṃ sukham.

(looking) Please close the door. What is it my wife is saying? "Your house has as many holes as an anthill." Even if there are other ways for tax collectors* to get in, still, since they're familiar with other houses, they will target the door. And anyway, that's really enough backtalk. Phew, I'm finished. *(walks about)* It is fitting indeed that the name of Pátali·putra should be established throughout the world simply as 'The City,' a distinction not shared by any other city. Many indeed are its lofty houses. People are amazed beholding all manner of prosperity stemming from masses of chattels and thronging crowds. What is astonishing about this? There are other prosperous cities, too. But let me proclaim its unique virtues. For—

Sponsors are easily found, art is respected, women can be won over by courtesy, the rich are not arrogant, the uneducated are not jealous, all are versed in polite conversation, all are appreciative of the merits of others, and affable. Even gods, upon my word, can find joy in the City, abandoning heaven :
You bump into creditors everywhere, interest is extortionate, women can be bought for a trifle, the rich are very arrogant,* the uneducated are jealous, everyone is a gossip, all consider each other unimportant,* the people are busybodies. Even demons,* upon my word, can find joy in the City, abandoning the quest for heaven.**

(parikramya) aye śreṣṭhi|putraḥ Kṛṣṇilakaḥ khalv asau veśa| prasaṅgāt saphalīkṛta|yauvano 'smad|vidha|jana|praṇaya|bhājana|bhūtaḥ kuṭumb'|âtyaya|bhīruṇā pitrā prayatnād rakṣyamāṇaḥ katham api veśaṃ gatvā priy"| ôpabhukta|śobhinā vapuṣā drutataram ita ev' âbhivartate. avaśyam abhinandayitavyaḥ. upagamiṣyāmas tāvad enam. *(upagamya)* bhoḥ Kṛṣṇilaka! evam eva saphalīkṛta|yauvano bhavatu bhavān. nanu khalu Mādhavasenāyā gṛhād āgamyate.

kiṃ bravīṣi? «kathaṃ vijñātavān?» iti. kim atra vijñeyam? sadṛśa|saṃyogī hi bhagavān Madanaḥ. na c' âpy ahaṃ bhavad|vyāpārān nivṛttaḥ. athav" âvirata|surata|tṛṣṇāṃ kāminīm utsṛjya kv' âsi prasthitaḥ?

4.25 kim āha bhavān? «etat tv idānīṃ kathaṃ vijñātavān?» iti. etad api n' âtisūkṣmaṃ. kutaḥ?

haste te parimṛjya s'|âśru|vadanaṃ
netr'|âñjanaṃ lakṣyate,
keś'|ânto viṣamaś ca pāda|patanād
ady' âpy ayaṃ tiṣṭhati.
vyaktaṃ tatra mano nidhāya bhavatā
muktā śarīreṇa sā.
mārgaṃ pota iv' ânila|pratihataḥ
kṛcchrāt tathā gāhase.

(walks about) Aha! That merchant boy Mr Shady hastens this way. Indeed he has lost his virginity by frequenting the bordello. He is a worthy vessel for the attentions of a person such as me. He is being scrupulously watched by his father who fears that his family will go down the drain. Somehow he has made it to the bordello, and now his body glows, taken pleasure in by his beloved. I absolutely must congratulate him. I will go up to him. *(approaches)* Master Shady! May you ever enjoy a fruitful youth. Surely you are coming from the house of Ms Spring's-Army.

What are you saying? "How do you know?" What is there to be known here? For Lord Spring makes a match of equals. And I am not unfamiliar with your affairs. By the way, where are you running away to, leaving behind your beloved who craves incessant love-making?*

What are you saying? "Now how can you know this?" This too is no mystery. How? 4.25

On your hand
  which you have rubbed around on her tearful
    face
one can see eye-liner.
Your coiffure is even now disheveled
  from falling at her feet.
It's obvious that you've abandoned her in body,
  leaving behind your heart.
You are cleaving a path with difficulty
like a boat tossed about by the wind.*

kiṃ bravīṣi? «tātaṃ tāvad avalokayiṣyāmi» iti. katham! anen' âiva veṣeṇa? avaskandaṃ dāsyati.

kiṃ bravīṣi? «yad' īdṛśīm avasthāṃ tāto me paśyej jīvita|parityāgam api kuryād» iti.

anavarata|surata|tṛṣṇāṃ kāminīṃ tyājayatā kiṃ tena na kṛtaṃ? pitā nāma khalu sa|yauvanasya puruṣasya mūrtimāñ chiro|rogaḥ. na ca kila bhoḥ pitṛmatā śakyam paraspar'|âmarṣa|vivardhita|paṇa|rāgasya s'|âdhikṣepa|vacan'|âlaṅkṛtasya tejasvi|puruṣa|nikaṣ'|ôpalasya dyūtasya darśana|mātram apy upalabdhum.

4.30 na ca kila śakyam samupahit'|ôtpala|khaṇḍakānāṃ sahakāra|tail'|âvasek'|ôdgata|candrakāṇāṃ kāminī|niḥśvāsa|vikṣobhita|taraṅgāṇāṃ pranṛtta|barhiṇ'|ākārāṇāṃ vāruṇī|caṣakāṇāṃ gandha|mātram api jñātum. na ca kila śakyaṃ dvidhā|bhūta|goṣṭhī|janeṣu vayasy'|ârdh'|āsan'|ôpaviṣṭa|gaṇikā|janeṣu kāminī|sāṃnidhyād a|mīmāṃsita|paṇeṣv āsakta|maṇḍaleṣu pakṣi|yuddheṣu prāśnikatvam api kartuṃ. na ca kila śakyaṃ vātāyan'|ābhoga|viniṣpatita|pīna|payodharābhiḥ sa|sambhram'|ôddhūta|lalit'|âgra|hastābhiḥ paura|vadhūbhiḥ sa|bahumānam avekṣyamānena mada|rabhasasya gaja|pateḥ

What are you saying? "Well, I have to see papa." What? In this outfit? He'll kill you.

What are you saying? "If my father sees me in such a condition he may perchance drop dead..."

What has he not done to try to make you leave this lusty woman who is addicted to incessant love-making? A father surely is an embodied headache for a man in his prime. It is truly impossible for someone who has a father to even get a glimpse of swagger-adorned gambling, the touchstone of spirited men, where the tension of betting is heightened by mutual rivalry.

It is even less possible to get even a whiff of wine-goblets 4.30
shaped like dancing peacocks, scattered with a trace of lotus petals, with moonlike circles produced by the sprinkling of mango-oil, rippling with the heaving breath of lovely women. Nor indeed is it possible to be a critic of cock-fights, where the spectators are divided into two camps, where courtesans are sharing seats with their companions, where, because of the proximity of their lovers, the stakes are not checked, in which there are intimate groups of enthusiasts. Nor is it possible for a man who is gazed upon admiringly by the wives of the citizens, whose lovely fingertips quiver with excitement and who put forward their large breasts through the openings of the windows, to tread the path of a lordly elephant who is violent with rut. Nor is it possible to haunt the high street on heroic nights red with blazing torches, girt in mail shirt, with a drawn sword for a sole companion, on the lookout for a major fracas,

panthānam anusartum. na ca kila śakyam ardh'|ōruka|parihiten' ākṛṣṭa|khaḍga|mātra|sahāyen' âkṛpaṇāṃ vṛttim ākāṅkṣatā mitr'|ârthe vā bandhana|bhed'|ôdyatena prajvalit'|ôlkā|piṅgalāsu vīra|rātriṣu nara|pati|mārgam avagāhitum. na ca kila śakyaṃ pratyupakāra|cint''|ôpahata|cittena saṃnivṛtta|ślāghā|doṣeṇa pratyupakāra|pīḍitena mitr'|ârthe sarvasva|tyāgaṃ kartum. sarvaṃ c' âitat sahyam. yat tu dāsī|putrāḥ pitaraḥ svayam apy an|anubhūta|yauvanā iva dhana|kupy'|ârthe veśa|vadhūbhyaḥ putrān vārayanti, atra me gṛhīta|tīkṣṇa|paraśor Jāmadagnyasya Rāmasya kṣatra|vadh'|ôdyatasy' êva lokam apaitṛkaṃ kartuṃ matir jāyate. atha vā yauvanam atilaṅghitaṃ nu ku|vṛddhaiḥ? na c' âitad vijānanti tapasvino yathā vikaca|kamal'|ântar|gata|salila|surabhir amṛta|rasa|sadṛś'|āsvādo mṛtam api puruṣaṃ saṃjīvayed veśyā|mukha|rasa iti. api ca,

kāñcī|tūryam asakta|pīna|jaghanaṃ
    visrambha|daṣṭ'|âdharaṃ
śvās'|ôtkampita|nartita|stana|taṭaṃ
    bhrū|bheda|jihm'|ēkṣaṇam
sītkār'|ânuviṣakta|roma|pulakaṃ
    kālena kop'|ânvitaṃ
veśyānāṃ ka ih' âsti bho mada|vaśād
    ājñā|rataṃ vismaret?

kiṃ bravīṣi? «anyac ca kaṣṭaṃ bhāvāya nivedayāmi» iti. kiṃ tat? kathayatu bhavān.

or ready to cut the fetters for a friend. Nor can someone give up everything for a friend, his heart tormented with concern to return a favor, free from the blemish of self-exaltation, obliged by debt. All this may be endured. But that those son-of-slave fathers ward off their sons from the women of the bordello for the sake of wealth which is just base metal, as if they had themselves never experienced youth: I have a mind to take up a sharp axe to de-father the world, just like the son of Jamad·agni, Rama, who was poised to exterminate the warriors. Or have these wretched elders perhaps simply missed out youth? The simpletons have no idea how the taste of a courtesans mouth, fragrant like the water inside a full-blown lotus, with a flavor comparable to ambrosia, can reanimate even a dead man. Moreover,

> The tinkle of the girdle,
> wide open plump thighs,
> lips bitten without hesitation,
> sloping breasts made to dance
>   by the tremor of sighs,
> side-glances with knitted brows,
> horripilation caused by love cries,
> eventually accompanied by anger—
> who in this world could forget
> the imperious love-making*
> with delirious courtesans?

What are you saying? "My friend, let me report you another disaster." What is it? Tell me, sir.

kiṃ bravīṣi? «tātaḥ kila māṃ dāra|karmaṇi niyuṅkte» iti. dhiṅ māṃ astu! mā tāvad bhoḥ! kaṣṭam īdṛśam api nāma mayā śrotavyaṃ? śakyam ūrdhva|hasten' ākranditum veśyā|mahāpatham kil' ôtsṛjya kula|vadhū|kumārgeṇa yāsyat' îti. paśyatu bhavān:

jāty|andhāṃ surateṣu dīna|vadanām
antar|mukh'|ābhāṣiṇīṃ
hṛṣṭasy' âpi janasya śoka|jananīṃ
lajjā|paṭen' āvṛtām
nirvyājaṃ svayam apy adṛṣṭa|jaghanāṃ
strī|rūpa|baddhāṃ paśuṃ
kartavyaṃ khalu n' âiva bhoḥ kula|vadhū|
kārāṃ praveṣṭuṃ manaḥ.

4.35 kiṃ bravīṣi? «eṣa eva me niścayaḥ» iti. yady eṣa bhavato niścayaḥ prītāḥ smaḥ. sadṛśam asmat|saṃsargasya. gacch' êdānīm. gṛham ev' āgamiṣyāmi punar api tvāṃ saṃjñām upalaṃbhayituṃ. *(parikramya)* ayaṃ hi tāvad atyākīrṇa|janatayā prakīrṇa|vīcī|valaya iva salila|nidhiḥ subhīma|darśano 'pi sukho 'vagāhituṃ Kusumapura|rāja|mārgaḥ. iha hi:

What are you saying? "It seems that papa has arranged a marriage for me." I'm doomed! Anything but that! Must I listen to such horrors? I could flail my arms and wail: straying from the highway of the courtesan he will take the dirt track of the wife of a good family. Observe, sir:

The heart really ought no to be condemned
to the prison of a chaste wife,
who is born blind in matters erotic,
has a dour visage, habitually mumbles,
inflicts dejection even upon the cheerful,
who is shrouded in a veil of modesty,
who plainly has never seen
even her own pudenda,
a dumb animal
appearing in the guise of a woman.*

What are you saying? "That is precisely my resolution." If 4.35
that truly is your resolution, sir, then I'm glad. This befits our friendship. Go for now. I'll come to your house and instruct you again. *(walks about)* So here is the High Street of Pátali·putra, delightful to plunge into even though it is terrifying to behold with its thronging crowds, like the ocean ringed with scattered waves. For here:

yo māṃ paśyati satvaro 'pi na kathāṃ

chitvā prayāty anyataḥ;

saṃbādhe 'pi dadāti c' ântaram asau

sarvaḥ prahṛṣṭo janaḥ;

kaś cin n' âticiraṃ vilambayati māṃ

kāry'|âtyay'|āśaṅkayā:

loka|jñaiḥ puruṣair aho pura|varasy'

āptaṃ yaśo lakṣyate.

(parikramya) aye! viṭa|matir iva veśa|gāmin" îyaṃ rathyā. ito yāsyāmaḥ. mayā hi:

kṛta iha kalaho hṛt" êha veśyā

cakitam iha drutam a|kṣaṇaṃ niśamya.

iti vayasi nave yad atra bhuktaṃ

tad anuvicintya samutsuko vrajāmi.

Whoever sees me, even if in hurry,
does not walk away interrupting his story.
Even in a congestion everybody happily gives way.
Nobody detains me for long,
fearing that they may obstruct my affairs.
Widely traveled men declare
the fame of this best of cities
to be well-deserved. ⁝
Whoever sees me flees elsewhere,
even if he is no hurry,
interrupting his chat.
Everybody rushes on,
their hair standing on end,
even if there is a danger of injury.
Within no time someone harasses me,
regardless of transgressing decorum.
Those who are familiar with its inhabitants
point out that the alleged fame
of this worst of cities is a mystery.**

(walks about) Oho! This road, like the mind of a pimp,* leads to the Courtesans' Quarter. I'm off. For,

Here I started a quarrel,
here I've "had" a courtesan,
here I was suddenly startled
hearing something improper.
Remembering all that I enjoyed here
in the flush of my youth,
I wander overcome with nostalgia.

(parikramya) hanta! labdhāḥ prāṇāḥ. eṣa veśam ev' âsmi praviṣṭaḥ. *(sparśaṃ rūpayitvā)*

4.40 niṣevya saṃlolita|mūrdhajāni
veśyā|mukhāny ardha|nirīkṣitāni
āyāti māly'|āsava|gandha|viddho
veśasya niśvāsa iv' âiṣa vāyuḥ.

aho nu khalu Kailāsa|śikhar'|ākāra|prāsāda|śikharasya veśa|vadhū|stana|taṭ'|âvanamyamāna|gavākṣasya sañcārit'|âgaru|dhūpa|durdinasya puṣp'|ôpahāra|prahasita|gṛh'|ôpadvārasya praṇādita|kāñcī|tūry'|ôtkaṇṭha|kāmi|janasya nūpura|svana|gadgada|bhāṣiṇaḥ Kāma|karm'|ânta|bhūtasya veśasya parā lakṣmīḥ! iha hi samudyata|kaṭākṣa|praharaṇāḥ sphuṭa|hasit'|ônmīlita|vimala|daśana|paṅktayo 'nibhṛta|bhrū|lat"|ânuvṛtta|vacana|vinyāsāḥ pīna|payodharatvād anavasthita|laghu|prāvaraṇā vibhramād a|prāvaraṇāś ca vibhrama|vilasita|capala|lalita|gatayaḥ Kāma|vijaya|patākā iva itas tataḥ saṃcaranti gaṇikā|paricārikāḥ. nitya|smit'|âlaṅkṛta|mukhānām a|vismaya|vismit'|âkṣīṇām snigdha|sukumāra|kuṭila|tanu|dīrgha|kṛṣṇa|keśīnāṃ śroṇī|cakr'|ôdvahana|manda|parikramāṇāṃ matta|dvirada|pati|gāminīnāṃ surata|prapāṇām iva tatra tatra vicarantīnām anibhṛta|madhura|cā-

(walks about) Yes! I breathe again. I've entered the brothel quarter. *(miming a touch)**

Here comes the breeze, 4.40
caressing the ruffled hair
and faces of courtesans
their eyes half-closed,
suffused with the fragrance
of garlands and wine,
like a sigh of the Courtesans' Quarter.

Behold the supreme splendor of the Courtesans' Quarter, where the turrets of the palaces resemble the peaks of Mount Káilasa, where the windowsills are leaned on by the sloping breasts of the hetaeras, which is cloudy with the diffused smoke of *ágaru* incense, whose side-doors laugh with flower-strings, where amorous men hope to hear the chimes of sounded girdles and musical instruments, whose halting speech is the sound of anklets, and which is the head office of Kāma. For here the courtesans' maids parade up and down like Kāma's triumphal banners, with readied glance-missiles, the rows of their stainless teeth displayed in open laughter, speaking words in consonance with provocative eyebrow movements; their flimsy blouses are uncontrollable because of their swelling breasts and they are unclothed as soon as they assume a pose; their delightful gait is unsteady with playful coquetry. One can see exquisite beauties, *petites dames* who are treasuries of coquetry, whose faces are adorned with perpetual smiles; their eyes are wide without wonder; their long, dark hair

ru|ceṣṭitānāṃ gaṇikā|dārikānāṃ dṛśyante vilāsa|nidhayo rūpa|viśesāḥ.

api ca, an|avarata|mṛdaṅga|niḥsvanāḥ sambhrānta|pārāvata|mithunā garjant' îva prāsāda|mālāḥ. ājñāpyamāna|śilpi|janāni sambhrānta|preṣya|varga|vilulita|puṣp'|ôpahārāṇi× spardhanta iv' ânyonyaṃ bhavana|dvārāṇi. rati|yuddha|śram'|âpahārīṇi saṃyojyante gandha|tailāni. pīna|stana|taṭa|visarpiṇaḥ piṣyante varṇakāḥ. manasvinī|jana|hṛdaya|sukumārā ādīyante māly"|âbhiyogāḥ. priyā|vacanam iva śrotr'|âvadhāna|karaṃ śrūyate vallakī|vādyaṃ. priya|jan'|âdhar'|ôpadaṃśa|praṇayī pracarati śīdhuḥ. api ca—

netrair ardha|nimīlitaiḥ stana|taṭaiḥ
savyāja|saṃdarśitair
hāsair vrīḍa|vibhūṣitaiḥ śruti|sukhair
alp'|âkṣarair bhāṣitaiḥ
mandair niśvasitaiḥ svabhāva|madhurair
gītaiś ca tāl'|ânvitair×
nity'|ākṛṣṭa|śarāsanaṃ Manasijaṃ
kurvanti veśy"|âṅganāḥ.

is smooth, soft, curly, and fine, they saunter slowly with the burden of the orb of their buttocks and carry themselves as rutting majestic elephants do; they are water fountains of carnal passion as it were, ranging hither and thither, and their attractive gestures are uninhibitedly sweet.

Furthermore, the rows of the mansions, thundering as it were with incessant drum-beats, alarm the pigeon couples. The gates of the mansions vie with each other, marshalling hosts of craftsmen, with their flower ornaments tossed about by bustling servants. Fragrant oils which allay the fatigue of the battle of love are being applied. Colored powders, to be spread on the slopes of swelling breasts, are being ground. Garland accoutrements, tender as the hearts of virtuous women, are being put on. The music of lutes, which engages the ear as much as the words of one's beloved, is audible. Wine, intimate friend of the lips of lovers and chutneys, flows. Moreover,

Courtesans
make the heart-born God of Love
  perpetually draw his bow
—with half closed eyes,
with sloping breasts flashed under any pretext,
with laughter adorned with bashfulness,
with measured words, delighting the ear,
with inherently sweet, deep sighs,
with songs perfectly in time.*

(parikramya) aye! iyaṃ khalu tāvad yauvana|madād ânavekṣita|stana|prāvaraṇā pelav'|âṃśuka|paridhānā jaghan'|ābharaṇa|kṛta|nīvī vibhram'|âvamukt'|âika|karṇa|pāśena vitrasta|hariṇī|cañcal'|âkṣeṇa nirbhukta|piṇḍit'|ôṣṭhena munīnām api manaḥ|kampana|samarthena su|labha|hasitena mukhena Madanasenāyāḥ paricārikā Vāruṇikā nāma vāma|hast'|âṅguli|saṃdaṃśena karṇ'|ôtpalaṃ racayantī kiṃ|cid|udyat'|âika|bhrūlatā mām avekṣya prahasy' âtikrāmati. asyā hi—

4.45 romāñcaṃ darśayatā
  kapola|deśe viśāla|jaghanāyāḥ
karṇ'|ôtpalena kṛta iva
  nirakṣaraṃ cumban'|ôdghātaḥ.

kā śaktir anabhibhāṣy" âtikramitum! abhibhāṣiṣye tāvad enāṃ. vāsu Vāruṇike! nigṛhyatām ātmā. katham! asmad|vacanaṃ skhalī|kṛtya gacchaty eva. sundari! anena skhalīkaraṇena prītāḥ smaḥ. kathaṃ! prahasya sthitā. *(upetya)* kṛtam añjalinā! pṛcchāmas tāvat kiṃ cit: ken' âsya *śarat/kamala/rajaḥ/puñja/piñjarasya gagana/tal'/ônmukhasy'* êva cakravāka|mithunasya stana|yugalasya te pratham'|âvatāraḥ sukham upabhujyate? katham! "hī!" ity ek'|âkṣaram uktvā sa|vrīḍam avekṣya māṃ vrajati tūrṇam anavasit'|ârtha|bhāṣiṇī. tat khalu kāmasya sarvasvam!

(walks about) Oho! Here comes Ms Tipsy, the maid servant of Ms Cupid's-Army! With her youthful exuberance she cares not for her breast coverlet; her garments are made of transparent fine muslin, and she has made a mini-skirt out of her hip-ornament. Her face lacks one earring because of her haste, her eyes are as flighty as those of a startled doe, her lower lip, bumpy because it has been severely enjoyed, is capable of shaking even the hearts of seers, and is quick to laughter. She is sticking a lily behind her ear, using the two fingers of her left hand as pincers, slightly raises one eyebrow as soon as she spots me, laughs, and strides on. For,

The ear-lotus displays goose pimples 4.45
on the cheek of this wide-hipped lady,
as though
it had silently kissed her.

What strength do I have to pass her by without talking to her? So I will greet her. My dear Ms Tipsy! Detain yourself! What! She ignores* my words and just carries on. My beauty! I am pleased by your insult. What? She has stopped, laughing. *(approaches)* You need not pay you respects. Let me ask you something. Who is it that happily enjoys this first swell of your pair of breasts, *golden like an autumn lotus with masses of cosmetic powder, pointing heavenwards,* as though they were a pair of sheldrakes, *yellowed with a mass of pollen of autumnal lotuses, flying up to the sky*? What? Squealing just the single syllable "hee"* she bashfully averts her eyes and hastens away, muttering to herself under her breath.

(parikramya) aye Bandhumatikā khalv eṣā sva|gṛha|dvāra|koṣṭha|gatā pārśv'|ôpaviṣṭayā Caturikayā paricārikayā pradīyamāna|prativacanā bhrūlatā|sañcāra|cikurām sāy'|âhna|nalina|sukumārām dṛṣṭiṃ kṛtvā svayam eva mekhalāṃ saṃyojayati. aho yauvan'|ânurūpo vyāpāraḥ! aho sukumāraṃ karm' ânuṣṭhitam! aho lalito 'bhiniveśaḥ! aho kārkaśyaṃ prakāśayate yatnaḥ! aho darpād raśanā|dāma|saṃyojayantyā kim iv' ânayā n' ôktaṃ bhavati? avaśyam asyā vihāra|kāla|caturatā pūjayitavyā. idam upagamyate. *(utpetya)* vāsu karma|siddhir astu te! bhavati kṛtam āsanena. pṛcchāmas tāvat kiṃ cit—

eṣā kāmi|kar'|âṅguli|priya|sakhī
nābhi|hrad'|âmbhaḥ|srutir
vidyut kṣauma|valāhakasya rucirā
kārkaśya|yogy" âraṇiḥ
maurvī Kāma|śar'|āsanasya lalitā
vāk śroṇi|bimbasya te
chinnā mānini mekhalā rati|sukh'|
âbhyās'|âkṣa|mālā katham?

That indeed is the essence of love!

(walks about) Oho, here is Ms Many-Affairs* in the doorway of her house, in conference with her maid Ms Crafty seated at her side. Casting a glance unsteady with the dance of her vine-like eyebrows and as tender as an evening lily, she adjusts her girdle unaided. O what a task befitting her youth! O how delicate her dexterity! O how lovely her industry! O her effort betrays her tenacity! O what insolent words will she not say, trying to affix the fillets of her girdle! I definitely must worship her skill at wasting her free time. So I approach her. *(approaching)* Darling, may your enterprise succeed. Madam! Don't bother offering me a seat. But let me ask you something:

O irascible woman!
How did this girdle of yours break,
the dear friend of the fingers of your lovers,
the stream of you navel-pond,
a lightning-flash bright upon the cloud
    of your silken garment,
a handhold suitable for manhandling,
the string of Kama's bow,
the sweet voice
    of the circumference of your buttocks
a rosary to count repeated orgasms?

athavā kim atra jñeyam?[×]

4.50 visrambh'|âpahṛt'|âṃśukasya[×] śayane
prīty" ēkṣitasya priye-
ṇ' ônmatta|dvirad'|êndra|masta|kaṭabhū|[×]
līl"|ôday'|ālambinaḥ
sparś'|âvāpti|kutūhalasya jaghanasy'
āvalgatas te dhruvaṃ
tantrī|cheda iv' âkarod virasatāṃ
tāmr'|âkṣi! kāñcī|vadhaḥ.[×]

katham! adho|mukhī saṃvṛttā.[×] kiṃ[×] n' âsti prativacanam? idaṃ gamyate.

kiṃ bravīṣi? «na gantavyam» iti. hanta! eṣo 'smi mantr'|âvaruddha iva bhujaṅgamo 'jaṅgamaḥ samvṛttaḥ. katham! vrajāmi. eṣa dhvasto 'smi. *(parikramya, karṇaṃ dattvā)* aye! Rāmadāsī|gṛhe strī prarudit" êva.[×] iha khalu bahubhiḥ kāraṇair upapadyate. tatra kena khalu kāraṇe-n' âiṣā roditi? kutaḥ?

syāt kopād rudita|dhvaniḥ[×] sarabhaso,
dainyāt tathā śīpharo,
vicchinnaḥ praṇayād, bhayena viraso,
harṣ'|ôdayād gadgadaḥ.
manye krodha|vaśaṃ|gatā praṇayiṇī
hy eṣā sa|dainyā tathā
prārambhe rabhasaṃ virāma|bahulaṃ
mandaṃ tathā roditi.

Rather, why should this be unclear?

When, on the bed, the skirt was intimately 4.50
removed from your buttocks
and your lover fondly gazed upon them*
as, eager to be fondled, they rose up playfully,
like the temples of a rutting elephant—
O red-eyed girl, the breaking of your girdle
surely must have made them uninspiring,
just like the snapping of a lute's wire.

What! She lowers her head. No reply? I better leave.

What are you saying? "Don't leave." Here I stand, immobilized like a snake transfixed by a spell. What! I can walk! I'm off now. *(walks around and listens)* Oho! It seems a woman is crying in the house of Rama·dasi. In this case we may postulate many causes. Which among these is the specific reason for her crying? For,

If sobbing is caused by anger
it swells to a *crescendo*,
if by misery
it fades in a *diminuendo*,
if by affection
it breaks in a *staccato*,
if by fear it is discordant,
if by the arising of joy it is vibrato.
I believe her to be under the sway of anger,
for she is in love, and also miserable:
her weeping is *crescendo* at its onset,
much interrupted, and then fades away.

āśaṅkate Rāmadāsīm eva me hṛdayam. praviśāmas tāvat. *(praviṣṭakena)* hanta s" âiv' êyam. katham! māṃ dṛṣṭvā bhṛśataraṃ praruditā.

4.55 asyā netr'|ânta|vibhraṣṭāḥ
kopa|sarvasva|sambhṛtāḥ
priy'|âparādha|gaṇanāṃ
kurvant" îv' âśru|bindavaḥ.

(upetya) mānini! kim idam?

āpūry' âbhinav'|âmbhuja|dyuti|hare
netre prayāto 'dharaṃ
tad|bhraṣṭaḥ kaṭhinau gataḥ stana|taṭau
tatr' âpy|alabdh'|āspadaḥ
bāṣpas te mṛdu|roma|rāji|lulitaḥ
śoka|prasaṅg'|ôjjhito
nābhiṃ pūrayati priy'|âṅguli|mukha|
prakṣepa|līl"|ôcitām.

na khalu kṛtam ātmanaḥ sadṛśaṃ Kuñjarakeṇa?

kiṃ bravīṣi? «so 'yam evaṃ para|yuvati|cihnit'|oṣṭho mām abhigataḥ, upālabhyamānaś ca mayā roṣa|calena nirgataḥ, adya bahūny ahāni n' āvartate» iti. ha ha ha! aho! aparādha|saṃmardaḥ! sarvath" âiken' âpy aparādhena tīkṣṇaṃ kul'|ôtsādakarāṇāṃ daṇḍam arhati, kiṃ punar

My heart suspects it to be Ramadasi herself. Let's enter now. *(mimes entering)* Oh dear! It really is her. What! Seeing me, she wails all the more.

Her tear-drops, 4.55
tumbling from the corners of her eyes,
brimming with the quintessence of wrath,
seem to count the offences of her lover.

(approaches) Angry woman! What's this all about?

Your tear-drop sent forth by grief
wells in your eyes
that steal the beauty of a fresh lotus,
rolls down to your lip, falls from that,
reaches the firm slopes of your breasts,
there too it finds no rest,
shivers along the fine line of hair,
and fills your navel,
which deserves to be fondled
by the fingertips of your lover.

Surely Jumbo has not committed something that befits him?

What are you saying? "That man came to me, his lip marked by another woman, and as I reproached him, ran off feigning anger. For many days he has not returned." Dear me! What a way to add insult to injury! He absolutely deserves the severe punishment of those who destroy their own clan for committing just a single one of these offences, how much more for such an aggravation

eteṣāṃ saṃnipātena? tad evam api tu gate baddha|megha|yūthaṃ kālam avekṣya sahāmahe dur|janasy' âvalepam. samprati pārthivānām api tāvad anyonya|baddha|vairāṇāṃ pratinivṛttāḥ kalahāḥ, kiṃ punaḥ śirīṣa|kusuma|sukumāra|cittasya kāminī|janasya? yadi te mad|vacanaṃ pramāṇaṃ bhavati kālam avaloky' âdy' âiva priyo 'bhisārayitavyaḥ.

4.60 śarvaryām avagāhya harmya|śikharāl
lagn'|âvalamb'|âṃbudān
mārgaṃ bhīru gṛha|praṇāli|salil'|ôd-
gāra|svan'|āpūritam
kāntaṃ prāpya tataḥ payoda|pavanair
udvepit'|âṅgyā tvayā
vaktr'|ôṣṇ'|âpahṛt'|oṣṭha|kampa|viśadaṃ
raty|antare kathyatām.

katham? udbhinna|romāñcau kapola|talau vacanasya naḥ pratigrahaṃ nivedayataḥ. sādhayāmas tāvat.

(parikramya) aye! eṣā khalu sā Ratisenā garbha|gṛh'|âvarodha|janita|sveda|bindu|seken' ârdh'|ônmīlita|cāru|nayana|viprekṣitena kapola|pārśva|lagna|mūrdhajena mukhena nūnaṃ s'|âvaśeṣa|madā sāṃpratam eva pratibuddhā, tathā hi gavākṣa|mukha|mārutasy' ātmānam upanayantī ramaṇīyāyāṃ khalv avasthāyāṃ vartate. abhi-

of insults. But even if this is how the matter stands, considering that it is the time when banks of clouds throng together, we may endure the insult of this wretch. For now even kings who hold each other in hostile contempt set aside their quarrels,* how much more lovers with hearts tender like *shirísha* flowers? If my words mean anything to you, take heed of the season and hasten to your lover at once.

At night descend 4.60
from the tower of your mansion
  wreathed in hanging clouds, to the street,
echoing with the sound of water
  gushing from the spouts on the houses,
O timid girl,
and when you reach your lover,
your body shivering with cloud-born wind,
speak your mind to him, clearly,
in between bouts of love-making,
the tremor of your lip
  allayed by the heat of his mouth.

What? The down on her cheeks standing on end reveals that she pays heed to my words. So I'm off.

(walks about) Here indeed is Ms Army-of-Lust, her face speckled with droplets of perspiration because of her confinement to the inner chambers, squinting with her half-closed, lovely eyes, her tresses clinging to the sides of her cheeks. She must have just woken up, for, still somewhat groggy, she exposes herself to the wind entering through the open window. How lovely she is to

bhāṣiṣye tāvad enāṃ. *(abhigamya)* vāsu! subhagā bhava! tvāṃ hy alp'|âvaśeṣa|madāṃ s'|âvaśeṣa|saṃdhyā|rāgām iva pratīcīṃ dṛṣṭvā diśaṃ prasrasta|śar'|āsanaḥ Kusumāyudho 'pi tāvad vyākulatāṃ gacchet, kim aṅga punar anyaḥ?

praṇaṣṭā na vyaktir,
bhavati vacasaḥ s" âiva mṛdutā,
na rāgo netr'|âbje
tyajati, na ca lajjā vyapagatā,
smṛtiḥ pratyāyātā,
parihṛṣitam ady' âpi ca mukhaṃ.
mado doṣān tyaktvā
tvayi pariṇatas tiṣṭhati guṇaiḥ.

Ratisene! visarjitum arhasi mām. bhavati, n' âham aprārambhas tvāṃ moktum utsahe. katham! prasahy' âvaghāṭito gavākṣaḥ. hanta! visṛṣṭāḥ smaḥ.

4.65 *(parikramya)* hanta! vimanāḥ khalv asmy atikrāntaḥ. iyaṃ hi Pradyumnadāsī prasakta|surata|glāna|kapolen' âtyāyata|nayana|sañcāreṇa tilak'|âvabheda|piñjarī|kṛta|lalāṭ'|ôddeśena vilulit'|âlaka|śobhinā lagnam iva rati|pariśramam udvahatā vadanena jaghana|bimb'|âṃśuk'|ântara|dṛśyamānābhir abhinava|nakha|kṣata|rājibhir vimala|salil'|ântargatābhir iva phull'|âśoka|chāyābhiḥ surat'|âvamarda|mṛdita|maṇḍan" âvasita|samara|śithil'|ākalp" êva nāga|vadhūḥ pravāta|pradīpam iva pāṇinā pracchādy'

behold! So I'll speak to her. *(approaches)* My dear, enjoy yourself! Seeing you, slightly tipsy, like the western quarter flushed with the redness of twilight, even Kama would be bewildered and drop his flower-bow, how much more someone else?

Your personality is not impaired,
the sweetness of your voice is the same,
passion does not leave your eyes,
and you've lost none of your modesty,
recollection has returned
and your mouth is still smiling.
Intoxication, setting aside its defects,
transformed, attends you with virtues.

O Army-of-Lust! Please permit me to take my leave. Madam, I dare not leave without your inchoation. What! She slammed the window. Well! I am dismissed.

(walks about) Damn! Absent-minded as I am, I almost passed her by. For here is Ms Slave-to-Kama, adorning the street in the red-light district, betraying her fatigue brought on by love-making, which seems to cling to her face, its cheeks wan from her addiction to sex, her large eyes rolling, her forehead yellowed with her *tilak* rubbed all over it, beautiful with disheveled locks. She has rows of fresh nail-wounds, visible through the transparent skirt covering the circumference of her buttocks, appearing like blossoming *áshoka* flowers fallen into clear water. With her ornaments broken in love-sport, she looks like a female elephant with her accoutrements hanging loose at the end of battle. She covers her lower lip with 4.65

âdhar'|oṣṭham anuyāta|kiśor" îva padāt pada|śataṃ gacchantī veśa|mārgam alaṅkurute. iṣṭā naḥ kāminī! parihasiṣyāmas tāvad enāṃ. *(upetya)* vāsu! kim idaṃ priya|daśana|pad'|âdhiṣṭhitasya daśana|vasanasya sa|vraṇasy' êva yodhasya *ślāghyaṃ vapuś* chādyate? kathaṃ! prahasitā! hā dhik! kṛta eva naḥ paurobhāgyena doṣaḥ, asyā hi mand'|ārambheṇ' âpi prahasitena vikṛtam eva danta|kṣateṣu. kutaḥ?

sītkār'|ôtpatita|stanī stana|taṭ'|ôt-
kṣep'|âti|nimn'|ôdarī
bhrū|bhed'|âñcita|locanā kṣata|ruj"|ā-
dhūt'|âgra|hast'|âmbujā
yady any" âpi samākṣipej jana|manāṃsy
evaṃ prahasy' âṅganā
kāminyā hasitavyam eva tu bhaved
daṣṭ'|âdhar'|oṣṭhe mukhe.

kiṃ bravīṣi? "cirasya khalu bhāvo dṛśyate." iti. anena durdina|pātakena gṛha|bandhane 'smin niruddhaḥ kṛtaḥ. atha bhavatyā ko 'nugṛhītaḥ?

kim āha bhavatī? "Rāmilakasy' ôdavasitād āgacchāmi" îti. sadṛśaḥ saṃyogaḥ sthāvaro 'stu. aho, ekena khalu Rāmilakena Madan'|âgrahāro hṛtaḥ.[×] kutaḥ?

her hand as if it were a lamp flickering in the wind, and moves with a hundred tiny steps as if trailed by a child. This passionate woman is to my liking! So lets have a joke with her. *(approaches)* My dear! Why do you conceal the *outstanding beauty* of your lip, which, invested with the marks of your lover's teeth, resembles the *glorious body* of a wounded hero? What! She smiles! Dear me! I have hurt her with my impertinence. For though she smiles but slightly, her bite-wounds cause her pain.* For,

Her breasts swell as she draws a deep breath,
her belly much deepened
  by the upward thrust of her breasts,
her eyes elongated
  by her raised eye-brows,
the fingers of her lotus-hands shaken
  with the agony of her bite-marks
—if just any woman can enchant the hearts of men
  smiling in this way,
a passionate woman surely is obliged to smile,
when her lower lip is bitten.

What are you saying? "Long time no see." I have been confined to the prison of my house by this criminal weather. But who has enjoyed your attentions madam?

What are you saying, miss? "I am coming form Rámilaka's* house." May such a good match be long lasting. I say! Rámilaka is the sole inheritor of the Love God's estates. Why?

saphalaṃ tasya kṛś'|ôdari
  yuvatvam asamasta|vihasitaṃ yas te
s'|ârdha|śaśāṅka|chāyaṃ
  caṣakam iva mukhaṃ samāpibati.

4.70 vāsu! durvihagebhyo rakṣitavyo 'dharaḥ. gamyatām. vayam api sādhayamaḥ.

(parikramya) aye! idaṃ tad adhvanīna|bhayād Kumbhakarṇa|vadanam iva nitya|nimīlitaṃ bhavana|dvāraṃ yatra dhūrta|dvayaṃ prativasati Viśvalakaḥ Sunandā ca. Viśvalako hi bhakṣita|sarvasvo nagna|śramaṇaka iva śarīra|mātr'|âvaśiṣṭaḥ kevalaṃ priya|gaṇikatvād āgata|keś'|ôpadravām api Sunandāṃ vāyasa iva grām'|ôpāntaṃ na muñcati. s" âpi c' âtra proṣita|yauvanā kāntāra|śuṣka|nad" îva kasya cid anabhigamyā Viśvalakaṃ kil' ânuvartate. tan na yuktam etad dvandvam anabhibhāṣy' âtikramitum. ayam ākrandaḥ kriyate. bho ko 'tra dharate? *(karṇaṃ dattvā)* prayātasy' êv' âśvasya khura|puṭa|nipāta|dhvaniḥ pād'|ôtkṣepa|sama|layaḥ kāṣṭha|pādukā|śabdaḥ śrūyate. sannihiten' âtra Viśvalakena bhavitavyaṃ. hanta! sa ev' âiṣa virauti!

O slender-waisted lady,
the youth of him has borne fruit,
who drinks deeply your mouth
  opened somewhat in a smile,
resembling a goblet
  reflecting the half-moon.

Darling! Please guard your lip from naughty birds. Off you 4.70
go, I'm also moving on.

(walks about.) At last! Here is the door of the hovel where the rogue-couple Mr Busybody and Ms Pleasing live, ever-shut in fear of unbidden guests like the demon Kumbha·karna's* mouth. For Mr Busybody, who squandered all he owns, stripped bare to his body like a naked mendicant, sticks to Ms Pleasing even though her hair is about to fall out only because he is addicted to prostitutes, just as a crow will hover about the outskirts of a village. As for her, well beyond her prime, whom it is pointless to approach, like a dried up river in the wilderness, she now, it seems, attends upon Mr Busybody. So it would not be right to pass this couple without paying my respects. I'll start shouting. Who lives here? *(listens)* I hear the clattering of wooden platform shoes in time with approaching footsteps, which is like the thundering of the hooves of a galloping horse. Mr Busybody must be close. Hark! It is he who bellows!

bhoḥ kiṃ bravīṣi? "ka eṣa gardabha|vratam anutiṣṭhati?" iti. aham Yama|dūtaḥ Sunand"|ârtham āgataḥ. katham! asmat|svaram abhijñāya tūṣṇīṃ|bhūtaḥ. aṃgho na prayacchasi dvāraṃ? tena hi sthirīkriyatām ātmā. eṣa śāp'|âgnim utsṛjāmi.

līl"|ôdyatasya kalahe
    nūpura|saṃkṣobha|ninada|mukharasya
dūrībhavatu śiras te
    vilāsinī|vāma|pādasya.

etad apāvṛta|dvāram. praviśāmas tāvat. *(praviṣṭakena)*

4.75 kim āha bhavān? «kiṃ na dayitāḥ smo bhāvasya? ayuktaṃ ×nām' ēdṛśaṃ śāp'|ôtsargaṃ kartum» iti. samyag abhihitam. īdṛśo hi śāpo Brahma|lokam api kampayet, kiṃ punar bhavantam? tad idānīm asya śapasya pratīkār'|ârthaṃ prāyaścittam. kutaḥ?

vikaca|nav'|ôtpala|tilakā
    sa|sambhram'|ôtkṣepa|cañcala|taraṅgā
tasyai deyā madirā
    yā hṛdaya|kuṭumbinī bhavataḥ.

evam upaviśāmaḥ. *(upaviśya)* kṛtaṃ pādyena, Kusumapura|rāja|mārgo hi prakṛti|niṣpaṅkatayā× harmya|talāny apy atiśete. na khalu me pādau durlalitau kartavyau.

Hullo, what are you saying? "Who is it who is observing the donkey-vow?" I'm Death's messenger come for Ms Pleasing. What! Recognizing my voice he has fallen silent. Well, won't you open the door? Then stand firm. Behold, I spew forth the fire of a curse.

May your head be far removed
 from the left foot of a dallying woman,
playfully lifted up in a love-quarrel,
jingling with the sound of a shaking anklet.

The door is open. So I enter. *(mimes entering)*

What are you saying, sir? "Aren't we dear to you? It is indeed not proper to cast such a curse." Well said. For such a curse could make even Brahma's world quake, how much more you? So now then the propitiation to countermand this curse. How? 4.75

Some liquor,
on which floats a new-blown lily,
rippling with waves when lifted too quickly,
must be given to her
 who keeps the household of your heart,
who has a vast forehead-mark
 patterned on a fresh lily
and who saunters about sportively
 with graceful swift movements.

With this I take a seat. *(sits down)* Don't trouble yourself to offer me water to lave my feet, for the high street of Pátali·putra* is by nature spotlessly clean, even more

kim āha bhavān? «Viṣṇudāsa | prabhṛtīnāṃ goṣṭhikānām Rāmilaka|goṣṭhake samāgatānāṃ paraspara|vivāda|ramyāḥ ke cit saṃśayāḥ samutpannāḥ kāma|tantre. tāṃś ca yadā kārtsnyena na śāknuvanti vaktuṃ, tato 'smy ahaṃ tair ātma|darśanaṃ śrāvayitum abhyarthitaḥ. tatra may" âpi sva|darśanam uktam. iccheyaṃ tāvad Devilaka|bhāvam api tam ev' ârthaṃ śrāvayitum. tatra yad bhāvo vakṣyati tan naḥ pramāṇaṃ bhaviṣyati. etam arthaṃ bhāvaṃ śrāvayituṃ gṛham ev' āgantumanāḥ. atha bhāvena svayam ev' ātmā darśitaḥ. yadi tāvad bhāvaḥ kṣaṇikas tataḥ pravakṣyāmi» iti.

ājñāpayatu bhavān. avahito 'smi. śaktito vakṣyāmaḥ. ayaṃ tu durlalita iva dārakaḥ *kaṭī/pradeśaṃ* na muñcati vāyuḥ. ataś cir' | âdhyāsanaṃ na śaknomi kartum. yady abhirucitaṃ bhavate parikrāntāv eva saṃbhāṣiṣyāvahe. vistīrṇ" êyaṃ goṣṭhī|śālā.

4.80 kiṃ bravīṣi? «evaṃ, n' âsti doṣaḥ» iti. *(utthāya)* bravītu bhavān.

kiṃ bravīṣi? «yady arth'|ârtham eva veśyānāṃ puruṣaiḥ saha saṃbandhaḥ kathaṃ tāsām uttam' | âdhama | madhyamatvaṃ vijñeyam?» iti. bho dānaṃ nāma sarva | sāmānyaṃ vaśīkaraṇaṃ lokasya, viśeṣatas tu veśa | vadhū-

than palatial terraces. My feet do not need to be cosseted.

What are you saying, sir? "Connoisseurs such as Vishnu·dasa gathered in Rámilaka's salon and some difficulties, delightful due to the clash of opinions, have arisen a propos the topic of *ars amatoria*. And when they found themselves incapable of fully unraveling these, then it was I who was solicited to put forth my hypotheses. And so I advanced my hypotheses. May I request now the honorable Dévilaka also to expound on this matter? Whatever you say on this topic we shall take as authority. I was on the verge calling upon you at home to hear you elaborate on this matter. Now you yourself have put in an appearance. So if you have a moment to spare, let me explain."

At your service, sir! I'm all ears. I'll hold forth to my ability. But wind refuses to leave my *backside** like a spoilt brat that clings to the *hip*. So I cannot remain seated for long. If it please you, then let us converse while perambulating; this salon is spacious.

What are you saying? "Sure, no problem." *(They stand up.)* 4.80
Please speak, sir.

What are you saying? "If it is money alone that binds courtesans to men, then how can they be classified into superior, inferior or middling types?"* Sir! Gifts are in fact a universal means of winning over people, but especially

nām. tath" âpi vidyate viśeṣaḥ. kuto 'pi c' ôktaṃ parā-para|jñaiḥ:

dānād rāgam upaiti veśa|yuvatir
niṣkāraṇād v" âdhamā,
madhyā rūpam avekṣya yauvana|yutaṃ
dānena vā hṛṣyati,
dātāraṃ vigata|spṛhaṃ su|vayasaṃ
rūp'|âdhikaṃ c' âiva bho
dākṣiṇyena vibhūṣitaṃ khalu naraṃ
nāry uttamā sevate.

kiṃ bravīṣi? «kāmayamānā veśyā kathaṃ vijñeyā?» iti.× tad vakṣyāmaḥ, śrūyatām:

kāntā netr'|ârdha|pātā,
vadana|ruci|karāḥ sasmitā bhrū|vilāsāḥ,
sākūtā× vākya|leśāḥ
saha|tala|ninadā dṛṣṭa|naṣṭāś ca hāsāḥ,
nābhī|kakṣa|stanānāṃ
vivaraṇam, asakṛt|sparśanaṃ mekhalānāṃ,
śvās'|āyāsāś ca dīrghā
Madana|śara|hatāṃ kāminīṃ sūcayanti.

so in the case of courtesans. Nevertheless there is a difference. In all cases those who understand esoteric and exoteric matters teach that:

A young prostitute of the inferior type
falls in love as a consequence of gifts,
  or without a cause;
the middling type becomes infatuated
  by seeing beauty in consort with youth,
  or due to gifts;
a lady of the superior type shows affection
  to a benefactor of a ripe age,
  free from craving,
  who is more than just handsome,
but instead, sir!,
is a man whose ornament is
  appreciation.

What are you saying? "How is one to detect that a courtesan is in love?" I'll explain, listen:

Lovely, sly side-glances,
dancing eye-brows
  with smiles enlivening her face,
innuendoes, fleeting giggles
  punctuated with claps,
flashing the navel,
  arm-pits, and breasts,
fiddling with the girdle,
and deep, drawn out sighs
reveal a passionate woman
  struck by Kama's arrows.

4.85 kiṃ bravīṣi? «tatra kāma|liṅgāni bahūni bruvate. śaṭha|prāyatvād veśyā|janasya niṣṭh"|ôcitatvāc ca ka etac chraddhāsyati? tat kāmayamānā kathaṃ vijñeyā?" iti. śrūyatām:

sāsrā niśvāsāḥ sneha|yuktā ca dṛṣṭiḥ
kārśyaṃ pāṇḍutvaṃ sveda | bind' | ûdgamaś ca
kṣīṇe dravye 'pi prārthanā kāminīnāṃ
bhāv'|āsaktānāṃ bhāva|śuddhiṃ vadanti.

(parikramya) kiṃ bravīṣi? «prathamaḥ samāgamaḥ kena kāraṇena saṃmoham utpādayati?» iti. śrūyatāṃ: prathamaḥ samāgamaḥ khalu yūnāṃ na kāminīnām a|niyoga|sthānam. tat sthāne khalu muhyanti tapasvinaḥ. kutaḥ?

duḥkhā śleṣayituṃ kathā, prativaco
labdhuṃ ca duḥkhaṃ, tato
jāte 'pi pracure kathā|vyatikare
visraṃbhaṇaṃ duṣkaram,
visrambhe 'pi sati svabhāva|sadṛśī
duḥkhā vidhātuṃ ratiḥ,
samyak|prāpta|rat" âpi veśa|yuvatī
rajyeta vā n' âiva vā.

What are you saying? "Many such signs of passion are taught. But because courtesans are generally deceptive and because these are the signs of their trade, who would place his trust in them?* So how is one to detect that she is in love?" Listen. 4.85

Tearful sighs, an affectionate gaze,
  emaciation, paleness,
  a mist of droplets of perspiration,
  showing an interest in a man
  even when his money is gone
betray the sincerity of a passionate woman in love.*

(walks about) What are you saying? "What is the logical reason that the first date is so confusing?" Listen. For young men—not for passionate woman, though—the first encounter is clearly not a suitable occasion to enact the theory. It is natural that the poor men are so confused. Why?

It's difficult strike up a conversation,
and hard to get an answer,
and even if a lively conversation should ensue
it's difficult to win her confidence,
and even if confidence be won
it's nearly impossible to have her at will,
and even if she is enjoyed
  to one's heart's content—
the young courtesan may
  or may not show interest.

api ca,

4.90 rājani vidvan|madhye
vara|yuvatīnāṃ ca saṃgame prathame
sādhvasa|dūṣita|hṛdayaś
paṭur api vāg|āturo bhavati.

(parikramya) kiṃ bravīṣi? «kena khalu kāraṇena nirguṇāsv api darśana|mātrakeṇ' âiva sneho bhavati? tāsu ca vyalīkam utpādayantīṣu kiṃ pratipattavyam?» iti. pratyakṣe hetu|vacanaṃ nirarthakam. asty etan mahad avakāśam Anaṅgasya. yāsu tu nirguṇāsv api rajyante manuṣyās tāsu vyalīkam utpādayantyaḥ śīghram eva parityājyāḥ. kutaḥ?

priya|virahe yad duḥkhaṃ
sahyaṃ tad bhavati sattva|yuktasya
priya|jana|vimānitānāṃ
na rohati parikṣataṃ hṛdayam.

kim āha bhavān? «yas tu nāryāḥ priyo bhavati tasya sā n' âtibahumānyā priyā bhavati: s" âpi kiṃ parityājyā?» iti. na na na! anyāsv api kāminīṣv āyatiṃ rakṣatā svaṃ ca dākṣiṇyam adūṣayatā tasyām api tasmin tasmin kāle raktavad viceṣṭitavyam. kutaḥ?

Furthermore,

Before the king, among scholars, 4.90
 and during the first encounter
 with a beautiful girl,
even a smart man, his heart spoiled by fear,
 becomes afflicted with stammering.

(walks about) What are you saying? "For what reason do men fall in love at first sight even with worthless women? And what line of action should we take when they cheat on us?" When something is directly perceived, there is no use in stating a reason for it.* Kama has great latitude in these matters. But the cheaters among the worthless women with whom men fall in love must be ditched instantaneously. Why?

A man of strong character
can endure the bitterness of separation
 from his beloved.
The grievously wounded heart
 of those scorned by their loved ones
will never mend.

What are you saying, sir? "What if a woman falls in love with a man, but for him she is not the beloved whom he really appreciates: should he leave her?" No, not at all! While maintaining his affairs with his other sweethearts too, and not slacking in his gallant behavior, he should act towards her from time to time as if he were a man in love. Why?

ye kāminīṃ guṇavatīṃ ca sa|yauvanāṃ ca
nārīṃ narāḥ praṇayinīṃ ca vimānayanti
te bhoḥ kṛṣīvala|vacaḥ|paridagdha|cittair
gobhiḥ samaṃ pṛthu|mukheṣu haleṣu yojyāḥ.

4.95 *(parikramya)* kiṃ bravīṣi? «yas tu kṛt'|âparādhas tena kathaṃ kāminī samanuneyā?» iti. sthāne khalu saṃśayaḥ, praṇayinīnāṃ hi kopo viṣama|jvara iva duś|cikitso bhavati. tath" âpy avaśyam asyāḥ kopa|pratyāvartakena bhavitavyam. sāmprata|kālikāś ca kaumārakāḥ pāda|patanam ev' âtr' âuṣadhaṃ paśyanti. tan mayā n' âtibahumanyate. yathā ca vṛddha|śrotriyāṇām api tāvat kaṭhina|kuṇṭhita|nakharā vṛddha|karkaṭ'|ākṛtayaḥ pādukā|kiṇa|karkaśāḥ purāṇa|ghṛt'|âbhyaṅga|dur|gandhāḥ pādā gṛhyante, ko 'tr' âbhimānaḥ pallava|sukumāreṣu kāminīnāṃ pādeṣu? api ca tat tu doṣavat. kutaḥ?

pāda|grahaṇe 'vaśyaṃ
bāṣpaḥ saṃjāyate praṇayinīnām.
aśru|vimokṣe dainyaṃ,
dainy'|ôtpattau kutaḥ kāmaḥ?

Those men
who have no respect for a lovely,
passionate woman
who is young and is in love,
should, upon my word,
be yoked to broad-shared ploughs
with oxen
whose hearts have been scorched
by the plowmen's words.

(walks about) What are you saying? "What if someone has committed an offence: how should he appease his beloved?" Your uncertainty is indeed appropriate, for the anger of women in love is as resistant to remedies as is a remittent fever. Nevertheless there must be a cure for her anger. Today's youth hold that falling at the feet is the only medicine in this case. I don't have a high opinion of that. Just as the feet of aged priests are also touched—feet with hard and blunt nails, feet which look like old crabs, which are rough with corns caused by sandals, and smell foul because they are rubbed with rancid ghee—how can this be a way of showing our respect towards the feet of lovely women which are as tender as flowers-buds? Furthermore it is also not free from defects. Why? 4.95

When a man grasps his beloved's feet
she will necessarily shed tears.
Flowing tears mean misery.
When spirits become low,
how could there be love?

anye tu bruvate: «śapatha|karaṇair anuneyā» iti. tad ap-

y aśiṣṭam.[X] kula|vadhvo 'pi tāvat kāmukānāṃ śapathaṃ

na śraddadhati, kiṃ punar veśyā? yā vā śraddadhyāt tayā

kim anunetavyayā bhavitavyam? uktaṃ ca:

grāme vāsaḥ śrotriya|

    kathanaṃ para|tantratā kṛpaṇa|bhāvaḥ

ārjava|yutā ca nārī

    puṃsāṃ madan'|ânta|kāriṇi.[X]

ke cid bruvate: «yena kena cid upāyena hāsayitavyā. hās'|

ântarita|dhairy" âbhijñāta|gādh" êva nadī sukh'|âvagāhā

bhavati» iti. atra brūmo, yady apy asty etat tath" âpi tu

kopa|phalaṃ[X] n' âvāptaṃ bhavati. kutaḥ?

Others, however, say the following: "She should be conciliated by repeated swearing of oaths." That, too, is an uneducated view. First, even women of good families do not believe the promises of their lovers, how much less courtesans? On the other hand, what point is there in conciliating a woman who might actually believe it? And it is taught:

Living in a village,
the prattling of priests,
dependence on others, poverty,
and an unsophisticated woman:
these are the factors
that kill a man's passion.

Some say: "She must be made laugh by any means whatsoever. Once laughter has removed her obduracy, she will become easy to enter into, like a river in which a ford has been discovered." In my opinion, although this is correct, nevertheless one cannot obtain the fruit of anger in this way. Why?

4.100 utkṛṣy' ālambam īṣat pratanu|nivasanaṃ
nartayitv" âdhar'|oṣṭhaṃ
tat|kāla|śrotra|ramyaṃ paruṣam aparuṣair
akṣaraiḥ śrāvayitvā
yat kopād vāma|pādaṃ nava|nalina|nibhaṃ
strī kṣipaty uttam'|âṅge
tac chlāghyaṃ yauvan'|ârghyaṃ rati|kalaha|phalaṃ
prāpta|kāmā vadanti.

tasmādd hāsya|prayogeṇ' âpi mānayitavyaḥ strī|prakopaḥ. evaṃ tu vimṛśyamāneṣu strīṇāṃ kopa|prasādan'|ôpāyeṣu sadyo|dṛṣṭa|phalatvād avamṛdya cumbanam ev' âsmākaṃ pakṣaḥ. kutaḥ?

keśeṣ' ûtkaṭa|dhūpa|vāsa|surabhiṣv
āsajya vāmaṃ karaṃ
hastau dvāv api dakṣiṇena sahitau
saṃgṛhya n' âtyāyatam
yo harṣaḥ pibato balāt priyatamā|
vaktr'|êndum utpadyate
ten' āpyāyita|manmatho hi puruṣo
jīrṇo 'pi na kṣīyate.

kiṃ bravīṣi? «yas tu pramāda|doṣāt priyāyāḥ samakṣam eva gotraṃ skhalayati tatra bhāvaḥ kaṃ pratīkāraṃ paśyati?» iti. bhoḥ! anya|strī|gotra|grahaṇaṃ hi mahān upaplavaḥ kāmukānām! āśī|viṣa|daṣṭasy' êv' âsya duḥkhā pratikriyā kartum. tan muhūrtaṃ nāma dhyānaṃ pravekṣyāmaḥ. kiṃ cid avadhānaṃ dīyatām. *(dhyātvā)* ā dṛṣṭam!

Pulling up slightly her very thin, draped garment, 4.100
making her lower lip dance,
saying something lewd with refined diction
which is, at that moment, pleasing to the ears,
when, enraged, a woman lets fall her left foot,
which resembles a fresh lotus,
on her lover's head:
those who have mastered love say
that this fruit of a love-quarrel
is a desirable offering to youth.

Therefore, female anger can be assuaged by the employment of humor, too. But having thus investigated the methods to allay women's anger, I propound nothing but "aggressive kissing," because its efficacy is immediately perceived. Why?

Grabbing her abundantly perfumed hair
with the left hand,
with the right clutching both of her hands for a while—
due to the joy that falls to his share
when forcibly kissing the moon-face of his beloved
even an old man, having gratified Kama,
will not wither.

What are you saying? "Do you know of a remedy for accidentally calling the beloved by another's name to her face?" Ah! Using another woman's name is a catastrophe for a lover! A cure for this is as difficult as a cure for someone bitten by a venomous serpent, so I must immerse myself in meditation for a moment. Permit me a moment of concentration. *(ponders)* Yes! I have it!

dhārṣṭyāt sarv'|âpahāraḥ
parisaṭham, athavā trastavan niṣkriyatvaṃ
nāryā vākya|prasaṅgāt,
tvaritataram atho hāsya|lakṣa|kriyā vā,
anyasmin vā prayogo
vacasi yadi bhavet tasya c' ânyena yogo,
nānā|gotra|graho vā
bhavati hi śaraṇaṃ gotra|vākya|kṣatasya.

4.105 kiṃ bravīṣi? «nakha|daśana|nipātāḥ kena kāraṇena sa|vedanā api prītim utpādayanti?» îti. ha ha ha! atimugdham abhihitaṃ! paśyatu bhavān: nakha|daśana|nipātāḥ sa|vedanā api prītimadbhyāṃ sukham utpādayanti. kutaḥ?

yathā pratodo 'vahitaṃ karoti
jave hayaṃ sārathi|saṃprayuktaḥ
tathā ratau danta|nakh'|âvapātaḥ
sparś'|âikatānaṃ hṛdayaṃ karoti.

(parikramya) kiṃ bravīṣi? «kathaṃ veśyā viraktā rakt" êva ceṣṭamānā vijñeyā?» iti. atha bhoḥ ko 'tra saṃśayaḥ? eṣa ev' ôpadeśaḥ: anuraktāyāṃ rāgo bhāvayitavyaḥ. tathā c' ôpadiṣṭam. paśyatu bhavān! ākāra|saṃvaraṇaṃ hi tāvan mahātmano 'pi na śaknuvanti kartuṃ, kiṃ punar akaṭhina|hṛdayāḥ svalp'|âvagamāḥ striyaḥ? ata ākāra ev' âvekṣitavyaḥ.

One can boldly and dishonestly deny everything,
or stay immobilized as if frightened
  because of what the woman says,
or quickly pretend it to be a joke,
or one should link it with another phrase
  and that one with yet another,
or one might blurt out many other names
—this is the remedy
  for the wound inflicted by a *lapsus linguae*.

What are you saying? "How can assault with nails and teeth, even though painful, arouse pleasure?" Ha ha ha! What a foolish remark! Look, sir: assault with nails and teeth, even though painful, arouses pleasure for those in love.* How? 4.105

As the whip,
  wielded by the charioteer,
makes a steed attentive to its speed,
just so stimulation by teeth and nails
  in lovesport
makes the heart
  focus onepointedly on touch.

(walks about) What are you saying? "How can one spot an indifferent courtesan feigning passion?" Now sir! What could be unclear in this matter? This is the teaching: One should substantiate passion in an infatuated woman. And it has been taught how. Consider Sir! Pro primo even the enlightened sages have no power to conceal their mien, how much less tenderhearted, dimwitted

kiṃ bravīṣi? «katham?» iti.

vyarthaṃ prasmayate, vadaty akathite,
s'|āvegam uttiṣṭhati,
proktaṃ na pratibudhyate, na kurute
strītv'|ôcitāṃ vāmatām,
gāḍhaṃ pratyupagūhya muñcati muhuḥ,
khinnā niyukte ratau,
rāg'|ânte nipuṇ" âpi vandhya|kusumā
jñeyā lat" êv' âṅganā.

4.110 kiṃ bravīṣi? «virāgaṃ samutpannaṃ kathaṃ śakyaṃ cikitsituṃ?[×] ut' âho apratīkāra ev' âiṣa bhāvaḥ?» iti. śṛṇotu bhavān: rāg'|ôtpattiḥ khalu dvividh" âiva bhavati: kāraṇād akāraṇād vā. tatra kāraṇ'|ôtpannasya rāgasya kāraṇād eva virāgo bhavati. evam ev' ākāraṇ'|ôtpannasy'[×] âkāraṇād eva. evaṃ rāga|virāgayor vaiṣamye kim iva śakyā pratikriyā kartuṃ? mandībhūte tu rāge yā pratikriyā tāṃ vakṣyāmaḥ:

women? Therefore it is the demeanor that must be carefully diagnosed.

What are you saying? "How?"

She bursts out laughing for no reason,
speaks without being addressed,
jumps up with a start,
does not understand what was said,
does not display the coyness natural to womankind,

when tightly embraced she lets go again and again,
she is exhausted after indulging in love-play—
a woman fallen out of love can be seen through,
no matter how clever she may be:
she is like a vine with barren flowers.

What are you saying? "How is it possible to cure estrangement once arisen? Or is there perhaps no remedy for this condition?" Listen sir: love arises only in two ways: because of a cause or without a cause. Of these, love that arises from a cause can only cease due to a cause. In the same way, that which arises without a cause can only cease without a cause. Thus, since neither infatuation nor estrangement is uniform, how could it be possible to effect a remedy? On the other hand, I shall expound the remedy for love which has become stale: 4.110

anya|strī|sevanaṃ vā
rati|vikritir atho dhīratā vigrahe vā,×
kṣāntiḥ kāle, sa|hāsyā
vacana|nipuṇatā, bandhu|pūjā stutir vā,
veśyā|vyāja|pravāsaḥ,
pura|vara|gamanaṃ sāhas'|ôpakramo vā
dānaṃ vā kāminīnāṃ
paricaya|śithilaṃ rāgam uddīpayanti.

api ca, śṛṇotu bhavān:

bālā bālatvād dravya|lubdhā pradānaiḥ
prājñā prājñatvāt kopanā sāntvanābhiḥ
stabdhā sevābhir dakṣiṇā dakṣiṇatvān
nārī saṃsevyā yā yathā sā tath" âiva.

(parikramya) kiṃ bravīṣi?

4.115 «darśayati kāma|liṅgaṃ
na vadaty alam iti na gacchati samīpam
yā strī viharati kāle
sā kartavyā kathaṃ vaśyā?» iti.

Frequenting other women,
or a change in love-sport,
a serious quarrel,
or forbearance at the right time,
clever words delivered with a smile,
worship of her relatives or their praise,
staying away on the pretext of going to a courtesan,
visiting a big city,
or some rash adventure,
or gifts
can rekindle the beloved's affection
when it has become dulled
by familiarity.

Moreover, listen sir:

Each woman must be courted as it suits her:
a young girl with being childish,
a greedy one with gifts,
an intelligent woman with being intelligent,
a short-tempered one with soothing words,
a stiff woman with devoted service,
a good-natured one with being affable.

(walks about) What are you saying?

"How can one captivate a woman 4.115
who shows the symptoms of love,
does not say 'enough'
but does not move close to you,
who bides her time?"

sādhv abhihitam etat. prathamaṃ tāvat kāmino vijñeyaḥ strī|svabhāvaḥ. eṣa eva strī|svabhāvaḥ syāt. kiṃ tu yāvaj|jīvitam api garvitā nir|upāyaṃ na śakyā vaśam upanetuṃ. yat tu strīṇāṃ rahasyaṃ tad idam udghāṭyate:

śūnye vā saṃpramathya
dvirada iva latāṃ yo haraty āśu nārīṃ,
mattāṃ vā yo viditvā
hy abhibhavati śanaiḥ rañjayan vākya|leśaiḥ,
anyaṃ kṛtv" ôpadhiṃ vā
cchalayati, kurute bhāva|saṃgūhanaṃ vā:
tasy' âitac ceṣṭitaṃ bho
na bhavati viphalaṃ vāma|śīlā hi nāryaḥ.

(parikramya) kiṃ bravīṣi?

«gate tu kope prathame samāgame
pravāsa|kāle punar|āgame tathā
vadanti catvāri ratāni kāmukāḥ.
tato bhavān kiṃ nv adhikaṃ vyavasyati?» iti

4.120 atra brūmo: yat tāvat prathama|samāgame rataṃ tad apy alabdha|visrambhāyāṃ kāminyām ajñāta|gādham iva saraḥ śaṅk"|âvagāhaṃ bhavati. yad api pravāsa|kāle rataṃ tad api tac|chok'|âbhibhūtatvān manda|rāgāyāḥ s'|

You've made a very good point. First of all the lover must know the nature of the woman. It can happen that the nature of the woman is just like that. But without the right means you won't be able to captivate a conceited woman even if you devote your whole life to this task. As for the secret of women, I hereby reveal it:

If he gets her down and ravishes her quickly
at a solitary place,
as an elephant ravishes a vine it has crushed,
or, knowing that she is drunk, arouses her gradually
with half-uttered sentences
and then lays her down,
or cheats her using some other trick,
or conceals his own feelings:
such a behavior of a man will never be fruitless,
for women have a perverse nature.

(walks about) What are you saying?

"Womanizers say
there are four kinds of lovemaking:
when her anger has gone,
when the lovers are together for the first time,
when the man sets out on a journey,
and when he returns.*
Which one do you consider the best, sir?"

Here is my opinion in this matter: To begin with, making love on the first date, and, what's more, to a lovely girl whose confidence you haven't yet won, is a dangerous enterprise to throw yourself into, just as jumping into a lake of unknown depth is dangerous. As for making 4.120

âsr'|âvil'|âkṣam upohyamāna|hṛday'|ôdvegam aramyaṃ karuṇaṃ grah'|ôpasṛṣṭaṃ candra|maṇḍalam iva na māṃ prīṇayati. yad api pravāsād āgate rataṃ tad apy akṛta|pratikarmatayā priyayā vrīḍitay" âvyaṃjitaṃ durdina|gāndharvam iva manda|rāgaṃ bhavati. yat punaḥ kop'|âpagamād āgataṃ tat sur'|âsur'|āviddha|Mandara|pīḍite sarv'|âuṣadhi|prakṣep"|âpyāyita|vīrye bhagavati salila|nidhau yad utpannam amṛta|saṃjñakaṃ kim api śrūyata āyur|vayo|'vasthāpanaṃ rasāyanaṃ tad apy ativartate. kutaḥ?

kop'|âpagame nāryāḥ
 tam eva hṛdayena bhāvam ajahantyāḥ
suratam atirabhasam anibhṛta|
 kara|ruha|daśana|pada|jarjaraṃ bhavati.

(parikramya) kiṃ bravīṣi? «veśyā|vañcitaṃ puruṣaṃ parihasanti dhūrtāḥ. kathaṃ veśyā|vañcanaṃ na prāpnuyāt kāmukaḥ?» iti. bho veśyā lipikāraś ca chidra|prahāritvāt tulyam ubhayaṃ. tatra lipikāro 'bhyāse hasta|gata|kalpaṃ kṛtvā muhūrtam avasthānaṃ prāpayati. veśyā punar vāta|roga iv' âtyarthaṃ vyayam utpādayayati. yadi

love when the man sets out on a journey: for a woman whose passion has cooled off because she is overwhelmed by sadness it will entail, when her eyes are clouded with tears and her heart-ache intensifies, it will become joyless and pathetic: as such it does not please me, like the disk of the moon when it is eclipsed. As for making love when the man returns from the journey: it is mildly exciting, like indistinct music on a rainy day, because your beloved has not made her toilette and is bashful. Quite a different matter is that lovemaking which comes when anger slips away: it surpasses that wonderful elixir called nectar witnessed by scripture, which arose from the Blessed Ocean—churned by the Mándara mountain wielded by the Gods and the Titans and its potency maximized by the admixture of every medical herb—, which strengthens health and vitality. Why?

The impetuous lovemaking
of a woman who, at the end of quarrel,
does not release that emotion from her heart
  becomes rugged
with unchecked scratches and bites.*

(walks about) What are you saying? "Sly foxes ridicule a man fooled by courtesans. How can an amoroso escape the courtesans' snares?" Oh, courtesans and scribes, both are equal in that they strike at one's vulnerable points.* Of these two the scribe, having made entries into his ledger (?),* gives you peace for a while. But a courtesan is like rheumatism: both drain you completely. But if someone

mac|carit'|ânugāmī bhavet tena veśaḥ praveṣṭavyaḥ. mayā hi

visrambho gata|yauvanāsu na kṛto,
bālāḥ parīkṣya sthitā,
dūrād eva sa|mātṛkāḥ parihṛtā
nadyaḥ sa|sattvā iva
manyur n' âsti vimānitasya na punaḥ
saṃprārthitasy' ādaraḥ.
veśe c' âsmi jarāṃ|gato na ca kṛtaḥ
svalpo 'pi mithyā|vyayaḥ.

(parikramya) kiṃ bravīṣi? «nāryor yugapad|āgame kā pratipattavyā kā parityājyā: kāla|vardhita|praṇayinī, ut' âho nava|praṇayinī? enaṃ praśnaṃ vadatu bhāvaḥ» iti. kaṣṭaḥ khalv ayaṃ praśnaḥ. dur|vaco mā pratibhāti. kim atra bhavān paśyati?

4.125 kim āha bhavān? «na kiṃ cid atra paśyāmi. mahat tv etat saṅkaṭam. bhāva eva vaktum arhati» iti. tena hi śrūyatām:

were to follow my lead, he could enter the courtesans' quarter. For

I placed no trust in women whose youth was spent.
Young girls stayed only after I vetted them.
I gave wide berth to those who had a madam:
they are like rivers full of crocodiles.
I do not lose my temper
  when I am treated with disrespect,
nor do I think much of it
  when someone asks me a favor.
I have turned grey in the courtesans' quarter,
yet I haven't wasted a penny if it was unnecessary.

(walks about) What are you saying? "If one manages to be involved with two women simultaneously, which one should be kept and which one dumped: the long-time girlfriend, or rather the new girlfriend? Please answer this question, sir." This is a tricky question indeed. I find it hard to answer. What is your opinion in this matter?

What are you saying, sir? "I see no way through. It remains 4.125
a huge dilemma. You alone are able to unravel it." Well, listen then:

rūḍha|snehān na yuktaṃ
nava|yuvati|kṛte svāṃ priyāṃ vipramoktuṃ.
tat|prīty|arthaṃ na heyā
svayam|abhipatitā kāminī jāta|kāmā.
tatr' ôpekṣ" âiva kāryā
vrajati paricitā yāvad udbhūta|kopā.
śūnye prāpya dvitīyām
atha tad|anumate saṃprasādyā priy" âiva.

(parikramya) kiṃ bravīṣi? «veśe saṃcaratā darśana|mātrakeṇ' âiva kathaṃ śakyaṃ jñātuṃ strīṇāṃ raho|naipuṇam?» iti. n' âsti kiṃ cin nipuṇasy' âjñeyam. striyaṃ khalu dṛṣṭvā puruṣeṇa dṛṣṭir eva prathamaṃ parīkṣyā bhavati. cakṣuṣi hi sarve bhāvā niyatāḥ. paśyatu bhavān:

sa|kekarā manda|nimeṣa|yuktā
tiryag|gatā snehavatī viśālā
dainyena hīnā cala|tārakā ca
strīṇāṃ raho|naipuṇam āha driṣṭiḥ.

api ca, yasyāś c' âbhugnam īṣat|pratanu|kapolaṃ bhrū|saṃcāri tiryak|kaṭākṣam ānanaṃ tasyā rati|kārkaśyaṃ. yasyā vā śyāna|mūlo 'dharaḥ sa|danta|nakha|padaṃ śarīraṃ pravirala|hasitaṃ ca mukhaṃ tasyā nirviśaṅkam eva rati|śauṇḍīryam avagantavyam. yāṃ vā bhavān paśyati kaṭi|pradeśa|vinyasta|vāma|hastāṃ pralamba|dakṣiṇa|karām eka|pārśv'|ônnata|jaghanāṃ tasyām apy āsthā kāryā. na

Since she is deeply in love,
it is unseemly to dump one's beloved
for the sake of a new girlfriend.
However, just for the sake of her pleasure
we ought not to reject a lusty wench
who has willingly fallen into our lap.
One should simply ignore the old acquaintance
until she flies into a temper and goes away.
Having had the other girl
in some lonely place agreed to with her,
one should conciliate one's beloved.

(walks about) What are you saying? "When someone strolls in the courtesans' quarter, how can he gauge at a mere glance the amorous prowess of women?" Nothing remains hidden for an expert. As soon as he notices a woman, a man should first of all examine her eyes. For the eye is the seat of all emotions. Observe, sir:

Eyes that squint,
close softly, cast side-glances, are affectionate,
large and immodest with lively pupils
proclaim the amorous prowess of women.

Furthermore, if her face is slightly screwed up, her cheeks somewhat hollowed, with dancing eyebrows and darting side-glances, she is a rough lover. Or, if her corners of her lower lip are shrunken, her body is covered with tooth- and nail-marks, and her mouth rarely flashes a smile, we may deduce that she is a champion of love-making.* Now then, if you notice a woman with her left hand put on her waist, her right arm hanging loose,

hy evam agarvitā tiṣṭhati. yāṃ ca nivasan'|ânt'|āvṛt'|âika|payodharāṃ sva|gṛha|dehalī|vilagn'|âika|rucira|caraṇāṃ dvāra|pārśv'|âvaruddha|śarīrāṃ paśyati sa khalu strī|mayaḥ pāśaḥ. cāru|līlatvam ev' âsyāḥ sarvaṃ kathayati. yā vā kavāṭa|go|stanaka|taṭam ālambya prakaṭī|kṛta|bāhu|pāśā śithilī|kṛta|nīvī|bandhanā sandarśita|nābhi|hradā dṛśyate tasyā ākṛtau rati|pūrva|raṅgāyām× anumeyaṃ× na vidyate. śakyam atra bahv api vaktum. saṃkṣepas tu śrūyatām×—

4.130 yasyās tāmra|tal'|âṅguliḥ śuci|nakho
gaṇḍ'|ânta|sevī karo
vāṇī s'|âbhinayā gatiḥ sa|lalitā
praspandit'|oṣṭhaṃ smitam
lolā dṛṣṭir aśaṅkitaṃ mukham adho
nābheś ca nīvī|kriyā
tāṃ vidyān nara|vāgurāṃ rati|raṇe
prāpt'|âgrya|śauryāṃ striyam.

and one side of her hips raised, you may approach her also with confidence. For she would not stand like that if she had no self-esteem. And if you see a girl who covers one of her breasts with the hem of her garment, keeps one dainty painted foot on the threshold of her house, her body hidden behind the door-panel: she is indeed a snare embodied as a woman. Everything indicates her bewitchingly coquettish nature. On the other hand a woman who appears holding on to the cow-udder-shaped studs fastening the door-panels, revealing the noose of her arms, with the knot of her mini-skirt loosened and the pool of her navel visible: since her appearance is a prelude to love, there is nothing left to be conjectured. Much might be said on this matter. To summarize:

She who holds her hand, 4.130
its palm and fingers painted red,
its nails bright, close to her cheek,
who accompanies her speech
  with graceful gestures,
whose gait is elegant,
whose lips quiver as she smiles,
who has a roving eye,
whose countenance knows no inhibition,
who has tied her mini-skirt below her navel,
one should identify her as a man-trap,
a woman who has attained
the non plus ultra of valor in the war of love.*

(parikramya) kiṃ bravīṣi? «dvividham eva strīṇāṃ kāmitaṃ bhavati prakāśaṃ pracchannaṃ ca. tayoḥ katarad vyatiricyate?» iti. bhoḥ! yat prakāśaṃ tad veśa|vadhūṣv ev' ôpapadyate. kṛtakam api c' âitad bhavati. yat tv idaṃ pracchannaṃ tat kula|vadhūṣu veśa|vadhūṣu ca. yat kevalam anurāgād utpadyate viśeṣataś c' âitad alpa|doṣatvād veśyā|vadhūṣv eva ramyaṃ bhavati. dur|labhatvād api puruṣāṇāṃ kula|vadhvas tu yaṃ kaṃ cit kāmayante. veśyayā tu na sarvaḥ kāmyate.

syān mataṃ kasya cin: «nirdoṣa|madanatvād veśyānāṃ prachanna|kāmitena kiṃ prayojanam?» iti. atra brūmaḥ: pūrva|saṃstuto rāja|vallabhaḥ kṛt'|ôpakāro bhaktimān nṛśaṃsa ity ete veśyā|jananī|sevitāḥ. eteṣām avaśyam akāmayamānā api veśyā anuvidheyā bhavanti. kiṃ|nimittam? prayojan'|ârtham iti. tasmād veśyayā pracchanna|madan'|ârthinyā yaḥ kāmyate tena janma|jīvitayoḥ phalam avāptaṃ bhavati.

kiṃ c' ânyad, yat tāvad viraham āsādya svayaṃ|dūtīnāṃ prāñjali|puraḥsarāṇi sa|bāṣpa|gadgadāni vākyāni śrūyante nanu tāny eva tasya paryāptāni bhavanti. yā vā tad|dhyāna|parā roga|vyapadeśena gatā pāṇḍu|bhāvaṃ candr'|ôdaye roditi prajāgar'|âbhitāmra|nayanā śithilīkṛta|bhūṣaṇā kāminī, «diṣṭyā tvad|artham eva nirghṛṇa! śarīrasy' êyam avasthā, bhadraṃ tav' âstu» iti svayam upālabhamānāyāḥ «prasīda kānta! yāce tvā dayasva me

(walks about) What are you saying? "Women's love can be of two types only: open or secret. Of these two which is better?" Sir, only courtesans can love openly. And that love is also artificial. As for secret love, that is possible in the case of respectable women as well as courtesans. When it arises simply from inclination, and especially because its drawbacks are few, it is delightful only with courtesans. Furthermore, respectable women, because they find it hard to get hold of men, will make love to anybody whomsoever. But a courtesan will not love just anybody.

Someone may opine: "Why would courtesans love someone secretly if love for them is not a sin?" On this I answer: Old flames, favorites of the king, benefactors, and the devoted but vile: such men are pampered by a bawd. For them courtesans will perforce be compliant even if they feel no affection. For what reason? Because they are motivated. Therefore a man loved by a courtesan seeking secret love will have reaped a double fruit of birth and life.

And what's more, he certainly will fully enjoy the words of women interceding on their own behalf, preceded by hands folded in supplication, tearfully stammering, suffering the pangs of separation. Or a beautiful woman whose thoughts are fixed on him, who becomes pale under the pretext of some disease, and weeps when the moon rises with eyes are blood-shot with sleeplessness and with her ornaments hanging loose—a man hearing these syllables interwoven with sighs: "Please, my love,

śarīrasya!» iti sītkār'|ânubaddh'|âkṣarāṇi śṛṇvatas, «tvarasva mā m" âivam» iti daśana|kara|ruhair vicodya radamānāyā «aham evaṃvidhā śraddadhātu bhavān may" âpi śāpitaḥ» ity evaṃ c' ôktāni rasāyana|prayog'|âtivartakāni vacāṃsi cintayato, «mad|artham ev' êyam īdṛśī saṃvṛttā» iti kāraṇato dūtī|vacanāc c' ôpalabhya puruṣasya kāruṇya|miśrā yā prītir utpadyate tat|sadṛśīṃ yad anyāṃ brūyād viṭa|bhāvam imaṃ parityajya śrotriyaiḥ samatāṃ gaccheyam. api ca,

hast'|ālambita|mekhalāṃ mṛdu|pada|
nyās'|âvabhugn'|ôdarīṃ
labdhv" âpi kṣaṇam āgatāṃ sa|madanāṃ
saṅketam ekāṃ niśi
yo nārīṃ sthita eva cumbati mukhe
bhītāṃ cal'|âkṣīṃ priyāṃ
tasy' êdaṃ sva|bhuj'|ātta|paṅkaja|mayaṃ
chattraṃ mayā dhāryate.

I beg you, show mercy to my body," from that woman reprimanding him herself: "Congratulations! For your sake alone, O merciless man, my body is reduced to this condition. I hope you are happy," and pondering these words which outperform the application of an elixir: "I am in such a state, you must believe me, my lord, I made you to take an oath," of that woman scratching and biting while urging him "Hurry! No, no, not like that!," having learnt from evidence and from the words of the go-between that "Just because of me she has been reduced to this state"—the pleasure admixed with pity which arises for a man, if someone can tell me of another like it, I shall give up my status of a pimp and become like a Vedic priest.

I will bear this lotus-parasol
won by my own arm for a man who,
winning even a fleeting tryst at night,
  while still standing,
kisses a woman as his beloved on the mouth,
come to him with passion all alone,
her eyes tremulous with fear,
her girdle stilled by her hand,
and her stomach curved
  as she creeps forward with soft foot-fall.

4.135 api ca,

> «tvarasva kānt' êti» bhayād bravīti
> yaṃ kāminī corita|saṃprayogā
> krītās tayā tasya bhavanti puṃsaḥ
> prāṇā yath"|êṣṭaṃ parikalpya mūlyam.

(parikramya) kiṃ bravīṣi? «rūpavatī ca strī dakṣiṇā c' êti tayoḥ kasyāṃ prīti|viśeṣaṃ bhāvaḥ paśyati?» iti. ubhayam etat striyaṃ bhūṣayati. yat tāvad virūpāyāṃ dākṣiṇyaṃ tad andhakāra|nṛttam iva vyarthaṃ bhavati. rūpam api dākṣiṇya|hīnam aṭavī|candr'|ôdaya iva kāṃ prītiṃ kariṣyati? māṃ prati rūpād dākṣiṇyaṃ bhavati pradhānam. kutaḥ? dākṣiṇyaṃ virūpām api striyaṃ bhūṣayati surūpām apy adākṣiṇyaṃ dūṣayati. dṛśyante hi puruṣāḥ surūpā api striyaḥ parityajya virūpāsv api dakṣiṇāsu rajyamānāḥ. rūpavatyā c' âvaśyaṃ stabdhayā bhavitavyaṃ. stabdhatā ca kāmasya mahāñ chatruḥ, anuvṛttir hi kāme mūlaṃ, sā ca dākṣiṇyāt saṃbhavati. yadi rūpa|mātraṃ kāraṇaṃ syāc citra|nāryām api prayojanaṃ nirvartayet. dākṣiṇya eva rūpa|guṇaṃ hitvā sarva eva guṇa|samudāyo 'ntarbhūtaḥ. kutaḥ?

> su|vāk su|veṣā nibhṛtā kṛtajñā
> bhāv'|ânvitā n' âpi ca dīrgha|kopā
> alolupā chanda|karī ca nityam
> dākṣiṇya|yuktā bhavat' îha nārī.

And, 4.135

To whom a passionate woman,
in secret love-making, fearfully whispers:
"Hurry my love!"
she has bought the life-breaths of this man,
fixing the price as she wills.

(walks about) What are you saying? "A beautiful woman or a warmhearted woman: which one pleases you more?" Both of these adorn a woman. As for kindliness in an ugly woman, it is wasted like dancing in darkness. On the other hand, beauty without kindliness is like a moonrise in the forest: what kind of pleasure will it produce? For me, kindliness wins over beauty. Why? Kindliness is an ornament even for an ugly woman, discourtesy ruins even a beautiful woman. For we see men leaving even beautiful women and attaching themselves even to misshapen, but kindly women. A beauty will invariably be haughty. And haughtiness is the great foe of love, for compliance is the root of love, and that springs from kindliness. If bare beauty were the cause, then it could generate the effect even in the case of a woman represented in a painting. Kindliness in itself contains the totality of all virtues except the virtue of beauty. Why?

A kindly women is always mellifluous,
dresses tastefully, is unassuming,
grateful, affectionate, and what's more,
is quickly reconciled,
not greedy and obedient.

kim āha bhavān? «veśyāḥ kṛtak'|ôpacāritvāt satām anabhigamyā bhavant' îti bruvanti. tat katham?» iti. iha khalu kāmyair viśeṣair upacaraṇam upacārah, etac ca svabhāvato nāryāḥ. dve ca labhyete veśyāyāṃ kriyā|niṣpatteḥ. syān matam: yac chāṭhyād upacaryate tat kṛtakam iti. tad apy adoṣaḥ. kutaḥ? śāṭhyād apy upacāraḥ prayuktaḥ prītim utpādayati. ārjavād apy upacāraḥ skhalīkṛtaḥ kasya prītiṃ janayati? śāṭhyaṃ nām' ârtha|nirvartako buddhi|viśeṣaḥ. tad apy adoṣaḥ. ātm'|ârtha|pradhānayā ca striyā puruṣa|viśeṣo 'vaśyaṃ mṛgayitavyah. yā ca puruṣa|viśeṣa|jñā strī tasyām rajyante puruṣāḥ. api ca,

4.140 *nīcair bhāvaḥ priya|vacanatā*
kṣamā nityam apramādaś ca
śāṭhyād utpadyante.
ken' âitad dūṣyate loke?

kiṃ bravīṣi? «visaṃvāditvaṃ hi śaṭhāyāḥ sāram. visaṃvāditasya kāminaḥ priyayā duḥkham utpadyate. n' âsti tasya pratikriyā» iti. bhoḥ! sarvaḥ khalu kāraṇam abhisamīkṣya visaṃvādyate. yas tu na śaknoti tat kāraṇaṃ parihartuṃ nanu tasy' âiva so 'parādhaḥ. anaikāntikaś ca visaṃvādane doṣaḥ. dṛśyante bahavo visaṃvāditā bhṛśataram anurajyamānāḥ.

What are you saying, sir? "People say that courtesans must be shunned by the virtuous because their polite behavior is feigned. What about that?" In fact here polite behavior means approaching with pleasing virtues, and it comes natural to women. And two kinds are found in the case of a courtesan, based on expedience.* There might be a view that whatever service is rendered dishonestly is artificial. That is no crime either. Why? Even if service be rendered dishonestly it generates pleasure. On the other hand, who will be pleased by honest service rendered clumsily? Dishonesty is in fact a specific mental state bringing about some result. That is no crime either. And a woman preoccupied with her own benefit will invariably seek an excellent man. And men prefer women who appreciate their excellences. What's more,

Humility : servility, kind words : flattery, 4.140
forbearance : intolerance,
continuous prudence : spying,
arise from dishonesty.
Who in the world censures this?

What are you saying? "The essential quality of a dishonest woman is perfidiousness. Suffering is the lot of a lover betrayed by his beloved. It cannot be cured." Sir! Everybody is betrayed as a consequence of some cause. But someone who cannot avoid that cause is surely himself to be blamed. And the fault you found in perfidy is inconclusive. We see that many deceived men love the woman even more.

āvalgita|stana|taṭāni ca bāṣpa|miśrā
bhāv'|âbhidhāna|paṭavaś ca kaṭākṣa|pātāḥ
avyakta|śobhita|padāś ca bhavanti vācaḥ
śāṭhyāt sato 'pi guṇavat parikalpayanti.

kiṃ bravīṣi? «veśyābhyo yad dīyate tan naṣṭam iti bahavo bruvanti. Dattaken' âpy uktaṃ ‹kāmo 'rtha|nāsaḥ puṃsām› iti. tatra bhāvaḥ kiṃ paśyati?» iti. bhoḥ! arthasya traya eva vidhayo: dānam upabhogo nidhānam iti. tatra dān'|ôpabhogau pradhānau, nidhānaṃ tu garhitam. kutaḥ?

nidhau kṛte 'rthe na hi vidyate phalaṃ,
bhavaty atuṣṭir viphalīkṛte punaḥ.
tato nidhānaṃ hi na yuktam. āgataṃ
sphurat|turaṅgasya jav'|ôpamaṃ dhanam.

4.145 artha|dharmau śarīra|sukham utpādayataḥ. tatr' êṣṭānāṃ śabd'|ādīnām avāptiḥ sukham ity ucyate. tac ca veśyā|janam upasevamāno yathāvat prāpnoti. sarva|śabdeṣu tāvad viśeṣataḥ priya|vacanaṃ nirvṛtti|karaṃ bhavati. tac ca veśyā|jano bravīti, na tath" ânyaḥ. katham iva?

Heaving breast-slopes,
sly side-glances intermingled with tears
and crafty at expressing emotions,
sentences with words indistinct and pretty:
even though these arise from dishonesty,
they accomplish something valuable.

What are you saying? "Many say: 'What is given to courtesans is wasted.' Dáttaka also has taught: 'Infatuation is the ruin of men's wealth.' What is the right honorable gentleman's view on this?' Sir, money has three uses: giving, spending, saving. Among these giving and spending take precedence, but saving is despised. Why?

When money is stashed away
  there accrues no gain.
When it yields no profit,
  there results dissatisfaction.
Therefore saving is not proper.
Income is as fleet as a racing horse.

Wealth and piety produce comfort. Here comfort is defined as the acquisition of words etc. that are agreeable. And someone frequenting courtesans attains that squarely. Now, among all words, it is especially sweet words that make one happy. And courtesans speak these, while others do not to that extent. How is this so? 4.145

priyaṃ priy'|ârthaṃ kaṭu vā priy'|ârthaṃ
vadanti kāle ca mitaṃ ca veśyāḥ
vadanti dākṣiṇya|dhanāḥ kadā cin
n' âiv' âpriyaṃ na priyam apriy'|ârtham.

yasyā anibhṛtam× aviṣam' | ōru | nitambam uddhṛt' | âṃśukam āviddha | mekhalā | kalāpaṃ jaghanam× abhivāhayataḥ sparśāḥ saṃbhavanti—kiṃ na tat|kṛte prāṇān api parityajanti, kiṃ punar dhanaṃ? sarvebhyaś ca rasebhyaḥ pānaṃ garhitam iva lakṣyate: tasy' âpi veśyā|viśiṣṭatvād upabhogo ramyo bhavati. paśyatu bhavān:

sa|saṃbhram'|ôddhūta|vighūrṇitāṃ vā
pīt'|âvaśeṣāṃ mukha|vicyutāṃ vā
oṣṭh'|ôpadaṃśāṃ madirāṃ nipīto
yo veśa|madhye sa rasaṃ viveda.

yena v'' ârdha|nimīlit'|âkṣīṇi praspandit'|âdharāṇy āyata|bhrū|latāni svinna|kapolāny ānanāni veśyā|janasy' âvalokitāni tasya cakṣuṣaḥ phalam avāptaṃ bhavati. api ca,

Courtesans articulate felicitously
and at the right time
agreeable words with a pleasant sense,
or sharp words with a pleasant sense.
Rich in courtesy,
they never voice either agreeable
or disagreeable words
with an unpleasant sense.*

Sensory delights arise for a man who boldly fondles her loins, with smooth thighs and buttocks, its petticoat pulled up, its girdles cast aside,—would men not even sacrifice their lives for such a woman, not to mention money? It is alleged that alcohol is the most contemptible, so to say, of all drinks, nevertheless, its consumption is a pleasure when transmuted by courtesans. Look, sir:

He who has drunk a cocktail
in the courtesans' quarter,
briskly swirled and tumbled,
or that which remained after her sipping,
or what slipped from her mouth,
with her lips as a canapé,
truly knows what flavor is.

Whoever has beheld the faces of courtesans, with heavy-lidded eyes, with quivering lower lips, with long eyebrows, glistening cheeks, has reaped the ultimate goal of sight. Furthermore,

4.150 keś'|ântaḥ snāna|rūkṣo viracita|kusumaḥ
keśa|hastaḥ pṛthur vā
vastraṃ vā bhukta|muktaṃ parimala|surabhiḥ
padma|tāmro 'dharo vā
veśyāyās tāmra|netraṃ mukham udita|madaṃ
candan'|ârdrā tanur vā
yen' āghrātāni tasya dhruvam abhipatito
ghrāṇa|mārgeṇa Kāmaḥ.

na tv asmākaṃ dharme 'dhikāraḥ. tath" âpi tu yathā dharm'|âvāptir bhavati tathā vakṣyāmaḥ. iha hi kṛta|ghnatā sarva|pāpīyasī. sa ca tataḥ kṛta|ghnataro yo veśyā|vadhūbhyaḥ sukham īpsitam anupamam āvāpya tābhyo na pratyupakurute. yadi ca ×kṛtajño bhavati tasya haste svargaḥ. tasmāt svarga|sukh'|âvāpty|arthaṃ nirviśaṅkena veśyābhyo 'vaśyaṃ vittaṃ dātavyam.

kim bravīṣi? «dākṣiṇya|yuktāyām api kula|vadhvāṃ kena kāraṇena tādṛso na bhavati yādṛśo veśyāyām?» iti. śrūyatāṃ: dākṣiṇya|viṣayas tāvad anyaḥ kula|vadhvām anya eva veśyāyām. ṛjus tu kula|vadhūr yadi tāvat priyaṃ vadaty akāle vā vadat' îti ×atīva priyam iti vā vipriyaṃ vadati. evaṃ sarvatra. kāmaś c' êcchā|viśeṣaḥ, prārthanā c' êcchā. prārthanā c' âsaṃprāpter utpadyate. sā ca veśyāyāṃ svādhīna|prāptāyām api mātsaryād utpadyate,

A man who has smelled the tips of a courtesan's hair, 4.150
dry after bathing,
or her rich locks of hair adorned with flowers,
or her dress, shed after wearing,
or her lower lip,
  scented with fragrant breath and pink
  like a lotus,
or her intoxicated face with red eyes,
or her body moist with sandal-paste,
is at once sought out by Kama,
  by way of the nose.

Admittedly, I am no authority in religious matters. Nevertheless, I will extemporize on how religious merit might be secured. In this world, ingratitude is the most horrendous sin. A man who has received that incomparable, sought-after bliss from courtesans and does not requite them is the worst of ingrates. But if he becomes grateful, then heaven is in his hand. So, in order to attain heavenly bliss one must by all means, without hesitation, give money to courtesans.

What are you saying? "How is it that this does not apply to a respectable woman, even though she is kindly, in the same way as it does to a courtesan?" Listen: the concept of 'kindliness' is one thing for a respectable woman and another for a courtesan. First of all, if a forthright respectable woman says something agreeable, she either says it at the wrong time or she says something acutely agreeable, and therefore what she speaks is disagreeable.

bahu|sādhāraṇatvāt. mātsaryaṃ ca lobhaṃ janayati. tasmāl labdh'|âvakāśo veśyāyāṃ kāmo na vyapaiti. kāma|mūlaś ca rāgah. api ca, —

veśyā|jaghana|ratha|sthaḥ
kula|nārīṃ kaḥ sa|cetano gacchet?
na hi ratham atītya kaś cid
go|yānena vrajet puruṣaḥ.

kiṃ bravīṣi? «lokasya veśyāṃ prati sakto manuṣyaḥ pūjyo na bhavati, saṃmatiś ca tasya n' êṣṭā. yatra ca guṇā dṛśyante tat kim|arthaṃ n' ânuṣṭheyam?» iti. ativiṭatvam abhihitaṃ. muhūrtam avadhānaṃ dīyatāṃ. *(dhyātvā)* iha hi dvividhā pūjā bhavati: phalavaty aphalā ca. tatra y" âphalā nagnasy' êva ceṣṭitaṃ bhavati hāsyaṃ. veśyāyām aprasaktasya kiṃ phalam iti. syān matam: «ayaśasyo veśa|prasaṅgaḥ» iti. tan na grāhyaṃ. sarvo hi sukhinaṃ dveṣṭi lokaḥ. yathā ca para|striyo na gamyā iti pratikaṇṭham abhihitaṃ na tathā veśyāḥ. syān mataṃ: «strīṣu prasaṅgo na śreyān veśyāś ca striyaḥ.» iti. atra brūmaḥ: na tu strīṣv āyattaṃ loko dūṣayitum arhati. api ca,

It is like this in all contingencies. Love is a variety of desire, and desire is entreaty. And entreaty arises from not getting what you want. And in the case of a courtesans, even though she is enjoyed at will, that arises from jealousy, because she is owned in common. And jealousy produces covetousness. Therefore desire for a courtesan will never diminish if given latitude. And desire is the root of passion. Furthermore,

What sentient man,
ensconced in the chariot of a courtesan's hips,
would approach a respectable woman?
For no man can overtake a chariot
with a cow-drawn cart.

What are you saying? "A man addicted to prostitutes is not respected by the public, and his opinion is not valued. Why should one be banned from indulging in that where virtues are evident?" You have declared that you are a super-pimp. Permit me a moment of concentration. *(reflects)* In this world, respect is of two kinds: fruitful and fruitless. Of these, the fruitless one is as ridiculous as the frolicking of a naked man. What fruit can there be for a man not attached to courtesans? Some may opine: "Addiction to prostitutes is disreputable." This view is not acceptable. The whole world resents a happy man. And while it is proclaimed with one voice that the wives of others should not be frequented, this does not apply to courtesans. Someone might opine: "Association with women is not salutary, and courtesans are women." On this I reply: Nevertheless people ought not

4.155 prāgalbhyaṃ sthāna|śauryaṃ
vacana|nipuṇatāṃ sauṣṭhavaṃ sattva|dīptiṃ
citta|jñānaṃ pramodaṃ
surata|guṇa|nidhiṃ rakta|nārī|nivṛttim,
citr'|ādīnāṃ kalānām
adhigamanam atho saukhyam agryaṃ ca kā-
mī
prāpnoty āśritya veśaṃ
yadi, katham ayaśas tasya loko bravīti?

(parikramya) kiṃ bravīṣi? «yad etad Bṛhaspaty|Uśanaḥ|prabhṛtibhir anyaiś ca śāstra|proktṛbhir upadiśyate: ‹strīṣu prasaṅgo na kartavyaḥ› ity atra bhāvaḥ kiṃ paśyati?» iti. bhoḥ! upadeśa|mātraṃ khalv etat. tam ahaṃ na paśyāmi yaḥ strīṣu prasaṅgaṃ na gacchet. śrūyante hi Mahendr'|ādayo 'py Ahaly"|ādyāsu vikṛtim āpannāḥ. dharm'|ârthayor api śreṣṭho viṣayaḥ, iṣṭa|viṣaya|prādurbhāva|phalatvāt. viṣaya|pradhānāś ca striyah. yo hi veśyāṃ parityajya kām'|ôpabhogān divyān kāmayate tam apy ahaṃ vañcitam ity avagacchāmi.

to defame a man who keeps the company of women. Moreover,

How can people defame a man 4.155
who by frequenting the brothel becomes bold,
becomes valorous in standing his ground,
  skilled in innuendos,
  light-bodied, radiant with virility,
perceives the intentions of others,
becomes joyful,
gains a storehouse of methods of love-making,
  beatitude with an impassioned woman,
learns the crafts headed by painting
and obtains supreme comfort?

(walks about) What are you saying? "How, sir, do you view the pronouncement of people like Brihas·pati, Úshanas, and other scientific authors who teach that one should not become attached to women?" Well, this serves only for instruction. I can see nobody who is not attached to women. For scripture reveals that even the great Indra etc. became lovesick for Ahálya and others. Sensuality is superior even to piety and wealth, since it results in the appearance of the desired entity. And women are the best of all such entities. For I also consider as deluded someone who rejects a courtesan and then lusts after the enjoyment of heavenly love.

ih' âpi tāvat tadātv'|āyatyos tadātvam eva garīyaḥ pratyakṣa|phalatvāt. kiṃ punar anyasmin deha|grahaṇe saṃśayite tapaś|caraṇa|duravāpe ramaṇīyam? paśyatu bhavān. jaladhara|nirvāpita|candra|dīpāsu dviguṇatara|timira|bhīma|darśanāsu śiśiratara|pavanāsu salila|pavana|duḥsañcārāsu jalada|kāla|nīlāsu rajanīṣu madana|śara|saṃtaptay" âikākinyā kāminy" âbhisāritasya pumso nūpura|svana|bodhitasya janma|jīvitayoḥ phalam avāptaṃ bhavati. kim āha bhavān? «nūpura|dhāraṇaṃ hi mahad upakurute 'bhisārikābhyaḥ» iti. evam etat. kutaḥ?

prathama|samāgama|nibhṛtaḥ
katham ātma|nivedanaṃ janaḥ kuryāt
pāda|spandana|rabhaso
yadi na syān nūpura|ninādaḥ?

evaṃ nūpura|śabda|nibodhito 'yaṃ jala|dhara|dhārā|dhauta|viśeṣakam āplut'|âñjan'|âkṣam anavasthit'|oṣṭham ānanaṃ samadaṃ pītvā yady avāk|cirā bahūni kalp'|ântarāṇi naraka|duḥkhāny anubhavati, tath" âpi tasya yuvati|jana|praṇaya|pratigrāhiṇas tāni ślāghyāni bhavanti. vigata|jalad'|âvakuṇṭhanāyāṃ viracita|vimala|grahapati|tilakāyāṃ vigata|mārutāyām asana|kusuma|vāsita|van'|ântarāyāṃ śaradi sārasa|ruta|saṃvādita|mekhalā|svanābhir bandhūka|kusum'|ôjjvala|viśeṣakābhiś

Now as regards actuality and future potentiality, actuality definitely outweighs because its result is directly perceptible. What is amusing about haphazardly taking on another body, laboriously won by ascetic torments? See here, sir. A man realizing from the tinkling of anklets that he is hastened to by an eloping beautiful woman all by herself, wounded by Kama's arrow, on nights when the lamp of the moon is extinguished by clouds, terrifying to behold with darkness twice as intense, with freezing winds, when roaming is made difficult by water laden breezes, dark in the rainy season—such a man has obtained the fruit of his birth and life. What are you saying, sir? "Indeed, the wearing of anklets renders good service to an eloping woman." So it is. Why?

How could someone silent on the first date
  announce herself
if her anklets did not tinkle intensely
  because of her shaking feet?

In this vein, if a man, informed by the sound of the anklets, drinks in the impassioned face, its make-up patterns washed off by could-bursts, with eyes replete with collyrium and with unsteady lower-lip, and then, his head hanging down, he experiences the hellish torments of many eons, nevertheless they are praiseworthy for him because he has assented to the love of a young woman. What use has a man for heaven if he plunges into the water of a pool with blossoming lotuses with his beloveds who have been taught affection by Brahminy ducks, their make-up patterns shining like *bandhúka* flowers,*

cakravāk'|ôpadiṣṭ'|ânurāgābhiḥ priyābhiḥ saha yena pratibuddha|paṅkaja|dīrghikā|salilam avagāḍhaṃ tasya kiṃ svargeṇa? athavā kunda|kusuma|miśrite phulla|lodhra|gandh'|āviddha|mārute priyaṅgu|mañjarī|kḷpta|keśa|haste prāpte hemanta|kāle him'|âparādha|kātar'|oṣṭhīnām adhar'|oṣṭha|rakṣiṇīnām× api cumbana|vivādinīnāṃ priyāṇāṃ praṇaya|balān mukhāny āpibato yā prītir utpadyate tasyā n' âsty aupamyam. athavā kālāgaru|dhūpa|durdineṣu garbha|gṛheṣu prakīrṇ'|âtimukta|kusumeṣu tuṣāra|muktā|varṣiṇīṣu paruṣa|pavanāsu śiśira|kālarātriṣu priyay" ânuraktayā pīnābhyāṃ stanābhyām avapīḍyamāna|vakṣā vara|śayana|tal'|ôpagato gāḍh'|ôpagūhana|janita|sveda|bindu|surabhi|gātro yaḥ surat'|ântareṣu nidrām upasevate tena kiṃ nāma n' âvāptaṃ bhavati? api ca —

4.160 adhar'|ôṣṭha|rakṣiṇīnām×
kaca|grah'|ôtkṣepa|cañcal'|âkṣiṇām
pātavyāni ca tṛṣitair
mukhāni sītkāra|sahitāni.

nidrā|virahite svarge kim avāpyate? athavā sveda|bindu|laṅghan'|âvaruddha|tilaka|mārgeṣu pravṛtta|madana|dūtī|saṃpāteṣu saṃyojyamāna|maṇi|raśaneṣu dṛṣṭa|sahakā-

and the resounding of their girdles accompanied by the warbling of water-fowl, when Lady Autumn reigns, her cloud-veil slipping away, her forehead-mark furnished by the stainless moon, when the winds have subsided, and the forest depths are perfumed by the flowers of the *ásana* tree?* Or rather, that bliss has no equal which arises for a man who, helped by love, softly drinks from the mouths of his beloveds, though, averse to kissing, they protect their lower lips, with lips trembling by the onset of the cold, when winter has arrived with the wind laden with the scent of blooming *lodhra* flowers* mingled with jasmine, and locks of hair are bound with bunches of *priyángu* flowers. Or rather, what remains to be achieved for a man who falls asleep between bouts of love-making lying on an exquisite bed in bed-chambers cloudy with the smoke of black aloe, his body fragrant with droplets of perspiration produced by tight embraces, his chest being pressed by the swelling breasts of his impassioned beloved, on the dark nights of late winter that rain with pearls of hail, when harsh winds blow and *atimúkta** flowers are scattered? Furthermore,

> The thirsty should drink the sighing mouths 4.160
> of women protecting their lower lips,
> their eyes tremulous
> because of their hair is being pulled.

What is gained in heaven where there is no sleep? Or rather, a man should not long for any other day if he is conciliated by his impassioned beloved, herself deserving

r'|âṅkureṣu surabhi|pavaneṣu vasanta|divaseṣv avidit'|āgatayā svayam eva mukta|mānayā yaḥ priyay" ânuraktay" ânunetavyay" ânunīyate tena n' ânyeṣu spṛhā kartavyā. ath' âpi yo vā śirīṣa|kusuma|śyāmilīkṛta|strī|kapole salila|maṇi|muktā|hāra|candan'|ôśīra|vyajana|pavan'|ôpabhoga|ramaṇīye pracaṇḍa|sūrya|kiraṇe nidāgha|kāle kusuma|śayana|śāyinyā navamālik"|ônmilita|keśa|hastayā candan'|ārdra|payodharayā tāla|vṛnta|māruten' ôpasevyamāno māruta|grāhiṇy udavasite priyayā saha madhyāhnam ativāhayati.

athavā gandha|salil'|âvasikta|bhūmi|bhāgeṣu prakīrṇa|bakula|mallik"|ôtpala|daleṣu māruta|grāhiṣu gṛha|madhyeṣu yo nirudhyate priyayā ten' âtipāti yauvanam anubhūtaṃ bhavati. api ca—

ādaṣṭa|sphurit'|âdhare bhavati yo
 vaktr'|âravinde rasaḥ,
 prītir y" âpahṛt'|âṃśuke ca jaghane
 kāñcī|prabh"|ôddyotite,
lakṣmīr yā ca nakha|kṣat'|âṅkura|dhare
 pīne kapole striyo
 raktaṃ tena virajyate na hṛdayam
 jāty|antare 'pi dhruvam.

conciliation, who has arrived without arranging a rendezvous, after giving up her pride by herself, on days of spring when the tracings of the make-up patterns are obscured by droplets of sweat rolling over them, when there are meetings with messengers of love, jeweled girdles are put on, mango-sprouts appear, and the breezes are fragrant. Or again, the man who passes the time of midday with his beloved, her hair tied up with jasmine flowers, her breasts moist with sandal-paste, reclining on a bed of flowers, being comforted by the breeze of palm-fans in a airy pavilion, in summertime when the cheeks of women are darkened by *shirísha* flowers,* which is delightful with the enjoyment of the breeze of fans, vetivert, sandal-paste, pearl necklaces, jewels, and water, when the rays of the sun are fierce.

Or a man who is detained by his beloved in her airy apartments, their floors sprinkled with perfumed water, scattered with petals of *bákula*,* jasmine and lotus, spends well his evanescent youth. Moreover,

A woman's flavor in her lotus-face,
its lower lip throbbing because it is bitten,
and the delight of her buttocks
released from the dress,
resplendent with the radiance of the girdle,
and the felicity of her swelling cheek,
bearing the curved wounds of nails
—the heart captivated by these
cannot possibly grow weary even in the next life.

ayaṃ tu tapasvi|lokaḥ pipīlikā|dharmo 'nyony'|ânucarit'|ânugāmī prāṇ'|âpāya|hetubhiḥ svayam aparīkṣya svargaḥ svarga iti mṛgatṛṣṇikā|sadṛśena ken' âpy asad|vādena vikṛṣyamāṇa|hṛdayo marut|prapāt'|âgni|praveśan'|ādibhir anyaiś ca ghorair japa|homa|vrata|niyama|veṣaiḥ svargam abhikāṅkṣate. parīkṣituṃ n' êcchati param'|ârtham. svarge saṃnihitāḥ pramadāḥ śrūyante. tasya tāsām amanuṣyatvāc ca paraspara|virodhitvāc ca sukh'|ôtpattir na vidyate. nitya|saṃnihitatvāc c' âvirahitāḥ kāṃ prītiṃ kariṣyanti? anyony'|ânabhibhavatvāc c' âvyakta|guṇ'|ôpabhoge 'py asamarthāś ca bhavanti. yad api c' âtra sauvarṇāni gṛhāṇi sauvarṇās taravaḥ śrūyante tat khalu vibudhānām adākṣiṇya|sarvasvaṃ. yadi tāvat sauvarṇāni gṛhāṇi sauvarṇās taravaḥ, ken' âlaṅkriyante striyaḥ? ko 'tra viśeṣaḥ? kathaṃ bhavana|viniyogād upanītaṃ kanakaṃ strīṇāṃ śobhām utpādayati? yaś ca kāminībhiḥ svayam eva putravat|saṃvardhita|saṃmānitānāṃ yuvati|keśa|hasta|saṃkrānta|kusuma|samudāyānāṃ gṛh'|ôpavana|bāla|vṛkṣāṇām upabhogo ramyo bhaviṣyati, kutaḥ sa jāti|kaṭhinānāṃ kanaka|tarūṇāṃ?

But these ascetics, each imitating the behavior of the other in the manner of ants, their hearts seduced by some false doctrine which is like a *fata morgana*, shouting 'Heaven, heaven!' without having examined it themselves, devoting themselves to such lethal means as subsisting on air alone, leaping off precipices, and entering fire, and other horrors such as mumbling prayers, burnt offerings, vows, and costumes, they hanker after heaven. They have no interest to investigate the facts of the matter. Scriptures reveal that women are at hand in heaven. And since they are not human, men cannot enjoy those women due to mutual incompatibility. And since they are always at hand, what pleasure can those women, from which one can never be separated, generate? And since none of them surpass the others, there is no chance to enjoy hidden qualities. And as for the scriptural revelation of golden mansions and golden trees, that clearly shows the essence of the gods' lack of consideration. Firstly, if the houses are golden, and the trees are golden, with what are the women adorned? What would be special about it? How on earth could gold taken from a construction site beautify women? And the pleasure one takes in young trees in orchards which are cherished and raised like sons by beautiful women with their own hands, their bunches of flowers transferred to the locks of virgins, how could that be possible with golden trees which are inherently clunky?

4.165 tāruṇya|baddha|kāma|tantrasya paraspara|darśan'|ôtsukasya madana|dūtī|vacan'|âbhitṛṣitasy' ânyonyam upālambhamānasya prīti|phal'|ēpsoḥ kāmi|janasya yā prītir utpadyate, kutaḥ sā śāpa|bhay'|ôdvigna|strī|jane svarge? ye ca praṇaya|kupitāsu kāminīṣu tat|kāl'|ôtkaṇṭh''|ânurūpa|ramyān prasādan'|ôpāyān mitraiḥ saha cintayataḥ s'|āyāmā iva divasā vrajanti, kutas ta īrṣyā|virahite svarge? yac ca bhāva|viniviṣṭ'|âṅgyo vakṣaḥ|sthala|śāyinyo bakula|kusuma|niśvāsa|mārutair ghrāṇam āghrāpayantyaḥ striyo nidrā|sukham utpādayanti, kutas tan nidrā|virahite svarge? yāni vāruṇī|mada|vilulit'|âkṣarāṇi kim api lajjāvanti priyāṇi priy'|ârthāni vacāṃsi strīṇāṃ, kutas tāni pāna|virahite svarge? sukṛta|sītkārāṇi śvasita|bahulāny upagūhana|dūtāni nava|vadhū|ratāni kuta eva svarge? bho māṃ prati varaṃ śrotriyair vṛddhaiḥ sah' āsituṃ n' âpsarobhiḥ! tās tu dīrgh'|āyuṣmatyaḥ saṃskṛta|bhāṣiṇyo mahā|prabhāvāś ca śrūyante. yāsu Vasiṣṭh'|Âgastya|prabhṛtayo maharṣayaḥ samutpannās tāsu ko visrambhaḥ? paśyatu bhavān:

And that joy which arises for lovers addicted to the study of love while still young, as they are eager to gaze at each other, thirsting for the words of a love-messenger, squabbling with each other, and striving for the rewards of union, how could that be possible in heaven where women are paranoid of curses? And the days that seem to grow long for a man who with his friends ponders upon the means of reconciliation, delightful and well suited to the yearning of the occasion, when passionate women feign anger—how could these days be possible in heaven which is devoid of jealousy? And when women lull a man to happy sleep, their bodies suffused with emotion, lying on his chest, giving his nose a *raison d'être* by their exhaled sighs fragrant like *bákula* flowers—how could that be possible in heaven where nobody ever sleeps? And as for women's words, their syllables slurred by intoxication with date-wine, a trifle bashful, pleasing and dear—how could these be possible in teetotal heaven? How could there be in heaven sex with newly-married women, with hissing that comes easily, full of moans, heralded by embraces? Ah! I'd rather bed down with senile bigots than with heavenly nymphs. Scriptures teach that they are ancient, speak Sanskrit, and are majestic. They gave birth to the great sages headed by Vasíshtha and Agástya: who could let himself go in their company? Look, sir: 4.165

śāṭhyam anṛtaṃ mado māt-
saryam avamataṃ tathā praṇaya|kopaḥ
madanasya yonayaḥ kila;
vidyante n' âiva tāḥ svarge.

tasmād yady asti kāmam avyāhatam anubhavituṃ spṛhā, bhos ten' êh' âiva rantavyaṃ, viśeṣeṇa veśa|vadhūbhiḥ saha. iha hi,

ā|dvārād anugamya s'|âśru|vadanaṃ
yaṃ prekṣate śambhalī,
vastr'|ânte parilambate yam anṛta|
krodha|prayātaṃ priyam
kruddhaś c' âpy anunīyamāna|kaṭhino
yo rudhyate kāntayā
Kāmas tena samuddhata|dhvaja|rathaḥ
saṃcūrṇya sammarditaḥ.

aye Sunandā! kiṃ bravīṣi? «sarvaṃ mayā śrutam» iti. hanta! vikrīta|paṇyāḥ smaḥ. vāsu na khalu vipralambhitam. kiṃ bravīṣi? «na khalu candrād andhakāro *niṣpatati*» iti. Sunande! tav' âiva sadṛśam etad vākyam. ata eva tvay" âitad ucyate. evam abhyantaraṃ praviśāvaḥ. *(praviśya)* bhavati, visarjitum icchāmi. saṃprati hi—

Slyness, dishonesty,
intoxication, jealousy,
contempt, feigned anger
are said to be the sources of lust;
they are non-existent in heaven.

Therefore if you yearn for the experience of unobstructed love then, sir, you must enjoy yourself here in this world, and above all with courtesans. For here,

He whom the bawd gazes at with tears in her eyes,
following him up to the door,
whom she detains by the edge of his garment as he,
her beloved, passes her by, feigning anger,
who, when really annoyed
and becoming obstinate when placated,
has his path blocked by the passionate woman,*
fells the God of love,
crushing him on his chariot
streaming with lofty banners.

O no, its Ms Pleasing. What are you saying? "I've heard everything." Look, my wares are sold. No trick has been played, darling. What are you saying? "Darkness clearly does not *fall out of: fly away due to* the moon." Ms Pleasing, these words undoubtedly portray you, that's why you speak like this.* So let's join her inside. *(They enter.)* Madam, I wish to be dismissed. For now,

4.170 baddhvā mānini mekhalāṃ praśithilāṃ
pītv"|âsakṛd vāruṇīṃ
kṛtvā kānta|kara|graha|praṇayinaḥ
puṣp'|ôtkaṭān mūrdhajān
hast'|ālambita|mekhalābhir asakṛt
strībhiḥ kaṭākṣ'|āhataḥ
haimaḥ kūrma iv' âvasīdati śanaiḥ
saṃkṣipta|pādo raviḥ.

kiṃ bravīṣi? «na śakyam adya tvay" ârdha|pādam ap' îto gantum» iti. bhoḥ! gantavyam eva. me bhāryā kalevaram anyathā grahīṣyati. kim āha bhavatī? «ahaṃ tām anuneṣyāmi» iti. rajovad|guhyatvād apratigṛhīt'|ânunaya iva durjano na śaky" ânunetum. idaṃ gamyate. katham? pādayor lagnā saha Viśvalakena. hanta! paṅgūkṛtāḥ smaḥ. Sunande.

na tv" âham ativartiṣye
velām iva mah"|ôdadhiḥ.
imām api mahīṃ pātu
rājā sāgara|mekhalām.

O sulky woman, 4.170
the sun is slowly setting, *its rays withdrawn,*
as a golden turtle diving under,
its feet retracted,
repeatedly struck by the side-glances of women
who have fastened their loose girdles
after drinking heartily date-wine,
adorning their hair,
friend of the lover's grasp,
with bunches of flowers,
and resting their hands on their girdles.

What are you saying? "You are not allowed to take even as much as half a step away from here." I really must go, sir. Otherwise my wife will lay hand on my body. What are you saying, madam? "I'll mollify her." Because she is menstruating, she is like a wicked person who does not accept conciliation: she cannot be conciliated. I'm off. What? She falls at my feet with Mr Busybody! Woe! I'm crippled. Ms Pleasing,

I will not offend you : I bow and take my leave*
as the sea
does not transgress its tides :
floods it shore.
May the king protect this earth
girdled by the sea!

niṣkrānto viṭaḥ

it' Īśvaradattasya kṛtir «Dhūrtaviṭasamvādo» nāma bhāṇaḥ samāptaḥ.

Exit the Pimp.

Thus ends the Causerie called "Rogue and Pimp Confer," a composition by Íshvara·datta.

NOTES

Bold *references are to the English text;* ***bold italic*** *references are to the Sanskrit text. An asterisk (*) in the body of the text marks the word or passage being annotated.*

1.2 This is a reference to Śiva burning Kāma with his third eye in a fit of temper (see e.g. *Kumārasambhava*, canto 3).

1.2 **lure**: If one followed the reading of Sed *(sādakāḥ)* one could translate "destroying, exhausting."

1.4 **hosts**: *Gaṇas*, the troops of Shiva. It is also possible that *gaṇapatibhir* is an honorific plural for Gaṇeśa.

1.5 Of the four old *bhāṇas* it is only the *Pādatāḍitaka* where we find the name of the poet and the title of his play mentioned in the Prologue.

1.6 Rājaśekhara in his *Kāvyamīmāṃsā* seems to refer to this verse when he says (p. 11), *kāvyakarmani kaveḥ samādhiḥ paraṃ vyāpriyata iti Śyāmadevaḥ. manasa ekāgratā samādhiḥ*, "In Śyāmadeva's view when composing poetry, the poet's activity is primarily concentration. Concentration is one-pointedness of mind."

1.8 An allusion to the allegory of cat- and heron-like fake ascetics in *Manusmṛti* 4.192–197.

1.8 **cynic mendicant**: The exact meaning of the term ***diṇḍi*** remains uncertain. Bisschop (p. 207, note ad *Skandapurāṇa* 167.116a) associates them with the Lāṭa country: 'Diṇḍimuṇḍa seems to be connected with the *māhātmya* of the *tīrtha* Ekaśālā (Eksāl), told in SkP Āvantyakhaṇḍa 3.212. Śiva once assumed the guise of a *bhikṣu* and went to Ekaśālā, where he laughed, danced, sang, etc., with a terrible appearance, showing his diṇḍirūpa.' Diṇḍins appear also as mercenary shaved Pāśupatas in the *Bṛhatkathāślokasaṃgraha* 18.202. Arcaṭa's *Hetubinduṭīkā* portrays them as bards: *diṇḍikāḥ nagnācāryāḥ*. Concerning the shaved appearance of certain *muṇḍa* Pāśupatas cf. the *muṇḍaśṛṅkhalikapāśupatācaryaparṣad* referred to in the in the Chattracaṇḍeśavara inscription from Nepal. DIWAKAR ACHARYA has argued that this refers to two sub-sects and not just one group as it is usually taken: 1) *muṇḍa-pāśupatas* and 2) *śṛṅkhalika-pāśupatas*. See his "The Role of Caṇḍa in the early history of the Pāśupata Cult," in: *Indo-Iranian Journal* 28, p. 210, n. 13. HANS BAKKER ("Thanesar, the Pāśupata Order and the Skandapurāṇa," in: *Studies in the History of Indian Thought*, 2007, p.3, n. 12) on the other hand rather views the *muṇḍaśṛṅkhalikas* mentioned here as a sub-sect of the *śṛṅkhalikas* because of the reference to *dānaśṛṅkhalikapāśupatas* in the same inscription and to *rudraśṛṅkhalikas* in an inscription from Mandasor. Śyāmilaka is called "bald" *(khalati)* below, and it is possible that he was one of the 'shaven-headed Pāśupatas,' i.e. *ḍiṇḍikas* mentioned in the *Bṛhatkathāślokasaṃgraha*. Considering this we are inclined to interpret *ḍiṇḍikavinarma* as *ḍiṇḍi+kavi+narma, pace* SCHOKKER who takes it as *ḍiṇḍika+vinarma* (*vinarma* does not seem to be recorded elsewhere).

1.8 It is possible that this is an allusion to *Śākuntalā* act 2 where the *vidūṣaka* uses a similar phrase: *kṛtaṃ bhavatā nirmakṣikam.*

1.11 In the *Avimāraka* (act 3, after verse 9) we read about a *śṛṅgāṭakasthā viṭasabhā,* "the hall of pimps at the mall."

1.11 We have translated as though the bard comes in with his own gong (or bell), but it is also possible that there was an announcement bell/gong in such halls. Could it be that such Pāśupatas carried a bell or gong, in the manner of the Buddhist mendicant's rattle-staff *(khakkhara)*?

1.12 As SCHOKKER remarks, 'doves' and 'donkeys' might be allusions to courtesans and *viṭas* (p. 146, note ad 6c). We may add that Śyāmilaka in a deprecatory manner compares his own poetry to the harsh braying of donkeys, and likens other poetic works to the soft cooing of doves in the morning. For the literal sense we have to understand that the donkeys might produce sounds similar to the cooing of doves if they did not have Śyāmilaka as a role-model for braying (=his harsh sounding poetry).

1.14 ***naipathye***: The usual form of this word in North Indian manuscripts is *nepathye*.

1.14 The proposed pun in ***vilāsinī*** as Pārvatī is tenuous, but it is likely this verse is meant to be readable as praise of a deity, and most likely is that the imagery of this verse inverts Śiva's triumph over Kāma. The *viṭa*'s reply in the next verse is precisely a specific application and of this universal benediction.

1.20 ***Dadruṇamādhava***, a ridiculous name meaning literally "Spring/Krishna (or black) among herpetics" that intends a person most virulently afflicted with herpes. Such curious names were often apotropaic in intention.

1.21 ***Madanasenikā*** = "Kāma's troop"

1.21 ***Tauṇḍikokir Viṣṇunāgaḥ*** = "Viṣṇu's Serpent, son of Tuṇḍikoki (Beaky Cuckoo?)" The joke in this name (if we interpret it correctly) seems to be that this small harmless bird, a sort of mini-Garuḍa, fathered the huge world-supporting serpent (Garuḍa is the natural enemy of serpents). The same character is called Viṣṇu later, where Tauṇḍikoki Sūryanāga (his brother?) is also mentioned (he is the husband of the sister of Viṣṇu's wife). At one point the whole Koki family is referred to.

1.24 ***Prayata*** here has the sense of "ritually pure" rather than just stretched out.

1.24 **Regardless of my prestige**: This could equally mean: "Regardless of the seriousness [of this offence]."

1.24 In the *Mṛcchakaṭikam* (act 8, verse 19) the Śakāra protests in a remarkably similar vein when Vasantasenā kicks him.

1.28 The use of ***mahāmātra*** in this meaning is curious, since after the Mauryan times it gradually fell into disuse, and in classical Sanskrit it usually means "elephant-driver."

1.28 **Authorized to issue royal writs:** For the duties of this official see *Arthaśāstra* 2.10.

1.29 Note the wordplay showing the transformation of ***śabda***: she desired of *śabda,* she attained the best *śabda,* then she paid the price of negative *śabda*.

1.29 ***śabdasya vyasanam:*** lit. "the vice afflicting speech." This is a reference to "harsh speech" as defined as an eighth vice at *Manusmṛti* 7.48c: *vāgdaṇḍajaṃ ca pāruṣyaṃ.*

1.32 The expression ***vaiyākaraṇakhasūcin*** ('a grammarian pointing to the sky') occurs in the *Mahābhāṣya* and the *Kāśikā* on *Aṣṭādhyāyī* 2.1.53 (in the latter it is interpreted as *niṣpratibhaḥ,* "stupid"). In the *Padmaprābhṛtaka* we find a similar expression: *vaiyākaraṇapāraśava*, "bastard grammarian."

1.32 **don't triturate...**: Abhinavagupta quotes this passage in his commentary to *Nāṭyaśāstra* 16.5 in a remarkably different form: *mā musalenāpakārṣīḥ, mā kusūlāgninā dhākṣīḥ,* "don't hurt with a pestle, don't burn with the fire of a frying-pan."

1.32 **distinction**, or reading v.l. *°saṃskāram*, "sanctifying ceremony"

1.34 **'Here I am...'** This parodies two passages in the *Manusmṛti* concerning theft and its punishment. In 8.314 a thief turns himself in seeking clemency, saying *evaṃkarm" âsmi śādhi mām!* In 9.237c: *steye tu śvapadaṃ kāryam*, the punishment is specified as branding with the mark of a dog's foot.

1.38 The expression *tṛṇaṃ dattvā* may intend no more than "slighted him," but note that in *Rāmāyaṇa Sundarakāṇḍa* 5.19.2–3: *... tṛṇam antarataḥ kṛtvā...,* Sītā holds up a blade of grass to Rāvaṇa. The commentators read multiple insults into this passage but we might also legitimately consider it an apotropaic action. See *Sundarakāṇḍa* p. 481 for further references. Note also that *Śatapathabrāhmaṇa* 11.5.2.20 records an expiatory ritual for an adulterous woman: the officiating priest asks the woman to hold up as many pieces of grass as she has had lovers before he removes her sin.

1.38 This "sin" refers presumably not to the kick, but rather to inferred sins she committed in a past life, the fruit of which is her association with such a wretched man.

1.48 **Shaibya**: belonging to the Śibi people. There were two countries called Śibi (or Śivi), one in the Swat valley and the other in Mewar.

1.48 **Dashéraka**: the Dāśeraka country might have been in Malwa or in Marwar.

1.48 **Avánti** was the country the capital of which was Ujjain.

1.48 **Abhíraka**: Ābhīra was the south-eastern part of Gujarat.

1.48 **the first king of Aparánta, Indra·varman from the mountains**: Aparānta(ka) was the name of Konkan. Indravarman may be identified with the Traikūṭaka king who ruled in the first half of the fifth century. The name of the dynasty derives from the Trikūṭa hill in Konkan.

1.48 **Anánda·pura** was probably identical with modern Vadnagar in northern Gujarat.

1.48 **from Suráshtra:** from Surat.

1.56 **Padma·nágara** might be the same as Padmapura in Vidarbha, the birthplace of the poet Bhavabhūti.

1.56 **crossbow bolt:** A rare early reference to the use of crossbows in India. *Yantreṣu* is lit. "mechanism-missile," so it is possible that some other type of projectile weapon such as a *balista* or catapult is intended.

1.56 **Váidisha** is the city near the river Vidiśā (modern Bes or Besali), itself also called Vidiśā (modern Besnagar or Bhilsa).

1.60 **Sarva·bhauma** is a name of Ujjain.

1.64 **Shakas:** name of a people of Central Asian origin who came to India around the beginning of the common era and established kingdoms there. The Śaka Kṣatrapas ruled in what is today Gujarat until the arrival of the Guptas. Of the above listed *viṭa*s Jayanandaka is called 'a Śaka prince,' *śakakumāra*.

1.64 **Tukháras:** Tukhāra was the name of the upper Oxus valley, including Balkh (Bactria) and Badakshan (cf. STEIN, *Rājataraṅgiṇī* vol. 1, p. 136); its inhabitants were called Tochari in the west.

1.64 **Kirátas:** tribes inhabiting the mountains. Kirātadeśa included Sylhet and Assam.

1.64 **Kalíngas:** the inhabitants of Kaliṅga in East India on the border of the sea, between the Mahānadī and Godāvarī rivers.

1.64 **Vangas:** the inhabitants of Vaṅga, the eastern part of historical Bengal.

1.64 **Kashas:** probably people from Kashi, Benares.

1.64 **Mahíshakas:** the inhabitants of Mahiṣamaṇḍala, a country on the Narmadā.

1.64 **Chólakas, Pandyas and Kéralas:** the three traditionally listed peoples of southernmost India.

1.65 ***caukṣa/cokṣa:*** According to Abhinavagupta's commentary to *Nāṭyaśāstra* 17.38, the *cokṣas* were a particular branch of the Vaiṣṇava Bhāgavatas *(cokṣā bhāgavataviśeṣā ye ekāyanā iti prasiddhāḥ).* They are also mentioned in the *Padmaprābhṛtaka.* In the *Kuṭṭanīmata* we read about Kuśakarṇa, another hypocrite Vaiṣṇava who is outwardly hyper-religious, but at the same time "ogles the women with desire" in a Śiva-temple (verses 748ff).

1.70 ***svasti:*** lit. "Hail!," an inappropriate, formal mode of address.

1.71 ***utkoṭanā*** = *utkoca.*

1.75 It is not clear at which stage in the manufacture of a knife or a sword it should be held against a conch-shell.

1.77 The function of grass or straw might be to drive away the birds, or to wrap the meat, or the grass might be sacrificial grass held to ward off evil. *Cf.* the above episode in the law-court. There may also be a humorous allusion to the *Rāmāyaṇa* (5.65.12) episode where Rāma empowers a blade of grass and hurls it at a crow.

1.80 **Purna·bhadra** is the name of a *yakṣa*, who was cursed by Kubera and was born as the bull-elephant of Mahāsena, king of Ujjain (see *Bṛhatkathāślokasaṃgraha* 5.312ff).

1.81 **Yodhéyaka**: the Yodheyakas or Yaudheyakas were a people in eastern Punjab, the Yaudheya country lay between the Vitastā (Jhelum) and the Sindhu (Indus).

1.81 **Róhitaka** or Rauhītaka was the name of a fort and a region in Multan, cf. Alberuni 1, p. 308, 316, STEIN's note ad *Rājataraṅgiṇī* 4.12, *Epigraphia Indica* 1, p. 10f.

1.81 We are tentatively translating the otherwise unattested ***apavartikā*** as a "fibula" (a "safety-pin" brooch used to fasten a toga).

1.81 It is possible that it is intentionally comical that he wears his toga on the wrong side, or that it is too short to cover him properly.

1.81 **Fellow**: the word ***dhāntra*** also occurs in the *Padmaprābhṛtaka*, but it is not recorded in any dictionary and we haven't found it in any other Sanskrit text yet. It probably means "fellow, bloke."

1.83 ***Kāmadevāyatanād...*** As SCHOKKER remarks, "the ablative [...] has to be constructed with [...] *makarayaṣṭiṃ pradakṣiṇīkaroti*." One might also consider emending to ***kāmadevatāyā upayācitaṃ nirvartya.***

1.83 **Mákara post**: the *makara*, a kind of sea-monster, is Kāma's emblem. It seems likely that a pillar possibly surmounted with a *makara* was standing in front of the Kāma-temple, just as a pillar with Garuḍa on the top stands in front of a Viṣṇu-temple.

1.85 **Curlew-elixir**: presumably a type of rejuvenating elixir or aphrodisiac. How this involves the drummer is unclear.

1.86 Kṣemendra quotes this verse in his *Aucityavicāracarcā* p.125–26 (he attributes it to Śyāmala), his variant readings are: *cumbanasaktaḥ, ātmano vadanāt,* and *jihvāmūlaprāptaṃ.*

1.89 **Kambója** was the northern and / or eastern part of what is today Afghanistan.

1.93 ***kākalīpañcama:*** SCHOKKER compares this expression with the *kākalīniṣāda* discussed in *Nāṭyaśāstra* 28.35, a microtonal variant of *niṣāda*. *Kaiśikīniṣāda* would be B flat and *kākalīniṣāda* B. Similarly *kākalīpañcama* should be a microtonal variant of *pañcama*. However, this violates a number of rules: *pañcama* is a fixed *(acala)* note *(svara)* without microtone variants. That she should be singing such an impossible off-key or "blue" note only adds to the absurdity of the situation.

1.94 **paragon of a friend:** lit. "city-of-a-friend"

1.94 **Harish·chandra** is the name of the celebrated physician of king Sāhasāṅka (possibly Candragupta II Vikramāditya, around 400) who wrote a commentary to the *Carakasaṃhitā*.

1.94 A certain **Íshana·chandra** is known from the *Rājataraṅgiṇī* (4.216), he was the physician of Caṅkuṇa, the minister of Lalitāditya (eight century).

1.94 **Kankáyana**, another physician from Balkh is known already from the *Carakasaṃhitā* (e.g. 1.12.6).

1.106 **Bhatti Makha·varman, the noble son of general Sénaka:** Dasharatha SHARMA (Journal of the G. Jha Res. Inst. XIV, pp. 20–21) identified him with the son of the *senāpati* Dharasena I of the Maitraka dynasty of Valabhī (end of the fifth century).

1.106 **cynic ascetics from Lata:** It is noteworthy that the *Diṇḍins* are associated here with the Lāṭa country in southern Gujarat, where Kārohaṇa was located, the place of origin of the Pāśupata sect where Śiva's four *avatāras* took place in the four *yugas*. Diṇḍi or Diṇḍimuṇḍi (or °muṇḍa) was Śiva's incarnation in the second (Tretā) *yuga* (cf. BISSCHOP, notes ad *Skandapurāṇa* 167.115ff).

1.106 **white wooden earrings:** The color associated with laughter is white. On the other hand the *viṭa* might consider these earrings laughable because they are made of wood instead of ivory (cf. SCHOKKER, note ad loc.).

1.108 **royal rank** v.l. *rājopacāro* T3, 'reverence due to a king'

1.109 **a one-man play without lutes and drums:** Cf. *Padmaprābhṛtaka* after verse 22: *amṛdaṅgo nāṭakāṅkaḥ saṃvṛttaḥ,* 'You've performed an act in a play, only the drums were missing.'; also *Cārudatta* act 4, after verse 7: *amudaṃkanāḍaaṃ saṃvuttaṃ.*

1.114 **Fruit** and **flower** can also mean "menstrual discharge."

1.121 **Blossoming** also means "menstruating."

1.130 The following verse seems to be a parody of *Bhagavadgītā* 12.15: *yasmān nodvijate loko lokān nodvijate ca yaḥ / harṣāmarṣabhayodvegair mukto yaḥ sa ca me priyaḥ //* "Whom people do not fear and who does not fear the people, who is free from lust, dread and agitation: that man is dear to me."

1.139 **breaths like amorous sighs:** lit. "breaths manifesting the sound 'hi'."

1.140 **Indra·svamin** is the same as Indra·varman above (aka Indra·datta), the Traikūṭaka king of Aparānta.

1.142 Consider emending to instrumentals *cāmara/grāhiṇyā Kuṭaṅgadāsyā,* as the *kartā* of a *karmaṇi prayoga* construction.

1.147 **Bhaga·datta** fought against Bhīma with the elephant with which Indra had defeated the demons (cf. *Mahābhārata* 7.25).

1.153 **round tooth-marks:** For various kinds of tooth-marks consult *Kāmasūtra* 2.5.4.

1.155 **Shurpáraka:** Śūrpāraka or Śūrpakāraka is probably the modern Sopārā in Konkan (north of Bombay).

1.155 **Bhadráyudha:** In the *Kathāsaritsāgara* (120.53ff.) Bhadrāyudha is said to be the *pratīhāra* of king Vikramāditya of Ujjain, son of Mahendrāditya. Since Mahendra is a well-known *biruda* of Kumāragupta I, Vikramāditya is probably identical with his son, Skandagupta.

1.155 **Kárushas and Máladas** lived around what is today Shahabad in Bihar.

1.156 **jugs:** SCHOKKER *ad loc.* refers to an Ajanta painting on which an ear-ring in the form of a barrel is depicted. One might consider, however, accepting *°śakalaḥ*, the reading of T1 and T3, meaning "chip, piece."

1.156 **with "ja" sounds** That is he pronounces the Sanskrit "ya"-s as "ja"-s, which is characteristic of the western Prakrit dialects. Lāṭī is a Prakrit dialect mentioned by Daṇḍin in *Kāvyādarśa* 1.35.

1.158 **with "sha" sounds:** In Māgadhī Prakrit the three Sanskrit sibilants become *ś*.

1.160 **Pigeon-gesture** is defined in *Nāṭyaśāstra* 9.130b–133a: *ubhābhyām api hastābhyām anyonyaṃ pārśvasaṃgrahāt // hastaḥ kapotako nāma karma cāsya nibodhata / eṣa vinayābhyupagame praṇāmakaraṇe guroś ca saṃbhāṣe // śīte bhaye ca kāryo vakṣasthaḥ kampitaḥ strībhiḥ / ayam evāṅguliparighṛṣyamāṇamuktas tu khedavākyeṣu // etāvad iti ca kāryo nedānīṃ kṛtyam iti cārthe* / "A gesture is called 'dove' when both hands are joined with each other at the side. Learn its function: [it is used] when someone is politely approached or bowed to, or when a senior person is addressed. Women should hold it trembling in front of their breasts when they are cold or afraid. The same [gesture] is released after rubbing the fingers together in the case of words expressing pain. It can be made in the sense of 'this much,' or in the meaning of 'it shouldn't be done now'." Abhinavagupta ad loc.: *vakṣastha iti sarvatra saṃbadhyate, bhītābhinaye tu kampito 'pi. (...) ayam eva ca kūrmākāratvāt kūrmaka iti loke prasiddhaḥ.*

1.162 **Aparánta:** Konkan. This might mean that Bhadrāyudha subjugated Indradatta, the Traikūṭaka king as well.

1.162 **Málavas:** inhabitants of Malwa.

1.162 **Mágadha dynasty**: the Guptas probably originated from Magadha (modern Bihar).

1.162 As already BURROW has pointed out (*Journal of the Royal Asiatic Society* 1946, p. 49, n. 1), this verse is remarkably reminiscent of a verse in Skandagupta's Bhitarī inscription glorifying the Gupta sovereign's campaign (*Corpus Inscriptionum Indicarum* vol. 3, second. rev. ed., p. 315, verse 6, lines 12–13): *pitari divam upete viplutāṃ vaṃśalakṣmīṃ bhujabalavijitārir yaḥ pratiṣṭhāpya bhūyaḥ / jitam iti paritoṣān mātaraṃ sāsranetrāṃ hataripur iva Kṛṣṇo Devakīm abhyupetaḥ //* "Who, after the death of his father, re-established the ruined fortune of his lineage defeating his enemies with the strength of his arms, and then, just as Krishna had approached Devaki, he betook himself to his mother, whose eyes were filled with tears, so delighted she was with his victory." H. BAKKER, The Vākāṭakas. An Essay in Hindu Iconology, Groningen 1997, p. 26: "These verses [i.e. verses 5–7 of the inscription] have often—and rightly so—been taken to mean that there had been a war of succession after Kumāragupta's death. It appears likely that Skandagupta [...] was not born of a *mahādevī*. The comparison in the Bhitari inscription with Kṛṣṇa make one look for an uncle who was more entitled to the throne than a bastard son; [...] the viceroy of Vidiśā, Ghaṭotkacagupta [...] was the uncle of Skandagupta, albeit a paternal, not a maternal uncle as Kaṃsa was of Kṛṣṇa."

1.164 This verse is quoted without attribution by Kuntaka (*Vakroktijīvita* 1.111, v.l. *līlānatāḥ* instead of *utkaṇṭhitāḥ*), and, as SCHOKKER observes (p. 22), it is comparable to the verse in the Bhitarī inscription preceding the above quoted one (*Corpus Inscriptionum Indicarum* vol. 3, second. rev. ed., p. 315, verse 5, line 12): ... *caritam amalakīrter gīyate yasya śubhraṃ diśi diśi parituṣṭair ākumāraṃ manuṣyaiḥ //* "... the splendid deeds of whom—a man of spotless fame—are sung in every direction by delighted people down to youngsters."

1.166 *aho mānuṣa iti Bhadrāyudhena na hi ko 'pi lipsate āyudhāni / na śauṇḍīrās (?) tasya karma/siddhiṃ viṭā hi khalu bhuñjanti sukara/siddhim //.* This tentative *chāyā* and translation precariously interprets the form *soṇṇāri* as *śauṇḍīrāḥ*. It is possible that a verbal form is intended, however, or some nom. pl. cognate of *sundarī*.

1.167 **Pradyúmna** was an incarnation of Kāma, born as the son of Kṛṣṇa.

1.167 Or: the ***asya*** might refer to Kāma.

1.169 **One's name...** Lit. "The name presents the essence of one's character." *arthaṃ* is SCHOKKER's emendation, if we accepted the reading of the MSS (*ardhaṃ*) we might translate "The name represents half of one's character."

1.169 **my dear friend** v.l. *naḥ priyasakhīṃ Rādhikām,* "my dear friend Radhika."

1.171 The passage is mocking the four Buddhist "immeasurables" *(brahmavihāra). Muditā* is specifically a feeling of altruistic joy in the success of others. Perhaps it is not accidental that the *ḍiṇḍin* 'Blasé' appears as a disciple of the Buddha. Cf. BISSCHOP, note ad *Skandapurāṇa* 167.116a: "Diṇḍimuṇḍa [one of Śiva's incarnations] seems to be connected with the *māhātmya* of the *tīrtha* Ekaśālā (Eksāl), told in Sk[anda]P[urāṇa] Āvantyakhaṇḍa 3.212. Śiva once assumed the guise of a *bhikṣu* and went to Ekaśālā, where he laughed, danced, sang, etc., with a terrible appearance, showing his *ḍiṇḍirūpa*."

1.182 We did not venture to provide a translation of this corrupt Prakrit passage.

1.182 ***Lāvaṇika***, as a noun, means 'salt-merchant,' while as an adjective it can mean 'beautiful,' so *lāvaṇikā* may refer to the beautiful women in the *veśa*.

1.183 **Shura·sena·súndari**: "The Beauty of Shúrasena" (country around Mathura).

1.188 **seat beside me:** The text could also be interpreted as "here in my lap."

1.188 **spherical buttocks** v.l. *śroṇīprayāmena*, "the expanse of her buttocks."

1.189 **someone's work** v.l. *kasyā api caritaṃ* "some woman's story."

1.210 The cpd. ***vanaṣaṇḍa*** (syn. *vanakhaṇḍa*) is commonly found only in Buddhist texts.

1.211 **water-jug:** The word appears as *alañjara* or *aliñjara* in other texts.

1.213 The animals with which the three men are identified appear to be listed in descending order of size. The identity of the *karabha* is obscure, most commonly the word denotes either an elephant or a camel.

1.213 **a domestic buffalo:** The translation is uncertain, *gomahiṣam* (neuter sg.) is normally a *samāhāradvandva* cpd., "a cow and a buffalo together."

1.214 ***pustaka/vācikā:*** A detailed description of the performance of such a (male) reciter can be found in *Harṣacarita* 3 p. 39 where a *pustakavācaka* called Sudṛṣṭi sings the *Vāyupurāṇa* to musical accompaniment. The *Svacchandatantra* 10.73ab: *etad eva hi pāṇḍityaṃ śeṣāḥ pustakavācakāḥ* derisively notes their lack of learning.

1.214 **Dáttaka's followers**: Dattaka was known as an author on *kāmaśāstra*, the sixth chapter of the *Kāmasūtra* on courtesans is ascribed to him (cf. *Kāmasūtra* 1.1.11: *tasya ṣaṣṭhaṃ vaiśikam adhikaraṇaṃ Pāṭaliputrikāṇāṃ gaṇikānāṃ niyogād Dattakaḥ pṛthak cakāra.*)

1.215 **"Mother"** and **"mother-in-law"** are used in a figurative sense, she is actually the bawd.

1.217 **the prince's minister:** *Kumārāmātya* was an official title during the Gupta period.

1.219 **his brother:** or her brother? A few lines above T3 had a v.l. *nivṛttakāmantadbhrātrā*, which contains the word *bhrātrā*, but we could not interpret it.

1.219 **Thug** translates *ḍāka*, which is a conjecture. *ḍāka*, according to CDIAL, could mean "imp, goblin, wizard."

1.221 **senior officers:** the meaning of *kāṣṭhaka* is uncertain, lit. "staff-bearer"?

1.227 **fragrant earth:** *āḍhakāṃl* is the emendation of the earlier editions, the manuscripts read *edhakān / edhakāl / akāl*. SCHOKKER interprets *āḍhaka* as a synonym of *āḍhakī*; *edha / edhas* means "fuel."

1.229 **Trina·pishácha:** "Worthless Goblin"

1.229 **Shárkara·pala** might be "the king of the Śarkaras," who lived in north-western India.

1.229 **Kira:** The Kīras were a tribe in the vicinity of Kashmir.

1.233 We considered and dismissed emending to *bhagavān eva jānīte,* "God alone knows!"

1.233 **divert** v.l. *viśrāmayeyam*, "rest."

1.236 **without hissing:** either she is too young to know about the *sūtkṛta* required by *Kāmasūtra* (2.7.6) as one of the eight cries of a woman striking a man, or, the experience is too unpleasant or intense for her to make such sounds of pleasure.

1.239 **Taundi·koki Surya·naga from Súpara:** Surya·naga is the husband of Vishnu·naga's wife's sister. Saupara is, according to the edition of MOTI CHANDRA & AGRAWALA, a short form of Saurpāraka.

1.239 **in the suburbs:** The meaning of *bahiḥśivike* is not clear, SCHOKKER translates it as "in the district outside the southern gate [of the town]"; *śivikadvāra* means "south gate [of a city]" in Buddhist Hybrid Sanskrit; *śibikā* means "palanquin, platform."

1.239 **banner-courtesans:** cheap prostitutes who live in the groves outside the city.

1.239 **interrogators:** The meaning of *śrāvaṇikair* is not certain, SCHOKKER translates it as "witnesses."

1.239 **general Skanda·kirti** is possibly identical with Skandasvāmin from Avanti mentioned above. The meaning of *baladarśaka* is not certain.

1.242 **Párashava** as a caste means the son of a Brahmin man and a Shudra woman.

1.243 There may be a pun intended with Lakshmi being a "formless and gaudy" Goddess.

1.245 SCHOKKER translates: "and is as it were distorted between its dark bones" (reading *kālāsthi-* with T1T2). T3 however reads *tālvasthinirbhugnam*: bent awry at he palate-bone? Cf. *Suśruta-saṃhitā* 3.10.42 *mastuluṅgakṣyād yasya vāyus tālvasthi nāmayet / tasya tṛddainyayuktasya sarpir madhurakaiḥ śṛtam //.*

1.247 **Rupa·dasi** might not be a proper name. KANGLE translates *rūpadāsī* as "a female slave living by her beauty" (R.P. KANGLE, *The Kauṭilīya Arthaśāstra*. Delhi, 1969, Part II, p. 160). Bhaṭṭasvāmin in his comm. to *Arthaśāstra* 2.27.17 interprets it as "a maid who does work in connection with perfumes, flowers, etc." (KANGLE, ibid.).

1.248 **lapwing:** In Monier-Williams' dictionary, *ṭiṭṭibhaka* = Parra jacana L., which however seems to be a South American bird. According to Salim ALI's *The Book of Indian Birds* (Oxford University Press 2002) the Red-wattled Lapwing is called Titeeri, Titi, Titori in Hindi, Titwi in Marathi (p.132). In K.N. DAVE's *Birds in Sanskrit Literature* (Delhi, 2005, p. 357) *ṭiṭṭibha* is identified with the Red-wattled or Yellow-wattled Lapwing, or the Spur-winged Plover.

1.252 SCHOKKER refers to *mukharata*, "coitus with the mouth."

1.267 **aloof man of Scripture:** The expression *āgama/pradhānatayā* occurs in the *Svapnavāsavadatta*, Act Two: Vāsavadattā remarks to the Nurse that Udayana, though his grief was great, is now indifferent, and is ready to marry another princess. The

Nurse replies: *āamappahāṇāṇi sulahapayyavatthāṇāṇi mahāpurusahiaāṇi honti,* "The hearts of the great are governed by Scripture, [and thus] they are easy to comfort." In the present passage the arbiters supported Hariśūdra because they knew him as someone for whom Scripture comes first and who is, therefore, impartial. (Of course, he was not.)

1.277 The **ashóka tree** is said to blossom when struck by ladies with the foot decked with jingling anklets and painted with lacquer.

1.289 The leaves float on the wine in the cup.

1.299 Reading with SHOKKER as a chiasm. It is possible to read it as saying that both her eyes and teeth are both black and white.

1.304 **Mayúra·kumára** = Mayúra·datta above.

1.304 **moon-apartment:** The *candraśālā* is a room at the top of the house provided with a moon-shaped ogee-arch window, in this case overlooking the main street of the courtesans' quarter.

1.304 **bought ... that poor wretch:** Consider emending to *tapasvī-kṛta*, "She has made even him a beggar...."

1.306 *Varāhadāsa* is an emendation of ed. sec. of T2 *varāhadāhasya*, all other MSS omit it. On the Mandasor inscription of Yaśodharman and Viṣṇuvardhana (AD 533/534) (J. F. FLEET, *Corpus Inscriptionum Indicarum*, vol. III, Calcutta, 1888, no. 35, pp. 150ff.), a Varāhadāsa appears as the son of Ṣaṣṭidatta. Varāhadāsa I and II were two feudatory chiefs of the Maitraka dynasty towards the end of the sixth century (cf. *Epigraphia Indica* XI, p. 17). Śārdūlavarman was the name of a Maukhari chieftain, his son was called Anantavarman (see FLEET, op. cit., pp. 221–28).

1.307 **Squint-eyed** is SCHOKKER's interpretation of *cikura*, presumably intending eyes that are barely open. The reading *cikura,* lit. "hair," is curious. Could it be that her hair and eyes resemble the plumage (?) and the eyes of a partridge? A derivative of *cikka* could also be possible, cf. CDIAL 4780 *cikka* "gummy matter in eyes, bird lime." Cat's eyes are often said to be *kācara*, "glassy," and here it could be "whiteness" that is intended to highlight the red-white contrasts in the verse.

1.316 **Kétaki**: Pandanus odoratissimus L. (Screwpine/Umbrella tree/ Kaldera bush), it has golden, fragrant, spike-like flowers.

1.320 ***Śatacandraṃ nabhastalam*** is a popular *samasyāpūraṇa*. The conjecture *cakraiḥ* for *candraiḥ* eliminates the possible defect of tautology *(punaruktidoṣa)*.

1.322 On *tādātvika* and *mūlahara* see *Arthaśāstra* 47.15–16.

1.341 **Dharáyaki Anánta·katha** (or Dhāyaki?) is possibly the same as Upāya Nirantakatha mentioned above.

1.348 Or, ***viṭabhāvadūṣitākāraḥ***, "his outfit/appearance ruined by his pimp life-style?"

1.352 **Wine** is a diagnostic conjecture for something is wrong with the text here: Mallasvāmin does not actually suggest a propitiation, so it does not make much sense for Āryarakṣita to dissent saying *na khalv idaṃ prāyaścittam.* Furthermore, it seems that Mallasvāmin might have suggested that the courtesan should spit wine on Viṣṇunāga's head. (Himself an alcoholic, Mallasvāmin would naturally arrive at this conclusion.)

1.353 SCHOKKER p. 291 notes that Bhartṛsthāna was a sacred place of pilgrimage, also known as same as Svāmitīrtha / Kumārasvāmin (26 miles from Hospet).

1.355 The first half of the verse is the result of a tentative conjecture.

1.357 **Bákula tree**: Mimusops elengi (L.), Indian medlar.

1.357 The verse is ascribed to Bhaṭṭa Śyāmala in the *Suvṛttatilaka* of Kṣemendra, 2.31, *v.l.: madhupa iva baddho 'bjavivare, sīdhoḥ, madhoḥ* (instead of *paśoḥ*) (quoted by SCHOKKER on p.292). De VREESE thinks *gaṇḍūṣaḥ sīdhuḥ* is better syntax than *sīdhoḥ.*

1.363 **kárana strokes:** *Karaṇa* is one of the four *dhātus* (aspects of strokes) in the playing of stringed instruments (for details see SCHOKKER p. 293).

1.363 Or, "in the matter of [producing] three kinds of instrumental music."

1.365 This intends not her two feet mentioned above, but his two feet to be bound by the girdle: the girdle is too good for him.

1.368 **Hasti·murkha:** A strange name, lit. "elephant-fool," perhaps an error for *Hastimūrta*, "elephant-bodied"?

1.368 **from Gandhára:** T3 adds: "who is famous for his poetry."

1.371 **Gupta** = Gupta Romaśa / Lomaśa Gupta

1.371 **who became poetically inspired:** or, if we read *upahata°* with T3, "whose poetic inspiration was enfeebled."

1.371 ***vārarucaṃ kāvyam***: A very early work mentioned already in the *Mahābhāṣya* (ca. 150 BC) 4.3.110; according to *Sūktimuktāvalī*, verse 46 its title was *Kaṇṭhābharaṇa*. F.W. THOMAS (*Journal of the Royal Asiatic Society* 1923, Centenary Supplement, p. 135, n. 1) states that a *vārarucaṃ kāvyam* was published in Cochin in 1876. See WARDER (1990, §614).

1.373 This verse is metrical only if we take the following *iti* with it, which would however be unusual. On the other hand some word meaning "his" might be missing. Consider something like *tasya prakṣālyatāṃ śiraḥ*.

1.379 See SCHOKKER pp. 297f. on the name Koki; on *mantrādhikāra* see *Arthaśāstra* 1.10.

1.380 **surely:** We are not certain about exact meaning of *kiṃ kila* here. The expression is used when someone considers something unlikely or when someone is angry *(anavakḷptyamarṣayoḥ)* according to *Kāśikā ad Aṣṭādhyāyī* 3.3.146. Perhaps it indicates the irony in Viṣṇunāga's words.

2.4 **lodh tree**: *Symplocos racemosa (Roxb.)*, also spelled *rodhra*; it blossoms in winter (*hemante*, cf. *Kirātārjunīya* 10.29, *Ṛtusaṃ-*

hāra 4.1). The red powder scattered during the spring festival is prepared from its bark. *Lodhra* powder was also used as a cosmetic (cf. *Meghadhūta* 65, *Kumārasambhava* 7.9, 7.17), and in curing diseases of women as well as an anti-inflammatory in Ayurvedic medicine. Note therefore the careful choice of this particular tree by our author, for allegorically the *viṭa* is also associated with such soothing properties. The verse is intended as a spoof on the common allegorical use of trees for generous donors who give shade and fruit even to wood-cutters about to chop them down.

2.9 **arrayed:** *viracita*; the previous editions read *viguṇita*, which VENKATACHARYA AND WARDER translate as "intensified" (p. 54), as if it were *dviguṇita*.

2.10 The soft fibers of the ***dukūla*** plant were used to produce valued white garments.

2.12 **temple:** VENKATACHARYA thinks that *bhagavato Nārāyaṇasya bhavane* refers to the palace of a king (p. 55). On the other hand the adjective *bhagavato*, "blessed," makes it more likely that Nārāyaṇa is a deity.

2.12 **recital / *saṅgītaka:*** "The music which is sung by the actresses who enter at the beginning [of the performance of a drama], as a religious rite, or as part of the play, is called *saṅgītaka*." (*Nāṭakalakṣaṇaratnakośa* 258: *ābhimukhye praviṣṭābhir naṭībhir yat pragīyate / puṇyārthaṃ nāṭakārthaṃ vā tat saṅgītakam iṣyate //* tr. DILLON-FOWLER-RAGHAVAN, p. 44, §2158.)

2.13 **Vaishikáchala** has a range of literal meanings: "Mountain of Harlotry," "Immovable / unperturbed in matters of prostitution," or "Summit of harlot-science." As we shall see below further jokes involving his name are possible.

2.13 ***madanānurāga***: an idiomatic expression meaning "intoxicating love."

2.19 ***avalokana***: There is a slight *arthaśleṣa* pun meaning both "gazing" (for the women) and "shining down upon" (for the lightning).

2.20 ***svargāyate:*** See *Aṣṭādhyāyī* 3.1.11. *svargāyate* means "acts / behaves like the heaven," *svarga ivācaratīti svargāyate.*

2.20 For a technical discussion of these various qualities and ornaments see Ruyyaka's *Sahṛdayalīlā.*

2.21 **Anánga·datta** means "Ms Cupid's Gift."

2.25 It seems that *vijñātā* is used in the sense of *vijñātavatī*. Later in the same play *samāsāditā* will also have an active transitive sense (cf. the meaning of *viditaḥ* in *Kirātārjunīya* 1.1). If we take *vijñātā* to be passive then we might translate as follows: "It took [you] long to recognize me" (*bhavantam* in this case would belong to the next sentence).

2.29 *Veṣalakṣmī* is reminiscent of *rājyalakṣmī* "the good fortune of a kingdom, glory of sovereignty."

2.32 *Nikṣiptapādaḥ* is problematic. Sukumar Sen emends it to *nikṣiptavādo* and translates "one who has ceased talking or left off boasting" (quoted in VWed, p. 60, note 9). VENKATACHARYA sees no reason to emend, he thinks it means *nikṣiptaḥ pādo yasmin gaṇikājane saḥ*; VENKATACHARYA AND WARDER translate as follows: "the harlots' profession is kicked off by your virtues" (p. 60).

2.36 The reading and meaning of the first line is not certain. T2 seems to read *na stotavyā mayā tvayi*. VENKATACHARYA AND WARDER translate (p. 61): "One's own qualities are all virtues, and (therefore) those that are found in you do not require to be praised." WARDER adds in a footnote: "Your own qualities are all good; but (if) they remain in you they are not praiseworthy (we should all be able to enjoy them)."

2.41 Note that T3 reads simply: *nāsti doṣaḥ parikliṣṭāyāḥ.*

2.58 ***vaiśeṣikam:*** SEN translates it as "amorous decorations" (quoted in VWed p. 64, note 11); VENKATACHARYA & WARDER translate it as "particularity" or "discrimination," or "expertise" (from *viśeṣikā* "female expert").

2.61 I.e. with nobodies. We follow VENKATACHARYA's interpretation: "*Saṭpadārtha* stands for the six positive categories [...], and *ṣaṭpadārthabahiṣkṛta* may mean *abhāva* (non-existence, the negative category). [...] By this statement she implies her contempt for the *viṭa* [...] She means that he is a bad person unworthy of honor (*asatpuruṣa*). [...] The *viṭa* is generally addressed as *bhāva* [...] which means 'worthy of honor.' Now she says that he is to be addressed as *abhāvavaiśikācala* [...]" (VWed, p. 26.)

2.63 *Dravya, guṇa, karman, sāmānya, viśeṣa, samavāya* are the six categories *(padārthas)* in Vaiśeṣika philosophy. The pimp adds *yoga* and *mokṣa* to show his superiority of knowledge.

2.65 We again follow VENKATACHARYA's interpretation: "[T]he *puruṣa*, the soul is *alepaka* (which represents the element of awareness or the principle of sentience, and being only *bhoktṛ*, an enjoyer, and not a *kartṛ*, an agent, is not affected by the actions good or bad), *nirguṇa* (i.e. without three constituents of the *prakṛti*, *sattva*, *rajas* and *tamas*) and *kṣetrajña* (i.e. knows only what takes place within the physical limitations like the body *(kṣetra)* with which it happens to be associated)." (VWed, p. 28.)

2.65 VENKATACHARYA has a different interpretation for the second meaning of the pun: "[I]t seems to be a retort implying thereby that her soul is not affected by what are supposed by the satirical *viṭa* as wrong actions, and therefore his concealed accusations are unwarranted and misdirected." (VWed, p. 28.) WARDER, however, understands the sentence as describing the "soul" on the one hand and "this man," i.e. the pimp, on the other. He translates *alepaka* and *nirguṇa* as we did, but for *kṣetrajña* he gives "libertine" as the second meaning. (ibid. p. 66.)

2.69 ***Kardanam*** (the reading of T2 and T3) means "passing wind, rumbling of the bowels," cf. *Pāḍatāḍitaka*: *kardanena na māṃ ḍhaukitum arhasi.* Alternatively, consider emending to *kūrdane* = *narmani*: "I was just joking and you reply with a curse?" VENKATACHARYA AND WARDER read *taddarśane*, which WARDER interprets as "a parenthesis to himself: 'seeing her'," while VENKATACHARYA wishes to emend to *tvaddarśane*. They translate as follows: "Hello, only a curse will be the reply to me when I see you (thus started). (Or: In your system only a curse will be the reply. (?))" (VWed, p. 67.)

2.72 **to draw away:** The infinitive of *ākṛṣ* should be *ākraṣṭum*. One might consider adopting T2's reading *ānetum*, though it might have been the replacement of an ungrammatical form.

2.75 **I shall bring:** The grammatically correct future form of *ānī* should be *āneṣyāmi*.

2.80 On the "third sex" see *Kāmasūtra* 2.9.1ff.

2.83 **vanquished:** Or, if we accept the reading of T3 *nirmitāḥ*, "fashioned."

2.84 Vākāṭaka royal names often end in *-sena,* though no Rāmasena is known.

2.86 Or, if we accept the reading of T3, *caturamadhuragatisahitaceṣṭitayā* "her gestures accompanied by quick and delightful gait." Alternatively one might emend the text to *caturamadhuragatihasita(/hasitagati)ceṣṭayā(/ceṣṭitayā)*.

2.96 **Submarine fire** or the fire of the lower regions was fabled to emerge from a cavity called the "mare's mouth" under the sea at the South Pole.

2.113 Both T2 and T3 omit *Kusumapura°*, T2 reads just *Purandarasya*, while T3 reads *Pākaśāsanasya.* Purandara (as well as Pākaśāsana) is a name of Indra, his "house" may be his temple.

Accordingly RAGHAVAN understands *Kusumapura-Purandara-sya bhavane* as "in the temple of Indra at Kusumapura" (*The Number of Rasas*, p. 1, quoted in VWed, p. 77, note 28). MOTI CHANDRA & AGRAWALA (quoted in VWed ibid.) take it as a reference to the emperor Kumāra Gupta, who was also known as Mahendra. In this case *bhavana* would be his palace. VENKATACHARYA AND WARDER think that the "Indra of Pāṭaliputra" means simply "our king," without special reference to the Gupta emperor (VWed, ibid.). On the other hand the adjective *bhagavato*, "blessed," makes it more likely that Purandara is a deity.

2.115 **four kinds of acting:** *āṅgika* (gestures), *vācika* (speech), *āhārya* (costume etc.), *sāttvika* (manifestation of feelings).

2.115 **hand-gestures:** As VENKATACHARYA remarks (VWed, p. 26), in the *Nāṭyaśāstra* (4.29f.) we find thirty-two *aṅgahāra*s (movements of the limbs) mentioned. MOTI CHANDRA & AGRAWALA identify these hand-gestures with the *nṛttahasta*s mentioned in *Nāṭyaśāstra* 9.11ff, but as VENKATACHARYA points out these are sixty-four in number (VWed, p. 17, note 4).

2.115 **eighteen:** or twenty-eight, according to T3?

2.115 **six postures:** *vaiṣṇava, samapāda, vaiśākha, maṇḍala, pratyālīḍha, ālīḍha*, see *Nāṭyaśāstra* 10.51.

2.115 **two kinds of gait:** in the *Nāṭyaśāstra* (12.12f.) three kinds of *gati*s are mentioned.

2.115 **eight aesthetic sentiments:** The well known eight (or nine) *rasas (śṛṅgāra, hāsya, karuṇa, raudra, vīra, bhayānaka, bībhatsa, adbhuta, + śānta)* are treated in *Nāṭyaśāstra* 6.

2.115 **three times:** *druta, madhya, vilambita*, cf. *Nāṭyaśāstra* 31.5.

2.125 **nearly full:** VENKATACHARYA AND WARDER construe *īṣat* with *darśana* and translate: "by partial glimpses of the disc of the full moon" (p. 79).

2.129 **your arrival:** VENKATACHARYA AND WARDER read *āyuṣmadāgamanam* and translate it as "the arrival of his lordship (Mr Kuberadatta)" (p. 80).

2.137 One might consider emending the text to *ātmaguṇagarvito 'nena* and translate: "proud as I am of my virtues, this time I have been cheated by spring…"

3.2 ***vilāsamūrtiḥ:*** there is a pun on *vilāsa*, "coquetry" and "shining," alluding to Śiva's burning of Kāma.

3.9 **Sinduvāra:** Vitex negundo, chaste tree shrub with lavender flower spikes. Bees are strongly attracted to Sinduvāra. Following Kuiper *ad loc.*, we translate *madana* as bee.

3.15 A legendary rogue and master of all disreputable arts. Cf. M. BLOOMFIELD, "The Character and Adventures of Mūladeva," in *Proceedings of the American Philosophical Society*, vol. 52, no. 212 (Nov.–Dec., 1913), 616–50.

3.20 I.e. Karni·putra.

3.23 Or maybe a "cross-word"? Lit. "circle-oppressor-game."

3.47 *Kātantra* (also called *Kalāpa* and *Kaumāra* is a grammatical system attributed to Śarvavarman, who devised it to teach Sanskrit easily to king Sātavāhana (cf. *Kathāsaritsāgara* 1.7.10ff.

3.48 Or possibly: " 'What do I care about the bastard Katántrika grammarians now?' May the same happen to you." The pimp's remark could be understood in various ways: "May you defeat them as you did before," "May you share their fortune," or, taking *yathātathā* differently, "Whatever may happen to you[, I don't really care]," or, as MOTI CHANDRA & AGRAWALA suggest, "May you suffer disgrace" (taking *yathātathā* in the sense of Hindi *aisī-taisī*).

3.49 If we retain *kāṣṭha*°, the meaning might be "as brutal as beating with a log."

3.50 As Kuiper remarks, *upahata* can also mean "defiled."

3.54 The meaning of *veśakoṣṭhaka* is not certain.

3.56 *bhaktaṃ anena kalpayati* seems to mean "prepares rice with him." Moti Chandra & Agrawala compare it with the Hindi idiom *bhāt-pānī rakhnā*.

3.72 ***Triphalā*** is a powder of the three myrobalans *(āmalakī, vibhītakī, harītakī)*, it purifies and stimulates the digestive system. Iron filings (sometimes mixed with *triphalā*) were used for dyeing the hair black. ***Gokṣura*** (Hindi *gokhrū*) is an aphrodisiac herb.

3.81 A Buddhist called **Sánghilaka** also figures in the *Avantisundarī/kathā/sāra* (4.179–180): he takes Shúdraka to a cave to murder him, but Shúdraka kills him in the end.

3.81 **Forest of Dharma** was possibly the name of a monastery. A place of pilgrimage not far from Bodhgayā was also called *Dharmāraṇya*.

3.84 Cf. *Raghuvaṃśa* 1.11, in which Manu Vaivasvata is compared to the sacred OṂ syllable.

3.95 **sandal powder** or saffron powder?

3.104 ***Bhaṇḍīra / bhāṇḍīra*** is the shrub *Clerondendrum infortunatum* (or *viscosum*), it is used in traditional Indian medicine. In the *Harivaṃśa*, *Bhāṇḍīra* is the name of a gigantic banyan tree on the Govardhana mountain.

3.109 ***Nīpa*** is a kind of *kadamba* tree, its flowers are red to orange, occurring in dense, globe-like heads.

3.114 **Shona** is a river that rises not far from the Narmadā and falls into the Ganges above Pāṭaliputra.

3.114 **Chandra·dhara**, "Moon-Bearer" can also be an epithet of Śiva.

3.114 The meaning of this sentence is not certain. Though we follow Ghosh's emendation, his interpretation is actually quite different.

3.122 ***Ṣaḍja*** is one of the two fundamental scales *(grāmas)* (the other being *madhyama*).

3.127 A lunar fast involves food being diminished every day by one mouthful for the waning fortnight, and increased during the waxing fortnight.

3.131 **Kumúdvati**'s story is mentioned in Aśvaghoṣa's "Handsome Nanda" (*Saundarananda*) 8.44: "They say that Sénajit's daughter slept with an outcaste, Kumúdvati with Mina·ripu and Brihad·ratha with a lion; there is nothing a woman will not do" (tr. COVILL). Mina·ripu is possibly the same as Abja·shatru in *Saundarananda* 10.53, who was burnt up by love. In "Life of the Buddha" (*Buddhacarita*) 13.11, Māra says: "I have raised this, the same arrow that I hurled at Shúrpaka, the enemy of fish [i.e. Mina·ripu]" (tr. OLIVELLE). As JOHNSON pointed out (note *ad loc.*), "The name [Śūrpaka] is known to the lexicographers as that of the enemy of Kāmadeva."

3.144 If we follow LOMAN's reading, the meaning may be: "She will speak when prodded."

3.144 The meaning of the last two sentences is not certain.

3.150 Or, as LOMAN and MOTI CHANDRA & AGRAWALA take it, "sighing has changed your complexion."

3.150 Both the reading and the sense of the last sentence are far from clear. LOMAN reads °*dhīrahastaiḥ* and translates "Tell me, you deceitful [lover], why is this little creature, so afflicted by illness, driven on by such a steadfast attitude?" MOTI CHANDRA & AGRAWALA read °*dhīrahastaḥ* and translate *"arī śaṭhatābhārī, batā jab yah jan yoṃ madanvyādhi se pīḍit hai, to phir itnī dhīrtā kyoṃ barat rahī hai?"*

4.2 It is noteworthy that Īśvaradatta considers his work erudite. Presumably he is referring to the long discussion about *kāmaśāstra* in the second half of the play.

4.2 **religious merit** A *prītinimitta* doctrine is criticized at *Ślokavārttika codanāsūtra* 272ab: *dharmaḥ prītinimittaṃ syāt tadā śyene 'pi dharmatā.*

4.2 Bhāmaha named proficiency *(vaicakṣaṇya)* among the four goals of man and arts, pleasure *(prīti)*, and fame *(kīrti)* as the threefold gift of poetry (*Kāvyālaṅkāra* 1.2).

4.3 **play:** Strictly speaking the genre of this play is *bhāṇa*, not *nāṭaka*.

4.3 The stage manager usually invites the actress / his wife to sing a song about the season, and the following song would do so. While it is composed in the *āryā* meter used by women for such songs it is in Sanskrit and not in the usual Māhārāṣṭrī Prakrit, and the introductory "Now, this above all is the time—" seems to also imply that it is the stage manager who sings the song, or perhaps they sing it together. Another possibility is that since this is a one man show there is no actress present, and so the stage director sings the song on her behalf in Sanskrit.

4.16 ***kumbhadāsī:*** A harlot, or prostitute, originally a female servant water-carrier, cf. *Kāmasūtra* 2.10.22.

4.17 In T2 (and, following it, in Ted*pc.*and MAed) we find a verse in the place of the last two sentences, but its clumsy features (one syllable too many in the first pāda and the misplaced / functionless *ca* at the end of the second) suggest a secondary versification.

4.17 ***upavīṇā***: "bindings," see 'The Parts of a Vīṇā,' A.K. Coomaraswamy, *Journal of the American Oriental Society*, vol. 57, no. 1 (Mar., 1937), pp. 101–103. The identity of the "bindings" is confirmed by a textual passage making a series of homologies involving sacrificial materials. The Pali Text Society dictionary also gives it as "neck of a lute." In that case the lute's neck might be bent.

4.21 **Tax collectors** *(nagaraghaṭṭakānāṃ)* is the interpretation of Ghosh (he actually wants to emend to *°ghāṭṭakānāṃ*), one might consider conjecturing *nagarabhaṭṭakānāṃ* "policemen" (?), or *nagaraghātakānāṃ*, "plunderers of the town."

4.22 One could also read: *kal" â / bahumat" â / dākṣiṇya / bhogyāḥ striyo.*

4.22 Construe: *n' ônmattā dhanino na.*

4.22 *guṇa* = "secondary."

4.22 Read: *nagare 'surair.*

4.22 Lit. "giving up on heaven."

4.24 If we follow T3, the reading will be *ath' âpagata/surata/tṛṣaṃ*, "whose lust for love-making has abated."

4.26 Or: "Like a baby bird, you are hopping around with difficulty, struck down by the wind."

4.31 On our translation of *ājñāratam* as "imperious love-making" cf. *Saptaśātīsāra* 10, where the commands are spelled out as: "let go, squeeze, hold, enliven, maintain it etc." *ājñāśatāni—muñca pīḍaya gṛhāṇa jīvaya trāhītyādi.*

4.34 The reading and interpretation of the verse is not certain.

4.36 Read as: *pur/avarasya.*

4.36 Read as: *puruṣai raho.*

4.37 Or, reading *viṭa/samitir* with T2, "the league of pimps."

4.39 This parodies the hero's conventional verse after he enters into the purifying sanctuary of a hermitage.

4.43 One might consider following T2 and read *kālānvitair*.

4.46 **ignores:** One might consider emending to *khalīkṛtya*, but *skhalīkaraṇa* and *skhalīkṛta* occur later again.

4.46 The *Bhāvaprakāśana* of Śāradātanaya (chapter 9, p.272) specifies that this sound is used by servants and buffoons: *hīhīśabdaḥ prayoktavyaḥ ceṭaceṭīvidūṣakaiḥ.*

4.47 **Ms Many-Affairs:** the translation blunts the "proper" sense "rich in relatives."

4.50 On the caesura *priye-ṇa* see Vāmana, *Kāvyālaṅkārasūtravṛtti* 2.2.4, the *nāmabhāgabheda* exception to the *yatibhraṣṭa* rule.

4.59 The rainy season is not suitable for military expeditions.

4.65 **cause her pain:** *vikṛta* could mean "changed for the worse," but also "decorated," and indeed the pimp says in the following verse that the girl's reaction has made her even more beautiful.

4.68 **Rámilaka:** Lit. "Little Kama"

4.71 **Kumbha·karna** is a demon notorious for his sleepiness.

4.77 **Pátali·putra:** "Ville-des-fleurs"

4.79 Cf. *Suśrutasaṃhitā* 2.1.77: *vāyuḥ kaṭyāṃ sthitaḥ sakthnaḥ kaṇḍarām ākṣiped yadā khañjas tadā bhavej jantuḥ, paṅguḥ sakthnor dvayor vadhāt.* "When the wind located in the bottom impacts on the tendon of the thigh, then the person becomes lame. If it impacts on both thighs, the person is a cripple." (tr. D. Wujastyk, *The Roots of Āyurveda*, Penguin 2001, p. 171.)

4.81 Cf. *Kāmasūtra* 6.1.1–3: *veśyānāṃ puruṣādhigame ratir vṛttiś ca sargāt. ratitaḥ pravartanaṃ svābhāvikaṃ, kṛtrimam arthārtham. tad api svābhāvikavad rūpayet, kāmaparāsu hi puṃsāṃ viśvāsayogāt.* "Courtesans obtain sexual pleasure and also make a living through having sexual intercourse with men. When they act for the sake of sexual pleasure, this action is natural; when they act for the sake of money, this is artificial. She should also pretend the latter to be natural, for men confide in women who are driven by love." Later Vātsyāyana repeats that profit and pleasure are the motivations of a courtesan, and adds (6.19): *arthas tu prītyā na bādhitaḥ, asya prādhānyāt.* "But profit is not to be frustrated by pleasure, since the former is predominant."

4.85 Cf. *Kāmasūtra* 6.2.2: *rañjayen na tu sajjeta saktavac ca viceṣṭeteti saṃkṣepoktiḥ.* "In a nutshell: she should beguile him but should not be attached to him, and she should behave as if she were attached."

4.86 These symptoms could be read as a parody of an Āyurvedic diagnosis: "Wheezing with watering eyes, a glazed over stare, loss of weight, an ashen complexion, outbreaks of feverish sweat, a craving even for the meanest of remedies..."

4.91 Cf. *Ślokavārttika* AKV29: *vahnir dahati nākāśaṃ ko 'tra paryanuyujyatām / na cānyā mṛgyate yuktir yathā sandṛśyate tathā.* "It is the fire that burns, not the air: who should be plied with questions in this matter? No other reason is sought: as we observe it, so it is."

4.105 Cf. *Kāmasūtra* 2.4.31: *nānyat paṭutaraṃ kiṃ cid asti rāgavivardhanam / nakhadantasamutthānāṃ karmaṇāṃ gatayo yathā //* "There is nothing that intensifies passion more than the various ways of using nails and teeth."

4.119 For a different classification see *Kāmasūtra* 2.10.14–26. Returning from a journey and union after a quarrel are classified under *rāgavat*, "passionate" sex.

4.121 *Kāmasūtra* 2.4.1–2 prescribes scratching when the couple is together for the first time, on a return from or a departure for a journey, and when the woman has just relented and is drunk.

4.122 **they strike at one's vulnerable points:** or, in the case of an engraver, should we understand "they engrave incisions [into the stone]"?

4.122 **ledger:** Both the reading and the interpretation of this sentence are uncertain.

4.129 This parodies the grim appearance of a champion warrior.

4.130 The ornament is a *samāsokti* (condensed speech) where the epithets refer also to a unstated second subject, here a great warrior: 'His hand, its palm and fingers reddened [with blood] and holding a glittering arrow, drawn back to the edge of his cheek, his bow fitted [with an arrow], advancing easily, smiling with his lower lip trembling [in wrath], rolling his eyes, his face showing no fear, his loins girt up to his navel...'

4.139 **expedience:** The reading and the intended meaning of this sentence is not entirely certain.

4.146 This verse is a parody of *Manusmṛti* 4.138: *satyaṃ brūyāt priyaṃ brūyān na brūyāt satyam apriyam. priyaṃ ca nānṛtaṃ brūyād eṣa dharmaḥ sanātanaḥ.* "Let him say what is true, let him say what is pleasing, let him utter no disagreeable truth, and let him utter no agreeable falsehood; that is the eternal law." (transl. BÜHLER).

4.159 ***bandhūka***: Pentapetes phoenicea, it has round, red flowers.

4.159 ***asana***: Terminalia tomentosa (Roxb.), or Indian laurel.

4.159 ***lodhra***: Symplocos racemosa (Roxb.), lodh tree.

4.159 ***atimukta***: Gaertnera racemosa (Roxb.), also called *mādhavī*.

4.161 ***śirīṣa***: Albizzia lebbek (L.), also called Woman's Tongue. Its flowers grow in showy, rounded clusters near stem tips, cream or yellowish-white; each flower with numerous long stamens.

4.162 ***bakula***: Mimusops elengi (L.), or Indian medlar.

4.168 **has his path blocked...** The translation is based on a conjectured reading.

4.169 Cf. Kālidāsa's *Śakuntalā* describing Priyaṃvadā as *priyaṃ vadasi.*

4.172 **I bow...** reading *natvā.*

NOTES TO THE EDITION

The sign × called *kāka/pāda*, "crow's foot" in Sanskrit, in the body of the Sanskrit text marks the word or passage being annotated.

The sign ⊔ represents a gap in the manuscript.

1.2 sādhakāḥ] M1, sādakāḥ MSSSed

1.7 tataḥ] B, kutaḥ Sed(T1T2), *omits* HM1

1.28 na dānakāmāv avekṣate] T2 DE VREESE, dānakāmāv apekṣate T1, dānakāmāv upekṣate Sed(HM1)

1.32 śiraḥsatkāram] HM1T3Sed, śiraḥsaṃskāram T1BT2

1.33 kliśnanti] T3T1T2B, kliśyanti Sed(HM1)

1.81 samaṃ cāyam] *conj.* Sed, samavāyam / samanacavāyam MSS

1.85 tayā] *conj.*, tathā Sed(MSS), kathā T3

1.93 yoṣitā] T3T1T2B, prauḍhayā HM1Sed

1.93 °āsya°] after this there is a long gap in H and M1 up to °karapālaṃ in 1.233.

1.108 rājabhāvo] Sed(MSS), rājopacāro T3

1.108 athavā] T3, *omits* Sed(MSS)

1.111 yadā tāvad] *conj.*, yadaitāvad MSSSed

1.156 °kalaśaḥ] Sed(B), °śakalaḥ T1T3, °śakalahaḥ T2

1.169 °sakhīm] Sed(MSS), °sakhīṃ rādhikām T3

1.182 The Prakrit text is corrupt, only part of it can be tentatively translated into Sanskrit: *Guptakulena paśyasi (pṛcchyase?) apavāritavanapañcadikṣu gaṇikākṛte … tṛṣṇā, nanu pauravīthyāṃ … kāpi gaṇikā na dṛśyate. tathāpi tasya … samaṃ khelantaḥ … ambā hi me śāpitā tava arthakena idānīṃ gaṇikā kāmotpūritā yasyeha (?) kulotthitena kāmukena (?) yasya yadi gacchāmi … daṇḍituṃ (T3 reads daṇḍido = daṇḍito) bhavāmi … eka evam.*

1.188 °bimbenā°] Sed(MSS), °prayāmenā° T3

1.189 kasyāpi] Sed(MSS), kasyā api T3

1.201 te mayā] T3, te Sed(T1T2), *omits* B

1.201 spṛṣṭayā durbhagayeti] T3, spṛṣṭayeti Sed(T1T2), *omits* B

1.204 kāmayayamānena iti] T2T3B, ⊔mayāmānena T1, kāmayānena Sed

1.211 kusūlo nv ayam] T3B, kulonvayam T2, kusūlodvayam T1, kusūladvayam Sed

1.213 karabho 'gaur] *conj.*, karabhogau T2T3, karabhaugau T1, kara⊔oghau B, karabhogair Sed

1.219 ḍākenā°] *conj.*, drāk tenā°SedB, pakenā° T1, ṭhakenā° T2, *omits* T3

1.227 āḍhakāl̃] Sed, edhakāl T3, edhakān T2, e-?-akal T1, akāl B

1.233 vinodayeyam] Sed(BT2T1), viśrāmayeyam T3HM1

1.237 aparaḥ kaḥ] Here end H and M1.

1.239 vyavahārārtham] M2begins here.

1.240 āḥ] T3, ā° B, a° T2, *omits* T1M2Sed

1.245 tālvasthi°] T3, tālāsthi° M2, kālāsthi° Sed(T1T2), tālān(n?)isthi° B

1.252 tāvat] T3, yāvat Sed(MSS)

1.261 bhavatā] T2T3B, bhavato Sed(T1M2)

1.265 tasyaiva] *conj.*, tasyaiṣaḥ Sed(T2B), tesyaiṣaḥ T3, tatraivaiṣaḥ M2, tatraivasyaṣaḥ T1

1.267 aparibhūtāyām eva sadasy] *conj.*, aparibhūtā me sadasyā Sed (T1T2M2), aparibhūtā mama sadasyā B, aparibhūtām eva sadasyā T3

1.274 °vihasitenaika°] T3, °vihasiteneka° B, °vikasitenaika° Sed (T1T2M2)

1.274 âikahastenâ°] *conj.*, âikahastâ° Sed(MSS)

1.298 anen' âiva tasmāt] T1T3M2, anen' âitasmāt Sed(T2B)

1.298 veśabarbaryā] T3, veśavad veśabarbaryā Sed(MSS)

1.298 yadā tāvat] *conj.*, yadā tāv T3, kiṃ ca tāvat Sed(MSS)

1.306 varāhadāsasya] Sed, varāhadāhasya T2, *omits* T1T3M2B

1.313 upekṣyānurakta] *em.* Sed, anapekṣyānuyukta T3, avekṣyānukta M2T1, avekṣyānurakta BT2

1.313 tat kāmam] T3, kāmam Sed(MSS)

1.313 °guṇṭhanās] *corr.*, °kuṇṭhanās Sed(MSS), °kuṇṭhanāt B, °kuṇḍanās T3

1.314 °samājam eva] T3, °samājaṃ Sed(MSS), °samīpaṃ B

1.320 cakraiḥ] *conj.*, candraiḥ Sed(MSS)

1.320 saparigham] T3, saparigraham Sed(typo?)

1.328 °mukhyā°] Sed, °mukhya° T3BT2, °mukha° M2T1

1.331 utkṣipyā°] T3, utkṣiptā° Sed(MSS)

1.335 niyukto dhuri] T3, niyukto Sed(MSS)

1.337 atra°] T3, tatra° Sed(MSS)

1.341 dhārayakir] Sed(T1M2), dhāyakir T3B, dhārayakir (with a mistake-mark on ra) T2

1.344 bhavān āha tayā] T3, bhavān āha tathā BT2, āha bhavān tathā Sed(T1M2)

1.346 cittāni nāma. ārtaś cāyam] *conj.*, °cittāni nāma ārtta⊔āyam T3, °cittāni ārtaś cāyam Sed(MSS)

1.347 kinnu] T3, kva nu Sed(MSS)

1.347 goglanaptā] T3, goglanaptā ya eṣa Sed(MSS)

1.349 tāvad bhoḥ ucyantām] *conj.*, tāvan nanūcyantām *em.* Sed, tāvan nocyantām MSS

1.350 dāsyāhaṃ] *conj.* Sed, dāsyā MSS

1.352 madya°] *conj.*, asmai SedMSS, asyai B

1.352 eṣa] T3, eṣa māṃ Sed(T1M2), eṣāṃ BT2

1.352 pratiṣedhati] T3T2, pratiṣedhayati Sed(T1M2B)

1.355 krīṇanti kavaya evaṃ] *conj.*, krīṇanti kavayo yady evaṃ T3, vikrīṇanti hi kavayo yady evaṃ Sed(MSS), *omits* B

1.355 kāvyāni hi madya°] *conj.*, kāvyāni madya° T3, kāvyam adya Sed(MSS), kāpy ayam adya T1

1.357 °karo] *em.* Sed, °karaiḥ MSS

1.357 sīdhuḥ] *em.* DE VREESE, sīdhoḥ *em.* Sed, śīthuḥ MSS

1.360 asya] T3T1M2, asyāḥ Sed(T2B)

1.368 gāndhārakeṇa] Sed(MSS), gāndhāreṇa kāvyacañcuna T3

1.380 sadānamitam] T3B, sadānandam Sed(T1M2), sadānamita° T2

1.384 sabhājayanti] M2T1T3, saṃbhāvayanti Sed(T2B)

2.9 vara°] T2T3Ted*vl.*, para° TedVWed

2.9 °viracita°] T2T3Ted*vl.*, °viguṇita° TedVWed

2.12 atha] T3, *omits* T2TedVWed

2.12 samadanayā] T3, *omits* T2TedVWed

2.12 abhinīyamāne] T3, abhinīyamāne tato T2TedVWed

2.13 tathāsya] T2T3, tathā cāsya TedVWed

2.14 abhijñātatayā madanaduḥkhasyāprasahyasya] *conj.*, abhijñātatayā madanaduḥkhasyāpy asahyasya T2, abhijñātayā madanaduḥkhasyāprasahyasya T3, abhijñātayā madanaduḥkhasyāpy asahyatvāt Ted, abhijñatayā madanaduḥkhasyāpy asahyatvāt VWed

2.14 °pariṇāmam] T3, pramāṇam T2TedVWed

2.14 eṣa] T2T3, tad eṣa TedVWed

2.15 °vibodhitaiḥ] *conj.* VENKATACHARYA, °nibodhitaiḥ T2T3Ted VWed

2.19 ruciraprāsāda°] T3, prāsāda° T2TedVWed

2.19 suravaranagarayuvatiśriyam] *conj.*, varanagarayuvatiśriyam T2, paranagarayuvatiśriyam T3, suranagaravarayuvatiśriyam TedVWed

2.21 nayanāmṛtāyamānarūpeta] T2, nayanāmṛtāyamānaruceta T3, sarvajananayanāmṛtāyamānarūpeta TedVWed

2.22 °cihnito°] T2T3Ted*vl.*, °citrito° TedVWed

2.23 °mātram] T3, *omits* T2TedVWed

2.24 kathaṃ] T2T3, kiṃ TedVWed

2.31 tvayā] T2T3, *omits* TedVWed

2.31 utpāditam] T2T3, upapāditam TedVWed

2.33 gṛham] T2T3, svagṛham TedVWed

2.36 stotavyāḥ sthitās] TedVWed, stotavyā sthitās T3, stotavyā tās T2*ac.*?, stotavyā mayā (?) T2*pc.*?

2.41 vāsu] T2TedVWed, *omits* T3

2.41 vāsu ... bhavanti] T2(parikliṣṭānāṃ)TedVWed, nāsti doṣaḥ parikliṣṭāyāḥ T3

2.47 adya°] T2T3, adyatana° TedVWed

2.47 °śvāsa°] T2T3, °śvasita° TedVWed

2.52 śāstratattvataś śrutiṃ] T2T3, śāstraṃ tattvatas tvā TedVWed, śāstraṃ tattvataḥ śrutiṃ VWed*vl.*(?)

2.54 °mattabhramaraganāś] T2, °mattabhramaramadhukaraganāś T3, °mattā bhramanto madhukaragaṇāś TedVWed

2.66 bhagavatī] T2, bhavatī T3TedVWed

2.69 °bhūtāyā] T2T3, bhūtāyā asyā TedVWed

2.69 asyāḥ] T2T3, *omits* TedVWed

2.69 kasya] T3T2, katarasya TedVWed

2.69 kardane] T2T3, tvaddarśane VWed, taddarśane Ted

2.72 °karṣitum] T3TedVWed, °netum T2

2.73 aho] T2T3, aho nu khalu VWed, aho tu khalu Ted

2.73 T2 has a lacuna from *kutaḥ? labdhayā (?)* to *yāny ahāni naiva* (VWed p.43, l.15).

2.75 śāstratattvataś śrutir] T3, śāstratattvaśrutiṃ TedVWed

2.80 aye] T3, aho TedVWed

2.80 tasmāt] T3, yasmāt TedVWed

2.86 °hasitaraticeṣṭayā] TedVWed, °gatisahitaceṣṭitayā T3

2.87 °yāny ahāni] T2 resumes.

2.87 āgacchati] T2T3, āgacchatīti TedVWed

2.87 bhartā saha] T2, *omits* T3TedVWed

2.89 hy evaṃ tvāṃ suguṇāṃ] T2T3, tvām evaṃ saguṇāṃ Ted VWed

2.90 tasy' âiv' ôdavasite] *conj.*, tasyaiva svodavasite TedVWed, tasyaivovasite T2, svodavasite T3

2.90 bhavatī] T2T3, bhavatī gataiṣā TedVWed

2.90 sādhayāmy] T2T3, gacchāmy TedVWed

2.91 prākṛta°] T2T3, prakṛti° TedVWed

2.92 abhigamya] T2T3, āgamya mām TedVWed

2.92 bhadramukha] T2 (kha cancelled?), *omits* T3TedVWed

2.92 °janānāṃ] T2T3, °jana° TedVWed

2.92 °paharaṇasya] T2, °pahasya TedVWed, °hāṇasya T3

2.92 antare] T2T3, antarā TedVWed

2.92 samācaratas] T2T3, ācaratas TedVWed

2.93 °roma°] T2T3, °loma° TedVWed

2.94 me] T2T3, mama TedVWed

2.94 saṃtyakṣyatī] T3, saṃsantyakṣyatī T2, tyakṣyatīti TedVWed

2.98 atrānṛtam] T3T2, ity anṛtam TedVWed

2.99 mayā] T2T3, mayā nāma TedVWed

2.99 roditi] T2T3, rodity ayam TedVWed

2.107 ratipariśrānta] *conj.*, atipariśrānta° TedVWed, rata° T2, surata° T3

2.108 °veṣāṃ] T2T3, °śobhāṃ TedVWed

2.108 yauvanoṣṇa°] T2T3, yauvanauṣṇya° TedVWed

2.109 idaṃ] T2T3, *omits* TedVWed

2.113 kusumapurapurandarasya] TedVWed, purandarasya T2, pākaśāsanasya T3

2.113 me paṇitaṃ saṃvṛttam] *em.* , me paṇitaḥ saṃvṛttaḥ T2TedVWed, paṇitaṃ saṃvṛttaṃ T3

2.113 bhāva eva] T2T3, bhāvaḥ TedVWed

2.115 priyaṅgusene aho] T2, aho T3TedVWed

2.115 °prasiddhiḥ] T2, °siddhiḥ T3TedVWed,

2.115 aṣṭādaśavidhaṃ] TedVWed, aṣṭādaśavidha° T2, aṣṭāviṃśan T3

2.115 °dvayam] T2T3TedVWed, °trayam *conj.* VWed

2.115 trayo] T2TedVWed, dvayo T3

2.115 °vāditra°] T2T3, °vāditrādi° TedVWed

2.122 naiṣa] T2T3, bhadre naiṣa TedVWed

2.125 °bhojanaśayanā°] T2, °śayanabhojanā° TedVWed, °bhojanā° T3; °ālaṅkārakathāyām] T2T3, °ālaṅkārāyām TedVWed

2.125 °kākalī°] *em.*, °kākalīṃ MSS*edd.*

2.126 caiva] *conj.* HAHN, yaḥ T2TedVWed, *omits* T3 *(unmetrical)*

2.126 vasante 'smin] T2T3, vasantake TedVWed

2.130 ayam āśīrvādaḥ] T2T3, iyam āśīḥ TedVWed

2.133 praviśāva iti] *em.*, praviśāma iti MSS*edd.*

2.134 praviśāvas] *em.*, praviśāmas MSS*edd.*

2.140 kāmijanaviśeṣair] T2, kāmijanavacanaviśeṣair TedVWed, vacanaviśeṣair T3

2.145 T2 col.: ity Ubhayābhisārikā ṇāma bhāṇas samāptaḥ. T3 col.: iti Vararucikṛtir Ubhayābhisārikā nāma bhāṇaḥ samāptaḥ.

3.9 sasindu°] T1T2HKUIPER, sindu° BT3, sasindhu° Ted MAedLed(M1?M2?)

3.9 samadamadanaḥ sapavanaḥ] BHM2T2TedMAedGhed KUIPER, samadamadanaḥ samadanaḥ T3, madanapavanaḥ samadanaḥ *conj.* Led

3.14 °vallīpinaddhaṃ vanaṃ] BT2T3(M2?)Ted(*corr.*)MAedGhed KUIPER, °vallīvanaṃ vanaṃ Led, °vallīpinaṃ vanaṃ H, °vallīviḍaṃ vanaṃ M1, °vallīviḍambhanaṃ T1

3.15 ṛtur ayam] M1M2T1KUIPER, ayam ṛtur BHT2T3*edd.*

3.15 °otsavasyāpi] BT2KUIPER, °otsavasya M1M2HT1T3*edd.*

3.15 parikramya] T2, *omits* MSS*edd.*

3.17 ślāghyaṃ] M2T3KUIPER, ślāghya° BHM1T1T2*edd.*

3.18 prāpīna°] *conj.* KUIPER, pīna° T3, prācīna° BM1T1T2*edd.*, prīcina° H, *omits* M2

3.18 cānibhṛtaḥ] T2T3KUIPER, cānibhṛta° *edd.*MSS • °madhuraḥ] BT1T2TedMAedGhedKUIPER, °madhurā M1, °caturaḥ HLed, °caturaṃ M2T3

3.19 ajjā] *conj.* KUIPER, ajū B, ajjū (?) T2, ajā M1T1, ajja H, adya M2Led, āryaputra T3, ajjukā TedMAedGhed

3.20 tu] *em.* KUIPER, nu MSS*edd.*

3.21 °kriyāḥ] BHT2T3KUIPER, °kriyā M1M2T1*edd.*

3.23 aye] T2, *omits* MSS*edd.*

3.23 °svāditān kāvyarasān akṣi°] T2, °svāditān akṣi° BT3, °svāditām akṣi° H, °svāditaṃ akṣi° M2Led, °svāditākārākṣi° M1?T1, °svāditākārān *em.* Ghed, °svāditāny *conj.* KUIPER

3.23 na śakyaṃ T2, *omits* MSS*edd.*

3.25 mā tāvad bhoḥ! aṃgho] KUIPER, mā tāvat bhoḥ aṃgho BM1 T1T2TedMAedGhed, mā tāvat. bho aho M2Led

3.28 °ālāpamūḍhaḥ] *conj.*, °ālāpamūkaḥ BKUIPER, °ālāpapūtaḥ T3, °ālāvadūkaḥ HM2TedMAedGhed, °ālāpadūtaḥ T2, °ālāpamūrkhaḥ M1T1?Led

3.28 °tārapra°] BKUIPER, °tāraḥ pra° M2T2T3*edd.*, °tāraṃ pra° T1

3.29 tāvan] BHM2T2KUIPER, etan M1T1T3*edd.*

3.31 arciṣyāma bhavantaṃ] BHKUIPER, arciṣāma bhavantaṃ T1, arcciciṣāma bhavantaṃ T2, arciṣāmo bhavantaṃ M1 M2, arcāmo bhagavantaṃ *edd.*

3.32 atha vā vasantakālo] T2, api ca vasantakālo BT1T3TedMAGh KUIPER, vasantakālo HM1M2Led

3.33 kāmadattaḥ] BT1T2T3GhedKUIPER, kāmadatta° HM1? M2?, kāmadattā° TedMAedLed

3.33 vaiśikavṛttyādho°] M1M2T1TedMAedGhedKUIPER, kaiśavṛttyādho° T2, kaiśikavṛttyādho° BHT3Led

3.33 avagacchati] *conj.* KUIPER, anugacchan T2, avagacchan MSS

3.35 kitavā°] BHM2KUIPER, kiṃ tavā° M1T1T2T3TedLedMAed, kiṃ tayā° Ghed

3.36 abhigataḥ] T1T2T3BM1GhedKUIPER, adhigataḥ HM2Ted MAedLed

3.38 T2 is available up to this point.

3.41 saubhāgyena] BHM2TedMAedGhedKUIPER, saubhāgya sya M1T1T3Led

3.43 kāntālābha°] BM1T1T3KUIPER, kāntālāpa° HM2*edd.*

3.44 eṣa upālabdhuṃ] *conj.* KUIPER, enām upālabdhuṃ T1T3 TedLedMAed, evopālabdhuṃ BHM2(°opa°)

3.45 °kaṇḍurā] B?T3KUIPER, °kandurā H, °kandhurā M2, °kaṇḍū|bandhurā M1T1TedMAedGhed, °bandhurā *conj.* Led

3.45 api] M1T1TedMAedGhedKUIPER, *omits* BHM2T3Led

3.49 saṃcicariṣuḥ] BT3, saṃcicīrṣuḥ *edd.*M1?, saṃcicirṣuḥ HM2, sañcariṣuḥ T1

3.49 dudrūṣuḥ] M2TedLedMAed, dudruṣuḥ M1T1HGhed, datruṣuḥ T3

3.49 nārhaty] BHM2KUIPER, nārhasy M1T1T3*edd.*

3.49 kaṣṭa°] *conj.*, kāṣṭha° MSS*edd.*

3.49 vācācaratv asmān] BHM2T3KUIPER, vācā vadayasmād M1 T1, vācā vada *edd.*

3.50 hā dhik, upahataḥ syām] M2T3KUIPER, kā dhik, upahata iti T1, *omits* BM1H*edd.*

3.52 asthāne] *conj.* KUIPER, sthāne BHM2T3, sthāne khalu M1T1 *edd.*

3.52 śībharam] *em.* KUIPER, śīpharam MSS

3.53 yā] BHM2T3KUIPER, yat M1T1*edd.*

3.54 tad uṣṭragāndharvaṃ] BHT3KUIPER, tat duṣṭagāndharvaṃ M1M2?T1*edd.*

3.55 °viśoṣaṇena] BKUIPER, °virecanena MSS*edd.*

3.56 śrutaṃ śrotrāvatarpaṇam] BHKUIPER, kṛtaṃ śrotratarpaṇam T3, śrutaṃ śrotrarasāyanam M1T1?*edd.*

3.57 caukṣavādiko] Ghed, caukṣyavādiko KUIPER, caukṣavādikau T3, caukṣavārito M1Ted, caukṣavādito T1LedMAed

3.57 saṃgṛhītārdranivasanaḥ] BHKUIPER, saṃgṛhivārdravasanaḥ M1T1, saṃgṛhītārdravasanaḥ M2?*edd.*, saṃgṛhītānuvasanaḥ T3

3.57 hāsyaḥ] B is available up to this point.

3.57 śrūyate] T1 is available up to this point.

3.57 kim ayam āmakumbhaṃ vahati] HT3KUIPER, kim ayam ākumbhaṃ vahati M2, kim ayaṃ kumbhaṃ vahati Led, (kim?) aham ākulo bhavati M1, kim ayam ākulo bhavati TedMAed Ghed

3.60 caukṣya°] *conj.* KUIPER, caukṣa° MSS

3.62 'si] TedMAedGhedKUIPER, 'smi M1M2HT3Led

3.62 °ācāra° M1TedMAedGhedKUIPER, °opacāra° HM2T3Led

3.63 ca cara] *em.* SCHOKKER (p.120) Ghed, cara T3, caraḥ M1H, c' ācāraḥ M2TedMAedLed. KUIPER's article ends with this sentence.

3.65 upaskāritaṃ] MAed, upadhāritaṃ Led

3.69 nīlīkarmasnānā°] MAed, nīlīkarmanānā° Led, nimīlakarmanānā° M2, nīlīkarmasnā° M1, nīvīkarmanānā° T3

3.77 kṛcchrārūḍhā°] *conj.*, kṛcchārūḍhā° M1M2T3, kṛcchraṃ rūḍhā° Led, kṛcchrād ruddhā° MAed

3.87 vṛthāmuṇḍa na śvitrī dadruṇā°] *conj.*, vṛthāmuṇḍanaśvitridadruṇā° T3, vṛthāmuṇḍanaścitridudrūṇā° M1, vṛthāmuṇḍanaś citridadruṇā° MAed, vṛthāmuṇḍanaś citritadrūṇā° Led (M2?)

3.88 °lopaḥ kṛtaḥ] MAedM2?, °lobhaḥ LedM1?, °vilopaḥ T3?

3.103 snehatyakta°] MAed, snehātyakta M1?Led, snehābhyakta° M2T3

3.110 °praveśa°] M1T3MAed, °praveśana° M2Led

3.110 °grāhyasya] MAed, °grāhasya Led

3.114 candradharād] *em.* GHOSH, candrodayād MSS

3.119 ramaṇaṃ] M1MAed, nipuṇaṃ M2T3Led

3.120 na] M2MAed, nu M1Led, nāma T3

3.121 iti] MAed, *omits* Led

3.129 kaṃ] *conj.*, kiṃ MSS

3.135 °pratāraṇāy' âbhi°] MAed, °pratāraṇābhi°] Led

3.135 °siddhiṃ] MAed, °siddhaṃ Led

3.140 °grāhyaḥ prākkevalo] M1MAed, °grāhyaḥ kevalo M2Led, °gṛhya prakevalo T3

3.144 eṣāpi marma] MAed, eṣā vimarde Led

3.145 bho nāyaṃ] M1MAed, bhajano 'yaṃ T3Led, bhajamāno M2

3.147 tvaṃ] *omits* Led *(unmetrical)*

3.150 dhīrahaste] M2, dhīrahastaḥ MAed, dhīrahastaiḥ M1Led, vīrahaste T3

3.154 atinibhṛte] *conj.*, anibhṛte MSS

3.159 evāsyā] MAed, eva Led

3.159 ajjā] KUIPER, adya MSS

3.159 te yathārthanāmatā] *conj.*, yathārthanāmatā M2MAed, te yathārthanāmā M1?T3?Led

3.164 asūyitaṃ] *conj.*, asūyita° M1T3, asūcita° M2LedMAed

4.3 °manaḥprīty°] T2, °prīty° *edd.*; ⊔ T3

4.3 prītivarddhanakarāyām ... hṛdayaprītijananaṃ] *conj.*, prītivarddhanakarāyām ... °mandabhāgyānāṃ śokavardhanakarāyāṃ ... hṛdayaprītijananaṃ Ted, prītikarāyām ... °mandabhāgyānāṃ śokavardhanakarāyāṃ ... hṛdayaprītijananaṃ MAed, prītivarddhanahṛdayaprītijananaṃ T2, prītivarddhanakarāyām adhanānāṃ cintāparāyaṇānāṃ śokavarddhanāyāṃ kumudakuvalayakalhārakamalaṣaṇḍamaṇḍitāyāṃ prāvṛṣi hṛdayaprītijananaṃ T3

4.4 °vijvalad°] T3, °vijvalan° T2, °vihvalad° *edd.*

4.17 °edānīṃ ... saṃprati hi] T2, °edānīṃ sudinaṃ saṃvṛttam Ted, ⊔āvat sudinaṃ saṃ⊔ṛttaṃ T3, *omits* MAed

4.17 °ravā meghā durdinadoṣacakitaḥ T3Ted(*ac.*), °nādā vigatā ghanāś ca T2*edd.*

4.17 pakṣau vitatya] T3Ted(*ac.*), vitatya pakṣau T2*edd.*

4.17 virauti gṛhamayūraḥ] Ted(*ac.*), virauty ayaṃ gehaśikhī prahṛṣṭaḥ T2Ted(*pc.*)MAed, virau⊔ T3

4.17 pramṛjyante] T2T3, saṃpramṛjyante *edd.*

4.18 saṃtvaryate] *conj.*, santāryate T2, santvāryate T3, saṃcāryate *edd.*

4.23 °bhājana°] T2T3, °bhājanī° *edd.*

4.24 na cāpy ahaṃ] T3, na cāhaṃ *edd.*, ⊔ T2

4.24 athavāvirata°] *edd.*, athāpagata° T3, ⊔ T2; °tṛṣṇāṃ] *edd.*, °tṛṣaṃ T3, ⊔ T2

4.30 °tailāvasekodgatacandra°] *conj.*, °tailodgatacandra° *edd.*, °tailāvasekodgatacandri° T2, °tailodgatacandri° T3

4.30 jñātuṃ] T2, vijñātum *edd.*, prāptum T3

4.30 avekṣyamāṇena] T2, avekṣyamānasya Ted, avekṣamānasya MAedGhed, avekṣyamāṇa T3

4.30 °ārthe vā] T2, °ārthe T3*edd.*

4.30 °bhedo°] T2T3, °cchedo° *edd.*

4.30 mitrārthe] T2T3, mitrārthaṃ *edd.*

4.30 yat tu dāsīputrāḥ] T3, yatta dāsīputrāḥ T2, yat tu dāsyāḥ putrāḥ *edd.*

4.30 vārayanti] *em.* , dhārayanti T2*edd.*, vārayati T3

4.30 °tīkṣṇaparaśor] T2T3, °paraśor *edd.*

4.30 kṣatra°] T3, kṣatriya° T2*edd.*

4.31 °daṣṭā°] T2T3, °dattā° *edd.*

4.32 kiṃ tat kathayatu bhavān] T2, kiṃ tat T3*edd.*

4.33 kaṣṭam īdṛśam] T2, īdṛśaṃ kaṣṭam. īdṛśam T3*edd.*

4.33 śakyam ūrddhvahastenākranditum] T2, śakyaṃ kilordhvahastenākranditum *edd.*, khalūrddhvahastenākranditum T3

4.33 °pathaṃ kilotsṛjya] T2T3, °patham utsṛjya *edd.*

4.34 °baddhāṃ] *edd.*, °bandhāṃ T2T3

4.34 naiva] T2*edd.*, tena T3

4.35 āgamiṣyāmi] T2, āgamya T3*edd.*

4.35 upalaṃbhayituṃ] T2, upālaṃbhayituṃ T3, upalambhayāmi *edd.*

4.35 °darśano 'pi sukho] T2T3, °darśano 'sukho *edd.*

4.37 °matir] T3*edd.*, °samitir T2

4.41 praṇādita°] T2, praṇādi° *edd.*, *omits* T3

4.41 °vimaladaśana°] T2T3, °daśana° *edd.*

4.41 'nibhṛta°] T2, nibhṛta° T3(?)*edd.*

4.41 °capalalalita°] T2T3, °lalitacapala° *edd.*

4.41 °pati°] T2, °patibhāva° T3°, paribhāva° *edd.*

4.42 °vilulita°] T2, ⊔lulita° T3, °lulita° *edd.*

4.43 tālā°] Ted*ac.*MAedGhed, kālā° T2Ted*pc.*, ⊔ T3

4.44 °madād ana°] T2T3, °madāna° *edd.*

4.44 °āṃśuka°] T2, °āṃśukakṛta° *edd.*, ⊔ T3

4.44 °hariṇī°] T2, °hariṇa° T3*edd.*

4.44 racayantī] T2T3, kalayantī *edd.*

4.46 °tārtha°] T2, °tarttha° T3, °tārdha° *edd.*

4.47 caturikayā paricārikayā] T2, caturikayā *edd.*, paricārikayā caturikayā T3

4.47 °sañcāra°] T2T3, °sañcārita° *edd.*

4.49 jñeyam] T2T3, vijñeyam *edd.*

4.50 visrambhāpa°] *conj.*, visrambhācca T2*edd.*, visrambhārya T3

4.50 °kaṭabhū°] *conj.*, °kavapur° *edd.*, °kavalul° T2, °kapur° T3

4.50 °vadhaḥ] T2, ⊔ T3, ślathaḥ *conj.*MAed, pathaḥ TedGhed

4.51 saṃvṛttā] T2, ⊔ T3, sthitā *edd.*

4.51 kiṃ] T2, kathaṃ *edd.*, ⊔ T3

4.52 °ruditeva] T3, °rudita iva T2, °ruditam iva *edd.*

4.53 °dhvaniḥ] T2, ⊔ T3, °svaraḥ *edd.*

4.54 hanta saiveyaṃ] T2, saiveyam *edd.*, saiva⊔ T3

4.54 kathaṃ māṃ] *conj.*, kathamān T2, ⊔ T3, saiṣā māṃ *edd.*

4.57 mṛdu°] T2T3, tanu° *edd.*

4.59 so 'yam evaṃ] T2, evaṃ T3*edd.*

4.59 °rādhena] T3, °rādhakāraṇena T2*edd.*

4.59 °karāṇāṃ] *conj.*, °nakaraṃ MSS*edd.*

4.62 gavākṣamukha°] T2, gavākṣa° T3*edd.*

4.62 upanayantī] T2, upanayati T3*edd.*

4.64 visarjitum] T2T3, visarjayitum *edd.*

4.64 arhasi mā bhavati] T2, arhati bhavatī mām *edd.*, a⊔ T3

4.64 aprārambhas] T2, prārambhas *edd.*, ⊔bhas T3

4.64 prasahyā°] *conj.*, prasaṃhya T2, prahasyā° T3*edd.*

4.65 °pradīpam] T2, °dīpam T3*edd.*

4.68 °hāro hṛtaḥ T2, °hāraḥ kṛtaḥ *edd.*, ⊔ T3

4.70 gamyatām. (em. : gamyatā ms.) vayam api sādhayāmaḥ] T2, gamyatām. sādhayamo vayam api *edd.*

4.71 °nimīlitaṃ] T2, °nimīlita° *edd.*, ⊔ T3

4.71 °śramaṇaka] T2, °śramaṇa *edd.*, ⊔ T3

4.71 °keśopadravām] *em.*, °keśopadrava⊔ T2, °kośopadravām *edd.*, ⊔ T3

4.71 bhoḥ ko] T2, ko *edd.*, ⊔ T3

4.71 dattvā] T2, dattvā bhoḥ *edd.*, ⊔ T3

4.71 °samalayaḥ] T2, °samaye *edd.*, ⊔ T3

4.75 bhāvasyāyuktaṃ] T2, bhāvasya yuktaṃ *edd.*, ⊔ T3

4.77 prakṛtiniṣpaṅkatayā] T2, niṣpaṅkatayā *edd.*, ⊔ T3

4.78 goṣṭhikānām] T2, goṣṭhīkānām *edd.*, ⊔ T3

4.78 samutpannāḥ] T2, pravṛttāḥ *edd.*, ⊔ T3

4.78 bhāvaṃ] T2T3, bhavantaṃ *edd.*

4.79 kaṭī°] T2, ⊔ T3, kuṭī° *edd.*

4.79 °ādhyāsanaṃ] T2T3, °ādhyāsaṃ *edd.*

4.81 yady arthārtham] *conj.*, ⊔ rttham T2, yady artthā⊔m T3, yady artham *edd.*

4.83 vijñeyeti] T2, ⊔ T3, vijñāyeta iti *edd.*

4.84 sākūtā] T2, sākārā T3*edd.*

4.85 °ocitatvāc ca] T2T3, °ocitatvāt *edd.*

4.85 chraddhāsyati] T2T3, chrāddhāsyantīti *edd.*

4.87 prathamas] T2, ⊔ T3, prathama° *edd.*

4.87 yūnāṃ na kāminīnām] *conj.*, kāminīnām *edd.*, yūnāṃ ta kāminīnām T2, ⊔ T3

4.89 The following verse is found in T2, missing from T3, inserted *pc.* in Ted, which is followed by the later editions. The verse is also found in the *Subhāṣitaratnakośa* with variant readings

(1646): *rājani vidvanmadhye varasuratasamāgame varastrīṇām / sādhvasadūṣitahṛdayo vākpaṭur api kātarībhavati //*

4.91 kena khalu] T2, kena T3*edd.*

4.95 duścikitso bhavati] *conj.*, duścitso bhavati T2, duścikitsaḥ T3 *edd.*

4.95 yathā] T2, yadā *edd.*, ⊔ T3

4.95 api] T2T3, api tat *edd.*

4.95 °kuṇṭhitanakharā°] T2, ⊔ T3, °kūṇita° *edd.*

4.97 apy aśiṣṭaṃ] *conj.*, avyaśiṣṭam T2, ⊔ T3, apy aśliṣṭam *edd.*

4.98 °kārīṇi] T2, °kārīṇī T3*ac.*, °kāriṇaḥ T3*pc.*, °kāriṇaḥ ke cit *edd.*, °kāriṇī bhavati Ted*pc.*

4.99 tu kopa°] T3, tu ko° T2, kopa° *edd.*

4.100 strī kṣipaty] *conj.*, strī kṣity T2, nikṣipaty *edd.*, ⊔ T3

4.100 tat prārthyaṃ] T2, tac chlāghyam *edd.*, ⊔āghyaṃ T3

4.101 strīprakopaḥ] T2, strīkopaḥ *edd.*, ⊔ T3

4.101 evaṃ tu] T2, evam astu *edd.*, ⊔ T3

4.103 kaṃ] T3, kiṃ T2*edd.*

4.103 tan muhūrtaṃ nāma] T2, ⊔nmuhūrtan T3, muhūrtaṃ nāma *edd.*

4.103 pravekṣyāmaḥ. kiñ cid avadhānaṃ dīyatām] T2, pravekṣyāmaḥ *edd.*, ⊔ T3

4.104 °prasaṃgāt] *conj.*, °prasaṃgā T2, °praśaṃsā T3*edd.*

4.104 °lakṣa°] T2, °pakṣa° *edd.*, ⊔ T3

4.107 tathā] T2, yathā *edd.*, ⊔ T3

4.107 hi tāvan mahātmano 'pi] T2, hi mahātmano *edd.*, ⊔ T3

4.107 °gamāḥ] *em.* , °gamā T2, °gatāḥ *edd.*, ⊔ T3

4.107 ata] T2, kuta] *edd.*, ⊔ T3

4.110 kathaṃ śakyaṃ cikitsituṃ] T2, kathaṃ cikitsituṃ śakyam *edd.*, ⊔ T3

4.110 evam evākāra°] T2, evam akāra° *edd.*, ⊔ T3

4.111 vigrahe] *conj.*, vigraho T2*edd.*, ⊔ T3

4.116 kāmino vijñeyaḥ] T2, kāminā jñeyaḥ *edd.*, ⊔ T3

4.120 °vegaṃ] T2, °vegakaraṇaṃ Ted*ac.*Ghed, °vegakāraṇaṃ *corr.* TedMAed

4.122 'bhyāse] *conj.*, 'py āste T2*edd.*, ⊔ T3

4.122 °arthaṃ] T2, °artha° *edd.*, ⊔ T3

4.123 parīkṣya sthitā] *conj.*, parīkṣyā sthitā T2, parīkṣya sthitaṃ *edd.*, ⊔ T3

4.125 cid] T2T3, cid apy *edd.*

4.127 puruṣeṇa] T2, puruṣeṇ' âiva *edd.*, ⊔ T3

4.129 °kapolaṃ] T2*edd.*, °kapola° T3

4.129 tasyā ākṛtau] *conj.*, tasyām ākṛti° T2*edd.*, ⊔ T3

4.129 anumeyaṃ] MAedGhed, anunemeyaṃ T2, ananumeyaṃ Ted*ac.*, ananuneyaṃ Ted*pc.*, ⊔ T3

4.129 śrūyatām] T2, brūyatām *edd.*, ⊔ T3

4.132 nṛśaṃsa] T2, anṛśaṃsa *edd.*, ⊔ T3

4.132 sevitāḥ] *conj.*, sevakāḥ T2, sevakā *edd.*, ⊔ T3

4.132 °mānā api veśyā anuvidheyā bhavanti] T2, °mānāpi veśyānuvidheyā bhavati *edd.*, ⊔ T3

4.133 śithilīkṛtabhūṣaṇā kāminī] T2, kāminī śithilīkṛtabhūṣaṇā *edd.*, ⊔ T3

4.133 prasīda] T2, *omits edd.*, ⊔ T3

4.133 mayāpi] T2, mayā ca *edd.*, ⊔ T3

4.133 utpadyate] T2, utpādyate *edd.*, ⊔ T3

4.138 bhavatīha] T2, bhavatī ca *edd.*, ⊔ T3

4.139 °viśeṣaḥ tad apy adoṣaḥ] T2, °viśeṣaḥ *edd.*, ⊔ T3

4.147 yasyā a°] T2, yasyā° Ted, ye asyā° Ghed, yasyām a° MAed, ⊔ T3

4.147 jaghanam] *conj.*, veśyājaghanam *edd.*, ⊔ T2T3

4.151 yadi ca] T2, yadi *edd.*, ⊔ T3

4.152 vadatīti] T2, vadaty *edd.*, ⊔ T3

4.154 āyattaṃ] *conj.*, āyatto T2*edd.*, ⊔ T3

4.155 °nidhiṃ] *conj.*, °vidhiṃ T2*edd.*, ⊔ T3

4.156 āpannāḥ] T2, āpannā iti *edd.*, ⊔ T3

4.159 avākchirā] T2, avakchirā TedMAed, avākśirā Ghed, ⊔ T3

4.159 °vanāntarāyāṃ] T2, °digantarāyāṃ *edd.*, ⊔ T3

4.159 °rakṣiṇīnām] T2, °rakṣaṇīnām *edd.*, ⊔ T3

4.160 °rakṣiṇīnāṃ] T2, °rakṣaṇīnāṃ *edd.*, ⊔ T3

4.161 °onmilita°] *conj.*, °onmīlita° T2*edd.*, ⊔ T3; °hastayā] T2 Ghed, °hastahastayā TedMAed, ⊔ T3

4.163 yāpahṛtāṃśuke] *conj.*, yā ca hṛtāṃśuke T2*edd.*, ⊔ T3

4.164 tapasvi°] *conj.*, tapasvī T2*edd.*, ⊔ T3

4.164 tāsām amanuṣyatvāc] T2, tasyāṃ manuṣyatvāc *edd.*, ⊔ T3

4.164 °bhibhavatvāc cāvyakta°] T2, °bhijñatvāc ca(ā) vyakta° *edd.*, ⊔ T3

4.164 tat khalu] T2, tad *edd.*, ⊔ T3

4.165 prāpti°] T2, prīti° *edd.*, ⊔ T3

4.165 °rūparamyān] T2, °rūpān ramyān *edd.*, ⊔ T3

4.165 yac ca] *conj.*, yasya T2Ghed, yasya (cca) TedMAed, ⊔ T3

4.165 kim api] T2, kim api kim api *edd.*, ⊔ T3

4.168 yo rudhyate] *conj.*, yaḥ krudhyate *edd.*, yat krudhyate T2, ⊔ T3

4.169 visarjitum] T2, visarjayitum *edd.*, ⊔ T3

4.170 mekhalābhir] *edd.*, mekhalābhir asa vijñāpanavyagre śabda iva T2(Pādatāḍitaka begins!), ⊔ T3

4.171 rajovadguhyatvād] *conj.*, rājavadguhyād TedMAed, rājapuruṣavad guhyād Ghed

4.171 śakyānunetum] *conj.*, śakyo 'nunetum *edd.*

THE CLAY SANSKRIT LIBRARY

Current Volumes

For further details please consult the CSL website.

1. The Emperor of the Sorcerers (*Bṛhatkathāślokasaṃgraha*) (vol. 1 of 2) by *Budhasvāmin*. SIR JAMES MALLINSON
2. Heavenly Exploits (*Divyāvadāna*). JOEL TATELMAN
3. Maha·bhárata III: The Forest (*Vanaparvan*) (vol. 4 of 4) WILLIAM J. JOHNSON
4. Much Ado about Religion (*Āgamaḍambara*) by *Bhaṭṭa Jayanta*. CSABA DEZSŐ
5. The Birth of Kumára (*Kumārasaṃbhava*) by *Kālidāsa*. DAVID SMITH
6. Ramáyana I: Boyhood (*Bālakāṇḍa*) by *Vālmīki*. ROBERT P. GOLDMAN
7. The Epitome of Queen Lilávati (*Līlāvatīsāra*) (vol. 1 of 2) by *Jinaratna*. R.C.C. FYNES
8. Ramáyana II: Ayódhya (*Ayodhyākāṇḍa*) by *Vālmīki*. SHELDON I. POLLOCK
9. Love Lyrics (*Amaruśataka, Śatakatraya & Caurapañcāśikā*) by *Amaru, Bhartṛhari & Bilhaṇa*. GREG BAILEY & RICHARD GOMBRICH
10. What Ten Young Men Did (*Daśakumāracarita*) by *Daṇḍin*. ISABELLE ONIANS
11. Three Satires (*Kaliviḍambana, Kalāvilāsa & Bhallaṭaśataka*) by *Nīlakaṇṭha, Kṣemendra & Bhallaṭa*. SOMADEVA VASUDEVA
12. Ramáyana IV: Kishkíndha (*Kiṣkindhākāṇḍa*) by *Vālmīki*. ROSALIND LEFEBER
13. The Emperor of the Sorcerers (*Bṛhatkathāślokasaṃgraha*) (vol. 2 of 2) by *Budhasvāmin*. SIR JAMES MALLINSON
14. Maha·bhárata IX: Shalya (*Śalyaparvan*) (vol. 1 of 2) JUSTIN MEILAND
15. Rákshasa's Ring (*Mudrārākṣasa*) by *Viśākhadatta*. MICHAEL COULSON

16. Messenger Poems (*Meghadūta, Pavanadūta & Haṃsadūta*)
by *Kālidāsa, Dhoyī & Rūpa Gosvāmin*. SIR JAMES MALLINSON
17. Ramáyana III: The Forest (*Araṇyakāṇḍa*)
by *Vālmīki*. SHELDON I. POLLOCK
18. The Epitome of Queen Lilávati (*Līlāvatīsāra*) (vol. 2 of 2)
by *Jinaratna*. R.C.C. FYNES
19. Five Discourses on Worldly Wisdom (*Pañcatantra*)
by *Viṣṇuśarman*. PATRICK OLIVELLE
20. Ramáyana V: Súndara (*Sundarakāṇḍa*) by *Vālmīki*.
ROBERT P. GOLDMAN & SALLY J. SUTHERLAND GOLDMAN
21. Maha·bhárata II: The Great Hall (*Sabhāparvan*)
PAUL WILMOT
22. The Recognition of Shakúntala (*Abhijñānaśākuntala*) (Kashmir Recension) by *Kālidāsa*. SOMADEVA VASUDEVA
23. Maha·bhárata VII: Drona (*Droṇaparvan*) (vol. 1 of 4)
VAUGHAN PILIKIAN
24. Rama Beyond Price (*Anargharāghava*)
by *Murāri*. JUDIT TÖRZSÖK
25. Maha·bhárata IV: Viráta (*Virāṭaparvan*)
KATHLEEN GARBUTT
26. Maha·bhárata VIII: Karna (*Karṇaparvan*) (vol. 1 of 2)
ADAM BOWLES
27. "The Lady of the Jewel Necklace" & "The Lady who Shows her Love" (*Ratnāvalī & Priyadarśikā*) by *Harṣa*.
WENDY DONIGER
28. The Ocean of the Rivers of Story (*Kathāsaritsāgara*) (vol. 1 of 7)
by *Somadeva*. SIR JAMES MALLINSON
29. Handsome Nanda (*Saundarananda*)
by *Aśvaghoṣa*. LINDA COVILL
30. Maha·bhárata IX: Shalya (*Śalyaparvan*) (vol. 2 of 2)
JUSTIN MEILAND
31. Rama's Last Act (*Uttararāmacarita*) by *Bhavabhūti*.
SHELDON POLLOCK. Foreword by GIRISH KARNAD
32. "Friendly Advice" (*Hitopadeśa*) by *Nārāyaṇa* &
"King Víkrama's Adventures" (*Vikramacarita*). JUDIT TÖRZSÖK

33. Life of the Buddha (*Buddhacarita*)
by *Aśvaghoṣa*. PATRICK OLIVELLE
34. Maha·bhárata V: Preparations for War (*Udyogaparvan*) (vol. 1 of 2)
KATHLEEN GARBUTT. Foreword by GURCHARAN DAS
35. Maha·bhárata VIII: Karna (*Karṇaparvan*) (vol. 2 of 2)
ADAM BOWLES
36. Maha·bhárata V: Preparations for War (*Udyogaparvan*) (vol. 2 of 2)
KATHLEEN GARBUTT
37. Maha·bhárata VI: Bhishma (*Bhīṣmaparvan*) (vol. 1 of 2)
Including the "Bhagavad Gita" in Context
ALEX CHERNIAK. Foreword by RANAJIT GUHA
38. The Ocean of the Rivers of Story (*Kathāsaritsāgara*) (vol. 2 of 7)
by *Somadeva*. SIR JAMES MALLINSON
39. "How the Nagas were Pleased" (*Nāgānanda*) by *Harṣa* &
"The Shattered Thighs" (*Ūrubhaṅga*) by *Bhāsa*.
ANDREW SKILTON
40. Gita·govínda: Love Songs of Radha and Krishna (*Gītagovinda*)
by *Jayadeva*. LEE SIEGEL. Foreword by SUDIPTA KAVIRAJ
41. "Bouquet of Rasa" & "River of Rasa" (*Rasamañjarī & Rasataraṅgiṇī*) by *Bhānudatta*. SHELDON POLLOCK
42. Garland of the Buddha's Past Lives (*Jātakamālā*) (vol. 1 of 2)
by *Āryaśūra*. JUSTIN MEILAND
43. Maha·bhárata XII: Peace (*Śāntiparvan*) (vol. 3 of 5)
"The Book of Liberation" (*Mokṣadharma*). ALEXANDER WYNNE
44. Little Clay Cart (*Mṛcchakaṭikā*) by *Śūdraka*.
DIWAKAR ACHARYA. Foreword by PARTHA CHATTERJEE
45. Bhatti's Poem: The Death of Rávana (*Bhaṭṭikāvya*)
by *Bhaṭṭi*. OLIVER FALLON
46. "Self-Surrender," "Peace," "Compassion," and "The Mission of the Goose": Poems and Prayers from South India
(*Ātmārpaṇastuti, Śāntivilāsa, Dayāśataka & Haṃsasaṃdeśa*)
by *Appayya Dīkṣita, Nīlakaṇṭha Dīkṣita & Vedānta Deśika*.
YIGAL BRONNER & DAVID SHULMAN
Foreword by GIEVE PATEL

47. Maha·bhárata VI: Bhishma (*Bhīṣmaparvan*) (vol. 2 of 2)
ALEX CHERNIAK
48. How Úrvashi Was Won (*Vikramorvaśīya*) by *Kālidāsa*
VELCHERU NARAYANA RAO & DAVID SHULMAN
49. The Quartet of Causeries (*Caturbhāṇī*)
by *Śūdraka, Śyāmilaka, Vararuci & Īśvaradatta.*
CSABA DEZSŐ & SOMADEVA VASUDEVA

To Appear in 2009

Garland of the Buddha's Past Lives (*Jātakamālā*) (vol. 2 of 2)
by *Āryaśūra*. JUSTIN MEILAND
Maha·bhárata VII: Drona (*Droṇaparvan*) (vol. 2 of 4)
VAUGHAN PILIKIAN
Maha·bhárata X & XI: Dead of the Night & The Women
(*Sauptikaparvan & Strīparvan*). KATE CROSBY
Málavika and Agni·mitra (*Mālavikāgnimitram*) by *Kālidāsa*.
DÁNIEL BALOGH & ESZTER SOMOGYI
Princess Kadámbari (*Kādambarī*) (vol. 1 of 3)
by *Bāṇa*. DAVID SMITH
The Rise of Wisdom Moon (*Prabodhacandrodaya*)
by *Kṛṣṇamiśra*. MATTHEW KAPSTEIN
Seven Hundred Elegant Verses (*Āryāsaptaśatī*)
by *Govardhana*. FRIEDHELM HARDY